Mi lengua

Mi lengua

*Spanish as a Heritage Language
in the United States,
Research and Practice*

Ana Roca
AND
M. Cecilia Colombi
EDITORS

GEORGETOWN UNIVERSITY PRESS
WASHINGTON, D.C.

Georgetown University Press, Washington, D.C.
© 2003 by Georgetown University Press. All rights reserved.
Printed in the United States of America.

10 9 8 7 6 5 4 3 2 1   2003

This volume is printed on acid-free offset book paper.

Design and composition by Melissa Ehn at Wilsted & Taylor Publishing Services

LIBRARY OF CONGRESS CATALOGING-IN-PUBLICATION DATA

Mi lengua : Spanish as a heritage language in the United States,
research and practice / Ana Roca and M. Cecilia Colombi, editors.
    p.   cm.
Includes bibliographical references and index.
    ISBN 0-87840-903-3 (pbk. : alk. paper)
    1. Spanish language — Study and teaching — United States.   2. Spanish
language — Acquisition.   3. Education, Bilingual — United States.   4. Hispanic
Americans — Education.   I. Roca, Ana.   II. Colombi, María Cecilia.
PC4068.U5 M55   2003
468'.0071'073 — dc21

                                                        2002014712

Table of Contents

Foreword   vii
  Guadalupe Valdés

1 *Insights from Research and Practice in Spanish
   as a Heritage Language*   1
   M. Cecilia Colombi and Ana Roca

PART I
SPANISH AS A HERITAGE LANGUAGE
THEORETICAL CONSIDERATIONS

2 *Toward a Theory of Heritage Language Acquisition*   25
   Spanish in the United States
   Andrew Lynch

3 *Profiles of SNS Students in the Twenty-first Century*   51
   Pedagogical Implications of the Changing Demographics and
   Social Status of U.S. Hispanics
   María M. Carreira

4 *Un enfoque funcional para la enseñanza del
   ensayo expositivo*   78
   M. Cecilia Colombi

5 *La enseñanza del español en Nuevo México*   96
   ¿Revitalización o erradicación de la variedad chicana?
   Ysaura Bernal-Enríquez and Eduardo Hernández Chávez

PART II
COMMUNITY AND CLASSROOM-BASED RESEARCH STUDIES
IMPLICATIONS FOR INSTRUCTION K–16

6 *"Spanish in My Blood"*   123
   Children's Spanish Language Development in Dual-Language
   Immersion Programs
   Ernestina Pesina Hernández, Hinako Takahashi-Breines,
   and Rebecca Blum-Martínez

7 *Minority Perspectives on Language* 154
Mexican and Mexican-American Adolescents' Attitudes
toward Spanish and English
    Karen Beckstead and Almeida Jacqueline Toribio

8 *META: A Model for the Continued Acquisition of Spanish
by Spanish/English Bilinguals in the United States* 170
    Roberto Luis Carrasco and Florencia Riegelhaupt

9 *La enseñanza del español a los hispanohablantes bilingües
y su efecto en la producción oral* 198
    Marta Fairclough and N. Ariana Mrak

10 *Academic Registers in Spanish in the U.S.* 213
A Study of Oral Texts Produced by Bilingual Speakers
in a University Graduate Program
    Mariana Achugar

11 *¡No me suena!* 235
Heritage Spanish Speakers' Writing Strategies
    Ana María Schwartz

12 *Navegando a través del registro formal* 257
Curso para hispanohablantes bilingües
    Rebeca Acevedo

13 *Spanish Print Environments* 269
Implications for Heritage Language Development
    Sandra Liliana Pucci

    Contributors 291

    Index 295

Foreword

For those of us concerned about the use and teaching of non-English languages in the United States, these are times of many contradictions. We are living in a moment when antibilingual education efforts have spread from California to Arizona to Colorado and more recently to Massachusetts. Teaching the mother tongue to young immigrant children, especially in Spanish, continues to be viewed by many as un-American and divisive. At the same time, the events of September 11 have once again made evident the importance of non-English languages for national security. It is clear that the very safety of Americans within their own homeland will depend on the availability of speakers of non-English languages who can support the efforts of the intelligence community at many levels. The dilemmas facing the country are obvious. If this society is to nurture and produce loyal Americans who are also speakers of non-English languages, public perspectives about the teaching and learning of non-English languages, of maintenance efforts by immigrant communities, and of early educational use of non-English languages must undergo a profound change.

Surprisingly, for those of us who are frequently pessimistic, there are already encouraging signs and beginning evidence of change. That this change in public perspective is happening with regard to Spanish is perhaps doubly surprising. I, for example, had prepared myself for a continuing anti-Latino and anti-Spanish hysteria fomented by a profound anti-immigrant sentiment. I had worried that in an intense xenophobic climate, differences between Latinos who are here legally, who were born here, whose families have been in this country for generations and newly arrived and undocumented aliens would become unimportant. I was concerned that questions about rights, concerns about equality, and arguments about the greater burden that might be placed on bilingual individuals would be viewed with suspicion.

As I pointed out some years ago (Valdés 1997), in certain climates, as Fishman (1992) has argued, facts appear not to matter. At the time that I wrote the article, the United States appeared to be in the process of what Nunberg (1992) has termed "reimagining" its national identity. Where in the past what was thought to hold the U.S. together were the democratic principles under which it was founded, it appeared that the country was moving into a period in which cultural bonds were considered more important. Fear of what the presence of large numbers of immigrants from the Third World would mean to the American context had led to the use of language as a symbolic rallying point. I viewed the United States as undergoing a transformation in which members of the majority or dominant group had deliberately chosen to use language as a strategy. Given such thinking, I argued that it mattered little that bilingual populations have already learned English. It mattered even less that, by definition, bilingual individuals were not identical to monolinguals. I considered it unlikely that language issues involving bilingual persons could be viewed as anything other than divisive and problematic.

But I was wrong. On February 17, 1999, the *San Jose Mercury News* published a front-page article titled "Latino Lawmakers Study Their Spanish: Some Were Fluent as Kids but Stumble Today." The article pointed out that newly elected Latino lawmakers, as products of a public school system that emphasized English and immigrant parents who wanted their children to assimilate, were wrestling to recover the Spanish that they had spoken fluently as children. Many found themselves struggling to discuss complicated issues of policy, such as health care, as they accompanied Governor Gray Davis to Mexico. They realized that the pressure to perfect Spanish-speaking skills was rising as Spanish language media covered the Capitol and as Latinos emerged as a major voting bloc. Faced with the need to campaign in Spanish and to court the Latino population, the article reported, many Latino lawmakers had begun to take intensive courses in Spanish and were immersing themselves in the language among family members and Spanish-speaking aides.

More recently, increasing evidence of this new perspective has been highlighted in many ways. For example, the importance of developing the language resources of Latinos who grew up in homes where Spanish was spoken was featured in articles in such major newspapers as the *Wall Street Journal*. In an article published December 28, 2001, and titled "Talking Spanish Is as Hot as Salsa for Latinos Who Never Learned Their Ancestral Tongue," the economic advantages, even for Latinos who have never learned Spanish, were clearly emphasized (Perez 2001). The significance of this change and its ramifications were further emphasized by political events in the March 2002 Texas primary elections. As Tijerina (2002, p. 1) pointed out in his *San Antonio Express-News* article,

> Barely a generation ago, Spanish was a liability in San Antonio and much of South Texas. Today, it's often seen as a valuable asset, even in politics. Last summer, Gov. Rich Perry went to San Miguel de Allende, Mexico to study Spanish.

And Texas soon may see its first gubernatorial debate in Spanish if Morales and Sanchez can stop quibbling about terms for such an event. This shift can be seen in the lives outside politics as well. Until a couple of years ago, Montemayor, like many Latinos in South Texas, spoke only a little Spanish. But he's studied it as a young adult, and when he has a family, plans to pass it along to his children. He is one of a small but growing number of young, professional Hispanics who are learning their ancestral tongue.

This volume is particularly important in the light of these changes and these dramatic shifts. What has happened in Texas and in California and in other parts of the United States will seriously impact the Spanish-teaching field. This book is a unique contribution in that it incorporates theory, research, and practice and moves us forward to the next stage in the development of this specialized field of inquiry and teaching. Roca and Colombi have brought together an exceptional set of papers that focus on the most important issues involving the teaching of Spanish as a heritage language today. What is exciting about this collection of articles is that it is poised to address many of the questions that have surfaced as Latino young professionals actively seek to develop their Spanish language proficiencies. It focuses on a number of relatively "new" topics in the field such as register, the development of expository writing, Spanish language print environments, and the creative use of Spanish. Additionally, it gives attention to areas that continue to challenge us, such as social status, language attitudes, issues of eradication versus revitalization, and the effect of early development of Spanish in young children. I am confident that we will build on this work to respond to the expectations of a new generation of students. I believe that these young future movers and shakers will impatiently push us to look beyond proficiencies required for the completion of the traditional Spanish major. They will demand that we develop new theories and new practices that will result in students' increased ability to use Spanish professionally during the course of their lifetimes in both Spanish-speaking communities in this country and in international business settings. *Mi lengua: Spanish as a Heritage Language in the United States* is an important first step. I predict that it will become a much-cited collection that will undoubtedly be used by future researchers and practitioners, not only in the teaching of Spanish to Spanish-speaking bilinguals, but also in the now growing broader field of heritage language policy, planning, and pedagogy. I congratulate both the editors and the authors for their outstanding work.

Guadalupe Valdés
Stanford University
March 2002

REFERENCES

Fishman, J. 1992. "The Displaced Anxieties of Anglo-Americans." In *Language Loyalties: A Source Book on the Official English Controversy*, ed. J. Crawford. Chicago: University of Chicago Press, 165–70.

Jordan, H. 1999. "Latino Lawmakers Study Their Spanish." *San Jose Mercury News*, February 17, pp. 1a, 18a.

Nunberg, G. 1992. "The Official Language Movement: Reimagining America." In *Language Loyalties: A Source Book on the Official English Controversy*, ed. J. Crawford. Chicago: University of Chicago Press, 479–94.

Perez, E. 2001. "Talking Spanish Is as Hot as Salsa for Latinos Who Never Learned Their Ancestral Tongue." *Wall Street Journal*, December 28, p. 1.

Tijerina, E. 2002. "Spanish Debate Stirs Talk about Spanish." *San Antonio Express-News*, March 10, pp. 1, 16A.

Valdés, G. 1997. "Bilinguals and Bilingualism: Language Policy in an Anti-Immigrant Age." *International Journal of the Sociology of Language* 127:25–52.

Mi lengua

Insights from Research and Practice in Spanish as a Heritage Language

M. Cecilia Colombi
University of California, Davis
Ana Roca
Florida International University

*M*i lengua: *Spanish as a Heritage Language in the United States* addresses the issues and challenges of developing and maintaining Spanish as a heritage language in the United States. Our book brings together work that addresses theoretical considerations in the field of Heritage Language Development (HLD), as well as community and classroom-based research studies at the elementary, secondary, and university level. Each chapter includes a practical section titled "Pedagogical Implications for the Teaching of Spanish as a Heritage Language in the U.S.," which provides practice-related suggestions for the teaching of Spanish as a heritage language to students from elementary grades through the secondary and college levels. The collection of essays in this volume was undertaken in response to the growing and urgent need for scholarly materials in applied linguistics and pedagogy in the specific areas of research on Spanish as a heritage language and the teaching of Spanish to U.S. Hispanic bilingual students in grades K–16.

U.S. Hispanic Population Growth

Unlike the past immigrant waves in this nation's history, in which sizeable linguistic enclaves of German, Japanese, Polish, and Italian communities gradually diminished, the populations of Spanish-speaking U.S. Latinos and newly arrived Latin American groups have continued to grow, resulting in increased use of the Spanish language. The city of Los Angeles alone has over

4.2 million Hispanics, the largest concentration of Hispanics in the U.S. In a CNN report titled "Will Spanish Become America's Second Language?" (Hochmuth 2001) the lead reads: "It's not just your imagination. In cities from coast to coast, the use of Spanish is booming and is proliferating in ways no other language has done before in U.S. history—other than English of course. It's a development that's making some people nervous. It's making others rich."

According to the 2000 U.S. Census, Hispanics are the fastest-growing segment of the population, totaling 35.3 million, a number that has surpassed the African-American population (34.6 million). If we add into the equation the estimated numbers of undocumented Latin Americans who come into the country every day via Mexico, Canada, and elsewhere (estimated at 4,500,000 undocumented workers by INS, 2002), then we can safely assume that Latinos in the United States likely number more than 40 million and are, without question, the largest minority group in the country. One consequence of this demographic trend is that the use of the Spanish language has increased in the U.S. As the new arrivals interact in Spanish within the community and the schools, we hear more Spanish in public settings and see more Spanish in media and advertising. It is as if the constant influx of new immigrants is providing "booster shots" of the language to Spanish speakers who have been here longer. The demographic changes and the increasing use of Spanish in public, business, and private settings have important implications in modern language education, teacher education programs, policy development, and curriculum and program planning for teachers and students in the twenty-first century.

The number of persons who classified themselves as Hispanic in the latest census has grown 60 percent since the previous census. In the 1990 U.S. Census out of a total population of 248,709,803, 9 percent of the population, or 22,354,059, were Hispanic. By the 2000 U.S. Census the number of Hispanics grew to 35,300,000 (12.5 percent of the population of 281,421,906). According to the most current census, persons of Mexican origin comprise approximately 66 percent of the U.S. Hispanic population. Among the Hispanic population, Mexicans have the largest proportion of persons under age 18 (38 percent) and in general, the Hispanic population is younger than the non-Hispanic white population.

The projected statistics in 1990 had already indicated that Hispanics (who could be of any racial group) would become the largest minority of the twenty-first century; however that milestone has been reached sooner rather than later than expected. After English, Spanish is the most frequently spo-

Figure 1.1 *U.S. Hispanic Population, 2000*

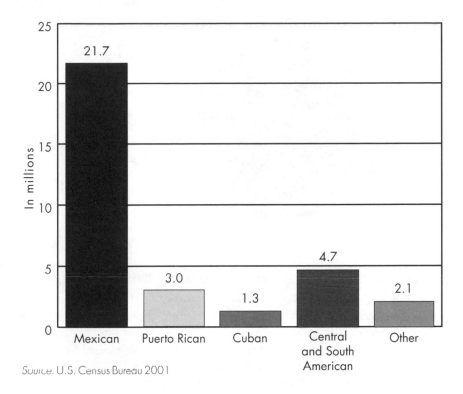

Source: U.S. Census Bureau 2001

ken language in the U.S. In some parts of the country, such as California, Spanish speakers make up more than a third of the total population. Spanish-speaking students make up more than 70 percent of all English learners in our schools, and one in seven school-aged children is from a non–English-speaking background (McKay and Wong 2000). In other words, multicultural classrooms are the norm in our schools today. Together with these demographic changes come new educational challenges.

Students who are heritage speakers of Spanish have typically spoken Spanish as a first or native language or interacted in both Spanish and English at home. The degrees of language proficiency in particular cases and the number of variables in the profiles of these students are complex and dependent on multiple circumstances. Some heritage learners of Spanish may understand basic informal communication but may have limited repertoires and registers and be unable to speak with much confidence in Spanish with-

Figure 1.2 *U.S. Hispanic Population in 2000*

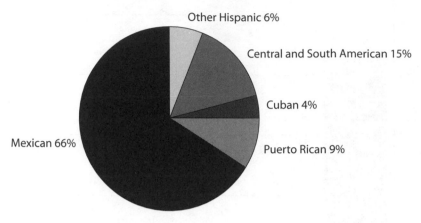

Other Hispanic 6%

Central and South American 15%

Cuban 4%

Mexican 66%

Puerto Rican 9%

Source: U.S. Census Bureau 2001

out resorting to English, their dominant language. Other students may be first-generation immigrants from Latin America who arrived in this country at an early age, having already had some schooling in Spanish. They may be placed in Spanish for Native Speakers (SNS) classes in the United States and find that they are the more advanced students in the class even if they had gaps in their schooling in Spanish in their place of origin. With so many complex variables, proficiency levels, and varied cultural backgrounds, how can heritage language instruction best serve these students who need to recover and/or develop and build upon the language abilities and cultural knowledge that they bring into the classroom? What can successful bilingual education programs teach us about the Spanish heritage language learner? How can the American public and educational policy provide support to help promote heritage language education in the United States that would result in a higher level of bilingualism? What conditions or environments have prevented this thus far?

Language Attitudes and Sociohistorical Factors

As language instructors we need to take into account the attitudinal and sociohistorical factors affecting students in the environment in which we teach. We should understand that teaching Spanish as a heritage language in Los Angeles can and will vary widely from the experience of teaching it in Miami. Even if there are many similarities in the objectives of such instruction, community attitudes toward Spanish and attitudes toward those who use the language may be very different in certain settings and contexts. The majority of Spanish speakers in California are of Mexican background and have a very different history from, say, today's Puerto Ricans and Dominicans in New York and Cubans and Colombians in Miami. In which cities and in which settings would students feel that being more proficient in both languages would be a personal and future professional or career asset (Boswell 2000)? Do students associate speaking Spanish with being punished in elementary school or do they associate it with praise for maintaining their heritage? Have students had an opportunity to learn about their historical and cultural background or have they been deprived of such instruction by its exclusion or by its stereotyped representation in the curriculum? Finally, what would help Spanish teachers who face classes of U.S. Latino bilingual students of varying backgrounds, cultures, and proficiency levels? What approaches have been used in the past and what could we be doing today to encourage the best practices possible based on research and experience? How can the profession best publicize, in communities and schools, important research results that show the benefits of heritage language education and bilingualism?

INCREASE IN SPANISH HERITAGE LANGUAGE STUDENTS IN SCHOOLS AND COLLEGES: THE GROWTH OF THE FIELD

In public schools and colleges around the nation we have seen a marked growth in the number of students who enroll in courses of Spanish as a second or native language (see Lynch, chapter 2 in this volume). Because of this growth of the Latino population in the schools and colleges, teachers in many cities and regions are voicing an urgent need for professional development in heritage language teaching approaches, new SNS courses, an expanded and articulated curriculum for Spanish speakers, and special tracks and programs that can better address the linguistic, cultural, and pedagogical needs of these students who reflect the wide variety of the peoples in Spanish-speaking Latin America.

These concerns for more materials and professional development workshops were corroborated in a recent national survey conducted by the American Association of Teachers of Spanish and Portuguese (AATSP). The area of teaching Spanish for Native Speakers (SNS), as it is often called, or Spanish as a heritage language (SHL), was rated by AATSP members as a top priority for the association and the profession at large. (To examine the survey, contact the AATSP at www.aatsp.org.) These K–16 teachers are voicing the concerns of many who increasingly find themselves in teaching situations for which they have received little or no training and practically no orientation during their college education or even their graduate training. In the majority of schools of education and foreign language and linguistics departments, most of the course work aimed at educating prospective Spanish language teachers offers little if any preparation in such areas as first language acquisition, theories of reading and writing, bilingualism, and pedagogical issues of heritage language learners (either generically or specifically applied to Spanish heritage speakers in the U.S.). In spite of the fact that the Spanish heritage language population has increased enormously during the last ten years, schools of education—almost without exception—do not require their majors to take courses in the field of heritage language learning and teaching as part of graduation requirements. Indeed, students are lucky to even find elective courses in this area as part of the curriculum.

The area of heritage language learning has been with us for many years now (Lipski 2000). In 1970 the American Association of Teachers of Spanish and Portuguese (AATSP 1972) commissioned a report on teaching Spanish to native speakers in high school and college. It was also during this period that linguists and educators began developing materials for university-level teaching of Spanish to Spanish-speaking college students. Guadalupe Valdés and Rodolfo García-Moya (1976) edited the first collection of scholarly articles on teaching Spanish to Spanish speakers in the U.S. context. This was followed by the first major commercial text for bilingual students: *Español escrito: curso para hispanohablantes bilingües* (Valdés and Teschner 1977). This pioneering foundational textbook for college level emphasized basic writing (spelling, accentuation, and vocabulary) and aimed at developing advanced literacy in Spanish without undermining the students' vernacular varieties.

According to the 1990 census, in the 1980s, as more immigrants entered the country, we witnessed an increase of 40 percent in the number of minority language speakers in the United States, as well as an increase in the number of fluent bilingual persons. Contrary to many opinions and as shown by Veltman (1983), immigrants are acquiring English at a rapid pace. It is the respective heritage languages which can erode as generations go by if these languages are not nurtured and supported by families, the communities, and the schools. At the same time, the decade of the 1980s also marked the beginning of the English-only movement's march on civil liberties. The battle is not over and today's social and political scenarios show contradictory signs (Crawford 1992, 1999, 2001). California, as an example, where one-third of the population is Latino, has seen the approval of Proposition 227 (against bilingual education, in 1998) and Proposition 187. (The latter, passed in 1994, denied access to education and health services to undocumented workers; it was declared unconstitutional by the federal government and was never implemented.) English as an official language was approved in the mid-1980s in California, as well as in many other states with significant Latino populations, such as Arizona and Florida.

In 1981 Guadalupe Valdés, Anthony Lozano, and Rodolfo García-Moya coedited *Teaching Spanish to the Hispanic Bilingual,* addressing issues related to Spanish language teaching in bilingual communities. As the title reflects, this book focuses on the maintenance and development of Spanish and includes theoretical studies in dialectology, pedagogical recommendations for SNS courses, sample course syllabi, and evaluation procedures. Although Spanish had been taught to Spanish bilingual students before, the sociolinguistic constraints of the Latino communities in the U.S. had not been totally acknowledged or dealt with in any significant and practical manner until the publication of this book. This is in spite of the AATSP's position on the subject, published in the 1970s in an issue of *Hispania* and reproduced by the Government Printing Office (AATSP 1972). In 1982 Joshua A. Fishman and Gary D. Keller published the anthology *Bilingual Education for Hispanic Students in the United States,* with a special emphasis on language attitudes, language variation, educational approaches, and child language acquisition.

In the 1990s many more programs and courses for native or bilingual speakers began to be implemented in colleges and universities across the country, although in many cases (as happens with bilingual education programs) these programs did not receive sufficient funding or have assigned teachers and instructors who were properly prepared for teaching Spanish to bilingual students. In 1993 Barbara Merino, Henry Trueba, and Fabián Samaniego edited a book titled *Language and Culture in Learning: Teaching Spanish to Native Speakers of Spanish* that addressed the challenges of developing Spanish as a minority language in the educational context. This book presents sociolinguistic and language acquisition studies, as well as sample practical curricular and program practices.

More recently, M. Cecilia Colombi and Francisco Alarcón (1997) coedited a collection of essays devoted to the teaching of Spanish to native speakers, called *La enseñanza del español a hispanohablantes: Praxis y teoría.* This volume focuses on linguistic, cultural, and institutional aspects of the teaching of Spanish to native speakers and provides theoretical and practical implications for the classroom.

In 2000 the AATSP asked its National Committee on Spanish for Native Speakers to write and edit the first practical handbook for teachers K–16 on

Spanish for Native Speakers (AATSP 2000). Since this handbook appeared, there has been no other book especially oriented toward the teaching of Spanish as a heritage language in the U.S. Therefore, our book fills this void with representative recent studies in the field from which practical implications for instruction can be drawn.

We have divided this collection into two parts: part I, Spanish as a Heritage Language: Theoretical Considerations and part II, Community and Classroom-based Research Studies: Implications for Instruction K–16. Part I covers the current state of Spanish heritage language development in the United States. Part II is a selection of community and classroom-based studies of various levels of education (elementary, secondary, and college) from different regions of the country as far-reaching and varied as Texas, Arizona, New Mexico, California, Wisconsin, and Maryland. These essays examine such aspects as young people's attitudes toward English and Spanish, writing strategies, reading acquisition, oral production and development, and issues of revitalization or eradication of a Chicano variety of the language.

Part I. Spanish as a Heritage Language: Theoretical Considerations

In "Toward a Theory of Heritage Language Acquisition: Spanish in the United States," Andrew Lynch offers an overview of the different theoretical models that have been applied to the study of Spanish as a native language in the U.S., most of which have been adapted from the field of sociolinguistics and Spanish language acquisition (SLA). He addresses the necessary relationship between heritage language acquisition (HLA) and SLA in view of the future of Spanish language instruction in the United States. He suggests nine principles to develop a model of HLA that researchers and practitioners should take into account when they focus on Spanish as a heritage language. These principles are: (1) the purposeful acquisition principle, (2) the incidental acquisition principle, (3) the simplification principle, (4) the variability principle, (5) the discourse principle, (6) the utility principle, (7) the social relevance principle, (8) the social identity principle, and (9) the language re-contact principle. Lynch presents a clear and thorough perspective of the directions that HLA studies should pursue to ensure a societal bilingualism that will legitimize Spanish and its speakers in the United States as well as expand its domains in the global future of our nation.

María Carreira, in "Profiles of SNS Students in the Twenty-first Century: Pedagogical Implications of the Changing Demographics and Social Status of U.S. Hispanics," describes the different language competency profiles of the heritage speakers according to the implications of different research studies and the census data. Carreira points out that while states like California, Arizona, and Colorado have severely restricted bilingual education in spite of the significant population of Latinos there, at the same time there is an increased demand for bilingual professionals in many job markets around the country. Carreira argues in favor of looking at different resources to help develop and maintain Spanish and also points to the importance of Spanish-language media as a way to familiarize U.S. Hispanics with dialectical and register variants that go beyond the range of everyday use. She also describes how religious education programs in Spanish and parental instruction could play a decisive role in the attainment of basic literacy skills in Spanish bilinguals.

One of the most important yet difficult aspects of Spanish language development for heritage speakers is academic writing. In our educational system, many Latinos fail to continue the development of advanced literacy in Spanish as they become proficient in English. Even when students are provided with instruction in their first language, such as in bilingual programs, the focus has typically been on developing their English skills so that they can make a transition into English-only classrooms. The courses for heritage or native speakers of Spanish aim at developing the literacy skills that go beyond merely basic reading and writing. Studies have shown that bilingualism and biliteracy provide cognitive and social advantages to students (Bialystock and Hakuta 1994; Cummins 1983, 1989; Hakuta 1986; Fantini 1985; Zentella 1997), and that L1 academic language skills can serve as a basis for development of L2 literacy skills (Cummins and Danesi 1990; Ellis 1994; see also papers in Faltis and Wolfe 1999; and Pérez 1998). Maintaining and developing the first language facilitates the development of the second language, particularly at the levels of advanced literacy, and promotes bilingualism, a benefit for us all as a society. Proficiency in academic writing is essential to gaining access to and succeeding in college and the job market. Academic writing, as well as writing at a professional level, requires a greater mastery of a more extensive range of linguistic features than does everyday, ordinary Spanish. Several chapters in this book address this topic.

In "Un enfoque funcional para la enseñanza del ensayo expositivo," M. Cecilia Colombi looks at the challenges involved in developing advanced literacy in Spanish in the United States. She presents a description of an academic essay from the perspective of Systemic Functional Linguistics (SFL). Looking at the genre and register theory that SFL has developed for teaching writing, she draws some implications for the analysis of the expository essay in SNS courses. This explicit approach to how language functions in different social contexts can help students become more aware of the lexical-grammatical features of language that will make their writing more effective. She takes an essay written by a native speaker of Spanish in an SNS course and deconstructs it into its functional components, showing how language works at different levels (interpersonal, ideational, and textual meta-functions) integrating meaning and form. She also points out certain characteristics of academic writing, such as condensation of meaning through a high lexical density and nominalizations. A list of questions can guide students into the analysis and writing of essays in Spanish. This approach helps students and practitioners to understand how language functions to achieve different purposes. She presents some pedagogical implications for putting into practice a functional approach to language in the heritage speaker classroom.

Ysaura Bernal-Enríquez and Eduardo Hernández Chávez are concerned with questions regarding language maintenance and language loss and the implications for the teaching of Spanish to heritage speakers in New Mexico today. They explore the consequences of deep assimilation factors that have resulted in extensive Spanish language loss in New Mexico, a loss that has been noted by other studies of the region (Bernal-Enríquez 2000; Bills and Vigil 2000). The authors discuss other possible directions, models, and strategies in the teaching of Spanish to Chicanos who have lost their Spanish or are about to lose what little they have left, in order to find alternative ways that can encourage the maintenance or reacquisition of their heritage language.

Part II. Community and Classroom-based Research Studies: Implications for Instruction K–16

The first essay in part II, called "'Spanish in My Blood': Childrens' Spanish Language Development in Dual-Language Immersion Programs," by Ernestina Pesina Hernández, Hinako Takahashi-Breines, and Rebecca Blum-Martínez, explores language development of Spanish-speaking children at the elementary level in a bilingual program in New Mexico. In many schools across the country, we see that dual language immersion programs, the majority of them in Spanish, are rapidly becoming the most prevalent models in bilingual education. Although we find a variety of program designs nationwide, typically these programs include language majority and language minority children in instruction periods for both first and second language learning. The Spanish language proficiency of the teachers in these programs also varies and represents a wide range of levels in a continuum of bilingualism, with some teachers being described as circumstantial bilinguals and others elective bilinguals (Valdés and Figueroa 1994). They may speak one of the standard varieties of Spanish that some would classify as "nonstandard" and therefore be stigmatized as such. Additionally, some of the teachers may have learned Spanish as a second language through schooling and study abroad. Because teachers often function as the main or only provider of the target language, this has become a point of great interest to language researchers. Thus, in this chapter, the authors examine the growth of the children's language as well as questions concerning the proficiency required of both elective and circumstantial bilinguals for teaching in second language programs.

In "Minority Perspectives on Language: Mexican and Mexican-American Adolescents' Attitudes toward Spanish and English," Karen Beckstead and Almeida Jacqueline Toribio study the language situation of Spanish-speaking students of various groups in relation to their length of residence in the United States. The study is based, in part, on an extensive sociocultural and educational questionnaire that was administered to discover heritage students' attitudes toward both Spanish and English. Interesting and informative questions are asked regarding links among culture, identity, and language relative to its prestige, and some answers are offered regarding provisions that schools should make for these Spanish-speaking students. Students' remarks, according to the authors, reflect an awareness that English, not Spanish, is highly valued in education but they also recognize that Spanish is an inseparable part of their identity and cultural background.

Roberto Luis Carrasco and Florencia Riegelhaupt, in their essay titled "META: A Model for the Continued Acquisition of Spanish by Spanish/English Bilinguals in the United States," present a holistic model for the acquisition of languages. While META was first developed and tested in language and culture immersion contexts in Mexico, it has since been implemented in an American university for heritage speakers. This chapter describes the theoretical concepts underlying META and a description of the curriculum design, with many practical examples for the classroom. The authors discuss pedagogical implications for the instruction of heritage language learners in the United States.

Marta Fairclough and N. Ariana Mrak, in their "La enseñanza del español a los hispanohablantes bilingües y su efecto en la producción oral," take into consideration the fact that many Latino children grow up using the local variety of the language used at home until they start their schooling in the dominant language, English. Often it is only when they are older and reach college age that these bilingual U.S. Latinos attempt to learn the standard variety of their heritage language, Spanish, via formal course work. We know all too well from the literature that these attempts commonly have mixed results. Fairclough and Mrak ask questions and explore issues related to the rate of acquisition of a second dialect (the standard variety), the systematicity of "interdialect" produced by heritage learners, and the developmental process or steps in this acquisition process. For example, are they different or similar to those of a traditional foreign or second language learner? Using a frequency analysis of production of forms (error analysis) as well as a qualitative analysis that looks at intra-learner variability, the authors attempt to identify systematicity as well as similarities and/or differences between these different groups of learners. They are interested in analyzing oral registers, comparing students who have taken SNS with Mexican-American residents from the Houston, Texas, area. By using error analysis, their study examines in detail the oral production of three groups of Spanish speakers: one that has no formal instruction in Spanish; another that has one year's experience with formal training; and a third that has benefited from an average of approximately three and a half years of instruction. The results show that formal instruction does not make a difference in these students, as the first group (with no formal instruction) was the one making the fewest errors. It is also important to emphasize that the frequency of errors is quite low in the three groups, with an average of 2 percent. Many implications can be drawn for teaching Spanish to native speakers from this study. Among these, it seems more productive to expand the lexicon of the student through more emphasis on materials that would allow students to feel more comfortable communicating with monolingual native speakers of Spanish. This study illustrates the need for materials and for teaching methodologies that would be more communicative and function-oriented.

Mariana Achugar, in "Academic Registers in Spanish in the U.S.: A Study of Oral Texts Produced by Bilingual Speakers in a University Graduate Program," also explores the linguistic and discursive features of oral Spanish academic registers in a bilingual context through analysis of one type of classroom speech event, oral academic presentations. Achugar presents as an example the oral presentations of two graduate students in a Spanish department who have two very different language socialization experiences and analyzes them using the systemic functional linguistics model to present a description of academic oral registers in Spanish. She finds significant differences in the registers of these students and argues for more academic discourse socialization in Spanish programs because there are few opportunities for this type of language development in other contexts in the U.S.

Rebeca Acevedo, like Colombi, also looks at academic writing in SNS courses. In "Navegando a través del registro formal: Curso para hispanohablantes bilingües," she presents some characterizations of oral and written language, establishing how highly our Western society values advanced literacy. In the context of Spanish-English bilingualism it is important to draw from the levels of literacy that have been achieved in English to develop advanced literacy in Spanish. Many heritage students of Spanish in the U.S. have used Spanish in interpersonal and familiar contexts with very little opportunity to use Spanish in a more formal academic environment. Acevedo points out the need to establish a program of SNS that will facilitate this transference of academic skills into Spanish by exposing the students to this formal register through texts, as well as helping students develop a critical awareness of the features of academic language. Based on her experience with an advanced-level SNS class, she presents five points that can facilitate academic writing and academic language development: (1) differentiate between oral and written register; (2) conceptualize the act of writing a composition as a process; (3) establish the message as the central focus; (4) organize the course by textual genres; and (5) emphasize the importance of the reader of the text. She concludes that a course focused on the written formal register can precede another one aimed at developing the oral formal register. The students' evaluations also show how the emphasis in the formal register increases their appreciation for the heritage language.

"¡*No me suena!* Heritage Spanish Speakers' Writing Strategies," by Ana María Schwartz, explains that because composition typically is a significant component in SNS courses, instructors need to better understand the interplay of the many factors and strategies that come into play in the process of writing in order for students to appreciate these complexities. Schwartz applauds the fact that the pedagogical focus in teaching writing in general has changed from one emphasizing the final product to one emphasizing the teaching of writing as a process that includes copious revision, editing, rewording, rethinking, and polishing before one achieves the "final" product. Schwartz examines various students' written discourse as they progress through the composing process in order to better observe what students go through as they work on their writing assignments.

Reading is also an area of great concern to teachers who teach bilingual Hispanics in the United States. Often, students who may be able to read aloud and sound fairly fluent in pronunciation will tell an instructor afterward that even though they can read in Spanish, they cannot really understand well what they are reading. We know now that extensive reading and reading for pleasure, as indicated by reviews of the literature (Krashen 1993, 2000), contribute greatly to literacy development. It is important that students are surrounded by a variety of reading material from which they can choose readings that they enjoy and that are appropriate to their reading capabilities as well. Availability and access are in many ways key to being able to develop and improve the language. In Sandra L. Pucci's contribution, "Spanish Print Environments: Implications for Heritage Language Development," the Spanish print environments in predominantly U.S. Hispanic areas in two different cities, one in Southern California and one in the Midwest, are explored. Keeping in mind that issues of adequate access to and availability of reading material are vital in terms of language instruction in Spanish for native speakers and bilingual education classrooms, Pucci investigates the range of potential Spanish reading materials available in these two communities for teenagers and young adults in SNS language classes and other secondary school bilingual education settings. In agreement with recent studies on extensive reading as a main contributor to literacy and language development (Krashen 1993), Pucci believes that extensive exposure to Spanish print also needs to be emphasized in SNS classes. Her results indicate that while there are a number of ample and rich sources of Spanish language reading materials available and there is also a tremendous demand for Spanish language materials in the libraries of both cities, the collections are limited and restricted and therefore do not adequately meet the needs of the communities. Literacy in the minority language depends to a great extent on availability of print materials from an early age, so that these experiences can serve as a bridge to more advanced biliteracy in the developing years and in secondary school and college.

New Directions in Spanish as a Heritage Language: National Initiatives, Projects, and Resources

In the last decade, concerned individuals, special interest groups, various universities and language centers, professional associations, funding agencies, and education offices of consulates have begun a public debate that addresses vital language needs by exploring the development of our heritage language resources in our own backyard. Some of these needs include: the need for government-related staff associated with the military and our national security; business needs related to a growing international or global economy; diplomatic needs; and the basic communication needs at the local community level in terms of daily interaction in more than one language. These areas of need may help to highlight for the general public why we must conserve and develop our heritage languages—in our case of interest here, Spanish. As James Crawford has pointed out: "Developing heritage language resources would be far more efficient, not to mention more economical, than to create them from scratch. Because this potential is unappreciated, however, it remains largely untapped" (Crawford 1999). But to these areas we must also add the benefits of cultural and linguistic vitality. Unfortunately Spanish has not been valued in this country for many years as a major world language with over 400 million speakers. It offers its speakers a rich world of music, literature, journalism, radio, television, and Internet communication, as well as the interpersonal interaction that could make this nation a more truly multilingual and multicultural community. In the United States, the public at large and the government cannot simply continue living with a blind spot in regard to the Spanish-speaking communities of the country.

THE AATSP AND THE NFLC

Under the leadership of its former executive director, Lynn Sandstedt, the AATSP has taken in recent years a more proactive and admirable role in the area of Spanish for Native Speakers instruction. By far the largest professional association of teachers of Spanish and Portuguese in the country (K–16), the AATSP now has a standing National Committee on Spanish for Native Speakers, has published a practical manual on the topic, and has conducted a national survey on SNS instruction. It is also a major player in the REACH (*Recursos para la Enseñanza y el Aprendizaje de la Culturas Hispánicas*) Project, a grant funded by the National Endowment for the Humanities, which aims to provide a web site of Internet linked resources designed for use by SNS teachers and students at all levels. The REACH Project, a joint project of the AATSP and the National Foreign Language Center (NFLC) now associated with the University of Maryland at College Park, is the first of its kind in the area of Spanish as a heritage language. The project will provide several web modules of selected topics that include: pedagogical considerations for instruction; U.S. Latinos; the Spanish language; and culture. These web resources are meant to facilitate access to specialist-selected resources and materials to supplement textbooks in the classroom. In addition, they may provide professional development material to help instructors who are searching for both a pedagogical orientation to instructional questions and content materials for class use.

The National Foreign Language Center, under the direction of Catherine Ingold, has also been at the forefront in other heritage language projects. In the late 1990s, the NFLC received major funding from various government sources for the development of the LangNet Project, a quality one-stop web site of foreign language resources and self-instruction for both instructors and students. (To find out more about the LangNet Project, visit their site at www.cal.org/heritage/sns/langnet.html.) The NFLC has been working closely with the AATSP and at times with the Center for Applied Linguistics (CAL) in relation to both REACH and LangNet. In addition to the modules described earlier, another collaboration has been the creation of a *List of SNS Materials with Annotations* (Winke and Peyton 2002), a list to be made available through the LangNet web site at www.langnet.org.

THE CENTER FOR APPLIED LINGUISTICS

Under the leadership of Joy Peyton and Donna Christian, the Center for Applied Linguistics has also been at the forefront of the Heritage Language Initiative that they have created through collaboration with other interested organizations such as the NFLC, language associations, and universities such as the University of California at Los Angeles (UCLA). The Initiative organized the first "National Conference on Heritage Languages in America" in 1999 in Long Beach, California. This was followed up by smaller symposia, and resulted in a book on education and public policy issues, *Heritage Languages in America: Preserving a National Resource* (Peyton, Ranard, and McGinnis 2001) as well as other projects and publication activities. In October 2002, the second National Conference on Heritage Languages in America was held in Tysons Corner, Virginia. It was well attended and well received.

For some time CAL has been steadily compiling and publishing informative and educational ERIC Digests and MiniBibs in the area of Spanish for Native Speakers (Roca 2000, 1992; Pino September 1997; Peyton, Lewelling, and Winke 2001), as well as an Internet Online Resource Guide for Spanish for Native Speakers (Roca and Marcos 1999; Roca, Marcos, and Winke 2001). Additionally, in the summer of 2000, CAL, together with UCLA with a grant from the National Endowment for the Humanities, organized a Summer Institute for Teachers of Spanish for Native Speakers, held at UCLA, with many nationally recognized faculty/scholars as the instructors. The Institute, which one can only hope can be duplicated periodically in different regions of the country, was organized to provide opportunities to secondary school teachers for professional development in the area of heritage language teaching.

THE AMERICAN COUNCIL ON THE TEACHING
OF FOREIGN LANGUAGES (ACTFL)

The American Council on the Teaching of Foreign Languages is the largest professional association of foreign language teachers. The ACTFL hosts a Special Interest Group (SIG) on Spanish for Native Speakers, now one of the largest and most active SIGs in the association. The SNS SIG conducts panels on the topic of Spanish as a heritage language at the annual ACTFL Conference. (To join the SNS SIG go to www.actfl.org.)

In the 1990s ACTFL, together with Hunter College High School and Hunter College, also took on a major national project in the area of Spanish as a heritage language via a FIPSE (Funds for the Improvement of Post Secondary Education) grant. Under the leadership of John Webb (at Hunter College and Hunter College High School at that time) and Jamie Draper (ACTFL), this grassroots professional development project involved working with a group of New York public school teachers of Spanish as a heritage language and teachers of Haitian Creole also as a heritage language. The three-year project surpassed its aims in professional development and in the creation of a model curriculum for heritage language education. It also resulted in an encouraging policy change at Hunter College: it is one of the first colleges to require modern language education majors to take courses in heritage language education as a degree requirement. Additionally, the project resulted in an important publication that was distributed to all registered ACTFL 2000 Conference participants, thereby assuring an impressive distribution to language professionals. Titled *Teaching Heritage Language Learners: Voices from the Classroom* and coedited by John B. Webb and Barbara Miller (2001), the book is an informative and inspiring collection of essays that will serve as a resource in professional development as well as a guide to those who wish to propose similar requirements at their own universities or at the state teacher certification level through their respective departments of education.

The National Foreign Language Standards

Finally, we cannot end our essay without at least saying a few words about what the national foreign language standards (National Standards in Foreign Language Education Project 1996) do and do not provide. It should be understood that they are not meant to offer a panacea to the profession or to provide either content or a model curriculum. The Spanish specific standards do give us, however, something much broader and more useful to explore and use as a framework than, for instance, the ACTFL Proficiency Guidelines in Spanish did. What the national foreign language standards offer SNS instructors is a fresher and more flexible and dynamic way of expanding the range of content possibilities, by looking at classroom activities, learning tasks, interactions, assignments, and designs of experiences in a way that goes beyond the more simplistic and rigid way of thinking of language learning, that is, the traditional four basic language skills (listening, speaking, reading, and writing). And unlike earlier guidelines, they take into account the Spanish heritage student's special needs and abilities. Finally, our students are not left out of this new paradigm that will help us think not only in terms of foreign language teaching but also heritage language development and bilingualism. In essence, the standards provide us with new ways to think about language learning and language teaching in terms of conveying communicative skills in various different modes: the interpersonal, the interpretive, the presentational. It is our role now as language instructors to explore further the usefulness and importance of the standards to Spanish both as a foreign language and as a heritage language. Nonnative students and native speakers of Spanish alike can then profit from a standards-based vision that can both formally and informally help us guide our instructional activities, materials, and curriculum design. It is our task now to experiment and look more carefully underneath the surface of instructional aims and place more attention in appropriate areas of content-based instruction, cooperative learning, educational linguistics, and instructional practice based on both research and classroom experience.

At the same time, while we concentrate on pedagogical issues, we cannot forget or underestimate the power of language attitudes or the politics of heritage language instruction and bilingualism. Given current and projected demographics, the profession should be urgently calling for serious public debates, and for government and private investing in Spanish as a foreign and heritage language in our schools, colleges, and libraries. The negative consequences of heritage language loss will, in the long run, have expensive and dangerous repercussions for the public at large. Spanish in the land that is the United States was here before English arrived and is not going to go away. It will change, however, and multiple varieties of the language will be spoken here, perhaps more so than in any other nation. It is our task as language professionals to see that it continues to grow in prestige and usefulness, both for its speakers and our nation.

REFERENCES

American Association of Teachers of Spanish and Portuguese (AATSP). 2000. *Spanish for Native Speakers. Professional Development Series Handbook* for *Teachers K–16*, Volume I. Fort Worth: Harcourt College Publishers. Available at www.aatsp.org.
———. 1972. *Teaching Spanish in School and College to Native Speakers of Spanish.* AATSP Report of the Executive Council. Wichita, KS: Author.
Bernal-Enríquez, Ysaura. 2000. "Factores socio-históricos en la pérdida del español del suroeste de los Estados Unidos y sus implicaciones para la revitalización." In *Research on Spanish in the United States: Linguistics Issues and Challenges*, ed. Ana Roca. Somerville, MA: Cascadilla Press.

Bialystok, Ellen, and Kenji Hakuta. 1994. *In Other Words: The Science and Psychology of Second Language Acquisition.* New York: Basic Books.

Bills, Garland D., and Neddy A. Vigil. 2000. "The Continuity of Change: Nahuatlisms in New Mexican Spanish." In *Research on Spanish in the United States: Linguistic Issues and Challenges*, ed. Ana Roca. Somerville, MA: Cascadilla Press.

Boswell, Thomas. 2000. "Demographic Changes in Florida and Their Importance for Effective Educational Policies and Practices." In *Research on Spanish in the United States: Linguistic Issues and Challenges*, ed. Ana Roca. Somerville, MA: Cascadilla Press.

Colombi, M. Cecilia, and Francisco X. Alarcón, eds. 1997. *La enseñanza del español a hispanohablantes: Praxis y teoría.* Boston: Houghton Mifflin.

Crawford, James. 2001. Language Policy Web Site and Emporium. Available from http://ourworld.compuserve.com/homepages/JWCRAWFORD. Accessed on May 30, 2001.

——. 1999. *Heritage Languages in America: Tapping a Hidden Resource.* October. Accessed at www.ourworld.compuserve.com/homepages/JWCRAWFORD/HL.htm.

——. 1992. *Hold Your Tongue: Bilingualism and the Politics of "English Only."* Reading, MA: Addison-Wesley.

——. 1989. "Language and Literacy Acquisition." *Journal of Multilingual and Multicultural Development,* 10 (1):17–31.

Cummins, James. 1983. "Language Proficiency, Biliteracy and French Immersion." *Canadian Journal of Education,* 8 (2):117–38.

Cummins, James, and M. Danesi. 1990. *Heritage Languages. The Development and Denial of Canada's Linguistic Resources.* Toronto: Garamond Press.

Ellis, Rod. 1994. *The Study of Second Language Acquisition.* Oxford: Oxford University Press.

Faltis, Christian, and Peter Wolfe, eds. 1999. *So Much to Say: Adolescents, Bilingualism and ESL in the Secondary School.* New York: Teachers College Press.

Fantini, Alvino. 1985. *Language Acquisition of a Bilingual Child: A Sociolinguistic Perspective.* vol. 17. Clevedon, England: Multilingual Matters.

Fishman, Joshua, and Gary Keller, eds. 1982. *Bilingual Education for Hispanic Students in the United States.* New York: Teachers College Press.

Hakuta, Kenji. 1986. *Mirror of Language: The Debate on Bilingualism.* New York: Basic Books.

"Heritage Language Research Priorities Conference Report." 2001. University of California, Los Angeles. Available online from the Center for Applied Linguistics at www.cal.org/heritage/priorities.html.

Hochmuth, Joel. 2001. *Will Spanish Become America's Second Language?* Accessed at CNN.com, September 21.

Krashen, Stephen. 2000. "Bilingual education, the Acquisition of English, and the Retention and Loss of Spanish." In *Research on Spanish in the United States: Linguistic Issues and Challenges*, ed. Ana Roca. Somerville, MA: Cascadilla Press.

——. 1993. *The Power of Reading.* Englewood, CO: Libraries Unlimited.

Lipski, John. 2000. "Back to Zero or Ahead to 2001: Issues and Challenges in U.S. Spanish Research." In *Research on Spanish in the United States: Linguistic Issues and Challenges*, ed. Ana Roca. Somerville, MA: Cascadilla Press.

McKay, Sandra Lee, and Sau-Ling Cynthia Wong, eds. 2000. *New Immigrants in the United States*. Cambridge: Cambridge University Press.

Merino, Barbara, Henry Trueba, and Fabián Samaniego, eds. 1993. *Language and Culture in Learning: Teaching Spanish to Native Speakers of Spanish*. Washington, D.C.: Falmer Press/Taylor & Francis.

National Standards in Foreign Language Eduation Project. 1996. *Standards for Foreign Language Learning: Preparing for the Twenty-first Century*. Yonkers, NY: Author.

Pérez, Bertha, ed. 1998. *Sociocultural Contexts of Language and Literacy*. Mahwah, NJ: Lawrence Erlbaum Associates.

Peyton, Joy Kreeft, Donald A. Ranard, and Scott McGinnis, eds. 2001. *Heritage Languages in America: Preserving a National Resource*. Washington, D.C.: Center for Applied Linguistics and Delta Systems Co.

Peyton, Joy Kreeft, Vickie W. Lewelling, and Paula Winke. 2001. "Spanish for Spanish Speakers: Developing Dual Language Proficiency." ERIC Digest. EDO-FL-01-09. Washington, D.C.: Center for Applied Linguistics. ERIC (EDO-FL-01-09).

Pino, Cecilia. 1997. "Teaching Spanish to Native Speakers: A New Perspective in the 1990s." ERIC Digest. vol. 2, no. 1 (Sept.). Also available at www.cal.org/ericcll/news/199709/9709spanish.htm.

Roca, Ana. 2000. Introduction. In *Research on Spanish in the United States: Linguistic Issues and Challenges*, ed. Ana Roca. Somerville, MA: Cascadilla Press.

———. 1999a. "Foreign Language Policy and Planning in Higher Education: The Case of the State of Florida." In *Sociopolitical Perspectives on Language Policy and Planning in the USA*, eds. Thom Huebner and Kathryn Davis. Amsterdam: John Benjamins.

———. 1999b. *Nuevos mundos: Lectura, Cultura y Comunicación*. New York: John Wiley and Sons.

———. 1997. "Retrospectives, Advances, and Current Needs in the Teaching of Spanish to United States Hispanic Bilingual Students." *ADFL Bulletin* 29: 37–43.

———. 1992. *Spanish for U.S. Hispanic Bilinguals in Higher Education*. ERIC Digest. ED350881. Washington, D.C.: Center for Applied Linguistics and ERIC Clearinghouse on Languages and Linguistics. Available at www.ed.gov/data bases/ERIC_Digests/ed350881.html.

Roca, Ana, and Kathkeen Marcos. 1999, Nov. "Resources for Teaching Spanish to Native Speakers." Washington, D.C.: ERIC/CLL Resource Guides Online. ERIC Clearinghouse on Languages and Linguistics.

Roca, Ana, Kathleen Marcos, and Paula Winke. 2001, Oct. "Resources for Teaching Spanish to Native Speakers." Washington, D.C.: ERIC/CLL Resource Guides Online. Updated publication of above-cited reference. ERIC Clearinghouse on Languages and Linguistics. Available at www.cal.org/ericcll/faqs/RGOS/sns.html.

U.S. Census Bureau. 2001. *United States Census 2000, Population Tables and Reports.* Accessed on May 30, 2001. Available at www.census.gov/main/www/cen2000.html.

Valdés, Guadalupe, and Richard A. Figueroa. 1994. *Bilingualism and Testing: A Special Case of Bias.* Norwood, NJ: Ablex.

Valdés, Guadalupe, and Rodolfo García-Moya, eds. 1976. *Teaching Spanish to Spanish Speakers: Theory and Practice.* San Antonio, TX: Trinity University.

Valdés, Guadalupe, Anthony G. Lozano, and Rodolfo García-Moya, eds. 1981. *Teaching Spanish to the Hispanic Bilingual in the United States: Issues, Aims, and Methods.* New York: Teachers College Press.

Valdés, Guadalupe, and Richard Teschner. 1977. *Español escrito: Curso para hispanohablantes bilingües.* New York: Scribner's.

Veltman, Calvin. 1983. *Language Shift in the United States.* Berlin: Mouton.

Webb, John, and Barbara Miller, eds. 2001. *Teaching Heritage Language Learners: Voices from the Classroom.* Yonkers, NY: ACTFL Series 2000.

Winke, Paula, and Joy Peyton, eds. 2002. *List of SNS Materials with Annotations.* A LangNet Annotated Bibliography Project, LangNet Project at the National Foreign Language Center. The materials were compiled by the Center for Applied Linguistics in summer of 2001. The information will be available at www.lang net.org.

Zentella, Ana Celia. 1997. *Growing Up Bilingual.* Malden, MA: Blackwell.

PART I

Spanish as a Heritage Language

Theoretical Considerations

2

Toward a Theory of
Heritage Language Acquisition
Spanish in the United States

Andrew Lynch
University of Florida

The sociolinguistic realities of English and Spanish, at the national and world levels, have evolved in fundamental ways since the 1960s. Traditional theoretical models of language variation, bilingualism, and language shift in the U.S. must be reconceptualized within the post-2000 context, and Spanish language educators must respond to the contemporary demands of their profession. In this essay, I give thought to the theoretical principles of Spanish heritage language acquisition (HLA) in the U.S. in the twenty-first century.

The Changing Nature of Spanish Language Study in the U.S.

Spanish language study in the U.S. has changed dramatically since the 1960s, both in purpose and in practice. Part of this change has been a direct result of the innovations that broadly swept the field of second language pedagogy in the U.S. from the late 1970s through the mid-1980s. With the formalization of more socially oriented notions of language in the 1970s, through sociological and anthropological perspectives, researchers and practitioners in the rapidly developing new field of second language acquisition (SLA) began to reconceptualize theories of second language (L2) learning. SLA debates did not take place in isolation; they were clearly reflective of what may be called the "social revolution" in linguistics in the 1960s and 1970s. Labov (1972) published a cogent methodology for analyzing languages as dynamic, variable systems rather than fixed, idealized ones, taking into account a wide array of synchronic extralinguistic factors that may condition diachronic internal changes. Hymes (1974) placed *communicative competence* as counterpoint to Chomsky's (1965) mentalist construct of *linguistic competence*, and Halliday (1975) and Hatch (1978) carefully made the case for discourse processes and interaction in first and second language development.[1] The seminal work of Terrell on the Natural Approach (1977) to language teaching, in explicit relationship to Krashen's (1981) Monitor model, provided Spanish language teachers with a groundbreaking textbook called *Dos Mundos* (1986), aimed at placing input and interaction at the center of the beginning classroom. The purpose of Terrell's methodology was to take students beyond the phonological, morphological, syntactic, and lexical levels of language to the social dimensions of semantics and pragmatics (cf. Klee 1998). Communication was to be the focus of the classroom; language *per se* would merely serve as the vehicle for interaction as learners followed natural routes of development. Grammar was placed at the service of lexicon and semantics rather than vice versa. What Widdowson (1988) called "grammar and nonsense" would, in the minds of Terrell, Krashen, and subsequent proponents of *communicative language teaching*, become a thing of the past.[2]

Although communicative methodologies impacted to some extent the way most L2s were taught in the U.S. in the 1980s, the circumstance of Spanish was unique. Not only was Spanish language teaching changing at the internal, professional level as a result of innovations in SLA, but it was also being importantly impacted at the external, social level by one of the most massive immigration waves in U.S. history, second only to the period 1901 to 1910 (Ricento 1995). Unlike the immigrations of the early twentieth century—of mostly European origin—the wave of the 1980s was principally Mexican, Caribbean, and Central and South American. Xenophobia in the 1980s became synonymous with Hispanophobia (Zentella 1995), and the political lobbying organization US English spent $28 million between 1983 and 1990 to promote English language legislation at the state and federal levels (Crawford 1992, p. 4).[3] But at the same time that political Hispanophobia flourished, so did nationwide Spanish language enrollments. Despite political efforts by organizations such as US English to weaken Hispanic visibility and ensure that English would cede no sociolinguistic territory to Latin American Spanish, many parents and students took notice and, in turn, took interest in the Spanish language that they increasingly heard spoken in their towns and neighborhoods. The growth of Spanish language programs at all educational levels—primary, secondary, and postsecondary—has remained steady until the present day, as the other traditional languages of study decline.[4] For example, a study carried out at Arizona State University by Guntermann, Hendrickson, and de Urioste (1996) showed that enrollments in the French lower division program at that institution dropped from nearly 800 in 1985 to fewer than 700 in 1995, while the Spanish lower division program grew from about 1,000 students to almost 2,400 within the same ten-year period. National enrollment figures in foreign languages compiled by the Modern Language Association (MLA) in 1998 reflected this same trend throughout the country (Brod and Welles 2000). French language enrollments continually declined from 34.4 percent of all U.S. postsecondary students studying a foreign language in 1968 to 26.9 percent in 1980, 23 percent in 1990, down to 16.7 percent in 1998. German enrollments decreased from 19.2 percent in 1968 to 13.7 percent in 1980, 11.3 percent in 1990, and 7.5 percent in 1998. In 1968, nationwide enrollments in postsecondary Spanish language programs were slightly under those of French, at 32.4 percent. By 1980, Spanish enrollments increased to 41 percent, up to 45.1 percent in 1990, and by 1998, more than half (55 percent) of all U.S. postsecondary students studying a foreign language were learning Spanish.

At a time in U.S. education when general interest in humanities is waning, one might think that the extraordinary growth experienced by Spanish language programs would be welcomed. But at many postsecondary institutions, the increasing popularity of Spanish among undergraduate students has not been met with open arms by some colleagues and administrators in humanities units. Nichols (2000) addressed the "rising tide" of Spanish, affirming that:

> The unequivocal primacy of Spanish in United States colleges and universities discomfits many who are not in the field, but it is a fact that must be faced. The irony of this rise to preeminence—in a time of general decline in support for the humanities—does not escape Spanish scholars of my generation, who endured decades of indifferent or disparaging treatment from colleagues in other languages and from equally biased administrators. Spanish has lived what might be termed a rags-to-riches story, except that it is still frequently dressed in rags, and its only apparent riches are unspendable student credit hours. In fact, there have not been increases in funding and tenure-line positions in Spanish commensurate with the spectacular growth in the language. . . .
>
> Faculty members in Spanish have borne and will continue to bear a much heavier teaching, advising, and service load than their colleagues. They have concomitantly less time for research, with all that generally implies in the university's reward system. (pp. 116–18)

Parallel to the problems of satisfying the expanding teaching and research demands in Spanish language at the university level are the problems faced by the multitude of Spanish-speaking children and adolescents in this country whose primary educational needs go unmet. Zentella (1990, 1996) has eloquently posited the need for bilingual education programs and has called for an "anthropolitical" linguistic approach to Spanish in the U.S. Her 1997 book, *Growing Up Bilingual,* documents in detail the social and economic forces that impact the patterns of language use among bilingual second-generation Puerto Ricans in New York City, as well as their ultimate access to formal education. Walker and Tedick (2000) made it convincingly clear that the need for planning and curriculum development across the three traditional subfields of L2 teaching—foreign language education, bilingual education, and English as a second language—have become crucial. They urged that the field as a whole must engage in "movement to a center," that is, the recognition that demographic changes have importantly altered the framework for language teaching in the U.S. The case of Spanish is, without any doubt, the most illustrative.

The growth of Spanish-English bilingualism in the U.S. has resulted in an ever-increasing demand for bilingual and heritage language education in Spanish. U.S. Census 2000 registered more than 35 million people who identified themselves as "Hispanic" or "Latino"; this represented a 57.9 percent increase over the 22 million documented by the 1990 census. Since this growth was mostly attributed to immigration, the "Hispanic" increase in the 1990s was synonymous with Spanish-language expansion. Projections suggest that the U.S. will become increasingly more Hispanic in the coming decades, solidifying its status as the world's fifth most populous Spanish-speaking nation. Roca (2000) observed that "today the Hispanic presence seems to be almost everywhere we look, even in areas where one would least expect it, such as small cities and towns in North Carolina, Minnesota, or Iowa. It is no longer only in New York, California, Texas, and South Florida" (p. viii). She affirmed that "one of the greatest challenges facing the United States in the twenty-first century is to deal with the new 'in your face' and 'in your ear' dimensions of the demographic changes that are happening at a lightning pace" (pp. vii–viii). Spanish heritage language (HL) education, a field which began building momentum in the U.S. in the early 1970s (cf. Roca 1997), will become continually more in demand as a consequence of this exponential population growth. Concomitantly, issues of language placement and the function of such classificatory terms as "native" versus "heritage" versus "nonnative" speaker will become more essential in the educational domain.

In response to the dramatic and very important changes that have affected our field since the 1960s, we must begin to focus carefully on a number of internal professional issues. Socially and demographically, it is clear that the language we teach is very much unlike the other "foreign" languages taught in the U.S. As the unofficial second language of the nation and the one with the most significant role in immigration, social transformation, bilingualism, and language contact, it is imperative that Spanish assume a contemporary theoretical framework to provide the basis for future discussions among researchers, teachers, administrators, and politicians. Valdés (1995) already observed that Spanish for Native Speakers (SNS) instruction "has developed multiple practices and pedagogies that are not directly based on coherent theories about the kinds of language learning with which they are concerned" (p. 308). She urged that "it is time for teachers and applied linguists working in this area to examine their research and practice and to begin to frame the agenda that will guide them in the years to come" (p. 321).

The situation of Spanish in the U.S. in the twenty-first-century context of globalization (and the inherent "Latinization" of the U.S. economy) does not afford educators and researchers the convenience of faithfully calling upon traditional models of bilingualism and sociolinguistics. Although only a few decades have passed since Ferguson (1959), Fishman (1967), and Labov (1966, 1972) formulated their respective hallmark theoretical models, the U.S. social, economic, and political realities have changed in very important ways since their time. In the U.S. in 1960, the effects of the cold war were still felt. Few Americans ever heard a language other than English spoken on the street, on television, or the radio. Signs, advertisements, product labels, and instructions did not appear in Spanish/English translation. The Spanish-language media was practically nonexistent. Computers, the Internet, and cellular telephones were not in use. International telephone service was limited. Air travel was highly restrictive in service, cost, and availability; only an elite few ever traveled or studied outside the U.S. The South, by law, remained racially segregated. Spanish speaking in the Southwest was social taboo. The civil rights movement had not begun, the voices of feminists were unheard, and "ethnic pride" was largely unknown by national minority groups. "Family" invoked a somewhat different social (and sociolinguistic) concept than the one many Americans think of today.

In sum, the monolingual anglophone communities of the northeastern U.S. studied by Labov in the 1960s, the urban ethnic enclaves studied by Fishman, Cooper, and Ma (1971) in the same decade and, certainly, the mid-twentieth-century societies of Haiti, Switzerland, and Egypt cited by Ferguson in support of his original (1959) theory of diglossia provide potentially misleading blueprints for understanding the ongoing construction of Spanish-English bilingualism in the global post-2000 context. As much as social, cultural, economic, and political realities have changed, so must our theories of language contact in the U.S.[5] A rich beginning will be to cultivate the largely undeveloped yet rapidly expanding field of Spanish HLA in our national and transnational context.

Approaching HLA through SLA and Bilingualism

In research and in practice, Spanish language education for the heritage speaker has usually been termed Spanish for Native Speakers (SNS) or Spanish for Bilinguals.[6] A heritage language (HL) learner of Spanish is generally considered to be someone born and educated entirely in the United States, whose family members use Spanish restrictedly. The term "heritage" learner should not invoke any lesser or greater degree of bilingual competence through classifications such as "second," "third," or "fourth" generation. I found in Miami, for example, that some third-generation Spanish speakers reflect higher levels of grammatical and discourse proficiency than some second-generation speakers (Lynch 1999). Issues of HL placement should be addressed in light of students' functional abilities in Spanish, independent of students' self-reports and administrators' classificatory debates about who is more "bilingual" or more "native." These terminological debates generally lack value in practice, and may result in learners being placed in classes where the level is inappropriate to their actual abilities. The terms "native" and "bilingual" in HL course titles may even discourage HL speakers from enrolling in such courses. Villa and Villa (1998) explained that HL speakers at New Mexico State University often opt out of SNS courses simply because of professional terminology. They stated: "Professionals may label certain students as 'native speakers,' while the students themselves may not share that vision of their language skills, and hence not identify with the label 'native speaker'" (Villa and Villa 1998, p. 512). These HL students then turn to courses of Spanish for nonnative speakers, where they lose valuable academic time which could have otherwise been devoted to developing their orthographic, grammatical, and discourse skills at a level appropriate to their needs.

In approaching HLA in practice, teachers might assume that HL learners bring to the classroom an immense advantage that many L2 learners do not have — lived experience with the language as a social reality. Perhaps this experience should be reflected in more "native-like" pronunciation, aptness in circumlocution, more fluid discourse (although vocabulary may be lacking), instrumental and integrative motivation for studying the language, as well as more positive attitudes toward the language in general. Reality sometimes demonstrates that our assumptions are equivocal, however. Those who have experience as teachers of Spanish HL classes in the U.S. are familiar with the circumstance of learners who sometimes refuse to speak Spanish in class — in group work or to the teacher individually; who make long pauses and hesitations in their HL discourse; who resort to English rather than attempting to circumlocute in Spanish; and who insist that they are only taking the class to fulfill a humanities requirement and that they have no concrete plans to use the language in the future. Reality informs us that HL professionals cannot enter the classroom with assumptions about the linguistic abilities of their students or their motivations for being there. Even though I would not agree with the suggestion that HL learners are no different than L2 learners, I would not disagree with it, either. Many HL learners proudly perceive themselves as "speakers" of Spanish, but many others do not. They may choose to think of themselves as L2 learners of Spanish, particularly those of the third and fourth generations. Solely at the linguistic level, some of them may be justified in their self-perceptions. In a study that I carried out at the University of Miami (Lynch 2001), I found consistent similarities between the grammatical systems of some second- and third-generation Spanish HL learners and the grammatical systems of advanced Spanish L2 learners. Through analysis of transcribed, tape-recorded conversations with individuals from both groups, I observed that many HL learners were grammatically indistinguishable from advanced L2 learners with regard to subject pronoun expression, adjective-noun agreement, *ser/estar* distinction, expression of aspect and hypotheticality, mood variability, and the occurrence of lexical "Anglicisms" (cf. Lipski 1993).

HL speakers are generally characterized by linguistic processes and social factors attributed to both SLA and to situations of language contact. HLA represents the interface of theory and research in the fields of SLA and language contact, so we must consider that the major factors taken into account by scholars and practitioners in both of these fields will be essential to our discussions of HLA. Moreno Fernández (1998) affirms that "cualquier situación de enseñanza de segundas lenguas o de lenguas extranjeras es, en realidad, una situación de lenguas en contacto . . . . [L]a colaboración entre los expertos en lenguas en contacto y en lingüística aplicada puede dar unos frutos beneficiosos para ambas especialidades" (p. 327). From the field of SLA, we should integrate the emphasis placed upon *input and interaction, acquisition orders and developmental sequences, cross-linguistic influence, language variability, communication strategies, learner motivations and attitudes*, and the *social context* of language learning.[7] We should further expand the definition of the *bilingual continuum* as it has been put forth in the field of language contact, and embark upon systematic, empirical exploration of the role of bilingual strategies, such as those posited by Silva-Corvalán (1995): *simplification of grammatical categories and lexical oppositions, over-generalization of forms, development of periphrastic constructions, direct and indirect transfer of forms across languages*, and *code-switching*. Silva-Corvalán makes explicit reference to the intricate and inevitable relationship between these separate fields of inquiry: "in language contact situations and in language acquisition we observe the same principles at work which characterize change in unstressed languages: *generality, frequency, distance, and semantic transparency*" (1995, p. 11). She also remarks (1990) that "it is arresting to note that language attrition in societal bilingualism is in fact to a large extent the mirror image of development in language acquisition" and that correspondences between the linguistic systems affected "may in fact reflect the freezing, at different levels of development of grammatical proficiency, of the bilingual's secondary language" (pp. 167–168). Klee (1996) revealed that second language acquisition processes can even be inherent in the norms of primary language use in a bilingual speech community. She found that L2 developmental orders of the Spanish clitic pronoun system has lead to the dramatic reduction of third-person forms (*lo, los, la, las*) in the normative Spanish of an Andean community which she studied in Peru. This was true even among speakers of the professional and middle socioeconomic classes whose first language was Spanish.

In spite of the obvious relationship between SLA and language contact, researchers have made only very scarce attempts to "cross party lines" from either field to bridge theory between the two, except in Creole language studies. This absence of dialogue seems puzzling if one assumes, as I do, that the ultimate goal of second language learning is bilingualism (be it to a lesser or greater degree), and that many bilinguals—especially U.S. Spanish-English bilinguals—embark upon some formal second language study of one or both of their languages at some point, or various points, in their lifetimes. How could SLA processes not somehow be inherent in bilingual language development? Why should educators and researchers not look to bilingual competence, as it is manifested in language contact settings, as the best potential baseline for comparison of non-L2 speakers' abilities at distinct stages of development?

In establishing dialogue between the fields of SLA and bilingualism, HLA scholars and practitioners must be careful to avoid what I would call the trap of the "never-native speaker" in research methodology. Several scholars in the field of SLA have, in recent years, highlighted the methodological imprecision, as much as practical inadequacy, of the pervasive tendency to describe and assess L2 development with reference to "native speaker" norms

(Cook 1999; Firth and Wagner 1997; Pavlenko 2001; Souto Silva 2000, to cite only a few). The theoretical quest to approximate "native" proficiency has, for some SLA researchers, seemingly turned into obsession with the notion that L2 learners will never be "native" speakers, and that they will forever be deficient in their language abilities. While researchers occupy their time comparing L2 development with monolingual native speaker norms, reality dictates that no L2 learner will ever become a monolingual speaker of the target language. The same is true of HL learners. With much reason, Cook (1999) declared that "if students and teachers see L2 learning as a battle that they are fated never to win, little wonder they become dispirited and give up. L2 learners' battle to become native speakers is lost before it has begun" (p. 204). Cook argues that we must "go beyond the native speaker" in L2 research and teaching by convincing learners that "they are successful multicompetent speakers, not failed native speakers" (p. 204).

Firth and Wagner (1997) argued that SLA's reliance upon the native speaker is symptomatic of the Chomskyan inheritance in linguistics. Within the Chomskyan paradigm, the idealized native speaker provides the basis for describing and assessing linguistic development. Chomsky's (1965) theory of the mental structures of language and an innate cerebral language acquisition device had, according to Firth and Wagner, a "cataclysmic effect" not only on SLA but on linguistics in general (p. 287). These researchers argued that because of the pervasive influence of such mentalist accounts of language, cognition and psychology have overshadowed the nature of language as a heterogeneous and highly variable social construct (cf. Caravedo 1990). Firth and Wagner remarked:

> Consonant with Chomskyan linguistics . . . in SLA as a whole, the NS [native speaker] is a seemingly omniscient figure . . . . NS data are thus viewed as the warranted baseline from which NNS [nonnnative speaker] data can be compared, and the benchmark from which judgements of appropriateness, markedness, and so forth, can be made. . . . NS and NNS are blanket terms, implying homogeneity throughout each group, and clear-cut distinctions between them. So a NS is assumed unproblematically to be a person with a mother tongue, acquired from birth. How bilingualism, multilingualism, "semi-lingualism," and (first) language loss relate to the concept of NS are in large measure ignored, as is the question of whether one can become a NS in a S/FL [second/foreign language].
> (1997, pp. 291–92)

Valdés and Figueroa (1994) cogently explained the fallacies and pitfalls of relying upon the native/nonnative speaker dichotomy in the assessment of bilingual language abilities. They raised a number of questions aimed at the problems inherent in educators' dependence upon the native speaker construct in formal assessment: "Is a bilingual speaker a native speaker of at least one of his languages? Is the native language always the language acquired first? If so, does the bilingual remain a native speaker of this language in spite of his almost exclusive use of a second language during most of his lifetime?" (p. 34); "To what degree is a circumstantial bilingual who is a fluent speaker of two languages still an *acquirer* or *learner* of his second language?" (p. 38); "Is it a fact that bilinguals have a dominant or 'stronger' language? Is it possible for bilinguals to be equally proficient in their two languages and thus not dominant in either?" (p. 55). The answer that Valdés and Figueroa provided us is that no clear, simple answer exists, to any of these questions. They stated:

> The fact of the matter is that there is no simple way of measuring language ability, language proficiency, or language competence in even one language. There is no exact set of procedures that can be used to determine how bilingual an individual is across a broad range of contexts and settings, and there are no strategies or instruments that can economically and easily assess either the language proficiency or the language dominance of large groups of individuals . . . . The point here is that procedures for measuring the range of abilities and skills that are involved in being a native speaker of a language have not been developed. They have not been developed for very good reasons. First, it is a difficult task, and second, it is doubtful that we need precise information about native speaker abilities (e.g., the nature of native fluency) except to carry out certain kinds of linguistic research . . . . (pp. 66–67)

The study of languages in contact is generally undertaken vis à vis the norms of some noncontact or "monolingual" variety of the same language. This tendency again probably reflects the inheritance of rationalist and mentalist paradigms in linguistics, ones which subsume language within a self-governing entity, at some "underlying" level as in the mind. Romaine (1995) suggested that the fallacy of most theoretical approaches to bilingualism stems from the prominent intellectual paradigms which informed the early foundations of the field: "Western modes of thought bear the legacy of structuralism—the belief that an entity, whether it is a society, language, etc., can be viewed as a structured, self-contained whole, an autonomous entity which is consistent with itself . . . . It is from this intellectual perspective that modern linguistic theory has been articulated and within it that much of the research on bilingualism has been conducted" (p. 326).

Bearing in mind these theoretical and methodological antecedents of research in SLA and bilingualism in the twentieth century, I turn to the focus and principles of a potential theory of HLA for future endeavors treating Spanish in the U.S.

Toward a Theory of HLA: Spanish in the U.S.

FOCUS

Research on Spanish in the U.S. in the twenty-first century will necessarily proceed from the bases established in the previous century. However, an important shift in focus must take place. Rather than the commonplace approach to understanding the Spanish of U.S.-born speakers through cross-generational variation (adapting Labov 1972) and social diglossia (adapting Ferguson 1959; Fishman 1967), the analysis of *intragenerational* variation and speaker social networks must move to center stage. In the study of intragenerational variation, we part from the Labovian model of language variation and change, and proceed with a fundamental and important methodological difference: rather than concentrating on the *uniformities* of variability in speech communities, we scrutinize *discontinuities*.[8] We thus not only intentionally sidestep the methodological trap of losing in group averages and statistics those individuals who manifest important sociolinguistic differences, but we focus specifically on those differences and search for explanations as to their existence. These *discontinuities* should lead us to investigate the *social networks* (Milroy 1980) of those IIL speakers who demonstrate greater and lesser degrees of language proficiency, yet who may reflect quite similar sociocultural backgrounds or perhaps even be members of the same social networks. Torres (1991) explained the value of a social network approach in research on Spanish in the U.S.:

> The informal groups in which people participate and have a clear consciousness of belonging to often reflect language use better than categories such as age, birthplace, etc. While these characteristics inform decisions on the type of networks people choose to be members of, they do not lead to any predetermined associations. Network analysis could help account for some of the individual variation that exists in a stable bilingual situation . . . . [W]e need to also look at the effect of network participation and style shifting on language usage in U.S. Spanish communities. (p. 263)

As we go about shifting our focus to *sociolinguistic discontinuities* and *speaker social networks* in research on Spanish-English bilingualism in the U.S., we should elaborate a series of theoretical principles related to the acquisition (and concomitant individual-level maintenance) of Spanish by U.S.-born speakers.

PRINCIPLES

I would initially propose at least nine principles for a theory of HLA relevant to Spanish in the U.S. context. These principles assume, based on a wealth of previous research on Spanish in the U.S., that: (1) English is the language of more frequent everyday use among most Spanish HL speakers; (2) English is the socially "preferred" language of interaction among Spanish HL speakers; (3) most HL speakers do not insist that one must speak Spanish to be considered "Hispanic" or "Latino"; (4) English literacy and formal discourse skills of the majority of U.S.-born bilinguals are prescriptively superior to their Spanish skills. Principles 1 and 2 describe the act of language acquisition; Principles 3, 4, and 5 refer to the process of language acquisition; Principles 6, 7, and 8 constitute macro-level issues of Spanish in the U.S. context; and Principle 9 encompasses the phenomenon of sociolinguistic recontact.

Principle 1. *The purposeful acquisition principle.* HL speakers are most apt to expand their linguistic repertoires through purposefully sought opportunities for acquisition. These opportunities may be formal, such as classroom or "on-the-job" learning, or they may be informal, such as watching Spanish-language television programs, attending Spanish-language religious services, purposefully conversing in Spanish with other Spanish speakers, or something as simple as choosing the Spanish-language option to carry out a bank ATM transaction or reading product labels/instructions printed in Spanish.

Principle 2. *The incidental acquisition principle.* HL speakers are likely to expand their linguistic repertoires through incidental experiences with the language, occurring naturally in social context. Incidental acquisition takes place, for example, when HL learners interact with family members who speak Spanish; overhear/observe conversations between other Spanish speakers outside the home; are placed in the position of having to converse with a Spanish-speaking immigrant, visitor, or customer/client; notice a sign or advertisement written in Spanish; or come across a radio or television broadcast in Spanish and tune in for a short (or long) time. Due to immigration, migration, the expansion of Spanish-language media, and the economic globalization of Spanish in North America and the Caribbean, the chances of incidental acquisition of Spanish among HL speakers in the U.S. are becoming increasingly greater.

Principle 3. *The simplification principle.* Due to the fact that English is the language of instruction and socialization in U.S. schools, it is the cognitively dominant language of HL speakers of Spanish. As a result, the Spanish linguistic system of these speakers will reflect a number of grammatical, lexical, and pragmatic simplifications that are not evident in English (Silva-Corvalán 1994). For this reason, the formal and academic discourse norms of Spanish HL speakers should not be compared to the formal and academic norms of first-generation Spanish speakers who were educated principally in their native countries. The most appropriate comparison—if one must be made for educational research purposes—might be that between Spanish HL learners and more advanced L2 learners of Spanish in the U.S. who are also academically English-dominant. Many educators and researchers place false and undue linguistic expectations upon HL learners by comparing them to monolingual or Spanish-dominant learners simply because of their family histories. This practice is as linguistically incorrect as it is socially unjust.

Principle 4. *The variability principle.* The grammar and discourse of HL speakers is highly variable in nature; therefore the most apt approach to HL development aims to build upon this variability. In the same way that L2 learners proceed in developing their proficiency according to extralinguistic factors such as task, interlocutor, register, and setting (cf. Tarone 1988, 1995 in SLA research), so does HL learner proficiency expand. Following Tarone (1995), we might postulate that HL proficiency grows most substantially outside the classroom and with interlocutors who are not teachers. Moreover, dialect and register issues are crucial for the HL learner. HL teachers must devote class time to tasks and explanations that build HL learners' awareness of dialect and register variation (cf. Valdés and Geoffrion-Vinci 1998). Teachers should oblige HL learners to produce language representative of formal as much as informal registers of their own dialects, through vertical discourse relationships and the imitation of illustrative oral and written texts.

Principle 5. *The discourse principle.* HL speakers will most readily and successfully expand their linguistic repertoires through vertical and horizontal discourse relationships with other speakers (cf. Hatch 1978 in SLA research). HL pedagogy should emphasize grammatical and lexical development through discourse-level activities (cf. McQuillan 1998; Roca 1999b; Valdés-Fallis 1978). Discrete-point activities, transformation exercises, grammar paradigms, metalinguistic rules, and long vocabulary lists will likely hinder HL learners more than help them.[9] Since their experience with the HL has been purely dialogic and socially discursive from the start, academic proficiency growth is most successful if a discourse-level focus is maintained. Faltis (1990) explained the contribution of Vygotskian and Freirian perspectives to

Spanish HL classrooms, where dialogue and discourse are fundamental. Colombi (2000) demonstrated how syntactic and semantic complexity expands through discourse-level writing activities in a Spanish HL course characterized by a communicative, coconstructive teaching methodology.

Principle 6. *The utility principle.* The more practically useful (or "instrumental") that HL speakers find the language to be in their immediate and/or broader social context, the more likely they are to seek out opportunities to use it and, in turn, to acquire it both purposefully and incidentally. HL teachers must integrate activities that require that learners use Spanish—and develop Spanish literacy skills—beyond the classroom. Fitting examples are chat rooms in cyberspace, community or family learning projects, service learning projects, and internships in businesses and corporations that deal with U.S. Spanish speakers or with the Spanish-speaking world. Educators must emphasize the advantage that Spanish-English bilinguals have in some career and professional paths, e.g., trade, sales, and marketing, human resources and management, health care, law, journalism, public social services, and the hotel and restaurant industry. They should emphasize that in some regions, such as the state of Florida, bilingual Hispanics earn considerably more money each year than do Hispanics who speak only English (Boswell 2000). The "utility principle" may also need to be taken into account in future research on Spanish SLA in the U.S., since this phenomenon would also feasibly impact L2 learners. Evidence from Spanish L2 learners in Miami, for example, already reflects its impact (Santiago 1998).

Principle 7. *The social relevance principle.* If HL speakers perceive their broader social environment to be a bilingual or multilingual one, they will be more likely to use and to acquire purposefully the HL. Spanish HL teachers are obligated to make learners aware of the longstanding historical and inevitable future presence of the Spanish language within U.S. borders. They should insist upon the recognition of Spanish as the unofficial second language of the U.S., and the vital contribution—both practical and ideological—made by those who speak and write Spanish in the public and private sectors. HL teachers must emphasize the notion of the U.S. as a multilingual, multicultural nation, and pay particular attention to local areas or neighborhoods where Spanish-English bilingualism is the norm. HL learners should be made aware that Spanish is one of the world's leading global languages in trade, commerce, and communication, and the world's third most-spoken language after Mandarin Chinese and World English.[10]

Principle 8. *The social identity principle.* HL speakers who psychologically relate one or more aspects of their social identity to the HL, either for reasons of utility or social relevance, will be more inclined to use it and purposefully acquire it (cf. Gardner 1985 in SLA research). HL teachers must instill in learners a sense of pride and prestige relevant to Spanish at the local, national, and world levels. With the consistently high immigration rates of young Spanish speakers in the U.S., and the expanding use of Spanish language in popular culture, the mass media, and the economy of the nation, HL learners will tend to identify the language less with an elderly generation or with "nostalgia for the homeland," and more with a younger, socially and economically active element of the U.S. population. Indeed, Ramírez (2000) found that nearly 95 percent of Los Angeles HL youths included in his study placed high value on using Spanish to "make more friends"; 87 percent of HL youths from Miami emphasized that Spanish was valuable for making friends as did 86 percent of HL youths from the Bronx (New York) and 81 percent in Albuquerque.

Principle 9. *The language recontact principle.* HL speakers who experience recontact with the language, either through contact with first-generation immigrants or visitors or through travel, work, or study abroad, will be more likely to acquire the HL both purposefully and incidentally. Recontact is presently the social phenomenon which is most vital and favorable to future maintenance of Spanish among U.S.-born speakers. HL teachers must implement activities that promote recontact of HL speakers with Spanish-language social networks, be they personal or professional. The best examples would be community and service learning projects as well as travel and study abroad. Fountain (2001) described such activities at a small private college in North Carolina, a state where a new Spanish heritage language population is rapidly emerging.[11] HL students at this college are provided internships at businesses, schools, and public organizations dealing directly with the Spanish-speaking population of the city and state. The college also sponsors learning experiences for HL speakers in New York, Miami, and nearby Washington, D.C., as well as educational travel and cross-cultural seminars in Mexico and Cuba. Fountain stated that these recontact experiences "have strengthened ties with

family members of heritage learners" and "provided a way in which
the college can highlight the importance of cultural understanding
in a Latin American context, but with relevance to the demographic
dynamics of the college's local setting—a county with a rapidly
expanding Hispanic population" (pp. 30–31). Nationwide, private and
public institutions alike will be required to make similar efforts in the
future in response to the increasing utility and social relevance of
Spanish in the U.S.

Each of the above principles serves, in the beginning, to focus our attention as researchers and pedagogues on factors that are more immediate to the
individual as a social *being* rather than a member of a social *category* (generation, sex, socioeconomic class, etc.). These principles do not adhere to notions such as the speech community, diglossia, or language dominance (cf.
Pedraza, Attinasi, and Hoffman 1980). Rather, they call upon more local,
concrete factors such as language utility, social relevance, and the continued acquisition and/or reacquisition of Spanish—at the discourse level—
through social interaction. In recognizing the impact of increasing numbers
of Spanish-speaking migrants and immigrants in the U.S., the increasing
monetary value of speaking Spanish, and the rapidly expanding visibility of
Spanish in much of the country, these principles attempt to account for the
complex arrangement of sociolinguistic factors that affect individuals in important, different ways, regardless of speaker generation or language preference. In research on HLA of Spanish in the U.S. in the decades to come, we
must focus on how these factors affect speakers who demonstrate social, functional abilities in Spanish as well as English. We must go far beyond analyses
of diglossia, language shift and loss, and intergenerational variation to understand qualitatively the processes which lead an ever-growing number of HL
speakers to develop their social and linguistic repertoires in both Spanish and
in English. These individuals must be at the core—instead of the periph-
ery—of our endeavors. Rather than considering them as "exceptions to the
rule" of Spanish "loss" in the U.S., we must look to them to guide us in elaborating the theoretical models, empirical research methodologies, and pedagogical principles of the ever-changing situation of Spanish in this nation in
the twenty-first century.

Future research efforts must be focused on explaining why and how some
third- and fourth-generation speakers of Spanish in the U.S. purposefully acquire the language and integrate it into their daily personal and professional
lives; why some third-generation speakers in places such as Miami maintain
the morphosyntactic and semantic norms of first-generation speakers with
few significant structural differences (Lynch 1999); how societal bilin-

gualism foments HL proficiency in some aspects of the linguistic system at the same time that other aspects become simplified and reduced (Silva-Corvalán 1994); how economic resources and family and social networks promote greater HL proficiency for some yet lead to more restricted use of HL for others of the same background (Zentella 1997)[12]; why the majority of a sample of Hispanic youths studying Spanish in Los Angeles (74 percent), Miami (60 percent), and San Antonio (58 percent) perceive that Spanish language ability is "very important" for finding a "good job" (Ramírez 2000); why Hispanic Spanish-English bilinguals have average yearly incomes more than $2,000 greater than those of Hispanic English monolinguals in the state of Florida, and nearly $7,000 greater in Miami-Dade County (Boswell 2000); why Spanish sometimes falls into disuse during late childhood and adolescence among HL speakers yet is later recovered in early adulthood (Language Policy Task Force 1983; Zentella 1987); why and how recontact with Spanish takes place among HL speakers in different U.S. contexts and how HL skills are beneficially impacted in turn (Cisneros and Leone 1983; Silva-Corvalán 1990; Elías-Olivares 2000; Lynch 2000); how cultural and economic globalization and steady Spanish-language immigration will impact societal bilingualism, particularly in urban settings, in the U.S. in the twenty-first century (Roca and Lynch 2000).

Pedagogical Implications for Instruction of Spanish as a Heritage Language in the United States

As the above principles of a theory of HLA suggest, we must insist upon the growing social and economic vitality of Spanish in the U.S. in formulating HL curricula, ancillary materials, and teaching methodologies. We must be proactive about encouraging HL learners to experience recontact, bearing in mind the potential that high nationwide rates of Spanish-speaking immigration have for stimulating HL development among the second, third, and fourth generations. We must aggressively encourage HL learners to travel or study abroad in the Spanish-speaking world, particularly in nearby Mexico and the Caribbean.

In the development of communication skills, we must be systematic about integrating the flourishing Spanish-language media. Local city and community newspapers (e.g., *El Nuevo Herald* in Miami) and national magazines (e.g., *People en español*) can be of great interest as well as great help to U.S. students in the acquisition of basic literacy skills in Spanish. National cable and local network television stations (Univisión, Telemundo, Discover en español, MTV Latino) are ideal resources for the development of aural

Spanish skills, as well as an entertaining way for HL speakers to enrich their formal and informal register vocabulary. Local radio stations as well as the World Wide Web provide further sources of authentic Spanish for outside-of-class activities aimed at expanding the HL speaker's linguistic repertoire.

In designing activities that integrate the U.S. Spanish-language media and in choosing materials and implementing exercises to develop literacy skills, writing style, and oral fluency, we must emphasize discursive and inter-active abilities as much as morphological and syntactic ones. Communica-tive approaches are essential to HL development. SNS and HL education in general have shown a quite delayed reaction to the communicative language teaching movement in this country. Despite the fact that a number of lead-ing researchers in the field have been advocating for communicatively-oriented approaches in the SNS classroom since the late 1970s (e.g., Valdés-Fallis 1978), many teachers across the country continue to insist upon the analysis of grammar rules and language paradigms and the use of transforma-tion drills and Spanish-English contrasts in their classrooms. As Krashen (2000) points out, this grammar-oriented practice often hinders HL develop-ment more than fomenting it. Teachers must bear in mind—and put into practice—the essence of *language learning through content* (cf. Stryker and Leaver 1997). Daily class themes should *not* be ones like "los participios pa-sados" or "comparación de los adjetivos" but rather ones like "la inmigración mexicana en California" or "movimientos feministas en Latinoamérica" or "la raza en el Caribe" (cf. Roca 1999b). The needs of HL learners are best and most appropriately served by discourse-level activities (Principle 5, above) that are based on a particular content and the expression of experiences, feel-ings, opinions, or arguments, be they academic or personal, formal or infor-mal. Grammar must be put at the service of these sorts of communicative activities, not vice versa. Widdowson (1988) advocates for this principle of language learning: "The question is how should grammar be learned so that its intrinsic communicative character is understood and acted upon. This cannot be done by restricting attention to its formal properties, the relations and regularities which make up the internal mechanism of the device . . . . Learners need to realize the *function* of the device as a way of mediating be-tween words and contexts, as a powerful resource for the purposeful achieve-ment of meaning"(p. 154).

Not only must we be strategic about placing grammar instruction in proper perspective in HL classrooms, we must also conscientiously and pro-actively guard against the referential use of idealized, grammar-book norms in our curricula. These norms are usually taken out of their proper sociolin-guistic context of *monolingual* regions of the Spanish-speaking world and brought into a classroom of learners whose social reality is entirely *bilingual*. It is imperative that Spanish language teachers in the U.S. put aside any prejudicial notions that they may have about what constitutes "good" or "pure" Spanish and what they consider "Spanglish" or *"español malhablado."* The opinion sometimes expressed by teachers that U.S.-based Spanish-language media, for example, should not be used in our Spanish language classrooms because of its alleged inferior, Anglicized quality, is not only sociolinguistically unsupported and professionally unethical, but it also politically denigrates the nature of Spanish in this country (cf. Zentella 1990, 1996). The most unfortunate consequence of such an opinion is that the students of these teachers are denied legitimate academic and social access to one of the most vital and influential sources of authentic Spanish language in their everyday lives. Anglicisms will inevitably occur in the Spanish used in the United States. Those more willing to address them objectively as acting professionals will, I believe, be more successful in their mission as language educators.

HL researchers, teachers, and administrators must never lose sight of the fact that the United States constitutes an autonomous social, cultural, political, and linguistic context for Spanish language usage in the Hispanic world. Just as none of us would expect a Spanish speaker from Buenos Aires to speak "the same way" as someone from Cuzco, Quito, Mexico City, or Havana, we cannot expect a Spanish speaker from the U.S. to speak "the same way" as someone from these other parts of the world, especially given the reality that the U.S. represents a language contact zone in which Spanish has historically been relegated to a politically subordinate status. Lipski (2000) asserts that "our legitimizing of Spanish as a national language through our research, teaching, and public presentations is a potent antidote to xenophobia and ignorance" (p. 28). Our pedagogical methods and aims must aspire to develop our students' fullest potential as *United States* speakers of Spanish, and not as *Mexican* or *Cuban* or *Colombian* speakers of Spanish. With this aspiration, we move toward a broader social legitimization of Spanish in the United States, toward the linguistic and political empowerment of its speakers as representatives of a distinct variety of World Spanish, and toward the global future of our nation.

NOTES

1. Hymes (1974) argued that "Chomsky's redefinition of linguistic goals appears . . . a halfway house. The term 'competence' promises more than it in fact contains. It is restricted to knowledge, and, within knowledge, to knowledge of grammar. Thus,

it leaves other aspects of speakers' tacit knowledge and ability in confusion, thrown together under a largely unexamined concept of 'performance' . . . . [L]inguistic theory must extend the notion of competence to include more than the grammatical . . . . A thorough going linguistics must move . . . from what is potential in human nature, and elementary in a grammar, to what is realizable and realized; and conceive of the social factors entering into realization as constitutive and rule-governed too" (p. 93).

2. Lee and VanPatten's (1995) *Making Communicative Language Teaching Happen* is one of the clearest and most popular illustrations of communicative language teaching as it is presently conceived in the U.S.

3. Fourteen states passed Official English legislation during the period 1981 to 1990, joining four other states with such previously existing laws. Official English activity continued through the 1990s, with seven more states being added to the list. In 2001, legislative debates around English language policy were still ongoing in a number of other states (Crawford 2001).

4. Reflecting upon the inadequacies of foreign language policy and planning at the secondary and postsecondary educational levels in Florida, Roca (1999a) concluded that foreign language professionals in the U.S. "have much work to do in the public relations arena in order to create a better-informed, more appreciative, more receptive public regarding a much needed orientation toward language-as-resource rather than language-as-problem" (p. 309). She urged that a first step in changing attitudes toward language education in this country may be to turn our attention to the oversights and misconceptions of professionals and academic colleagues in other fields, influential citizens who are often misinformed about the necessity and efficacy of bilingual, heritage, and second language education.

5. Wilson (1997) offers an insightful collection of articles that describe the impact of globalization in U.S. urban change through the 1980s and 1990s. Wilson states that globalization "exhibits a new character and intensity that places cities within dramatically transforming economic and social networks . . . . In this city, a heightened commodification and search for global purpose alter urban culture, politics, and civic life in fundamental ways" (p. 8). In my estimation, language use would also be a part of this process.

6. Valdés, Lozano, and García-Moya (1981), Merino, Trueba, and Samaniego (1993), and Colombi and Alarcón (1997) are milestone volumes dealing specifically with research and practice in the teaching of Spanish to native/heritage speakers in the U.S. AATSP (2000) provides a practical and highly accessible guide to basic issues in SNS education for teachers at all levels.

7. A synthetic overview of these areas of investigation in SLA is provided by Ellis (1994).

8. One of the key characteristics of the Labovian speech community is the sharedness of linguistic elements and linguistic rules, a criterion equally as important as the sharedness of norms of language usage. The principle of uniformity of variable linguistic usage states that speakers of the same speech community share the same linguistic rules and structural constraints determining rule application. How-

ever, Mougeon and Nadasdi (1998) observe that studies from a number of majority and minority language communities have revealed that there may be subgroups, or even numbers of noncollective individuals—within the same speech community—who manifest differences with respect to the rest of the community. These differences are not necessarily cross-generational, and they may relate not only to the variants used but also to the grammatical and semantic-pragmatic constraints applied in usage. These nonuniform tendencies of some speakers may be considered *discontinuities* in the speech community (Mougeon and Nadasdi 1998).

9. Krashen (2000) observed that: "Often, classes focus on conscious learning of grammatical rules that are late acquired. Some HL speakers may not have learned or acquired these items. Non-speakers of the HL who are good at grammar sometimes outperform HL speakers on grammar tests and get higher grades in the language class, even though the non-speaker of the HL may be incapable of communicating the simplest idea in the language while the HL speaker may be quite competent in everyday conversation. Such events could be psychologically devastating, a message to the HL speaker that he or she does not know his or her own language, while an outsider does. Even though the kind of knowledge the outsider has is not genuine, the HL speaker may not understand this, given the authority of the classroom and the value the teacher places on conscious knowledge of grammar" (p. 441).

10. According to the *Cambridge Encyclopedia*, fourth edition, Spanish claims approximately 332 million native speakers worldwide. Mandarin Chinese is the world's most populous language (885 million), followed by World English (400 million).

11. According to U.S. Census 2000, North Carolina's Hispanic population grew nearly 400 percent during the period 1990–2000, meaning that Hispanics represented more than one in every five individuals added to the state's population. An article in *USA Today* stated that "this seismic demographic shift in a state that has long been made up primarily of blacks and whites is certain to be followed by a change in the state's political dynamic" (22 March 2001, 8A).

12. Zentella (1997) found that: "Despite the impact of family migration histories and schooling, children from the same type of background could differ markedly in their ability to speak, read, and/or write Spanish or English . . . . As the profiles of three families proved, specifying the language dyads, or who speaks what to whom in each family . . . provides a limited view of children's linguistic input . . . . It is incorrect to assume that children with monolingual Spanish parents did not speak English with adults, or that those whose parents spoke only English heard no Spanish conversations. The presence of overlapping networks guaranteed constant visiting, sharing, and exposure to both languages" (p. 78).

REFERENCES

American Association of Teachers of Spanish and Portuguese (AATSP). 2000. *Spanish for Native Speakers*. Professional Development Series Handbook for Teachers K–16, Volume I. Fort Worth: Harcourt College Publishers.

Boswell, Thomas. 2000. "Demographic Changes in Florida and Their Importance for Effective Educational Policies and Practices." In *Research on Spanish in the United States: Linguistic Issues and Challenges*, ed. Ana Roca. Somerville, MA: Cascadilla Press.

Brod, Richard, and Elizabeth B. Welles. 2000. "Foreign Language Enrollments in United States Institutions of Higher Education." *ADFL Bulletin* 31 (fall 1998):22–29.

Caravedo, Rocío. 1990. *La competencia lingüística: Crítica de la génesis y del desarrollo de la teoría de Chomsky.* Madrid: Editorial Gredos.

Chomsky, Noam. 1965. *Aspects of the Theory of Syntax.* Cambridge, MA: MIT Press.

Cisneros, René, and Elizabeth Leone. 1983. "Mexican-American Language Communities in the Twin Cities: An Example of Contact and Recontact." In *Spanish in the U.S. Setting: Beyond the Southwest*, ed. Lucía Elías-Olivares. Rosslyn, VA: National Clearinghouse for Bilingual Education.

Colombi, M. Cecilia. 2000. "En vías del desarrollo del lenguaje académico en español en hablantes nativos de español en los Estados Unidos." In *Research on Spanish in the United States: Linguistic Issues and Challenges*, ed. Ana Roca. Somerville, MA: Cascadilla Press.

Colombi, M. Cecilia and Francisco X. Alarcón, eds. 1997. *La enseñanza del español a hispanohablantes: Praxis y teoría.* Boston: Houghton Mifflin.

Cook, Vivan. 1999. "Going Beyond the Native Speaker in Language Teaching." *TESOL Quarterly* 33:185–209.

Crawford, James. 2001. Language Policy Web Site and Emporium. Available at http://ourworld.compuserve.com/homepages/JWCrawford. Accessed on May 30, 2001.

———. 1992. *Hold Your Tongue: Bilingualism and the Politics of "English Only."* Reading, MA: Addison-Wesley.

Elías-Olivares, Lucía. 2000. Plenary address. Eighteenth National Conference on Spanish in the United States, 7 April, University of California at Davis.

Ellis, Rod. 1994. *The Study of Second Language Acquisition.* New York: Oxford University Press.

Faltis, Christian. 1990. "Spanish for Native Speakers: Freirian and Vygotskian Perspectives." *Foreign Language Annals* 23:117–26.

Ferguson, Charles. 1959. "Diglossia." *Word* 15:325–40.

Firth, Alan, and Johannes Wagner. 1997. "On Discourse, Communication, and (Some) Fundamental Concepts in SLA Research." *Modern Language Journal* 81:285–300.

Fishman, Joshua. 1967. "Bilingualism with and without Diglossia; Diglossia with and without bilingualism." *Journal of Social Issues* 23:29–38.

Fishman, Joshua A., Robert L. Cooper, and Roxana Ma. 1971. *Bilingualism in the Barrio.* Bloomington: Indiana University Press.

Fountain, Anne. 2001. "Developing a Program for Spanish Heritage Learners in a Small College Setting." *ADFL Bulletin* 32:29–32.

Gardner, Robert. 1985. *Social Psychology and Second Language Learning: The Role of Attitude and Motivation.* London: Edward Arnold.

Guntermann, Gail, Suzanne Hendrickson, and Carmen de Urioste. 1996. "Basic Assumptions Revisited: Today's French and Spanish Students at a Large Metropolitan University." In *Patterns and Policies: The Changing Demographics of Foreign Language Instruction*, ed. Judith Liskin-Gasparro. Boston: Heinle & Heinle.

Hatch, Evelyn. 1978. "Discourse Analysis and Second Language Acquisition." In *Second Language Acquisition*, ed. Evelyn Hatch. Rowley, MA: Newbury House.

Halliday, M. A. K. 1975. *Learning How to Mean*. London: Edward Arnold.

Hymes, Dell. 1974. *Foundations in Sociolinguistics*. Philadelphia: University of Pennsylvania Press.

Klee, Carol. 1998. "Communication as an Organizing Principle in the National Standards: Sociolinguistic Aspects of Spanish Language Teaching." *Hispania* 81:339–51.

———. 1996. "The Spanish of the Peruvian Andes: The Influence of Quechua on Spanish Language Structure." In *Spanish in Contact: Issues in Bilingualism*, eds. Ana Roca and John Jensen. Somerville, MA: Cascadilla Press.

Krashen, Stephen. 2000. "Bilingual Education, the Acquisition of English, and the Retention and Loss of Spanish." In *Research on Spanish in the United States: Linguistic Issues and Challenges*, ed. Ana Roca. Somerville, MA: Cascadilla Press.

———. 1981. *Second Language Acquisition and Second Language Learning*. Oxford: Pergamon.

Labov, William. 1972. *Sociolinguistic Patterns*. Philadelphia: University of Pennsylvania Press.

———. 1966. *The Social Stratification of English in New York City*. Washington, D.C.: Center for Applied Linguistics.

Language Policy Task Force. 1983. *Intergenerational Perspectives on Bilingualism*. New York: Centro de Estudios Puerorriqueños.

Lee, James, and Bill VanPatten. 1995. *Making Communicative Language Teaching Happen*. New York: McGraw-Hill.

Lipski, John. 2000. "Back to Zero or Ahead to 2001: Issues and Challenges in U.S. Spanish Research." In *Research on Spanish in the United States: Linguistic Issues and Challenges*, ed. Ana Roca. Somerville, MA: Cascadilla Press.

———. 1993. "Creoloid Phenomena in the Spanish of Transitional Bilinguals." In *Spanish in the United States: Linguistic Contact and Diversity*, eds. Ana Roca and John Lipski. Berlin: Mouton de Gruyter.

Lynch, Andrew. 2001. "'Will the True Bilingual Please Step Forward?' Implications of the Similarities between Heritage and Nonnative Learners for SLA Theory." Paper presented at the 2001 Annual Conference of the American Association of Applied Linguistics, 24 February, St. Louis, MO.

———. 2000. "Spanish-Speaking Miami in Sociolinguistic Perspective: Bilingualism, Recontact and Language Maintenance among the Cuban-Origin Population." In *Research on Spanish in the United States: Linguistic Issues and Challenges*, ed. Ana Roca. Somerville, MA: Cascadilla Press.

———. 1999. The Subjunctive in Miami Cuban Spanish: Bilingualism, Contact, and Language Variability. Ph.D. diss., University of Minnesota, Minneapolis.

McQuillan, Jeff. 1998. "The Use of Self-Selected and Free Voluntary Reading in Heritage Language Programs: A Review of Research." In *Heritage Language Development*, eds. Stephen Krashen, Lucy Tse, and Jeff McQuillan. Culver City, CA: Language Education Associates.

Merino, Barbara, Henry Trueba, and Fabián Samaniego, eds. 1993. *Language and Culture in Learning: Teaching Spanish to Native Speakers of Spanish*. Washington, D.C.: Falmer Press/Taylor & Francis.

Milroy, Leslie. 1980. *Language and Social Networks*. Baltimore, MD: University Park Press.

Moreno Fernández, Francisco. 1998. *Principios de sociolingüística y sociología del lenguaje*. Barcelona: Editorial Ariel.

Mougeon, Raymond, and Terry Nadasdi. 1998. "Sociolinguistic Discontinuities in Minority Language Communities." *Language* 74:40–55.

Nichols, Geraldine Cleary. 2000. "Spanish and the Multilingual Department: Ways to Use the Rising Tide." *Profession* 2000:115–23.

Pavlenko, Aneta. 2001. "'I Never Knew I Was Bilingual': Re-Imagining Identities in TESOL Classrooms." Paper presented at the 2001 Annual Conference of the American Association of Applied Linguistics, 25 February, St. Louis, MO.

Pedraza, Pedro, John Attinasi, and G. Hoffman. 1980. "Rethinking Diglossia." Language Policy Task Force Working Paper 9. NY: Centro de Estudios Puertorriqueños.

Ramírez, Arnulfo. 2000. "Linguistic Notions of Spanish among Youths from Different Hispanic Groups." In *Research on Spanish in the United States: Linguistic Issues and Challenges*, ed. Ana Roca. Somerville, MA: Cascadilla Press.

Ricento, Thomas. 1995. "A Brief History of Language Restrictionism in the United States." In *Official English? No!*, eds. Susan Dicker, Ruth Jackson, Thomas Ricento, and Kathleen Romstedt. Alexandria, VA: TESOL.

Roca, Ana. 2000. Introduction. *Research on Spanish in the United States: Linguistic Issues and Challenges*, ed. Ana Roca. Somerville, MA: Cascadilla Press.

——. 1999a. "Foreign Language Policy and Planning in Higher Education: The Case of the State of Florida." In *Sociopolitical Perspectives on Language Policy and Planning in the USA*, ed. Thom Huebner and Kathryn Davis. Amsterdam: John Benjamins.

——. 1999b. *Nuevos mundos*. New York: John Wiley and Sons.

——. 1997. "Retrospectives, Advances, and Current Needs in the Teaching of Spanish to United States Hispanic Bilingual Students." *ADFL Bulletin* 29:37–43.

Roca, Ana, and Andrew Lynch. 2000. "Spanish and English in Miami: Toward a New Model of Bilingualism in the US Context." Paper presented at the Eighteenth National Conference on Spanish in the United States, 7 April, University of California at Davis.

Romaine, Suzanne. 1995. *Bilingualism*, 2d ed. Malden, MA: Blackwell.

Santiago, Fabiola. 1998. "A Second Language Opens New Doors in Diverse Region." *Miami Herald*, 10 September.

Silva-Corvalán, Carmen. 1995. Introduction. *Spanish in Four Continents: Studies in Language Contact and Bilingualism*, ed. Carmen Silva-Corvalán. Washington, D.C.: Georgetown University Press.

———. 1994. *Language Contact and Change: Spanish in Los Angeles*. New York: Oxford University Press.

———. 1990. "Current Issues in Studies of Language Contact." *Hispania* 73:162–76.

Souto Silva, Rosângela. 2000. "Pragmatics, Bilingualism, and the Native Speaker." *Language and Communication* 20:161–78.

Stryker, Stephen, and Betty Lou Leaver, eds. 1997. *Content-based Instruction in Foreign Language Education*. Washington, D.C.: Georgetown University Press.

Tarone, Elaine. 1995. "A Variationist Framework for SLA Research: Examples and Pedagogical Insights." In *Second Language Acquisition Theory and Pedagogy*, eds. Fred Eckman, Diane Highland, Peter Lee, Jean Mileham, and Rita Rutkowski Weber. Mahwah, NJ: Lawrence Erlbaum.

———. 1988. *Variation in Interlanguage*. London: Edward Arnold.

Terrell, Tracy. 1977. "A Natural Approach to Second Language Acquisition and Learning." *Modern Language Journal* 61:325–36.

Terrell, Tracy, Magdalena Andrade, Jeanne Egasse, and Elías Miguel Muñoz. 1986. *Dos Mundos*. New York: McGraw-Hill.

Torres, Lourdes. 1991. "The Study of U.S. Spanish Varieties: Some Theoretical and Methodological Issues." In *Sociolinguistics of the Spanish-speaking World: Iberia, Latin America, the United States*, eds. Carol Klee and Luis Ramos-García. Tempe, AZ: Bilingual Press.

U.S. Census Bureau. 2001. United States Census 2000 Population Tables and Reports. Available at www.census.gov/main/www/cen2000.html. Accessed May 30.

Valdés, Guadalupe. 1995. "The Teaching of Minority Languages as Academic Subjects: Pedagogical and Theoretical Challenges." *Modern Language Journal* 79:299–328.

Valdés, Guadalupe, and Richard Figueroa. 1994. *Bilingualism and Testing: A Special Case of Bias*. Norwood, NJ: Ablex.

Valdés, Guadalupe, and Michelle Geoffrion-Vinci. 1998. "Chicano Spanish: The Problem of the 'Underdeveloped' Code in Bilingual Repertoires." *Modern Language Journal* 82:473–501.

Valdés, Guadalupe, Anthony G. Lozano, and Rodolfo García-Moya, eds. 1981. *Teaching Spanish to the Hispanic Bilingual in the United States: Issues, Aims, and Methods*. New York: Teachers College Press.

Valdés-Fallis, Guadalupe. 1978. "A Comprehensive Approach to the Teaching of Spanish to Bilingual Spanish-speaking Students." *Modern Language Journal* 3:102–10.

Villa, Daniel, and Jennifer Villa. 1998. "Identity Labels and Self-reported Language Use: Implications for Spanish Language Programs." *Foreign Language Annals* 31:505–16.

Walker, Constance, and Diane Tedick. 2000. "Bilingual Education, English as a Second Language, and Foreign Language Education: Movement to a Center." In *Reflecting on the Past to Shape the Future*, eds. Diane Birckbichler and Robert Terry. Chicago: National Textbook.

Widdowson, H. G. 1988. "Grammar, and Nonsense, and Learning." In *Grammar and Second Language Teaching*, eds. William Rutherford and Michael Sharwood Smith. New York: Newbury House.

Wilson, David, ed. 1997. "Globalization and the Changing U.S. City." *The Annals of the American Academy of Political and Social Science* 551. Thousand Oaks, CA: SAGE Publications.

Zentella, Ana Celia. 1997. *Growing up Bilingual.* Malden, MA: Blackwell.

———. 1996. "The 'Chiquitification' of U.S. Latinos and Their Languages, or Why We Need an Anthropolitical Linguistics." *SALSA III: Proceedings of the Third Annual Symposium about Language and Society-Austin. Texas Linguistic Forum* 36:1–18.

———. 1995. "La hispanofobia del movimiento 'Inglés oficial' en los Estados Unidos por la oficialización del inglés." *Alteridades* 5:55–65.

———. 1990. "El impacto de la realidad socioeconómica en las comunidades hispanoparlantes de los Estados Unidos: Reto a la teoría y metodología lingüística." In *Spanish in the United States: Sociolinguistic Issues*, ed. John Bergen. Washington, D.C.: Georgetown University Press.

———. 1987. "Language and Female Identity in the Puerto Rican Community." In *Women and Language in Transition,* ed. J. Penfield. Albany, New York: SUNY Press.

3

Profiles of SNS Students in the Twenty-first Century
Pedagogical Implications of the Changing Demographics and Social Status of U.S. Hispanics

María M. Carreira

California State University, Long Beach

Marketing surveys, socioeconomic studies of U.S. Hispanics, and census data provide a basis for making a number of projections regarding the composition of future heritage language students of Spanish. Specifically, they suggest that the number of students with intermediate to low levels of fluency in informal varieties of spoken Spanish will likely increase in the coming decades, and that those with higher levels of Spanish language proficiency will decrease. With respect to academic skills, students with basic to low levels of academic skills in Spanish are likely to greatly outnumber those with solid academic skills in this language. The evidence presented in this essay also suggests that the Spanish-language media may serve to familiarize U.S. Hispanics with dialectal and register variants that are outside their range of everyday use. In addition, religious education programs in Spanish, parental instruction, and general gains in education by U.S. Hispanics may play a positive role in the attainment of basic literacy skills in Spanish by bilinguals. The repercussions of these and other projections for the field of Spanish for Native Speakers (SNS) are examined in detail in this chapter.

Changing Student Profiles

The diversity of academic experiences and the range of Spanish language proficiency levels represented among U.S. Hispanics constitute one of the biggest challenges facing the teaching of Spanish as a heritage language. In table 3.1, Valdés (1997, p. 14) identifies eight different types of students who enroll in SNS courses. Two areas of knowledge crucial to SNS instruction are distinguished within these categories: Spanish language proficiency and general academic skills in English and Spanish.

With respect to proficiency, the students identified by Valdés range from those who are fluent speakers of a prestigious variety of Spanish (Newly arrived: Type A; Bilingual: Type C) to those who have only receptive skills in a contact variety of rural Spanish (Bilingual: Type F). The academic skills of these students also exhibit wide variation. Some students have basic to good academic skills in English and Spanish (Bilingual: Type A). Others have well-developed skills in one language but not the other (Bilingual: Types B, C; Newly arrived: Type A). Still others have minimal to nonexistent academic skills in both languages (Bilingual: Types D, E, F).

Each of the above categories differs with respect to the needs and expectations of students. While students with relatively high proficiency levels in Spanish may enroll in SNS classes to prepare for exacting academic or professional use of Spanish, those at the lowest levels of competence may seek to develop very basic skills in the language for personal reasons, such as connecting with family members. In each case, the pedagogical materials, course objectives, and classroom practices must be fine-tuned to the needs and expectations of particular populations of students.

Given the diversity of U.S. Hispanics, the success of SNS instruction depends as much on sound pedagogical practices as it does on the availability of up-to-date information on the linguistic and academic skills that Hispanic students bring to SNS classes. Literature dedicated to the topic of student profiles (Valdés 1997, 2001; Webb and Miller 2000; Walqui 1997) without exception support Valdés's conclusions regarding the wide range of abilities and needs among SNS students, particularly when examined from a national rather than regional perspective. However, the rapidly changing demographics of U.S. Hispanics and the evolving social and political conditions currently affecting this population may result in substantial changes in the student composition of SNS classes.

What is the range of the linguistic and academic skills that we can expect to find in the SNS classrooms of the twenty-first century? Marketing surveys, socioeconomic studies of U.S. Hispanics, and census data suggest that the number of students with intermediate to low levels of fluency in informal varieties of spoken Spanish will likely increase, as those with higher levels of Spanish language proficiency will decrease. With respect to academic skills,

Table 3.1 *Selected Characteristics of Students Who Enroll in SNS Language Courses*

TYPES OF STUDENTS	CHARACTERISTICS
Newly arrived: Type A	Well schooled in Spanish-speaking country Speakers of prestige variety of Spanish
Newly arrived: Type B	Poorly schooled in Spanish-speaking country Speakers of stigmatized variety of Spanish
Bilingual: Type A	Access to bilingual instruction in U.S. Basic academic skills in Spanish Good academic skills in English Fluent functional speakers of contact variety of rural Spanish
Bilingual: Type B	No academic skills in Spanish Good academic skills in English Fluent but limited speakers of contact variety of rural Spanish
Bilingual: Type C	No academic skills in Spanish Good academic skills in English Fluent but limited speakers of prestige variety of Spanish Some contact phenomena present
Bilingual: Type D	No academic skills in Spanish Poor academic skills in English Fluent but limited speakers of contact variety of rural Spanish
Bilingual: Type E	No academic skills in Spanish Poor academic skills in English Very limited speakers of contact variety of rural Spanish
Bilingual: Type F	No academic skills in Spanish Poor academic skills in English Receptive bilingual in contact variety of rural Spanish

Source: Valdés 1997, p. 14

students with basic to low levels of academic skills in Spanish are likely to greatly outnumber those with solid academic skills in this language.

However, not all of the projections bode badly for SNS instruction. Given the growing popularity of Spanish-language media, U.S. Hispanics will be increasingly exposed to mainstream, albeit informal, varieties of Spanish. Moreover, as the social prestige and economic value of Spanish in the U.S. continue to rise, the attitudes and experiences of SNS students with this language are also likely to become more positive. The repercussions of these and other projections for the field of SNS are examined in detail in this essay.

The Future of Spanish Language Proficiency

THE SIGNIFICANCE OF DEMOGRAPHIC AND ECONOMIC PROJECTIONS

According to census records, there are nearly 13 million foreign-born Hispanics in the U.S. In 2000, these accounted for approximately 36 percent of the total U.S. Hispanic population (U.S. Census Bureau 2000). However, with Hispanic birthrates in the U.S. rapidly outpacing immigration rates, the proportion of foreign-born Hispanics will shrink drastically in the coming decades. Indeed, it is estimated that 82 percent of the babies born in El Paso, Texas, between 1997 and 2000 were of Hispanic origin. In San Antonio, Los Angeles, San Diego, and Miami, the percentage of Hispanic babies born during this period were 66 percent, 53 percent, 37 percent, and 32 percent, respectively. Given this growth rate, by the year 2100 it is estimated that more than 90 percent of all Hispanics will be American-born ("As American as Apple Flan" 2000).

At the same time, census reports project a substantial growth in the Hispanic middle class in the coming decades. They also point to the fact that the number of Hispanics moving toward professional and managerial jobs is on the rise, while the number of those who are employed as laborers or service workers continues to decline (Brischetto 2001, p. 28).

These demographic and socioeconomic predictions are likely to have significant repercussions on the general linguistic profile of U.S. Hispanics, as well as that of SNS students in particular. If the demographic projections are accurate, it is reasonable to assume that as the percentage of foreign-born Hispanics in the total Hispanic population declines, the percentage of foreign-born Hispanics in secondary and postsecondary institutions will also decline. Conversely, as the percentage of second- and third-generation Hispanics in the population rises, so will it rise in these institutions. Extrapolating to the field of SNS, this means that a smaller proportion of students in SNS courses at the high school and university levels will come from the Newly arrived: Types A and B categories, in Valdés's schema.

The validity of the above assumptions is supported by the fact that second- and third-generation Hispanics are more likely than first-generation immigrants to attend college. Williams (2001) notes: "The distinction between foreign-born Hispanics and the native born is that most immigrants, regardless of their origin, attain relatively low educational levels, drawing down the over-all averages for education and income" (p. 34). In 2000, two out of three Mexican immigrants did not have a high school diploma, whereas three out of four American-born Mexicans did. In 1999, 22 percent of American-born middle class Hispanics held college degrees. By contrast, 17 percent of foreign-born middle class Hispanics earned a college degree that same year (Brischetto 2001, p. 34).

If borne out, census projections are bound to impact the linguistic practices of future generations of U.S. Hispanics. Sociolinguistic studies point to the fact that language attrition accelerates with each successive generation of immigrants in the U.S. The typical scenario documented for Spanish, for example, is that first-generation immigrants are Spanish-dominant. The second generation is bilingual, with a preference for English. The third generation has very limited, if any, skills in Spanish (Valdés 1997; Silva-Corvalán 1997).

Studies also point to the crucial importance of foreign-born Hispanics in preserving Spanish across the United States. Regarding Spanish in Miami-Dade, Lynch (2000) argues that

> the continuous influx of Spanish monolingual immigrants is quite significant. First, it points to the continued use of Spanish at the societal level. Second, in a city where new immigration is at a high rate and where Hispanics are the demographic majority, there is a high probability that already established immigrants and their offspring will have intimate social contact with recently arrived Spanish monolinguals (p. 279).

In their study of the Spanish population in New York City, García, Morín and Rivera (2001) note:

> Whereas in 1970 almost 60 percent of the U.S. Puerto Rican population had been born in Puerto Rico, in 1990 only 40 percent remained island born. *Because most of the other Latino groups are more recent arrivals, they are generally Spanish speakers, helping to pull the Spanish of Puerto Ricans as they communicate with each other* (emphasis added).

Similarly, the findings of Hudson, Hernández Chávez, and Bills (1995) suggest that

> the maintenance of Spanish in the Southwest, in terms of raw numbers of speakers only, is heavily dependent upon a steady transfusion of speakers from Mexico to communities in the United States, and offer no warrant for the survival of Spanish beyond a point when such speakers are no longer available to replace speakers north of the border lost through mortality or linguistic assimilation (p. 182).

Furthermore, large-scale market research studies at the national level concur with the above conclusions (2000 U.S. Hispanic Market Survey).

> Immigration levels drive the use of Spanish in this segment to some degree; new immigrants will tend to refresh the use of the Spanish language among those already in the country. As a result, new Latino immigrants are required to maintain the "Hispanic-ness" of the segment. Without relatively high immigration levels, the Hispanic segment will adopt English and in time, fully acculturate into mainstream American culture (p. 45).

Positive socioeconomic projections for Hispanics may also not bode well for the future of U.S. Spanish, at least in some parts of this country. In their study of Spanish in the Southwest, Hudson, Hernández Chávez, and Bills (1995) conclude:

> The high negative correlations between language loyalty and educational and economic attainment in the Spanish origin population, as well as the high positive correlation with the level of poverty, argue forcefully for the proposition that, in the Southwest at least, educational and economic success in the Spanish origin population are purchased at the expense of Spanish language maintenance (p. 179).

Similarly, a 1995 national survey of U.S. Hispanics supports the conclusion that improvements in socioeconomic status among U.S. Hispanics go hand in hand with increasing levels of English dominance (Roy 1997).

> Latinos are a heterogeneous group with their Spanish language as the dominant linkage. Many studies mentioned earlier have portrayed a socioeconomic relationship to income and adequacy in the dominant culture's language. Middle-class LEAS (Latino Ethnic Attitude Survey) respondents prove these findings accurate. Almost 40 percent of Latino respondents prefer English as their dominant language, and 92 percent prefer either monolingual English or bilingual English and Spanish. LEAS preference for monolingual Spanish averaged 9 percent. Over time, and as Latino socioeconomic status improves, Latino language preferences, while bilingual, move closer to an English predominance for LEAS respondents.

A 1997 study of Hispanics in the New Orleans area further suggests that Spanish language dominance correlates with a variety of social problems.

> The majority of Hispanics (60 percent) say that they are quite comfortable with the English language, that is, they are either better in English or equally able in both languages. The remaining 40 percent who are better in Spanish are more likely to have a variety of problems: They are concentrated in service occupations. They are less likely to be managers or professionals. They are less likely to have a college degree. They have lower incomes. They are more likely to have experienced discrimination in the past year (Howell 1997, p. 27).

A recent survey of the income patterns of Hispanics in eight metropolitan areas in the U.S. suggests that there is a fair amount of regional variation with respect to the economic value of Spanish. The survey found three metropolitan areas where there are discernible economic advantages to knowing both English and Spanish, namely, Miami, Jersey City, and San Antonio. However, this study found negative economic consequences for bilingualism in Los Angeles, San Francisco, Houston, New York, and Chicago. Overall, the study concludes: "In most metropolitan areas, English-only Hispanics/Latinos born in the United States had lower percentages living below the poverty level than those who spoke English very well and also spoke Spanish" (Fradd and Boswell 1999, p. 5).

MITIGATING FACTORS

While it is true that demographic and socioeconomic trends may adversely affect the use of Spanish in this country, there are also a number of factors that may keep Spanish alive in the U.S. well into the next century.

To begin with, although the percentage of foreign-born Hispanics in the U.S. will decrease in this century, the absolute number of such individuals will still be very high. In fact, according to census projections, by the year 2100 there will be approximately 17 million foreign-born Hispanics in the U.S., a number that corresponds to roughly 4 million more foreign-born Hispanics than there are in this country at the present time ("As American as Apple Flan" 2000). If to this sizable number of Spanish-dominant speakers we add the number of second-generation *bilingual* Hispanics, it is apparent that the Spanish language will remain well represented in the U.S.

This situation makes it highly likely that many current and new commercial ventures and social services available in Spanish in this country will exist well into the coming century. To the extent that these ventures offer valuable Spanish language input to U.S. Hispanics, provide professional opportunities to bilingual individuals, and keep Spanish in a position of high visibility, they will play a role in promoting and preserving this language in the U.S.

Of all of such ventures, none may prove as valuable to linguistic preservation as the Spanish-language media. According to a 1996 study, Hispanics in general spend an average of thirty-five hours a week with Spanish-language media, while the Spanish-dominant spend sixty-nine hours per week (Reveron 2001, p. 60). Valdés (2000) reports

> Most Hispanics use both English and Spanish media. The frequency with which they choose one or the other, however, varies drastically depending on age, language proficiency, length of residence in the United States and formal educational level. As would be expected, the fewer the number of years that Hispanic adults have lived in the United States, the lower their English proficiency and the greater the use of Spanish-language media. This rule, however, does not apply across the board. Many long-term U.S. residents and even second-generation Hispanics choose more Spanish-language media than English-language media (p. 28).

In light of this, the rapid proliferation of Spanish-language media in the recent past comes as no surprise. Between 1970 and 2000, the number of Hispanic newspapers in the U.S. increased from 232 to 543 and circulation increased from 1 to 14.1 million readers. By contrast, during that same time, total U.S. newspaper circulation fell from 62 million to 56 million and readership dropped by 21 percent (McCoy 2001, p. 25). Similarly, between 1986 and 1999, the number of Spanish-language radio stations nearly tripled from 213 to 600. The 538 Spanish-language commercial stations in existence in 1999 were ranked sixth nationwide in number of listeners, after country, news/talk, adult contemporary, oldies, and adult standards ("Radio Is Exploding" 2000).

Of all Spanish-language media ventures, none enjoys as much success as television. *Hispanic Business* reports that Telemundo and Univisión are the two fastest-growing television networks in the U.S. In many cities, including Miami, Los Angeles, and Chicago, Univisión's stations regularly capture a bigger share of the audience between the ages of eighteen and thirty-four, than NBC, CBS, ABC, Fox, and Telemundo (Reveron 2001, p. 62).

A recent poll of the Hispanic electorate conducted by Hispanic Trends found that while ten years ago the percentage of the Hispanic electorate that received its news from Spanish-language television was less than 25 percent, in 2000, 46 percent of Latino registered voters turned to Spanish-language television for news. During the last presidential campaign, 32 percent of U.S. Hispanics who were registered to vote turned to Univisión for coverage of political issues. Telemundo placed second with 16 percent, followed by NBC (15 percent), CNN (11 percent), ABC (10 percent), and CBS (7 percent) (Lobaco 2000).

From a linguistic perspective, the impact of the Spanish-language media is highly significant. The media provide accessible, authentic, and relevant Spanish language input to U.S. Hispanics. Hence, by watching television, listening to the radio, or reading newspapers in Spanish, U.S. Hispanics are exposed to a range of topics, grammatical constructions, and vocabulary that are outside the scope of everyday use in the home or the immediate community. Furthermore, the media, and television in particular, provide U.S. Hispanics with access to variants of Spanish from many different regions of the Spanish-speaking world.

Among Univisión's most popular shows are *telenovelas* (soap operas), the majority of which are produced outside the U.S.: *Betty la Fea* (Colombia), *Amigas y Rivales* (Mexico), *El Derecho de Nacer* (Venezuela), *Por tu Amor* (Mexico), *El Día que me Quieras* (Argentina), and *Secreto de Amor* (Venezuela and the U.S.). Other popular television formats that feature speakers from different dialectal regions of the Spanish-speaking world include talk shows, news magazines, celebrity profiles, and coverage of sporting events.

To my knowledge, no studies exist on how this multidialectal lineup of television shows impacts the use of Spanish by Hispanics in the U.S. However, it is reasonable to assume that given the popularity and ubiquitousness of Spanish-language television, a substantial number of U.S. Hispanics from all socioeconomic classes and national backgrounds are exposed on a regular basis to linguistic registers and dialectal variants of Spanish not necessarily represented in their immediate communities. In many cases, these variants conform to the conventions of a standard, albeit informal, variant of Spanish widely understood throughout the Spanish-speaking world. It follows that Hispanics who access Spanish-language media in this country must have some understanding of such variants, or they would probably not watch or listen to the programs.

In terms of Valdés's categories, this situation may well correlate with a decrease in the number of SNS students who have only receptive skills in a contact variety of rural Spanish (Bilingual: Type F). Naturally, the validity of this hypothesis hinges on the assumption that students who enroll in SNS courses use or have used the Spanish-language media. However, this is not an unreasonable assumption in light of the popularity of Spanish-language television and radio among young Hispanics. A national survey commissioned by Univisión finds that three-quarters of Hispanic teenagers watched at least one hour of Spanish-language television a day in 2001 ("Young Hispanics Embrace Their Culture as Cool" 2001). Arbitron data indicate that in the year 2000, 95 percent of U.S. Hispanics between the ages of 12 and 18, and 96 percent of those between 18 and 34, listened to Spanish-language radio (*Radio*

Marketing Guide and Fact Book for Advertisers 2001–2002 Edition). Another study of the media habits of Hispanics further underscores the popularity of radio. "The Hispanic population often listens to the radio all day. The entire family often listens to one station, and tunes in an average of 26–30 hours per week. This ranks more than 13 percent above the general population" ("Spanish-language Radio: A Cultural Forum" 2001). Television viewing also tends to be a family activity among U.S. Hispanics. According to a recent study, Spanish-only parents of bilingual children often perceive English-language media to be a threat since they cannot understand its content. For this reason, such parents often pressure their children to watch Spanish-language television with them (Valdés 2000, p. 64).

Interestingly, in their study of second- and third-generation bilingual Chicano students, Valdés and Geoffrion-Vinci (1998, p. 478) find that these students manifested an awareness of the properties of formal registers, despite the limited functional use of Spanish in Chicano communities. They hypothesize that "speakers of Chicano Spanish have a verbal repertoire that includes what we are calling 'approximative' high registers of Spanish, based perhaps on the high registers of English or perhaps on incomplete data about the characteristics of the high registers of Spanish." Given the findings of market research, it is probable that for this population of students, as well as for many others, the Spanish-language media may be an important source of data about the characteristics of the medium-high registers of spoken Spanish. This hypothesis finds support in Hinton (1999, p. 4). According to this study, Asian American students often identify television as being helpful in maintaining or improving their proficiency in their ancestral language.

To sum up, the decrease in the relative number of foreign-born Hispanics combined with the growing affluence of U.S. Hispanics may lead to a decline in the proficiency levels of U.S. Hispanics in general, and of SNS students in particular. However, the impact of the Spanish-language media may result in fewer numbers of Spanish speakers with no receptive skills outside their own contact rural variety of Spanish. All in all, this information suggests that we can anticipate fewer students from the extreme ends of Valdés's proficiency categories. That is, we can anticipate fewer students in the number of Newly arrived: Types A and B students, as well as Bilingual: Type F.

The Academic Skills of Future Generations of SNS Students

In 1998, California voters overwhelmingly approved Proposition 227, thereby severely restraining and downsizing bilingual education in the state with the largest number of Hispanics in the U.S. Two years later, Arizona voters cast their vote in favor of more restrictive antibilingual education legislation, Proposition 203. A still more draconian proposal is currently under consideration in Colorado. Bilingual education laws have also come under the scrutiny of a growing antibilingual education movement in Massachusetts and New York.

As bilingual education faces growing uncertainty in some states and disintegration in others, many future students will likely approach the SNS classroom with little or no formal reading and writing instruction in Spanish and without much exposure to a print-rich environment in this language. Indeed, in many key states, Valdés's Bilingual: Type A (Access to bilingual instruction in the U.S., good academic skills in English, basic academic skills in Spanish) may well become a rarity.

At least in one Southern California university, such students already appear to be a small minority of the total SNS student population. A survey I conducted during the 2000–2001 school year reveals that only 10 percent or 13 out of 127 SNS students at California State University Long Beach attended bilingual education classes as children. Over 60 percent (77 students) reported having learned to read and write in Spanish in their religious education classes, 20 percent reported learning it from parents or grandparents, and the remaining 10 percent had no recollection of where they had acquired these skills. Interestingly, when encouraged to speculate as to how they learned to read and write in Spanish, many students in the latter group felt that the task of simultaneously reading and listening to commercials on television had helped them decipher the sound/symbol correspondences of the Spanish writing system. Other activities mentioned included following along visually as parents read letters from relatives, looking at magazines and newspapers at home, and reading bilingual labels on household products.

Despite their limited academic background in Spanish, it is noteworthy that the students who did not participate in bilingual education programs demonstrated basic reading and writing abilities in Spanish. To be sure, a significant number of them exhibited many of the characteristics typically found in unschooled writers (Colombi 1997). However, all students were able to complete fairly advanced reading and writing assignments, albeit with varying degrees of effort and success.

This finding suggests that basic academic skills in Spanish are not confined to the Bilingual: Type A category.[2] They are also found among SNS students who did not have the benefit of bilingual education (Bilingual Types: B, C, D, etc.). Does this mean that informal learning scenarios such as those found in the home or those where literacy is a by-product rather than an end goal of instruction, as in religious education programs, can replace bilingual education as native-language literacy instruction?

Without the benefit of comparative studies it is, of course, impossible to render a definitive answer to this question. However, it is unlikely that such learning scenarios offer the same range, depth, and quality of experience with the written word that are available in bilingual education programs. For one, despite their best intentions, neither parents nor catechists are specialists in literacy instruction. Nor are the resources of an entire school system available to them. Furthermore, it is highly unlikely that they are able to dedicate as much time to native-language literacy as bilingual instructors. Catholic education for First Communion or Confirmation, for example, is typically offered for one to two hours a week over a period of two years. Even if all activities in religious education classes were dedicated to developing literacy skills (which, of course, they aren't), the amount of time given to reading and writing in Spanish would still be well below that allocated to these skills in most bilingual education programs. It stands to reason, therefore, that with fewer U.S. Hispanics receiving bilingual education and literacy instruction being relegated to nonspecialists, the Spanish reading and writing proficiency levels of future SNS students will suffer.

However, the transparency of the Spanish writing system and the dedication of parents and religious education instructors will likely continue to provide students with basic reading and writing skills in Spanish. For these students, literacy skills acquired in English may facilitate the learning of higher-level academic skills in Spanish. In their study of Chicano students, Valdés and Geoffrion-Vinci (1998, p. 493) hypothesize that these students fall back on their knowledge of English when attempting to express themselves in the higher registers of Spanish. They note: "It is important to stress the fact that in carrying out their presentations, the students appeared to transfer their sense of the lexical choices appropriate for academic discussion in English and their awareness of the need to utilize certain more formal expressions and terms to Spanish."

If linguistic skills learned in English can transfer to Spanish, the educational gains posted by U.S. Hispanics bode well for future generations of SNS students. The American Council on Education reports that from 1976 to 1996, the number of Hispanics in college grew by 202 percent (Williams 2001, p. 34). Statistics from the Advanced Placement Board also point to significant progress by U.S. Hispanics in the area of education. From 1974 to 2001, the participation of this population in AP exams went up by seven percentage points, growing from 2 percent to 9 percent of total test takers

("Then and Now" 2002).[3] By all projections, these trends will continue in the coming decades, as the Hispanic middle class comes of age (Brischetto 2001). In terms of Valdés's schema, this means that more students will be classified as having good to basic academic skills in English, while fewer such students will manifest poor academic skills in this language.

In sum, the situation with respect to the academic skills of future generations of SNS students is mixed. On the one hand, the loss of bilingual education in certain key states will likely result in a drop in the Spanish-language academic skills of U.S. Hispanics. The work of parents and religious education programs, however, may serve to instruct U.S. Hispanics on the basic rules of the Spanish writing system. General gains by U.S. Hispanics in academic skills and in English may further counteract some of the consequences stemming from the loss of bilingual education.

The Growing Economic Value and Prestige of U.S. Spanish

Paradoxically, as the impact of bilingual education recedes in some states, the professional opportunities available to bilingual Hispanics are rapidly proliferating in this country, as well as in the global market. The *LA Times* reports:

> countless U.S. companies are feeling the Latino talent pinch, not only to staff their operations in Mexico and Central and South America, but to serve the 35-million-strong Latino market at home, a sector whose population, purchasing power and businesses are growing faster than that of the U.S. as a whole (Kraul 2000).

Carreira and Armengol (2001) document the growing number and variety of professional opportunities available to bilingual Hispanics in the fields of law enforcement, translation and interpretation, marketing, the media, business, health, and education. These opportunities present both benefits and challenges to the field of SNS. On the one hand, the promise of interesting and lucrative employment represents a powerful motivation for U.S. Hispanics to hone their bilingual skills. On the other hand, the linguistic and cultural demands of the workplace can be very high. Such demands can include making correct and appropriate use of the oral and written modes of a standard variant, as well as understanding the cultural and dialectal nuances of the main Hispanic nationalities and social classes represented in this country.

Despite these challenges, the teaching of these and other skills to bilingual Hispanics constitutes one of the most important means for improving the economic future of this population and for preserving the Spanish language in the U.S. Linguists have argued that one of the greatest barriers to attaining the latter goal is the low social and economic value attached to Spanish in this country. Bills (1997) notes "despite a massive influx of Spanish-speaking immigrants, the shift to English is inexorable. The reasons for the shift are moderately clear in broad outline. The finding of clear associations between using Spanish and low socioeconomic status is repeated in study after study. Furthermore, these associations are transparent to everyone in the society, and the clarity of the evidence to Hispanic youth and young adults surely pushes the process of the shift" (p. 280).

Conversely, a language's perceived economic advantage may serve to preserve it in conditions otherwise known to accelerate linguistic loss. For example, in San Antonio, Texas, where 85 percent of the Hispanic population is U.S.-born, most Hispanics maintain proficiency in Spanish (Fradd and Boswell 1996, p. 4). This situation goes against the general pattern noted earlier that linguistic proficiency declines with each successive generation born in the U.S. Interestingly, an analysis of mean income for U.S. Hispanics in ten metropolitan areas indicates that there are economic advantages to knowing Spanish and English in San Antonio. Only two other cities share this distinction: Miami, with an 80 percent foreign-born population, and Jersey City, with a 71 percent foreign-born population. These findings offer the tantalizing possibility that economic advantage may play an important role in explaining the survivability of Spanish in San Antonio despite the high number of U.S.-born Hispanics that reside in this city.

Social prestige, a factor often closely aligned with economic power, may also favor the maintenance of U.S. Spanish. A national study conducted by Univisión in 2001 finds that three-quarters of Hispanic teenagers surveyed see Hispanic culture as "cool and hip" and closely identify with their home culture ("Young Hispanics Embrace Their Culture as Cool" 2001). A 1999 *Newsweek* poll found that although Latinos over thirty-five were most likely to identify themselves as American, most under that age preferred to think of themselves as Latino or Hispanic (*Latin USA* 1999). The 2000 Yankelovich Hispanic Monitor reports that 69 percent of Hispanics of all ages in the top seven markets in the U.S. find the Spanish language to be more important to them than it was five years ago, up from 63 percent in 1997 ("Yankelovich Releases the 2000 Hispanic Monitor Report Results" 2000).

Highly favorable views of the Spanish language are also to be found among the general American population. *USA Today* reports that enrollments in Spanish-language classes have soared more than 90 percent since the 1970s (Sharp 2001). Similarly, a recent *Time*/CNN poll reveals that 78 percent of adult Americans would encourage their children to learn Spanish (*Time*/CNN Poll 2001).

Recognition of the emerging power of U.S. Spanish and Hispanics is even to be found among traditional linguistic circles in the Spanish-speaking world. In his closing address at the II Congreso Internacional de la Lengua Española, Carlos Fuentes notes: "Las intervenciones de fuerza norteamericanas en Latinoamérica están siendo contestadas por una invasión pacífica de Latinoamérica a los Estados Unidos, y sus legiones hablan español" ("Clausural Fuentes congreso de la lengua" 2001).

All in all, young Hispanics in this country are growing up at a time of unprecedented prestige and economic power for Spanish. In the current climate, many Hispanics approach the learning of Spanish with a great deal of pride in their roots and a sense of general acceptance by mainstream America. In this regard, they differ significantly from those of earlier generations who may have experienced discrimination or faced punishment for using Spanish (MacGregor-Mendoza 2000). This difference is underscored in a 1999 *Newsweek* poll that asked U.S. Hispanics: "All in all, do you think the situation for the younger generation of Hispanic or Latino Americans is better, worse, or about the same as their parents' situation was when they were the same age?" Forty-nine percent of respondents between the ages of eighteen and thirty-four answered "better" to this question and 37 percent in this age group answered "worse." By contrast, only 39 percent of those older than thirty-five answered "better" and 45 percent answered "worse" to this question (*Latin USA* 1999). This generational difference in perspective is one that SNS teachers would do well to keep in mind in their presentation of cultural topics.

The Diversity of U.S. Hispanics

Notwithstanding the statistical reality of national trends, it is important to keep in mind that there is a great deal of variation between communities of U.S. Hispanics with regard to factors known to affect linguistic loyalty and preservation. For example, as shown in Table 3.2, the percentage of U.S.-born Hispanics relative to the total Hispanic population varies widely across metropolitan areas in the U.S.

There is also a great deal of variation to be found along geographical lines with regard to density. Table 3.3 represents the percentage of residents in given metropolitan areas that claim to be Hispanic. As shown, this number ranges from nearly 97 percent in East Los Angeles, to 5 percent in Detroit.

There are also significant differences to be encountered along ethnic or

Table 3.2 *Proportion of U.S. Hispanics Born in the U.S., by City*

CITY	PERCENT
San Antonio	85.5
El Paso	65.6
Houston	58.3
San Diego	55.1
Chicago	47.8
Los Angeles	45.4
San Francisco	43.2
New York	41.0
Jersey City	29.1
Miami	20.2

Source: Fradd and Boswell 1999, p. 2

national lines. Market research, for example, reveals that Cubans are less likely than Mexicans or Puerto Ricans to report feeling discriminated against (Valdés 2000, p. 113). Undoubtedly, in Miami, this situation stems in part from the important socioeconomic role of this language. Lynch (2000, p. 279) notes:

> Miami's sociocultural, economic and geographic intimacy with many countries of the Spanish-speaking world make its relationship to the Spanish language inevitable in the globalization of the coming decades. Miami will keep growing as an economic center for Latin American trade and finance, so Spanish will continue to have an instrumental value for Miami businesses and a bilingual workforce will be essential (Fradd 1996). The rise of Miami in the 1990s as the capital of worldwide Spanish-language mass communication and popular entertainment (Mac-Swam 1996) will additionally secure the vitality of the language there.

A strikingly different situation holds in the Southwest, where Hudson, Hernández Chávez, and Bills (1995) find that general socioeconomic advancement shows a strong negative correlation with Spanish-language use and retention among Hispanics. Similar findings are reported by Rivera-Mills (2001) for a Northern California community. Not surprisingly, in some regions of the Southwest, there is a long-standing history of societal stigma attached to Spanish. MacGregor-Mendoza (2000), for example, documents the physical punishment and humiliation endured by previous generations of schoolchildren in Las Cruces, New Mexico, for using Spanish.

Table 3.3 *Hispanics as a Fraction of the Total Population*

CITY	PERCENT
East Los Angeles	96.8
Laredo	94.1
El Paso	76.6
Miami	65.8
San Antonio	58.7
Los Angeles	46.5
Houston	37.4
Dallas	35.6
Phoenix	34.1
San Jose	30.2
New York	27
Chicago	26
San Diego	25.4
Philadelphia	8.5
Detroit	5

Source: U.S. Census Bureau, Population Division, Ethnic and Hispanic Statistics Branch, 2002

Another set of sociolinguistic circumstances characterizes the Puerto Rican experience in New York. According to García, Morín, and Rivera (2001), "Spanish and English have reversed roles in the Puerto Rican community, with Spanish, most often associated with poverty, being now linked also to middle-class status, and English, most often associated with prestige, being also linked to poverty" (p. 259). Moreover, Puerto Ricans are increasingly perceived as English-speaking by New Yorkers, while Dominicans are now viewed as the Spanish speakers in this city. In this context, Puerto Ricans sprinkle in Spanish linguistic and extra-linguistic features when speaking English as a way to mark their ethnic identity.

In this diverse landscape, it is not surprising to find that the attitudes of Hispanics towards their ancestral language vary according to geographical and national lines. A national survey of Hispanic youths finds that Cubans in Miami assign more instrumental than integrative value to Spanish. Mexican-Americans in San Antonio, Albuquerque, and Los Angeles, in turn, favor Spanish for instrumental and ethnic reasons. Puerto Ricans in the Bronx and Amsterdam, New York, on the other hand, evaluate Spanish as being less important to meeting instrumental or integrative goals (Ramírez 2000, p. 288).

The pedagogical significance of these differences is evident: SNS instruction must be regionally anchored. Pedagogical goals and materials that may be appropriate in Miami, for example, may be entirely out of place in the Southwest. Therefore, it is essential for SNS teachers to know the student population and local Hispanic communities they are dealing with.

Other Pedagogical Implications

A general picture emerges from the foregoing discussion.

- The projected drop in the percentage of foreign-born Hispanics, along with the growing affluence of second- and third-generation U.S. Hispanics, is likely to result in an overall decline in the Spanish language proficiency of future SNS students.
- The number of U.S. Hispanics exposed to mainstream informal varieties of Spanish will increase due to the influence of the Spanish-language media.
- The disintegration of bilingual education in some key immigrant states will undermine the academic skills in Spanish of a significant number of SNS students. However, parents, religious education programs, and other sources may provide basic reading and writing instruction in Spanish.
- As Hispanics make unprecedented gains in education, the general academic skills and English-language competence of SNS students will become stronger.
- Future generations of SNS students are likely to differ from those of earlier generations with respect to their experience with Spanish as a purveyor of economic opportunities and a language of social prestige.
- Despite these national trends, there remain significant differences between communities of U.S. Hispanics with regard to variables known to affect linguistic preservation.

In terms of Valdés's schema, we can anticipate fewer students from the Newly Arrived: Types A and B, and Bilingual: Types A and F categories. The remaining categories (Bilingual: Types B, C, D, E) are likely to differ from those proposed by Valdés with respect to three variables. First, we can expect to find basic reading and writing skills in Spanish in a significant number of students within these categories. Second, we can expect a rising number of students in these categories to have intermediate to good academic skills in English. Finally, we can anticipate fewer students whose exposure to Spanish is strictly limited to the rural or contact varieties represented in their community of residence. The latter does not imply, of course, that SNS students will have productive abilities in mainstream varieties of Spanish by virtue of their exposure to the media. It merely suggests that the language classroom is not likely to be the first point of contact with mainstream Spanish for many such students.

The above projections are fraught with implications for SNS instruction.

The anticipated decline in the proficiency levels and academic skills in Spanish of SNS students calls for the development of pedagogical materials for students with intermediate to low levels of speaking abilities and minimal levels of reading and writing skills. With regard to this population of students, it is important for SNS instructors to bear in mind that just because Hispanic students are able to sound out and transcribe the written word in Spanish, it does not mean that they have practiced the many skills underlying literacy in this language. Therefore, SNS instruction should focus on developing and practicing literacy strategies such as scanning, skimming, and analyzing the organizational structure of a text, as well as making appropriate use of traditional and electronic dictionaries.

Readings should present an idea that is not entirely novel to students in relatively familiar language and a short format. Advertisements, informal letters, e-mails, application forms, recipes, menus, personal ads, and video or music labels all represent accessible formats for this type of reader. In addition, texts that make use of graphs and charts, such as survey reports, and those that are based on the spoken word, such as interviews, words to songs, and television transcripts are particularly apropos for beginning readers.[4]

These formats are also appropriate as writing assignments at beginning levels, provided students are given sample texts to model their work after and are provided with ways to contextualize the task. For example, if instructed to design an advertisement for a restaurant, students should have the opportunity to view and study numerous samples of ads in Spanish. They should also study the population of Hispanics for which their ad is intended by, for example, conducting a poll of local Hispanics to find out about their eating preferences and habits. Additional information can be found on the Internet, through local chambers of commerce, or in marketing reports. Interviews of local Hispanics, Spanish-language menus, and recipes for Hispanic dishes can serve to inform linguistic decisions such as those involving the use of regional vocabulary, register, and the amount of English to include in the ad. All of this information can accompany the ad in a portfolio that serves as a dictionary of restaurant-related language, a reference on U.S. Hispanics, and a roadmap to community and electronic sources of information.

Given the familiarity of young Hispanics with the Spanish-language media (particularly television), activities that engage students in analyzing selected programs can serve as the basis of many interesting activities in the SNS classroom. For example, in classroom discussions students can compare and contrast television news in English and Spanish with respect to factors such as the lineup of the stories, the coverage of issues involving the Latino community in the U.S., and the coverage of international news. Students for whom the language of newscasts may be too advanced can do comparative studies of commercials, soap operas, or talk shows. The latter two formats also lend themselves well to writing programming summaries and critical reviews.[5]

Another instructive project involves comparing and contrasting televised news stories to those appearing in newspapers. First, students videotape a newscast in Spanish and transcribe three or four of the news stories. Next, they find newspaper stories in Spanish that cover the same topics as the transcribed television stories. They then compare the two formats with respect to the amount and type of information presented, average number of words per sentence, average number of unfamiliar words, and other variables. This activity is a particularly effective way to teach some of the differences between the spoken and written modes of language. Furthermore, as students compare their transcriptions to the newspaper stories, they correct their own spelling errors, learn synonyms, and see different ways of conveying the same information.

Projects such as these provide rich and authentic input in the aural and written modalities of Spanish, and engage students in exploring issues pertaining to communities of U.S. Hispanics. In so doing, they offer valuable practice with the skills and information needed to make personal, social, and professional use of Spanish in this country.

By and large, the most lucrative and prestigious professional opportunities available in Spanish in the U.S. require highly developed literacy skills in this language. All too often, however, such proficiency is not readily found among U.S.-born Hispanics. For example, according to Fradd and Boswell (1996, p. 284), many businesses in the Miami-Dade County area find that their employees are not fluent enough in Spanish to read or write at a level appropriate to creating reports or making presentations in a work environment. Therefore, companies in that area often import foreign-born speakers of Spanish to conduct business with Latin America. Thus, in a market that is in dire need of Spanish-English bilinguals, the best positions in Spanish are going to foreign-educated Spanish speakers, not to U.S. Hispanics. Not surprisingly, companies often find that these foreign-nationals lack the level of proficiency in English and the social skills to navigate the complex linguistic and social situations that arise in bilingual settings in the U.S. (Morán 1999).

The field of SNS can play an important role in reversing the current situation by bringing its linguistic, pedagogical, and cultural know-how to bear on the professional training of U.S. Hispanics. With this goal in mind, SNS specialists must forge alliances with experts in other fields to develop linked courses, internship opportunities, and study-abroad programs that target U.S. Hispanics aiming to make professional use of Spanish. Fields that would benefit from this type of collaboration are those where the opportunities for Spanish/English bilinguals are most abundant: journalism, marketing, business, health, the law, translation and interpretation, and technology (Kenig 1999).

In addition to focusing on the development of linguistic and professional skills, SNS instruction must emphasize three areas of cultural competence. First, as the proportion of second- and third-generation Hispanics increases relative to that of the foreign-born, the customs, culture, and history of the Spanish-speaking world may seem more remote to SNS students. For this reason, in the future, considerable effort must go into providing instruction on these topics to students with distant personal connections to the Spanish-speaking world. At the same time, SNS instruction must focus on presenting two complementary perspectives of the U.S. as a Spanish-speaking country. On the one hand, the U.S. is a microcosm of the Spanish-speaking world where different communities maintain their traditions and sense of identity. On the other hand, in the U.S., Hispanics are forging a new multicultural and multilingual identity that blends the traditions of the Spanish-speaking world with those of this country.

In keeping with the latter perspective, the SNS classroom of the future should provide a forum for U.S. Hispanics across the U.S. to explore their vastly different experiences as they forge a common identity. Technology affords unprecedented opportunities to accomplish this important goal. Through the use of electronic mail and two-way videoconferencing, SNS students from different regions of the U.S. can discuss their perspectives and experiences as bilingual Hispanics. Educational exchanges between American universities can also serve to familiarize SNS students from one region of the U.S. with communities of Hispanics from another region.

Undoubtedly, in their search to define what it means to be Hispanic in this country, many students will point to discrimination, poverty, and other social injustices as defining experiences. However, as the economic power, educational status, and demographic representation of U.S. Hispanics continue to rise, the experiences of many SNS students with mainstream American culture will become increasingly positive. The goal for SNS instruction must be to present both sides of the U.S. Hispanic experience. By acknowledging the social problems that continue to plague some immigrant communities, SNS instruction can galvanize students to eradicate them. At the same time, by displaying the many achievements of U.S. Hispanics, the SNS classroom can open up a world of possibilities for future generations of students.

Finally, it is important to bear in mind the changing status of U.S. Hispanics and Spanish. This fluidity manifests itself along time as well as space. Because of this, SNS teachers must devise ways to refresh and revise their understanding of the experiences, abilities, and expectations that every new set of students brings to the classroom. Carefully constructed class discussions and projects may help teachers accomplish this goal. Classroom surveys, such as the one included in the appendix to this essay, may further contribute to this end. Additional questions that teachers may want to consider can be found in Webb and Miller (2000, p. 48).

Directions for Future Work

Hispanics are radically altering the profile of SNS students. The challenge for SNS specialists is to mold instructional practices to the needs of this diverse population. SNS teachers must familiarize themselves with the particular sociolinguistic conditions that apply to the populations of their students. At the same time, SNS specialists must carefully study the pedagogical and linguistic implications of census data, marketing studies, and other reports on U.S. Hispanics. A national poll of SNS students would further serve to delineate the profile of this population for curricular purposes.

Student Questionnaire

1. As you were growing up, in which of the following environments did you speak **Spanish**? Mark as many as apply:
   □ Home □ School □ Church □ Spanish-speaking country

2. Where were you born? □ U.S. □ Other country
   If you were born in the U.S., where were your parents born?
   Country: _____ City/Town/Village: _____
   If you were born outside the U.S., what is your country of birth?
   _____
   How old were you when you arrived in the U.S.? _____

3. What language(s) do you speak in the following situations?
   At home, with parents: _____
   With siblings: _____
   With grandparents: _____
   With other relatives: _____
   At work: _____
   On social occasions: _____
   At church: _____

4. Did you attend religious education classes in Spanish as you were growing up? _____
   If yes, for how many years? _____ How many hours per week? _____

5. Do you currently attend church services or functions in Spanish? _____

6. Did you watch Spanish-language television as you were growing up?
   _____

7. Do you currently watch Spanish-language TV?
   If yes, how many hours a week: _____

8. Did you listen to Spanish-language radio as you were growing up? _____

9. Do you currently listen to Spanish-language radio?
   If yes, how many hours a week? _____

10. Do you read any of the following **in Spanish**? If so, how many hours/minutes a week?
    □ Magazines   Hours/minutes per week: _____
    □ Newspapers   Hours/minutes per week: _____

☐ Bible   Hours/minutes per week: _____
☐ Novels, short stories, etc.   Hours/minutes per week: _____

11. Where did you learn to read and write **in Spanish**? Answer as many as apply:
    ☐ At home
    ☐ In a bilingual education program. If so, for how many years? _____
    ☐ At church
    ☐ In a Spanish-speaking country. If so, what is the highest grade level you completed in this country? _____
    ☐ In high school in the U.S. If so, for how many years? _____
    ☐ At the university or community-college level in the U.S. If so, for how many semesters/quarters _____?
    ☐ I taught myself. If so, how did you accomplish this?

12. What are your reasons for wanting to improve your Spanish?

13. In the future, do you expect to make professional use of your Spanish-language skills? If so, how?

14. How would you rate your speaking abilities **in Spanish**?
    ☐ Excellent   ☐ Fair
    ☐ Very good   ☐ Poor
    ☐ Good   ☐ Very poor

15. How would you rate your writing abilities **in Spanish**?
    ☐ Excellent   ☐ Fair
    ☐ Very good   ☐ Poor
    ☐ Good   ☐ Very poor

16. How would you rate your speaking abilities **in English**?
    ☐ Excellent   ☐ Fair
    ☐ Very good   ☐ Poor
    ☐ Good   ☐ Very poor

17. How would you rate your writing abilities **in English**?
    ☐ Excellent   ☐ Fair
    ☐ Very good   ☐ Poor
    ☐ Good   ☐ Very poor

NOTES

1. In terms of absolute numbers of Hispanic college graduates, the disparity between the foreign-born and the American-born is much greater, as far more of the latter are middle class than the former.

2. We use "basic academic skills" to refer to (a) the ability to sound out the written word in Spanish, (b) to understand the basic idea of a text in the medium to low levels of register, and (c) to express a thought in writing, albeit with possible spelling and grammar errors.

3. By comparison, during that same time period, the participation of Asian-Americans increased from 5 percent to 14 percent, that of African Americans increased from 3 percent to 4 percent, and that of Native Americans did not change.

4. Many of these formats correspond to the mid-to-low register levels identified in Valdés and Geoffrion-Vinci (1998).

5. For additional activities that are based on texts from the mid-to-low register levels see Samaniego and Pino (2000).

REFERENCES

"As American as Apple Flan." 2000. *Hispanic Market Weekly* (August 7). Available from www.awool.com/hmw/rp080700.pdf. Accessed on April 15, 2001.

Bills, Garland. 1997. "Language Shift, Linguistic Variation and Teaching Spanish to Native Speakers in the United States." In *La enseñanza del español a hispanohablantes*, eds. M. C. Colombi and F. X. Alarcón. Boston: Houghton Mifflin.

Brischetto, Robert R. 2001. "The Hispanic Middle Class Comes of Age." *Hispanic Business*, December, 21–33.

Carreira, María, and Regla Armengol. 2001. "Professional Opportunities for Heritage Language Speakers." In *Heritage Languages in America: Preserving a National Resource*, eds. J. K. Peyton, D. A. Ranard, and S. McGinnis. McHenry, IL: Center for Applied Linguistics (CAL).

"Clausural Fuentes congreso de la lengua." 2001. *Reforma*. Available at www.reforma.com/cultura/articulo/136036/. Accessed on October 19.

Colombi, M. Cecilia. 1997. "Perfil del discurso escrito en textos de hispanohablantes: teoría y práctica." In *La enseñanza del español a hispanohablantes*, eds. M. C. Colombi and F. X. Alarcón. Boston: Houghton Mifflin.

Fradd, Sandra H., and Thomas D. Boswell. 1999. "Income Patterns of Bilingual and English-only Hispanics in Selected Metropolitan Areas." Available at www.ncbe.gwu.edu/miscpubs/florida/workforce99/income.htm. Accessed on November 7.

———. 1996. "Spanish as an Economic Resource in Metropolitan Miami." *Bilingual Research Journal* 20 (3):283–338.

García, Ofelia, José Luis Morín, and Klaudia Rivera. 2001. "How Threatened Is the Spanish of New York Puerto Ricans?" In *Can Threatened Languages Be Saved?*, ed. J. Fishman. Clevedon, U.K.: Multilingual Matters.

Hinton, Leanne. 1999. "Involuntary Language Loss among Immigrants: Asian-American Linguistic Autobiographies." *ERIC Digest*. Available at www/cal.org/ericll/digest/involuntary.html. Accessed on May 31, 2000.

Howell, Susan. 1997. "Hispanic Social Needs Survey: New Orleans Metropolitan Area." Available at www.uno.edu/-poli/hispan.htm. Accessed on April 21, 2001.

Hudson, Alan, Eduardo Hernández Chávez, and Garland Bills. 1995. "The Many Faces of Language Maintenance." In *Spanish in Four Continents*, ed. C. Silva-Corvalán. Washington, D.C.: Georgetown University Press.

Kenig, Graciela. 1999. *Best Careers for Bilingual Latinos*. Chicago: VGM Career Horizons.

Kraul, Christopher. 2000. "Latino Talent Pinch Hobbling U.S. Firms' Expansion Plans." *Los Angeles Times*, June 25.

"Latin USA." 1999. Available at www.pollingreport.com/race.htm. Accessed in August 2000.

Lobaco, Julia Bencomo. 2000. "Spanish Language News a Latino Favorite." Vista (September). Available at www.vistamagazine.com/seppol.htm.

Lynch, Andrew. 2000. "Spanish-speaking Miami in Sociolinguistic Perspective: Bilingualism, Recontact, and Language Maintenance among the Cuban-origin Population." In *Research on Spanish in the United States: Linguistic Issues and Challenges*, ed. A. Roca. Somerville, MA: Cascadilla Press.

MacGregor-Mendoza, Patricia. 2000. "Aquí no se habla español: Stories of linguistic repression in Southwest schools." *Bilingual Research Journal* 24 (4):355–67.

McCoy, Frank. 2001. "The Small Press Turns into a Big Deal." *Hispanic Business*, April 2001, 24–26.

Morán, Julio. 1999. Executive director, California Chicano News Media Association, October 17, 1999. Personal communication.

"Radio Is Exploding." 2000. *Hispanic Market Weekly*, (February 14.) Available at www.awool.com/hmw/o21400.html.

Radio Marketing Guide and Fact Book for Advertisers 2001–2002 Edition. Arbitron.

Ramírez, Arnulfo G. 2000. "Linguistic Notions of Spanish among Youths from Different Hispanic Groups." In *Research on Spanish in the United States: Linguistic Issues and Challenges*, ed. A. Roca. Somerville, MA: Cascadilla Press.

Reveron, Derek. 2001. "On with the Show." *Hispanic Business*, December, 60-62.

Rivera-Mills, Susana. 2001. "Acculturation and Communicative Need: Language Shift in an Ethnically Diverse Hispanic Community." *Southwest Journal of Linguistics* 20 (2):211–23.

Roy, Daniel. 1997. "Summary Results from the Latino Ethnic Attitude Survey." Available at www.falcon.cc.ukans.edu/droy. Accessed on March 10, 2001.

Samaniego, Fabián, and Cecilia Pino. 2000. "Frequently Asked Questions about SNS Programs." In *Spanish for Native Speakers*. Vol. 1 of Professional Development Series Handbook for Teachers K-16, edited by American Association of Teachers of Spanish and Portuguese. Fort Worth, TX: Harcourt College.

Silva-Corvalán, Carmen. 1997. "El español hablado en Los Angeles: Aspectos sociolingüísticos." In *La enseñanza del español a hispanohablantes*, eds. M. C. Colombi and F. Alarcón. Boston: Houghton Mifflin.

"Spanish-language Radio: A Cultural Forum." 2001. *Market Place Media*. Available at www.marketmedia.com/amm/ammradio.htm. Accessed on March 8, 2002.

"Then and Now." 2002. The College Board and collegeboard.com. Available at www.collegeboard.com/ap/techman/chap1/. Accessed on March 8.

Time/CNN Poll: "Evolving Perceptions." *Time Magazine*, June 11, 2001, 46–47.

U.S. Census Bureau. 2000. "Overview of Race and Hispanic Origin, Census 2000 Briefs." Available at www.census.gov/population/www/cen2000/briefs.html. Accessed on March 8, 2002.

U.S. Census Bureau, Population Division, Ethnic and Hispanic Statistics Branch. 2002. "Hispanic or Latino Origin for the United States, Regions, Divisions, States and for Puerto Rico: 2000 (PHC-T-10)." Available at www.census.gov/population/www/cen2000/phc-t10.html. Accessed on March 10.

Valdés, Guadalupe. 2001. "Heritage Language Students: Profiles and Possibilities." In *Heritage Languages in America: Preserving a National Resource*, eds. J. K. Peyton, D. A. Ranard and S. McGinnis. McHenry, IL: Center for Applied Linguistics (CAL).

———. 1997. "The Teaching of Spanish to Bilingual Spanish-Speaking Students: Outstanding Issues and Unanswered Questions." In *La enseñanza del español a hispanohablantes*, eds. M. C. Colombi and F. X. Alarcón. Boston: Houghton Mifflin.

Valdés, Guadalupe, and Michelle Geoffrion-Vinci. 1998. "Chicano Spanish: The Problem of 'Underdeveloped' Code in Bilingual Repertoires." *The Modern Language Journal* 82:473–501.

Valdés, M. Isabel. 2000. *Marketing to American Latinos*. Vol. 1. Ithaca, NY: Paramount Market Publishing, Inc.

Walqui, Aída. 1997. "Algunas consideraciones acerca de la enseñanza del español a hispanohablantes a nivel secundario." In *La enseñanza del español a hispanohablantes*, eds. M. C. Colombi and F. X. Alarcón. Boston: Houghton Mifflin.

Webb, John B., and Barbara L. Miller, eds. 2000. *Teaching Heritage Language Learners: Voices from the Classroom*. Yonkers, NY: ACTFL Series 2000.

Williams, Scott. "A Positive Learning Curve." *Hispanic Business*, December 2001, 34–36.

"Yankelovich Releases the 2000 Hispanic Monitor Report Results." 2000. Press release. Available at http://secure.yankelovich.com/about_us/hispanic_release.asp. Accessed on January 7, 2001.

"Young Hispanics Embrace Their Culture as Cool." 2001. *San Francisco Chronicle* (May 17), F3.

4

Un enfoque funcional para la enseñanza del ensayo expositivo

M. Cecilia Colombi

University of California, Davis

En el sistema educacional actual, las clases multiculturales son la norma en los Estados Unidos. Gran parte de la diversidad en nuestras escuelas es lingüística y está directamente relacionada con los desafíos que implica desarrollar una alfabetización académica. Desafortunadamente en las escuelas existen pocas posibilidades de desarrollar un lenguaje académico en otras lenguas que no sea inglés. Proposiciones como la 227, que se sancionó en California en 1998 y otras semejantes que han sido aprobadas o están siendo consideradas en estados como Arizona, Colorado y Massachusetts, promovidas por reacciones xenofóbicas y sin bases en los conocimientos que las investigaciones acerca del desarrollo de una segunda lengua nos han dado, son una amenaza seria en contra de la educación bilingüe en los Estados Unidos. Esto tiene serias implicaciones para la habilidad de los hispanohablantes de poder obtener un alto nivel de competencia académica en español (Bartolomé 1998; Pérez 1999; Faltis y Wolfe 1999).

El desarrollo del lenguaje académico va más allá de saber leer y escribir; es necesario aprender a usar el lenguaje en formas que demandan un conocimiento específico del lenguaje, de los textos y de los nuevos instrumentos tecnológicos para convertirse en participantes activos en nuestra sociedad actual. La competencia académica ("advanced literacy") se puede investigar desde distintas perspectivas, como una habilidad individual concentrándonos en las etapas cognitivas del desarrollo o a través de perspectivas socioculturales que se enfocan en los contextos históricos e ideológicos y en el rol de la cultura en la comunidad (Valdés y Geoffrion-Vinci 1998; Colombi y Schleppegrell 2002).

Cuando se analiza el desarrollo de la escritura en hablantes nativos del español en un contexto bilingüe como el de California, es claro que los estudiantes traen consigo características orales típicas de los registros interpersonales a los que están acostumbrados. Ellos están mucho más familiarizados con los registros informales de conversación en español que con los académicos, pero a través de una instrucción explícita avanzan en el continuo del lenguaje desarrollando los registros académicos (Colombi 1997a, 1997b, 2000, 2002). La lingüística sistémica funcional nos permite un marco teórico para el análisis del lenguaje académico (Halliday 1978, 1994; Martin 1992).

Este trabajo presenta una aplicación de la teoría de registro y género de la lingüística sistémica funcional en las clases de escritura de español avanzado. En este capítulo se analiza el ensayo expositivo escrito por un estudiante hispanohablante al final de tres trimestres de instrucción (véase apéndice). El ensayo expositivo es uno de los géneros textuales más relevantes para el desarrollo del lenguaje académico; los estudiantes deben saber escribir ensayos expositivos para poder avanzar en sus carreras universitarias y profesionales en español. A través de este análisis se identifican las características del registro académico que son funcionales para la escritura del ensayo académico en español. Se examinan los constituyentes funcionales del ensayo al nivel del género textual y las elecciones lexicogramaticales del registro (campo, tenor y modo) que le permiten a este estudiante escribir un ensayo académico efectivo. En este capítulo también se ofrece una guía de preguntas que los instructores pueden hacerles a sus estudiantes para que ellos mismos analicen su escritura desde la perspectiva de la lingüística sistémica funcional.

Género

La lingüística sistémica funcional (LSF) tiene una larga trayectoria de uso en la lingüística educacional en Australia y Europa para la enseñanza del inglés principalmente como primera y segunda lengua (Christie 1986, 1991; Halliday 1985, 1996; Halliday y Hasan 1989; Martin 1984, 1985, 1997, 1998; Martin y Christie 1997; Martin, Christie y Rothery 1987). La LSF es una teoría semiótica que considera el lenguaje inserto en un contexto social y con un rol primordial en la construcción de los contextos sociales en los que vivimos. Para Halliday (1978, 1994) el lenguaje se forma en un contexto social al mismo tiempo que también construye ese contexto social. El lenguaje siempre tiene lugar en un contexto, es influenciado por el contexto y cambia para reflejar el contexto extralingüístico de su creación; el contexto general o contexto de la cultura y el específico o el de la situación:

a. **El contexto de la cultura** se puede ver como la suma de todos los significados que son posibles para identificar una cultura.

b. **El contexto de la situación** es una abstracción que se puede definir como la suma de las características que motivan la construcción del texto y que hacen que sea lo que es.

Un componente esencial en esta teoría es el concepto de **género** como punto de partida para desarrollar una alfabetización crítica y consciente. Martin y otros caracterizan los géneros como procesos sociales, secuenciales y con un propósito claro en los cuales las personas interactúan como miembros de la cultura (Martin 1984, p. 25). La pregunta que nos ayuda a identificar un género es **¿qué es lo que hacemos con la lengua?**

El género está determinado por el contexto de la cultura y es más abstracto y general que el registro; podemos reconocer un género particular sin saber exactamente a qué contexto situacional pertenece; por ejemplo: un anuncio, una propaganda, una carta, etc. El género se puede ver como un marco o estructura que le da significado a interacciones de distinto tipo, es decir, el género se adapta a los contextos sociales en los que se usa. Así la

Figura 4.1 *Género y registro en relación con el lenguaje*

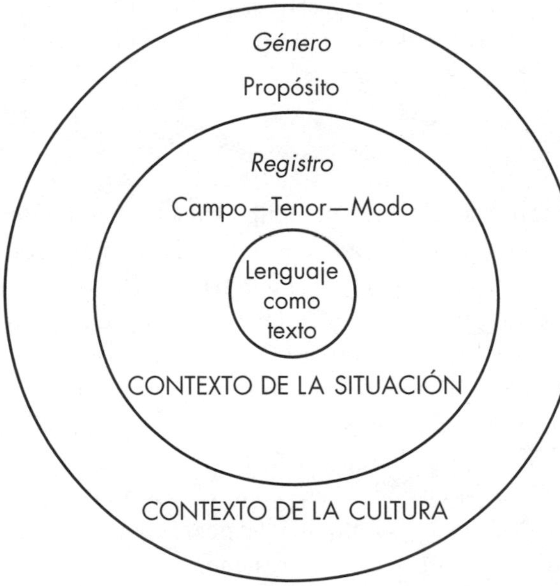

Fuente: Adaptado de Eggins 1994, p. 34.

lingüística sistémica funcional caracteriza a los contextos sociales como sistemas de géneros. Algunos de estos procesos (o géneros) reciben especial atención por la importancia que se les da en los contextos educacionales, por ejemplo: el informe, reportaje, ensayo expositivo, argumentativo, monografías, etc. (Martin 1996; Jones, Gollin, Drury y Economou 1989; Drury 1991; Er 1993; Unsworth 1999; Ventola 1996; Ventola y Mauranen 1991, 1996).

Cada género se caracteriza por una **estructura esquemática** o sea la organización en etapas y con un propósito del género que se expresa lingüísticamente a través de los constituyentes funcionales del texto. La segunda dimensión es la de los patrones de realización que marcan los límites en los distintos constituyentes funcionales y se expresan por medio de elecciones lingüísticas en el texto (discursivas-semánticas y léxicogramaticales).

Los conceptos hasta aquí elaborados se pueden examinar en la primera versión de la composición del estudiante que se ha transcripto textualmente en el apéndice. Esta composición pertenece al tercer trimestre en el programa de hispanohablantes y forma parte de un estudio longitudinal de un grupo de 30 estudiantes durante un año académico. El género al que pertenece este trabajo se puede reconocer a primera vista; es un ensayo expositivo porque propone algunas ideas que luego va a explicar y fundamentar.

Con respecto a la estructura esquemática del ensayo, se pueden ver claramente los constituyentes funcionales del mismo:

1. **La introducción** se encuentra en el primer párrafo, tiene como propósito explicarnos de qué se va a hablar y cuál es la idea que se quiere desarrollar. Esta idea se encuentra en la tesis de la introducción: "La revolución mexicana fue el inicio de la superación de la mujer mexicana". En el siguiente enunciado va a explicar cómo se va a elaborar esta idea.

2. El **cuerpo o desarrollo** del ensayo se encuentra localizado en los párrafos segundo, tercero y cuarto. Tiene como propósito fundamentar la tesis que se expuso en la introducción. En este caso vemos que el segundo párrafo se refiere al trabajo de las mujeres en el ejército durante la revolución. El tercero elabora la idea de que las mujeres por primera vez empiezan a ocupar distintas posiciones laborales en la sociedad. Y el cuarto comenta el cambio de rol de la mujer dentro de la familia donde se convierte en la mayoría de los casos en jefe del hogar.

3. La **conclusión** se encuentra en el quinto y último párrafo. El propósito de este párrafo es reiterar las ideas expuestas en la introducción explicando cómo se han fundamentado en el desarrollo de la composición.

Registro

El lenguaje en la LSF es visto como un sistema de significados, donde las elecciones se originan de acuerdo con el propósito por el cual se usa la lengua. El siguiente paso del análisis de este texto es verlo a través del nivel del contexto situacional o específico que lo determina. Halliday (1978; Halliday y Hasan 1989) menciona tres variables funcionales que son determinantes para el registro: campo, tenor y modo. El contexto de la situación motiva el significado de los textos en tres formas:

1. El **campo** se define como la actividad o tema en que los participantes están involucrados. Responde a las preguntas: **¿Qué ocurre? ¿De qué tema se habla?** En este caso el campo es la revolución mexicana. Evidentemente este estudiante usa varias fuentes como la novela *Hasta no verte Jesús mío* (Poniatowska), películas como *Flor Silvestre* y otras fuentes, probablemente artículos de periódicos, etc. para apoyar sus premisas. En general en estas clases se han discutido distintos textos, películas, etc. que tratan sobre el mismo tema, pero que muchas veces presentan opiniones diferentes para estimular distintas posiciones en los estudiantes.

2. El **tenor** se refiere a los roles sociales que existen en el contexto situacional entre el o la hablante y la audiencia. Las preguntas que nos hacemos para determinar el tenor son: **¿quiénes son los participantes en esta situación? ¿Cuál es la relación entre estos participantes?** En este caso es un ensayo académico, es decir que el escritor o la escritora va a recibir una nota de su instructor o instructora como resultado de su trabajo y por lo tanto la relación de los participantes en este contexto no es simétrica. Estas características van a influir sobre el tipo de lengua que se usa en el ensayo: el lenguaje es más formal.

3. El **modo** se refiere al rol del lenguaje o sea la naturaleza del texto en sí mismo y su función en ese contexto, incluyendo el canal (¿es hablado o escrito, o una combinación de los dos?). Responde a la pregunta **¿qué se espera que la lengua haga en esta situación?** En este caso existen las expectativas de la profesora (espera que el estudiante o la estudiante pueda argumentar, o sea apoyar su posición [tesis] por medio de ideas, referencias, datos claros y precisos). El canal es escrito; por lo tanto toda la información tiene que estar presente y sin posibilidad de diálogo o aclaración.

Campo, tenor y modo son variables extralingüísticas del contexto de la situación que van a ser relevantes para determinar el tipo de lengua que se usará en ese registro. El registro según Halliday y Hasan (1989) es un concepto semántico, una configuración de significados que están típicamente asociados con una situación particular y que se realizan a través de elecciones léxicas y gramaticales. La LSF considera tres metafunciones dentro del lenguaje que permiten dar significados textuales, interpersonales e ideacionales. Estas metafunciones se dan simultáneamente y están directamente influenciadas por las variables extralingüísticas del registro (campo, tenor y modo). La siguiente figura ejemplifica estas ideas:

Figura 4.2 *Registro en relación con las metafunciones del lenguaje*

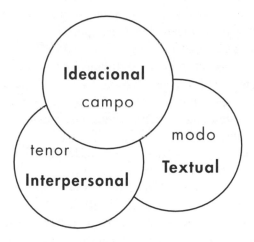

Metafunciones textuales

A través del análisis de las metafunciones (interpersonal, ideacional y textual) la LSF permite explicar cómo el lenguaje es funcional para lograr ciertos propósitos. En este caso particular de la composición de este estudiante, la LSF nos permite ver cuáles elementos lingüísticos han sido usados apropiadamente y cuáles no. La LSF nos permite ver cómo las elecciones léxicas y gramaticales funcionan en un contexto social. Esta teoría educacional y lingüística nos da un marco de referencia para analizar las asignaciones que nosotros les damos a nuestros estudiantes y nos permite identificar áreas de instrucción importantes para el desarrollo del lenguaje académico. A través de las herramientas de la LSF los maestros pueden trabajar con los estudiantes identificando los significados textuales, interpersonales e ideacionales que se realizan en sus textos y de este modo entender cómo las diferentes elecciones gramaticales y léxicas expresan los significados esperados.

La metafunción ideacional corresponde al lenguaje que se usa para organizar, comprender y expresar nuestras percepciones del mundo y de nuestra conciencia. Tiene dos subfunciones: la experimental (contenido e ideas) y la lógica (la relación entre las ideas).

La metafunción interpersonal es la que nos permite participar en actos comunicativos con otra gente, para expresar y comprender sentimientos, actitudes y juicios.

La metafunción textual corresponde a la lengua que se usa para relacionar lo que se dice con el mundo real y con otros eventos lingüísticos.

Estas tres metafunciones operan simultáneamente en la expresión del significado. La funcionalidad intrínseca de estas tres metafunciones interactúan con la organización social del contexto (con el campo, tenor y modo) respectivamente (véase figura 4.2). La realización entre el lenguaje y el contexto social se construye como algo natural. Para distinguir los textos es interesante notar como tantas diferencias se pueden revelar a través de los factores extralingüísticos del campo, tenor y modo del discurso. Estos tres elementos forman el aparato (scaffolding) o relevancias motivacionales que construyen el significado del texto.

A modo de ejemplo se pueden marcar algunas de las características que se dan en cada una de estas metafunciones en el ensayo expositivo.

La metafunción textual explica cómo se logra la **textura** en el texto y cómo el texto se adapta al canal en este caso **escrito** del género. Es la metafunción que estructura el texto. Los recursos textuales para organizar los ensayos expositivos incluyen la selección temática, la organización y combinación de las cláusulas y los recursos cohesivos. El desarrollo del tema o sea, el primer constituyente en la cláusula o el punto de partida del enunciado (Halliday 1994, p. 37) es crucial para la organización del texto e indica el método de desarrollo que ha sido escogido por el escritor o la escritora. El tema puede consistir de un nombre, adverbio, frase preposicional u otro elemento

---

Tabla 4.1 *Temas de la introducción*

· **El conflicto armado de México**
· Se alega
· En **este discurso intelectual**
· **La revolución mexicana**
· Estos cambios

Nota: Las nominalizaciones están marcadas en negrillas.

Tabla 4.2 *Nominalizaciones del primer párrafo*

· El conflicto armado de México
· el sistema social, económico y político del país
· las consecuencias de la revolución
· En este discurso intelectual
· el cambio social de las mujeres de México
· La revolución mexicana
· el inicio de la superación de la mujer mexicana
· las acciones de las mujeres en tres áreas

---

gramatical. Por medio de la identificación de los distintos temas, los estudiantes pueden analizar la estructura temática y el método de desarrollo que ellos usan (Mauranen 1996). En este ensayo se puede ver que el estudiante ha usado grupos nominales como temas principalmente en la introducción. El uso de las nominalizaciones en el ensayo expositivo ha sido ampliamente estudiado por Martin (1993) quien resalta este uso de las nominalizaciones como un recurso muy importante para nombrar los argumentos que se van a desarrollar y al mismo tiempo usar un lenguaje impersonal que le permite al estudiante tomar la postura objetiva de un experto en el tema.

Por medio de las nominalizaciones este estudiante se aleja de la organización secuencial del habla (actores, acciones) y organiza el texto en función de las ideas, como texto escrito, al mismo tiempo que condensa la información. Por ejemplo, el estudiante usa la nominalización "El conflicto armado en México" para comenzar su composición. En un lenguaje más congruente y secuencial él podría haber dicho: "La gente mexicana luchó con armas para cambiar la situación . . ." Este enunciado sería más característico de un discurso oral que escrito.

Este estudiante hace un uso muy efectivo de las nominalizaciones en su ensayo (véase tabla 4.2). La nominalización es un ejemplo de lo que Halliday llama metáfora gramatical (1994, 1998) que describe situaciones en las que significados que son típicamente congruentes se realizan en un patrón que es típicamente menos congruente. Se caracteriza como congruente un lenguaje en el que el sentido del enunciado se expresa de una forma explícita y lineal. El ejemplo presentado anteriormente "La gente mexicana luchó . . .", representa un ejemplo más congruente que "el conflicto armado en México"; en el último ejemplo no se especifica quiénes son los agentes de ese conflicto o cuándo ocurrió.

Nominalización es la conversión de verbos y otras partes del lenguaje en

Figura 4.3 *Metáfora gramatical*

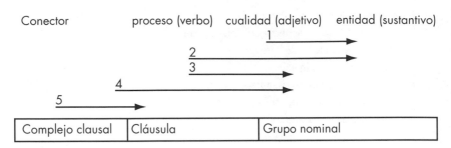

Fuente: Adaptado de Halliday 1998.

nombres, de modo tal que aumenta el contenido semántico de nuestro texto. El alto número de nominalizaciones nos da una mayor **densidad léxica.** La densidad léxica se calcula por medio de la proporción de palabras que poseen contenido semántico (nombres, verbos, adverbios, adjetivos) en relación con las palabras que no llevan contenido semántico (preposiciones, conjunciones, auxiliares, etc.) en el texto. En la tabla 4.3 se ve la densidad léxica de cada párrafo. Este ensayo refleja una densidad léxica apropiada al discurso escrito. Las implicaciones de estas características léxicogramaticales del registro del ensayo para la enseñanza son varias. En principio se observa que el uso de nominalizaciones permite una densidad léxica mayor y refleja un lenguaje más condensado e incongruente, típico del medio académico. Una instrucción explícita del uso de nominalizaciones en el ensayo (p. ej., como tema en la introducción, conclusión) puede facilitar y acelerar el desarrollo del lenguaje académico en los cursos de hispanohablantes.

Otras características de la textura de este texto están asociadas con la estructura de las cláusulas (Schleppegrell y Colombi 1997) y con la cohesividad (Burdach, Millán y Tonselli 1994). La cohesión se puede realizar dentro de las oraciones (estructural) como entre las oraciones (textual). Los com-

Tabla 4.3 *Densidad léxica de cada párrafo*

1. 44/93   = .47
2. 58/134 = .43
3. 37/78   = .47
4. 76/179 = .42
5. 34/74   = .45

Tabla 4.4 *Uso de paralelismo en el texto*

Primer párrafo:	como miembros activos del militar, escritores y organizadoras políticas
	como encargadas de hogares sin la ayuda de un hombre
Segundo párrafo:	Varias mujeres . . .
	Algunas . . .
	Otras . . .
Tercer párrafo	Algunas mexicanas . . .
	Otras . . .
Quinto párrafo	Algunas . . .
	Otras . . .
	Otras . . .
	Todas . . .
	No conocer esta historia **es** ignorancia.
	No aceptarla **es** un fracaso.

ponentes cohesivos gramaticales como la referencia, elipsis y sustitución; léxicos (sinónimos, antónimos, etc.) junto con los estructurales (tema, rema, paralelismo, etc.) y los conectores cohesivos son algunas de las herramientas que este tipo de análisis nos puede dar para organizar el texto. Este ensayo logra textura usando varios de esos componentes como la referencia, el paralelismo y las cadenas cohesivas. En un análisis posterior se puede ver el uso de conectores como guías para la organización lógica del texto. La tabla 4.4 ejemplifica el uso de paralelismo en el texto.

La metafunción interpersonal se realiza en el nivel léxico gramatical a través de adverbios de modo, conectores y en la estructura de las cláusulas. En español el proceso verbal indica la relación de los participantes en la conjugación verbal. Esta metafunción se relaciona con la variable tenor, o sea con los participantes de la interacción, en este caso el estudiante y su audiencia (su profesora). Cate Poynton (1989) en sus estudios pioneros de la variación del lenguaje en relación con el rol de los participantes ha propuesto tres continuos para analizar el tenor. Estos se relacionan con la formalidad, cortesía y reciprocidad de la interacción. Los tres continuos que Poynton identifica son el poder que existe entre los participantes, el contacto y el envolvimiento afectivo. La figura 4.3 presenta un diagrama de estos continuos.

El ensayo académico requiere un lenguaje formal y despersonalizado, alejándose de la subjetivización y presentando un lenguaje objetivo y menos expuesto al cuestionamiento. Es claro que el estudiante ha sido efectivo en mantener el nivel formal en los tres continuos.

Figura 4.4 *Tres continuos de la relación interpersonal del tenor*

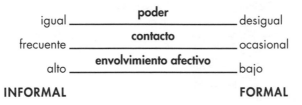

igual _____ **poder** _____ desigual

frecuente _____ **contacto** _____ ocasional

alto _____ **envolvimiento afectivo** _____ bajo

INFORMAL   **FORMAL**

Fuente: Poynton 1989.

El poder, como se ha mencionado anteriormente es desigual, el contacto por este medio, un trabajo académico para ser evaluado se puede considerar ocasional y el envolvimiento afectivo sin duda es bajo; por lo tanto ha omitido toda referencia a su opinión personal protegiéndose bajo una tercera persona singular o plural y una voz pasiva con 'se'. La tabla 4.5 presenta los ejemplos de voz pasiva. Estas variables resultan muy útiles para que los estudiantes reconozcan y produzcan un tipo de lenguaje adecuado al propósito de la interacción comunicativa.

En la descripción de las metafunciones textual e interpersonal se ha enfatizado el uso de parte del estudiante de algunas características léxico gramaticales que hacen que su ensayo sea efectivo en expresar un registro académico según la LSF. La tercera metafunción es **ideacional.** Esta metafunción se relaciona directamente con el campo y es la que refleja la realidad del mundo que queremos expresar a través del lenguaje. La metafunción ideacional enfatiza el uso del vocabulario (ya se vio cómo el uso del léxico también contribuye a la estructura textual (nominalizaciones, densidad léxica) en la metafunción textual y a la estructura interpersonal en el uso de expresiones impersonales (voz pasiva) en la metafunción interpersonal). La elección léxica permite la utilización de circunstancias y personas como agentes de los procesos verbales. En el ensayo expositivo los procesos más frecuentes son los relacionales en la introducción y conclusión para presentar y relacionar

Tabla 4.5 *Uso de la voz pasiva en el texto*

· Se alega
· . . . se olvida
· . . . se cambió
· . . . se vio

> **Tabla 4.6 *Uso de procesos relacionales en la introducción y conclusión***
>
> · La revolución mexicana **fue** el inicio de la superación de las mujeres de México.
> · (La revolución) **fue** el inicio de un cambio social para las mujeres.
> · No conocer esta historia **es** ignorancia.
> · No aceptarla **es** un fracaso.

las ideas expuestas (ej.: La revolución mexicana **fue** el inicio de la superación de la mujer mexicana).

Los procesos materiales son más frecuentes en el desarrollo donde el lenguaje se vuelve más secuencial y personalizado. Los procesos materiales sirven para marcar hechos y acciones, la mayoría de los procesos materiales en el ensayo sirven para apoyar las ideas a través de hechos históricos. En el ensayo del estudiante la mayoría de los procesos materiales del desarrollo se encuentran en el pasado como una descripción de eventos históricos que le ayudan a apoyar su premisa del cambio de rol de las mujeres después de la revolución en la sociedad mexicana (ej.: dieron, peleó, llegó a recibir, etc.). Si bien se encuentran varias equivocaciones en el uso del léxico en este ensayo, en general y siguiendo estas líneas léxico-gramaticales se puede decir que este estudiante ha sido efectivo en conferir un lenguaje formal a través del uso de procesos relacionales en la introducción y conclusión. La tabla 4.6 presenta los procesos relacionales que se encuentran en la introducción y conclusión.

Conclusión

Este trabajo ha presentado un análisis textual, interpersonal e ideacional de un ensayo expositivo escrito por un estudiante hispanohablante con el propósito de identificar maneras de facilitar el desarrollo del lenguaje académico. Un análisis funcional de los recursos gramaticales nos permite un marco teórico para que los estudiantes puedan analizar sus propios ensayos e identificar áreas de desarrollo.

Implicaciones pedagógicas para la enseñanza del español a hispanohablantes

El valor de este acercamiento funcional al texto para los maestros y estudiantes es evidente. Una vez que las distintas etapas de cada género se analizan, se puede ir más allá y hacer notar las familias de géneros: los diferentes tipos de informes, editoriales, reportajes, narraciones, etc. que adaptan su forma y significado más detalladamente a las distintas actividades sociales. En nuestro programa hemos comprobado que la estructura genérica es directa y bastante fácil de aprender aún con la terminología técnica para los distintos géneros y las diferentes etapas (constituyentes funcionales).

Por otra parte el estudio al nivel del registro con la estratificación del contexto en las categorías de campo, tenor y modo y las metafunciones respectivas: ideacional, interpersonal y textual, nos da herramientas para poder llegar a niveles más detallados que los componentes funcionales del género únicamente. Estas conexiones entre el lenguaje y el contexto son invaluables cuando nos permiten un mejor manejo de la gramática en los contextos educacionales, o sea, un conocimiento técnico (campo), la complementariedad de la lengua hablada y escrita (modo) y las ventajas de una pedagogía explícita (tenor). Muchos lingüistas educacionales sienten que sin una guía explícita muchos estudiantes que no han estado expuestos a discursos académicos en sus casas, se encuentran perdidos y separados de los discursos públicos de poder en esta cultura. El énfasis se centra en una presentación explícita y efectiva del discurso que se espera adquieran los estudiantes. Estas prácticas educacionales que abogan por una pedagogía clara y explícita se han desarrollado según las teorías del aprendizaje de Vygotsky y Halliday (Vygotsky 1986; Wells 1994). Por ejemplo, en nuestro programa de lengua, los cursos de escritura se basan en la enseñanza de los géneros textuales. En ellos seguimos los siguientes pasos pedagógicos que, por supuesto, se llevan a cabo en muchas lecciones:

a. negociación del campo (discurso académico). Los estudiantes realizan distintos tipos de escritura (privada, para compartir, para ser evaluada).

b. deconstrucción de los géneros más relevantes. Los estudiantes interactúan con una variedad de textos que tienen un tema común. Por ejemplo, en el caso presentado: la revolución mexicana vista a través de la literatura (Poniatowska), películas, fuentes sociológicas, históricas, etc.

c. construcción conjunta del texto. Presentación explícita de los constituyentes funcionales del género: introducción (con la tesis), desarrollo, conclusión. Características del registro.

d. construcción independiente del texto. Primer borrador de la versión para ser evaluada.

e. revisión y edición de la primera versión del texto con los compañeros de clase. En este paso se les proporciona a los estudiantes una guía de preguntas que ellos pueden usar para analizar sus ensayos expositivos.

Tabla 4.7 *Guía de preguntas para los estudiantes y profesores*

- ¿Qué género textual quiero desarrollar?
- ¿Conozco los diferentes constituyentes funcionales? ¿Puedo explicar sus diferencias?
- Si estoy escribiendo un ensayo: ¿he definido mi tesis claramente? ¿He marcado las premisas que voy a desarrollar?
- ¿Cuál es el campo del trabajo? ¿Puedo pensar en una lista de palabras técnicas que se asocien a este tema?
- ¿Cuán a menudo repito las mismas palabras? ¿Puedo usar sinónimos u otras formas de expresar el mismo concepto?
- ¿Cuál es el tenor de esta interacción? ¿Cómo va a influenciar el tipo de lengua que voy a usar?
- ¿Voy a asumir una posición impersonal en este trabajo académico?
- ¿Puedo expresar mi opinión a través de otros adverbios de modalidad o procesos verbales (ej. subjuntivo)?
- ¿En este trabajo académico he seleccionado los temas efectivamente para desarrollar el texto?
- ¿Dan los conectores que he escogido el significado que quiero?

Si volvemos al ensayo estudiado podemos utilizar este mismo aparato teórico para marcar algunas pautas que este estudiante puede seguir en la revisión de esta primera versión:

a. metafunción textual: temas, conectores y revisión de la referencia.

b. metafunción interpersonal: el modo en el uso de las secuencias verbales, adverbios de modalidad, voz pasiva.

c. metafunción ideacional: uso del léxico técnico o académico.

Sin duda este estudiante ha realizado un ensayo muy efectivo en su primera versión y usando estos recursos gramaticales se le puede dar un "feedback" para que revise y escriba una segunda versión más apropiada.

En conclusión, este trabajo intenta demostrar cómo los instructores y estudiantes pueden utilizar las herramientas de la gramática sistémica funcional para analizar el texto como un todo, enfatizando las características del género y el registro. Este marco teórico hace explícitas las características discursivo-semánticas y léxico-gramaticales de los textos permitiéndoles a los estudiantes un conocimiento más claro y accesible que rompe con los mitos acerca de la dificultad de aprender a escribir.

Las revolucionarias[1]

El conflicto armado de México cambió para siempre el sistema social, económico y político del país. Se alega mucho las consequencias de la revolución y si realmente tuvo un impacto positivo. En este descurso intelectual muchas veces se olvida el cambio social de las mujeres de México. La revolución mexicana fue el inicio de la superación de la mujer mexicana. Estos cambios salieron directamente de las acciones de las mujeres en tres áreas: como miembras activas del militar, escritoras y organizadoras políticas y como encargadas de hogares sin la ayuda de un hombre.

Varias mujeres dieron sus vidas por la revolución. Algunas fueron víctimas inocentes. Otras fueron soldaderas, peleando juntas con los hombres. En esta capacidad las mujeres desafían la idea cultural que ellas eran débiles. Una de ellas fue Juana Belén Gutiérrez de Mendoza. Ella peleó junto con Emiliano Zapata. Llegó a recibirla posición de coronel durante la revolución[2]. En la historia por Elena Poniatowska, *Hasta no verte Jesús mío,* se ve la transformación de una mujer que peleaba junto a su esposo. Con los nuevos ideales que aprendió durante la revolución se cuenta dio cuenta que ella no tenía porque ser víctima de los abusos de su esposo. Con demostrando las abilidades y tomando control de sus destinos, las mujeres mexicanas recibieron respeto, algunas hasta llegando hasta el nivel de recibir posiciones de generalas.

La revolución por primera vez dio una oportunidad a la mujer mexicana para destacarse en áreas en que dominaba el hombre. Salieron de lo escuro y se transformaron en agentes de la paz por medio de la revolución armada. Algunas mexicanas tomaron trabajos como operadoras de telégrafos y como traficantes. Otras ayudaron en partidos políticos como el Partido Liberal Mexicano (PML) que publicaba la *Regeneración.*[3] Por sus influencias directa la *Regeneración* publicaba varios temas sobre la mujer mexicana.

Muchas veces los cambios eran más simples. Una mujer durante la revolución no tuvo porque salirse del hogar para sentir el cambio social. Con el hecho que la mayoría de los hombres andaban en combate dejó muchas mujeres solas en cargo del hogar. Esto independizó a las mujeres. Ahora tenían que salir de casa y hacer compras. La economía era controlada por mayormente mujeres. En esa epoca andaban varios bandidos robando. Por esta razón mujeres tuvieron que aprender a defenderse. Se cambió su forma de vivir, algunas para siempre porque nunca volvieron muchos hombres de la guerra. La mayor influencia y cambio social que pasó la mujer fue con la transformación de la familia. Hijos y hijas vieron una mama fuerte y encargada del hogar. Un ejemplo de esto se ve en le película *Flor Silvestre*. Esmeralda tuvo sola que criar a su hijo sola después de que su marido fue fusilado por unos bandidos. Seguramente su hijo solamente tendrá la influencia de su madre y la verá diferentemente que un hijo que tuvo un padre y una madre.

La mujer formó y cambió el sistema social, económico y político durante la revolución y al mismo tiempo fue el inicio de un cambio social para las mujeres. Algunas tomaron papeles iguales a los hombres. Otras tomaron el lugar del hombre. Otras se quedaron en su lugar de mujeres. Todas contribuyeron al sistema actual de lo que conocemos como el país de México. No conocer esta historia es ignorancia. No aceptarla es un fracaso.

NOTAS DEL APÉNDICE

1. Este ensayo es una reproducción fidedigna del original.

2. Amott, Teresa y Julie Matthei. 1991. "The Soul of Tierra Madre: Chicana Women." In *Race, Gender and Work: A Multicultural Economic History of Women in the United States*, Boston, MA: South End Press.

3. Ídem.

BIBLIOGRAFÍA

Bartolomé, Liliana. 1998. *The Misteaching of Academic Discourses: The Politics of Language in the Classroom*. Boulder, CO: Westview Press.

Burdach, Ana María, Ana María Millán y Ana María Tonselli. 1994. "Aplicación del modelo de conjunción como recurso de cohesión de Halliday y Hasan a una muestra del español." *Revista del Instituto de Letras de la Pontificia Universidad Católica de Chile* 19:167–80.

Christie, Frances. 1991. "First- and Second-Order Registers in Education." En *Functional and Systemic Linguistics*, ed. E. Ventola, 235–36. Berlin: Mouton de Gruyter.

——. 1986. "Writing in Schools: Generic Structures as Ways of Meaning." En *Functional Approaches to Writing: Research Perspectives*, ed. B. Couture, 221–39. London: Frances Pinter.

Colombi, M. Cecilia. 2002. "Academic Language Development in Latino Students' Writing in Spanish." En *Developing Advanced Literacy in First and Second Languages: Meaning with Power*, eds. M. Schleppegrell y M. C. Colombi, 67–87. Mahwah, NJ: Lawrence Erlbaum Associates.

——. 2000. "En vías del desarrollo del lenguaje académico en español en hablantes nativos de español en los Estados Unidos." En *Research on Spanish in the United State: Linguistic Issues and Challenges*, ed. A. Roca, 296–309. Somerville, MA: Cascadilla Press.

———. 1997a. "La enseñanza de los géneros textuales como proceso." En *Los procesos de la lectura y la escritura*, ed. M. C. Martínez, 95–105. Cali, Colombia: Universidad del Valle.

———. 1997b. "Perfil del discurso escrito en textos de hispanohablantes: teoría y práctica." En *La enseñanza del español a hispanohablantes*, ed. M. C. Colombi y F. X. Alarcón, 175–89. Boston: Houghton Mifflin.

Colombi, M. Cecilia, y Mary Schleppegrell. 2002. "Developing Advanced Literacy." En *Developing Advanced Literacy in First and Second Languages: Meaning with Power*, ed. M. Schleppegrell y M. C. Colombi, 1–21. Mahwah, NJ: Lawrence Erlbaum Associates.

Drury, Helen. 1991. "The Use of Systemic Linguistics to Describe Students' Summaries at University Level." En *Functional and Systemic Linguistics*, ed. E. Ventola, 431–56. Berlin: Mouton de Gruyter.

Er, Eleanor. 1993. "Text Analysis and Diagnostic Assessment: Finding Teaching Directions for Adult ESL Learners through Text Analyses of Student Writing." *Prospect* 8 (3):63–77.

Faltis, Christian, y Peter Wolfe, eds. 1999. *So Much to Say: Adolescents, Bilingualism and ESL in the Secondary School*. New York: Teachers College.

Halliday, M. A. K. 1998. "Things and Relations." En *Reading Science: Critical and Functional Perspectives on Discourse of Science*, eds. J. R. Martin y R. Veel, 185–235. London and New York: Routledge.

———. 1996. "Literacy and Linguistics: a Functional Perspective." En *Literacy in Society*, eds. R. Hasan y G. Williams, 339–76. London and New York: Longman.

———. 1994. *Introduction to Functional Grammar*. London: Edward Arnold.

———. 1985. *Spoken and Written Language*. Deakin, Victoria: Deakin University Press.

———. 1978. *Language as Social Semiotic: The Social Interpretation of Language and Meaning*. London: Edward Arnold.

Halliday, M. A. K., y Ruqaiya Hasan. 1989. *Language Context and Text: Aspects of Language in a Social-semiotic Perspective*. Oxford: Oxford University Press.

Jones, Janet, Sandra Gollin, Helen Drury y Dorothy Economou. 1989. "Systemic-Functional Linguistics and Its Application to the TESOL Curriculum." En *Language Development: Learning Language, Learning Culture*, eds. R. Hasan y J. R. Martin, 257–328. Norwood, NJ: Ablex Publishing Corporation.

Martin, James R. 1998. "Mentoring Semogenesis: 'Genre-Based' Literacy Pedagogy." En *Pedagogy and the Shaping of Consciousness: Linguistic and Social Processes*, ed. F. Christie. London: Cassell.

———. 1997. "Analysing Genre: Functional Parameters." En *Genre and Institutions: Social Processes in the Workplace and School*, eds. F. Christie y J. R. Martin, 3–39. London: Cassell.

———. 1996. "Waves of Abstraction: Organising Exposition." En *The Journal of TESOL France 2.2: Functional Approaches to Written Text: Classroom Applications*, ed. T. Miller, 87–104. Paris: TESOL France and U.S. Information Service.

———. 1993. "Life as a Noun." En *Writing Science: Literacy as Discursive Power,* eds. M. A. K. Halliday y J. R. Martin, 221–67. London: Falmer.

———. 1992. *English Text: System and Structure.* Amsterdam: John Benjamins.

———. 1985. "Process and Text: Two Aspects of Human Semiosis." En *Systemic Perspectives on Discourse,* eds. J. Benson y W. Greaves, vol. 1, 248–74. *Advances In Discourse Processes, Vol XXVI.* Norwood, NJ: Ablex Publishing Corporation.

———. 1984. "Language, Register and Genre." En *Language Studies: Children Writing: B. Ed. Course Study Guide,* 21–30. Geelong, Australia: Deakin University Press.

Martin, James R., y Frances Christie, eds. 1997. *Genre and Institutions.* London and Washington, D.C.: Casell.

Martin, James R., Frances Christie, y Joan Rothery. 1987. "Social Processes in Education: A Reply to Sawyer and Watson and Others." *University of Sydney Working Papers in Linguistics* 5:116–52.

Mauranen, Anne. 1996. "Discourse Competence: Evidence from Thematic Development in Native and Non-Native Texts." En *Academic Writing,* eds. E. Ventola y A. Mauranen, 195–230. Amsterdam: John Benjamins.

Pérez, Bertha, ed. 1999. *Sociocultural Contexts of Language and Literacy.* Mahwah, NJ: Lawrence Erlbaum Associates.

Poynton, Cate. 1989. *Language and Gender: Making the Difference.* Oxford: Oxford University Press.

Schleppegrell, Mary J., y M. Cecilia Colombi. 1997. "Text Organization by Bilingual Writers: Clause Structure as a Reflection of Discourse Structure." *Written Communication* 14 (4):481–503.

Unsworth, Len. 1999. "Developing Critical Understanding of the Specialised Language of School of Science and History Texts: A Functional Grammatical Perspective." *Journal of Adolescent and Adult Literacy,* 42 (7):508–21.

Valdés, Guadalupe, y Michelle Geoffrion-Vinci. 1998. "Chicano Spanish: The Problem of the 'Underdeveloped' Code in Bilingual Repertoires." *The Modern Language Journal,* 82 (4):473–501.

Ventola, Eija 1996. "Packing and Unpacking of Information in Academic Texts." En *Academic Writing,* eds. E. Ventola y A. Mauranen, 151–94. Amsterdam: John Benjamins.

Ventola, E., y Anna Mauranen., eds. 1996. *Academic Writing.* Amsterdam: John Benjamins.

———. 1991. "Non-Native Writing and Native Revising of Scientific Articles." En *Functional and Systemic Linguistics,* ed. E. Ventola, 457–93. Berlin: Mouton de Gruyter.

Vygotsky, Leo S. 1986. *Thought and Language,* ed. A. Kozulin. Cambridge, MA: The MIT Press.

Wells, Gordon. 1994. "The Complementary Contributions of Halliday and Vygotsky to a 'Language-Based Theory of Learning.'" *Linguistics and Education* 6 (1):41–90.

5

La enseñanza del español en Nuevo México
¿Revitalización o erradicación de la variedad chicana?

Ysaura Bernal-Enríquez
Eduardo Hernández Chávez
University of New Mexico

Introducción

A principios del siglo XX, el español dejó de ser el medio de instrucción en las escuelas públicas de Nuevo México, siendo reemplazado por el inglés según una estipulación de la Constitución de 1911 (Meyer 1977; Milk 1980; Hernández Chávez 1994a, 1995). Como consecuencia de esta política, el estudio lingüístico formal de los hispanos neomexicanos, así como el de los mexicanos de otras regiones de EE.UU., ha sido casi completamente en el idioma anglosajón. Para los hispanohablantes, el aprendizaje del español formal y normativo se ha relegado en las escuelas públicas y en las universidades casi totalmente a los cursos sobre el idioma mismo.

En la gran mayoría de los casos, las metodologías usadas en estos cursos son diseñadas para estudiantes angloparlantes que aprenden el español como lengua extranjera. Estas metodologías también se encuentran en programas de español para bilingües, aunque en éstos la mayoría de los estudiantes son hispanos que ya usan alguna variante del lenguaje regional. Además, por más que toleran cierto uso de las variedades locales, los cursos tienen como meta principal la enseñanza de la norma culta con el resultado de que no sólo debilitan el uso del lenguaje comunitario, sino también contribuyen a la falta de su desarrollo a nivel individual.

La estigmatización del español nuevomexicano

El enfoque en el español culto y el desprecio concomitante del lenguaje comunitario tienen su justificación en la estigmatización de las variedades lingüísticas locales. Ciertos sectores de la sociedad hispanohablante, en particular los educadores, consideran las hablas regionales como un español degenerado, inválido, y corrupto que no tiene lugar en el discurso gentil, menos en el aula de clase. Estas hablas, se dice, están repletas de solecismos, barbarismos (Ordóñez Sabido 1977) y otros vicios de lenguaje, todos los cuales deberían extirparse del idioma. El uso entre los chicanos en el discurso familiar del cambio de códigos, o sea un español-inglés mixto llamado despectivamente *Spanglish*, refuerza la percepción de la corrupción lingüística.

Adicionalmente, se cree que el uso del habla no estándar sirve solamente para privar a los hablantes de la norma culta y mantenerlos en condiciones sociales subordinadas. Por el contrario, se supone que el español normativo da acceso al mundo hispánico culto, a la cultura alta, y a las capas socioeconómicas superiores.

Agudiza esta estigmatización del español chicano el uso de formas inmaduras, análogas a las usadas por hablantes jóvenes en el desarrollo lingüístico; por ejemplo, *yo sabo* en lugar de *yo sé*, o *ponió* por *puso* (Sánchez 1993), que se incorporan al lenguaje adulto a causa de las condiciones sociales que conducen a la ADQUISICIÓN PARCIAL del idioma. Entre las condiciones más destacadas son las políticas lingüísticas norteamericanas, las presiones socioculturales, y las condiciones sociolingüísticas que aceleran la pérdida lingüística.

Históricamente, los Estados Unidos han seguido una política abiertamente asimiladora hacia las etnias no anglosajonas, dando lugar al desplazamiento lingüístico (Kloss 1977). Además, en la última mitad de este siglo, la urbanización, acompañada de la tecnología moderna, la centralización de empleos, y la cultura de masas, ha ejercido presiones fuertes hacia el uso dominante del inglés y la disminución de la competencia en español (Ortiz 1975; Chávez 1988; Hernández Chávez 1994b). Los factores sociolingüísticos sobresalientes de esta disminución de competencia incluyen el uso en el hogar del inglés junto con el español durante la niñez, el aprendizaje del inglés a muy temprana edad, la residencia urbana, y, el factor clave, los años de educación en inglés (Hernández Chávez 1974; Wong-Fillmore 1991a, 1991b; Liu, Bates, y Li 1992; Bernal-Enríquez 1996; Hernández Chávez, Bills, y Hudson 1996). Hudson, Hernández Chávez, y Bills (1995, p. 180) argumentan que la educación "es el vehículo principal de la integración sociocultural a la sociedad mayoritaria, y como resultado, de la pérdida intergeneracional de la lengua minoritaria".

A continuación, describiremos primero las características dialectales del español chicano de Nuevo México y los procesos lingüísticos y sociolingüísticos que operan en el desarrollo incompleto del idioma. Trataremos de demostrar que el español chicano es toda una variedad legítima que obedece procesos históricos y sociolingüísticos universales y válidos, y que no es un lenguaje ni "corrupto" ni "degenerado".

Después, analizaremos las prácticas que producen la estigmatización lingüística y sus efectos socioculturales y educativos. Se examinarán también los problemas que resultan del énfasis en el uso exclusivo en el aula del español estándar y de la desconsideración del español en desarrollo parcial. Finalmente, discutiremos la importancia, tanto para el educando y su comunidad como para la pedagogía de la enseñanza del español local.

Las características del español chicano

EL CHICANO, EL NUEVOMEXICANO Y EL ESPAÑOL GENERAL

En un estudio previo, Bernal-Enríquez (1997a) demostró que el español chicano y el nuevomexicano componen subvariedades del español mexicano, el cual es una variante del español general (véase la figura 5.1, pp. 100–101). Todas éstas son variedades del español que se han venido desarrollando del castellano hablado en México desde tiempos coloniales (Sánchez 1993), y todas tienen en común formas fronterizas, rurales y jergales que comprenden un grupo no estándar. Estas formas tienen sus usos específicos, como los tienen todos los idiomas, en ciertos contextos y situaciones sociolingüísticos.

Más importante, hay que notar que la mayor parte de las formas que comparten estas variedades están incluidas bajo la categoría ESTÁNDAR GENERAL (columna 3 de la figura 5.1), lo que significa que el tanto español chicano, el nuevomexicano, como el mexicano, tienen como su corpus común (Hockett 1958) formas normativas usadas en todo el mundo hispánico. A estas formas no se les puede acusar de ser "corruptas" o "degeneradas", aunque incluyan innovaciones o palabras de otras lenguas. La diferencia principal entre las variedades es que el mexicano, en contraste con el nuevomexicano y el chicano general, tiene acceso a las formas "cultas", o sea formas adquiridas por medio del estudio formal.

LA VARIACIÓN REGIONAL Y SOCIOLINGÜÍSTICA

Por razones de la separación geográfica, cultural, socioeconómica, y política, todos los idiomas tienden a desarrollarse en variedades regionales y sociales distintas. Cada uno de estos factores ha operado en el español de EE.UU.

Hasta tiempos muy recientes en que se han convertido predominantemente en un pueblo urbano, los chicanos han sido una sociedad agraria aislada de los centros metropolitanos mexicanos. Por lo tanto, la variedad chicana, incluso la nuevomexicana, retiene ciertos ARCAÍSMOS, o sea voces del español general histórico que se han perdido en otras regiones (aunque también se usan en zonas rurales en otros países; véase la figura 5.1, columna 5). Así, por ejemplo, muchos chicanos del suroeste de EE.UU. usan formas como *asina*, *arrear* (por "manejar un auto"), *truje*, y *semos*. Los nuevomexicanos usan estas formas y además expresiones como *dos reales* ("moneda de 25 centavos"), *turnio* ("bisco"), y *creigo* ("creo") (columna 9).

El aislamiento también produce INNOVACIONES que tienden a seguir procesos universales del cambio lingüístico. El español chicano, como el de las zonas rurales de otros países hispánicos, no ha sido una excepción a estos procesos, creando formas como *aguelo*, *andábanos*, *caiba*, *coltura*, y muchas más (columna 5). El nuevomexicano también usa estas formas (véanse las columnas 8 y 9), y además otras como *si'a*, *e'a*, *nojotroj*, *ajuero*, *antonces*, *ganso*, e *idomia*. Dentro de Nuevo México mismo, existen regiones dialectales en las que se usan formas distintas. Por ejemplo, para el pavo, en unas regiones se dice *terque*, en otras *cócano*, y en otras *ganso* (Bills 1997). Ciertas regiones usan la *e* "paragógica", un arcaísmo en palabras como *comere*, *honore*, *sone* que se ha extendido a otros contextos no históricos, convirtiéndose en innovación, por ejemplo, en apellidos como *Salazare* o *Bernale* y en anglicismos como *magazine* y *gaseline* (Hernández Chávez y Pérez 1991).

Los idiomas en contacto suelen tomar ciertas palabras o estructuras de los otros idiomas, adaptándolas al sistema lingüístico del primer idioma (compárese los múltiples arabismos e indigenismos que han pasado a formar parte del español general, por ejemplo, *alfombra*, *naranja*, *almohada*, *maíz*, *tomate*, *papa*, etc., figura 5.1, columna 3). Esta clase de palabras se denomina PRÉSTAMO. Los chicanos, por estar en contacto íntimo con la sociedad angloparlante, han incorporado al español una abundancia de palabras y expresiones inglesas, préstamos como *troca* ("camión"), *magazín* ("revista"), *lonche* ("comida de mediodía"), *máscara de gas* ("cámara anti-gas"), y *llamar para atrás* ("regresar una llamada") (columnas 6 y 7). Los nuevomexicanos se distinguen de los otros chicanos por usar adicionalmente expresiones como *casa de corte*, *fone* ("gracioso"), y *jaitón* ("de la élite") (columna 8), además de por usar los indigenismos locales como *oshá* ("raíz medicinal"), *chaquegüe* ("atole espeso"), y *cunques* ("migajas") (columna 9).

Como ya se ha indicado, en los idiomas existen VARIACIONES relacionadas con las diferencias sociales o con la formalidad del contexto comunicativo. Así, ciertos grupos mexicanos usan la forma *háigamos* (columna 5) mientras

Figura 5.1 *El español mexicano*

ESTÁNDAR			NO ESTÁNDAR	
Culto		General	Jergal	Rural
1	2	3	4	5
PRÉSTAMOS ESCRITOS suéter formatizar computadora disquet	**ACADÉMICO** indómito paquidermo neurosis léxico ubicar geopolítica algoritmo arteriosclerosis correlacionar reumatismo anglicismos esdrújula	**METROPOLITANO** valiente elefante nervios palabras localizar silla fumar no, sí zapatos riumas tengamos hayamos andábamos maestro el idioma nadie ahi nos vemos así desarrollar yo traje mucho **ARABISMOS** naranja almohada arroz **INNOVACIONES** autopista avión manejar frenos de automóvil **NAHUATLISMOS Y OTROS INDIGENISMOS** posol(e) chile tocayo tamal papa huracán maíz	**CALÓ** bato chale chiva chota ranfla mota ruca **INNOVACIONES** ése, ésa ahi nos vidrios naranjas, simón leño trapos greña **RESIDUOS** cuete órale firme	**ARCAÍSMOS** arrear asina muncho naide(n) semos yo truje vide chupar freno (de silla de montar a caballo) plebe **INNOVACIONES** agüelo andábanos caiba coltura fuites, juites háigamos la idioma leyer mayestro riezo ve a tra[y]lo téngamos **NAHUATLISMOS Y OTROS INDIGENISMOS** ajolote cajete jumate maíz

CLAVE
Español Nacional
Español Chicano
Español Nuevomexicano
Anglicismos

NO ESTÁNDAR			
Fronterizo		*Nuevomexicano*	
6	7	8	9
	PRÉSTAMOS INTEGRADOS	clas	**INNOVACIONES**
brecas	suera	casa (de)	ajuero
mofle	cuara	corte(s)	antonces
		jaitón	
picap	daime	fone	dijir
yonque	lonche	terque/torque	e'os/e'as
comerciales	reque	telefón	tortías
	suiche	R inglesa ante	gradarse
	llamar para atrás	otra consonante:	la idomia
	dar para atrás	peRla, caRne	mestro
	PRÉSTAMOS		nojotros
	ESPONTÁNEOS		soterrano
	mirio		ganso
	riyunio		("pavo")
	PÉRDIDA		**ARCAÍSMOS E**
			INNOVACIONES
	CAMBIOS		yo seigo ("soy")
	FONOLÓGICOS		casorio
	el bario		el común
	muvimiento		
	televish[ə]n		comere
	l[ə] nuev[ə] ?ond[ə]		Taosi
	el c[ə]mún		silleta
	CALCOS DEL INGLÉS		**ARCAÍSMOS**
	gracias por viniendo		yo creigo
	el correcto español		reales
	yo fui nacida en __		turnio
			que vaiga
	RESIDUOS		
	bueno		**INDIGENISMOS**
	tío/tía		**PUEBLO**
			oxá
	(p)apá/(m)amá		chaquegüe o
	(my) 'jito/a		
			shaquegüe
	SIMPLIFICACIONES		cunques
	subjuntivo=indicativo		
	ser=estar		**PRÉSTAMO DEL**
	imperfecto=condicional		**FRANCÉS**
	imperfecto=pretérito		puela

que otros suelen usar *hayamos* (columna 3). Entre los chicanos, las diferencias sociales tienden a no expresarse lingüísticamente en español ya que estas distinciones generalmente se aprenden en contextos formales y la preparación académica de los estudiantes chicanos se lleva a cabo exclusivamente en inglés y no en español. No obstante, por el contacto con hablantes oriundos de otros países o con los medios de comunicación en español, o posiblemente por el haber estudiado el español formalmente, algunos chicanos alternan en su uso ciertas expresiones según el contexto social. En situaciones familiares se pueden oir formas como *jeguro que jí, 'onde juites*, o *túnico* (columnas 5 y 9) mientras que los mismos hablantes en contextos más formales usarían las pronunciaciones y las formas del habla general culta.

EL CAMBIO DE CÓDIGOS

Uno de los comportamientos lingüísticos que más distingue a los chicanos (y nuyorriqueños) de los hispanohablantes en otros países es el CODESWITCHING, o sea la alternancia rápida del inglés y el español dentro de un discurso y aún dentro de la oración misma. Este fenómeno, denominado el CAMBIO DE CÓDIGOS, fue documentado entre los chicanos en un estudio temprano por Gumperz y Hernández Chávez (1970), y en años recientes ha sido investigado en otros países en una multitud de situaciones bilingües (Myers-Scotton 1993). Lo que se ha aprendido es que el cambio de códigos es un comportamiento lingüístico regular que tiene funciones sistemáticas y obedece principios lingüísticos definidos.

El cambio de códigos se encuentra, por lo normal, en situaciones de bilingüismo natural en que uno de los idiomas tiene un estatus subordinado, siendo usado como el medio de comunicación regular en la comunidad minoritaria. No tiende a usarse en condiciones de bilingüismo culto, aprendido en contextos formales. En situaciones bilingües donde es apropiada la lengua predominante, el inglés en nuestro caso, el cambio a la lengua subordinada tiende a expresar eventos, prácticas, lugares, u objetos de la comunidad minoritaria, así evocando metafóricamente la identidad cultural (Gumperz 1964). En situaciones en que la lengua subordinada guía la comunicación, por ejemplo, el uso del español por chicanos, las alternancias con el inglés tienden a tener un valor más instrumental, es decir para expresiones que no se conocen en la lengua minoritaria o nociones sobresalientes en la vida diaria cuyo uso en el idioma dominante es habitual.

El cambio de códigos intraoracional no consiste en una mixtura esporádica de palabras sino que es regido por pautas estructurales que parecen tener su base en la gramática universal (Pfaff 1982). Así, por ejemplo, en una conversación bilingüe sería aceptable decir: "Y *espérate los chicharrones*, **you** *know, when they start school,"* pero ningún hablante diría **"gente que **have** chamaquitos"* (Gumperz y Hernández Chávez 1970).

En el concepto popular, se refiere como *Spanglish* tanto al cambio de código, que acabamos de describir, como a los préstamos, discutidos arriba. En cierto sentido esta designación es correcta por el hecho de que ambos fenómenos mezclan el español y el inglés. Sin embargo, la distinción técnica es importante para comprender a fondo las características del español chicano. Los préstamos son expresiones adaptadas fonológica y morfológicamente e incorporadas a la estructura del español. Muchas de ellas llegan a formar parte íntegra del habla regional (por ejemplo, *yonque* o *picap*, figura 5.1, columna 6). Por otro lado, en el cambio de códigos, las estructuras de los dos idiomas se mantienen fonética y gramaticalmente separadas, aunque mezcladas dentro de la misma oración.

El español parcial

LA ADQUISICIÓN PARCIAL

Por el hecho de que, en la gran mayoría de los casos, los chicanos no han tenido la oportunidad de estudiar en español, y por el bilingüismo consecuente que es usado en todos los contextos comunicativos entre chicanos, es muy insuficiente la cantidad de español al que está expuesto el aprendiz.

El patrón típico de aprendizaje de idiomas en la comunidad chicana de Nuevo México ha sido que la generación mayor (personas que ahora sobrepasan los 80 años de edad) es esencialmente monolingüe en español. Las generaciones intermedias (de 60 a 80 años de edad y de 40 a 60) son bilingües, el grupo menor dominante en inglés. Las generaciones jóvenes (menores de 40 años) apenas entienden el español (Bernal-Enríquez 1995).

El resultado de esta situación para muchos jóvenes es la PÉRDIDA o la ADQUISICIÓN PARCIAL del español. Esta adquisición incompleta puede tomar varias formas: el APRENDIZAJE DILATADO en que las estructuras se adquieren más tarde de lo normal; el APRENDIZAJE INTERRUMPIDO en que el hablante cesa de adquirir más (Burt, Dulay, y Hernández Chávez 1976; Dulay, Burt, y Hernández Chávez 1978; Hernández Chávez 1993); y el OLVIDO en que ciertas estructuras antes adquiridas se hacen inaccesibles a la memoria (Weltens y Grendel 1993).

Existe un debate académico acerca del olvido. Según la teoría de interferencia, las estructuras de un idioma se extinguen, o se olvidan, por el desuso o por la influencia de las estructuras de otro idioma. Sin embargo, muchos psicólogos afirman que lo aprendido de memoria jamás se borra de ella. En este concepto, el olvido simplemente representa la inhabilidad temporal de recuperar la información deseada (Weltens and Grendel 1993). El olvido, en este sentido, se ha comparado al proceso de no poder encontrar un objeto que se ha colocado fuera de su lugar (Loftus and Loftus 1976).

De acuerdo con esta teoría, Dulay et al. (1978) sugieren que los conocimientos lingüísticos profundos no se olvidan. Lo que es afectado es el funcionamiento, o sea la manifestación externalizada de los conocimientos. Esta realización lingüística involucra la fluidez, la memoria, o la planeación de las estructuras de la frase. La actuación es muy variable aún cuando el conocimiento profundo sigue intacto, indicando que las estructuras "olvidadas" son recuperables en un momento dado más no en otro (Hagoort 1990, citado en Weltens y Grendel 1993).

En términos de producción y comprensión, "la comprensión se retiene hasta el punto que primero se adquirió" (Burt et al. 1976, p. 13). Aunque haya una pérdida virtualmente completa de la habilidad de producir, esta pérdida es más cuestión de "desactivación" de la facilidad de hablar que de un verdadero olvido. Por esto es que los programas de lenguas universitarios diseñados para hablantes nativos han visto "estudiantes chicanos y puertorriqueños que habían dejado de hablar español en su niñez, y que lo hablaban después con gran dificultad, recobrar su dominio de la lengua muy rápidamente cuando se les presentan oralmente cantidades substanciales de la lengua y se les dan oportunidades de usarla" (Burt et al. 1976, p. 13).

Los procesos psicolingüísticos de la adquisición parcial son muy parecidos a los de la adquisición regular, ya que en ambos casos reflejan principios universales del aprendizaje de idiomas (Bernal-Enríquez 1997b; Dorian 1992; Gal 1992; Seliger and Vago 1991; Silva-Corvalán 1990, 1991). Los procesos naturales que se encuentran en la adquisición parcial incluyen generalizaciones, extensiones de significado, neutralizaciones, y otros tipos de simplificaciones.

Una simplificación gramatical se encuentra en el uso del imperfecto y el pretérito (Silva-Corvalán 1994) como en *Cuando yo era niña, hablé con mi abuelita en español* por *Cuando yo era niña, hablaba con mi abuelita en español*. Una simplificación fonológica que se oye con mucha frecuencia entre los jóvenes es la neutralización [r] de la oposición fonemática[rr]:[r], como en [baryo] por *barrio* (figura 5.1, columna 7; véase también Bernal-Enríquez 1995).

LOS PRÉSTAMOS EN LA ADQUISICIÓN PARCIAL

Otra clase de cambios que se encuentra en la adquisición parcial es la de los préstamos del inglés, a los cuales se ha referido arriba en relación con las características del español chicano. En la adquisición parcial, la influencia del inglés es mayor, con el resultado que los hablantes usan mucho más los préstamos léxicos e idiomáticos que los hablantes de competencia completa.

Otra clase de préstamo, intitulado CALCOS DEL INGLÉS (columna 7) y usado muy a menudo por los hablantes de adquisición parcial, se trata del uso en la lengua minoritaria de la estructura del idioma dominante. Así, en el español parcial se oyen locuciones como *el correcto español*, modelando la estructura inglesa que coloca el adjetivo antes del sustantivo (Bernal-Enríquez 1995, 1997a). Otro ejemplo sería *gracias por viniendo* que reproduce la estructura **preposición más gerundio**, al estilo inglés (Hernández Chávez 1990a).

El mayor uso de estas clases de préstamo por los hablantes de competencia parcial es debido seguramente al hecho de que las locuciones y las estructuras prestadas o no están al alcance productivo del hablante en español o no se han aprendido del todo.

Para terminar esta sección, se puede concluir que el español chicano/nuevomexicano, incluso con las variedades locales y el español parcial, no son, como es caracterizado por muchos educadores, un lenguaje degenerado sin sistema gramatical cualquiera. Al contrario, aunque no conforman con las reglas del español normativo, siguen procesos lingüísticos naturales y universales los cuales también siguen todas las lenguas expuestas a condiciones sociales y psicolingüísticas similares. En fin, el lenguaje de los chicanos tiene que considerarse lingüísticamente diferente pero legítimo en vez de deficiente e inválido. Es puro elitismo tanto la estigmatización de esta variedad como la falta de tomarla en cuenta en la instrucción formal.

El desprecio por el español chicano en la educación

INATENCIÓN A LA ADQUISICIÓN PARCIAL

Uno de los problemas más sobresalientes en la enseñanza del español a estudiantes chicanos es que ni los métodos ni los materiales usados en el salón de clase consideran los procesos naturales de la adquisición lingüística y la condición de aprendizaje que hemos denominado el español parcial. Las metodologías y los libros usados con estos estudiantes, aún en cursos diseñados para bilingües, son más apropiados para la enseñanza del español como idioma extranjero. Al empezar su estudio, se supone que los estudiantes en estos cursos no saben nada de español y que el método de enseñanza se debe enfocar en las formas gramaticales.

Por el contrario, los chicanos bilingües llegan a la clase con conocimientos del idioma ya desarrollados, aunque no completamente, y aprendidos en condiciones naturales de adquisición del idioma. El maestro debe usar esta base como punto de partida para desarrollar el idioma antes de introducir conceptos gramaticales abstractos. De otra manera, el estudiante entenderá muy pronto que su lenguaje no es valorado y le será difícil aprender por medio de métodos inapropiados.

DESPRECIO POR LA VARIEDAD CHICANA

Como ya se ha notado, generalmente se cree que el uso de la variedad regional sirve sólo para crearle desventaja al hablante y para prevenir el aprendizaje ordenado del español estándar. Consta que el español normativo tiene un lugar muy importante en el mundo hispánico (véase la discusión más abajo sobre el asunto). Es importante enseñarlo, y no hay nadie que sugiera lo contrario.

Pero lo que pasa comúnmente en la enseñanza del español a chicanos es que se introduce el estándar desde el principio y sólo esta forma se enseña o ignorando la variedad local o deliberadamente intentando desarraigarla del habla del estudiante. Esto se hace usando una variedad de estrategias. La más directa consiste en decirle al estudiante que su manera de hablar es incorrecta y que tiene que cambiarla. Comúnmente se caracteriza su habla como *Spanglish*, *slang*, o "lleno de barbarismos," poniendo en ridículo la variedad en cuestión (Ordóñez Sabido 1977).

Otro procedimiento que se usa para estigmatizar la variedad local es la comparación negativa con las formas cultas, por ejemplo diciéndole al estudiante *No se dice 'juites', se dice 'fuiste'*, o diciendo *Tú dices 'naiden'; en el español estándar se dice 'nadie'* (Hidalgo 1993). La justificación de esta comparación es que se le tienen que enseñar ambas maneras de decir la misma cosa, pero el mensaje que recibe el estudiante es que su manera de hablar no es válida.

EFECTOS DEL DESPRECIO POR EL IDIOMA

Estos intentos de cambiar el lenguaje del estudiante no sólo no tienen el efecto deseado sino que comunican el desprecio del maestro hacia la situación cultural del alumno. La lengua de la comunidad, siendo su idioma ancestral, representa para el alumno su identidad cultural como chicano y mexicano (Hernández Chávez 1994b). Ha aprendido su idioma en el seno de su madre y en los brazos de su padre y a veces de sus abuelos, y para el estudiante, la negación de su lengua equivale a la negación de sí mismo. Además, como la mayoría de los chicanos son de origen campesino u obrero, el desprestigio de su lenguaje también desprestigia su situación socioeconómica y la de su familia.

Una respondiente para un proyecto de la Universidad de Nuevo México, la *Encuesta sobre el Español de Nuevo México y el Sur de Colorado*, quien es ahora maestra bilingüe (Respondiente #53), habló de cómo las clases universitarias de español la habían confundido en cuanto a cuáles formas había aprendido de su abuelita y cuáles eran del español estándar. Esta comparación con la norma culta no sólo niega al idioma ancestral legitimidad y validez, sino que crea en el estudiante o la estudiante un sentido de inferioridad. Ella tomó estas clases para mejorar su español, pero en lugar de haberle dado más facilidad y confianza, le causaron inseguridad.

Otra joven entrevistada para el mismo proyecto (Respondiente #340), quien recuerda haber aprendido y hablado el español en su niñez con su bisabuela, describe su clase de español (Bernal-Enríquez 1997a):

Cita

Everything about our language is inferior: "This is how Spain does it." But yet, when I talk about way back when I was little, this is a word I remember, "Oh, no, you're not supposed to say that!"

Now, 'bote', and they say it's something (like a sailboat) . . . I say, "No, no, no! Wait!" 'Cause my greatgrandma said that 'bote' was a bucket: 'Ve a trae [trái] un bote de agua'. And now they say, "No, no, it's a different word." And I'm totally confused 'cause I always knew 'bote' was a bucket . . .

Traducción

Todo de nuestra lengua es inferior: "Así es como se dice en España." Pero cuando hablo de cuando era niña, esta es una palabra que recuerdo, "¡Oh, no, no debes de decirlo así!"

Ahora, 'bote', dicen que es algo (como un barco de vela) . . . Yo les digo, "¡No, no, no! Esperen." Porque mi bisabuelita decía que 'bote' era un balde: 'Ve a trae [trái] un bote de agua'. Y ahora me dicen, "No, no, es otra palabra." Y me quedo totalmente confusa porque yo siempre supe que 'bote' era un balde . . .

Este tipo de enseñanza no sólo crea un fuerte sentido de inferioridad, sino que causa enajenamiento tanto del maestro como de la lengua y de la comunidad del estudiante. Esto a su vez frustra al estudiante en su deseo de aprender mejor el español y además explica por qué los estudiantes chicanos fracasan con mucha más frecuencia que los angloamericanos en las clases de español y abandonan el intento de aprenderlo. Al mismo tiempo, el enajenamiento y el fracaso crean grandes choques psicológicos para el estudiante: la vergüenza de su lengua y cultura, el rechazo de sus padres y de su comunidad, y el autodesprecio.

El papel del español chicano en el aula

SU IMPORTANCIA CULTURAL

Por necesario que sea el español estándar, para el educando chicano es de importancia secundaria. Es el español hogareño el que es crucial para la identidad étnica del estudiante y para su sentido de ser parte de una comunidad: es el vínculo imprescindible con su cultura y con la historia de su pueblo. El español estándar no puede cumplir estos propósitos afectivos.

LAS METAS LINGÜÍSTICAS DEL ESTUDIANTE CHICANO

Las metas del estudiante chicano en estudiar y aprender el español son la reintegración a su comunidad lingüística y cultural, la revitalización o reaprendizaje de su idioma ancestral, la legitimización de su manera de hablar, y la comunicación con otros hablantes chicanos y mexicanos en la vida cotidiana. En contraste, las metas explícitas de los cursos de español son la preparación del estudiante para poder leer obras de literatura como el *Quixote*, el *Lazarillo de Tormes*, o *Cien años de soledad*; para viajar a países hispanohablantes; o para participar en negocios o en la diplomacia internacionales. Las metas implícitas son el eliminar del habla de los chicanos el cambio de códigos, los anglicismos, y los "errores" de las formas intermedias en desarrollo y del español no estándar.

Pero estas metas son *secundarias* para este grupo lingüístico. Como dijo la misma joven citada anteriormente (Respondiente #340),

Cita

When am I ever going to Spain? . . . What I want is to stop being a 'Chicana falsa' and really speak my language like I once did with my great-grandma. I want to be able to read the message on this beautiful little card that she wrote to my great-grandfather way back then (c. 1900).

Traducción

¿Cuándo en la vida voy a ir yo a España? . . . Lo que quiero es dejar de ser una 'chicana falsa' y verdaderamente hablar mi lengua como lo podía hacer hace mucho tiempo con mi mi bisabuelita . . . Quiero poder leer y entender el mensaje en esta tarjetita que ella le escribió a mi bisabuelito en aquel entonces (c. 1900).

EL VALOR AFECTIVO

Este valor afectivo del español local, expresado por tantos chicanos, realza el aprendizaje del idioma mismo y el de otras materias. En primer lugar, al adquirir la variedad local, *en forma completa,* el problema de las formas "incorrectas" debidas a la adquisición parcial desaparece. Este mismo hecho, y la conciencia de él, fortalece la autoestima y la confianza del estudiante, abriendo un deseo de aprender más de su lengua y de su cultura, incluso el estándar escrito. En una cascada de efectos, el fuerte sentido de identidad cultural que resulta del haber logrado sus metas lingüísticas permite al estudiante enfocar con mayor confianza sus otros estudios y actividades, mejorando su calidad de vida en general. La lengua y la cultura materna tienen un poder inmenso.

EL VALOR SOCIOLINGÜÍSTICO

Quizás más importantes que nada son los efectos sociolingüísticos sobre el mantenimiento del español en las comunidades chicanas. Se sabe que el desplazamiento tiende a ocurrir cuando el idioma minoritario es desprestigiado en la comunidad por una serie de razones (Campbell y Muntzel 1992). El aprendizaje del lenguaje comunitario en contextos formales, con la adición del idioma estándar, reforzaría el uso del español en todos los demás contextos, produciendo una situación en que empezaría a recuperar las funciones comunicativas que antes tenía. El español chicano, como el español comunitario de cualquier otro país, ya no se vería desprestigiado. Al contrario, se establecería no sólo una DIGLOSIA entre el inglés y el español (Fishman 1967) sino lo que podremos titular POLIGLOSIA, o sea, una situación en que el español chicano y el español estándar (en relación diglósica en el sentido de Ferguson, 1959), más el inglés (en relación diglósica en el sentido de Fishman 1967) formarían parte del repertorio lingüístico estable de la comunidad, cada uno manteniendo fuertes sus funciones comunicativas particulares.

EL VALOR PEDAGÓGICO DEL ESPAÑOL CHICANO

Aparte de su importancia psicológica y cultural, el uso del español chicano en el aula de clase ofrece al maestro una herramienta poderosa no sólo para la enseñanza de lenguaje sino también como base para toda clase de aprendizaje. Afirma esto uno de los principios fundamentales de la educación, a saber, que la enseñanza siempre debe partir de las bases cognoscitivas, afectivas, y sociales del educando.

Como se ha acentuado anteriormente, la variedad chicana, incluso el español parcial, engloba una estructura lingüística ya desarrollada y sistemática que respeta patrones universales. Dado este fundamento, no sería lógico ignorar los conocimientos que lleva consigo el estudiante y, a causa de prejuicios lingüísticos y culturales, no sólo no usarlos sino tratar de eliminarlos.

Por más de cuarenta años, se ha sabido que la alfabetización es mejor efectuada por medio del vernáculo que por un idioma extranjero y, por extensión, por una norma ajena (UNESCO 1953; Hernández Chávez 1973; Cummins 1981; entre muchos). A su vez, la alfabetización forma la base imprescindible para el aprendizaje de las estructuras y los términos más complejos del español estándar (figura 5.1, columnas 1 a 3). De este modo, el español comunitario, y la alfabetización que emerge de él, en vez de interferir con el aprendizaje del estándar, lo promueven.

IMPLICACIONES PEDAGÓGICAS PARA LA ENSEÑANZA DEL ESPAÑOL COMO LENGUA HEREDADA EN LOS ESTADOS UNIDOS

Existe un número de implicaciones claves para la educación bilingüe de las ideas enunciadas arriba que conciernen el valor de las variedades dialectales del español. Enfocaremos en esta sección principalmente la escuela primaria, pero los principios aquí expuestos seguramente se podrán aplicar a nivel de principiantes en las escuelas secundarias, y aún en las universidades.

En primer lugar, en aquellos casos en que los estudiantes todavía no hayan desarrollado el español en un nivel que corresponda a su edad, o sea que experimenten lo que hemos llamado la *adquisición parcial*, es importante que no se haga hincapié en la corrección de las formas lingüísticas. Los niños que se encuentran en estas situaciones suelen estar bien conscientes de sus propias insuficiencias lingüísticas, y el énfasis en ellas tenderá a confundir o a avergonzarlos, cohibiendo el aprendizaje del idioma. Además, es bien conocido por los psicolingüistas que la corrección de errores de adquisición tiene muy poco efecto en el desarrollo natural de un idioma y que el aprendiz seguramente los corregirá él mismo dada una interacción lingüística frecuente, suficiente y significativa (Krashen 1981; Garton 1992; Harris 1992). Será mucho más eficaz la creación por el maestro de una multitud de experiencias lingüísticas no amenazantes que promuevan la comprensión y el uso del idioma y, así, el desarrollo natural del español según los principios de la adquisición lingüística.

De igual manera, las mezclas interlingüísticas que usan muchos de estos hablantes para suplir sus conocimientos parciales del español no deben censurarse, ya que este comportamiento concuerda con las normas lingüísticas de la comunidad del estudiante. Por supuesto, nada de esto implica que se le deben dar clases al alumno en cómo usar el CODESWITCHING: los niños aprenden solos a alternar los códigos, y no hay que ni aprobar este uso ni prohibirlo. De todas maneras, se sabe que el cambio de códigos y los anglicismos en general tienden a disminuir siempre y cuando aumenten las habilidades en el español. Por razones análogas, tampoco debe sancionarse el uso de inglés en el aula, estimulando más bien al alumno a usar cuánto español sepa.

Con respecto al dialecto local, consta que el maestro deberá considerar que todas las variedades lingüísticas son legítimas dentro de sus propios contextos y para sus propios propósitos. Por todas las razones culturales, sociales, y pedagógicas que hemos enumerado arriba, el español local tiene que tomar su lugar como el primer medio de instrucción. Además, debe estimularse en los estudiantes el uso de la variedad comunitaria en todos los contextos dentro y fuera de la clase. El personal docente y no docente, si es de esa comunidad, deberá usar la variedad local en todas las interacciones informales. Los primeros materiales usados para la lectura han de estar escritos en el español comunitario, especialmente las historias orales y lo que denominamos la TRADICIÓN MORAL de su comunidad, la cual incluye los dichos, los cuentos, las experiencias, y la literatura chicana. La enseñanza de la escritura debe partir de las experiencias del alumno, usando su propio lenguaje, incluso los préstamos y el cambio de códigos. También es importante aprovecharse de la sabiduría de la comunidad (lo que titula Atencio [1988] *el oro del barrio*) invitando al aula a individuos peritos en varios aspectos de la historia y la cultura populares.

La práctica general recomendada aquí es que no sólo se le permita al estudiante usar su lenguaje local dentro de los discursos informales, sino que refuerce tal uso la maestra, usándolo ella misma hasta donde se lo permitan su propios conocimientos de las variantes locales, sin acudir, por supuesto, a usos forzados y afectados.

Como una de las consecuencias de estos principios, las variantes fonéticas locales deberán aceptarse así como se pronuncian, sin atraer a ellas la atención de los estudiantes y sin tratar de cambiarlas. Podremos comparar esta situación con la de otras regiones hispanoparlantes: en áreas del Caribe, así como en otras regiones, la /s/ ante consonante y al final de palabra se pronuncia como [h] o [Ø]; y en la Argentina la /y/ en ciertos contextos se pronuncia como [š] o [ž]. En estos países, muy pocas maestras intentarían requerir de sus estudiantes que pronunciaran estos fonemas de una manera ajena y artificial.

En cuanto a la ortografía, se debería usar la normativa universal para estos sonidos, ya que la ortografía es fundamentalmente fonemática y supradialectal en vez de fonética y regional. Así que las pronunciaciones nuevomexicanas [sïeta] y [ea] se escribirán "silleta" y "ella"; [nohotroh] y [komere] deberán escribirse "nosotros" y "comer".

Por otro lado, las pronunciaciones locales de vocablos específicos, por ejemplo, [fyerro] o [xalar], (en contraste con las variaciones puramente fonéticas arriba discutidas) forman parte de las representaciones fonológicas del léxico dialectal y, por lo tanto, simbolizan un valor cultural para la comunidad de hablantes. Estas palabras deberían escribirse como "fierro" y "jalar", de acuerdo con las normas locales. Las formas del español estándar se introducirán más tarde muy naturalmente dentro de contextos textuales específicos, y en esas oportunidades se les puede enseñar a los estudiantes su valor sociolingüístico.

En el salón de clase, la maestra debe usar textos orales y escritos, de muchos tipos diferentes, escritos tanto en el lenguaje local como en el de otras variedades regionales, incluso en el español estándar. La práctica recomendada al leerse estos textos es la de señalarles a los estudiantes el significado, la forma, y la ortografía de aquellas palabras y estructuras que no conocen, incluso formas de la variedad local, ya que muy posiblemente habrá algunas o muchas de éstas que desconozcan. Claro está que la idea de esta recomendación es mejorar los conocimientos de los estudiantes del vocabulario y la estructura gramatical de cualquier variedad lingüística.

Aún más, para aumentar el aprecio de los estudiantes por las normas comunitarias, es importante evitar las comparaciones frecuentes con las formas de otras variedades. A menudo, al encontrar locuciones locales, las maestras de la educación bilingüe, con el propósito de ayudar a los estudiantes a aprender las formas alternativas, suelen explicar a los alumnos que "existen dos maneras de decir esto: como se dice aquí, y como se dice en otros países". Pero tales advertencias más bien llaman la atención a las formas alternativas y, como fue la maestra quien las señaló, y como tales formas se encuentran generalmente en los libros, dan la impresión que la maestra las estima más y que las formas locales son incorrectas.

Así que las formas que pertenecen a variedades externas deben traducirse a formas locales, y no del modo contrario. Por ejemplo, las palabras *acera* y *foto*, formas no locales en Nuevo México, se pueden traducir como *banqueta* y *retrato*, mientras que no debería de comentarse sobre *camalta* y *arrear* (en el sentido de *manejar un coche*), a menos que no las conozcan los estudiantes. En tal caso, se pueden definir usando un diccionario dialectal como el de Rubén Cobos (1983), o se pueden explicar de la misma manera como se hace con cualquier palabra nueva y no con referencia a un supuesto estándar. Este procedimiento es análogo al de una maestra mexicana, digamos, que les traduce a los estudiantes la palabra *ordenador* como *computadora*, indicando que así se dice esta palabra en España, y quizás en otros lugares. Por otro lado, si sus estudiantes no comprenden las palabras *elote* o *recámara*, la maestra se las explica, las define, o las ilustra, en vez de usar una equivalente de otra variedad regional, por ejemplo, *choclo* o *alcoba*, ¡las cuales los estudiantes tampoco entenderían!

Estos comentarios seguramente tienen su aplicación principalmente en lo que Cummins (1981, 1991) llama BICS, o sea las habilidades comunicativas básicas e interpersonales, el uso del lenguaje en las comunicaciones orales o en la producción informal escrita, por ejemplo, en descripciones personales, cuentos, o en escritos que reflejen la cultura comunitaria. Para los escritos más formales como ensayos o reportes de investigaciones, se les ayuda a los estudiantes a usar la ortografía y las estructuras normativas.

Es algo más problemático el tratamiento de las construcciones gramaticales no estándar que el del vocabulario y el de la pronunciación. Es preciso que la maestra entienda bien la distinción entre *las formas en desarrollo* y las que reflejan *las normas comunitarias*. Las formas en desarrollo son construcciones inmaduras como *cabió* o el uso del pasado imperfecto en aquellos contextos donde se requiere el pasado pretérito. Estas faltas mejor se corrigen modelando para el estudiante las formas correctas y exponiéndolo a una abundancia de lenguaje completamente desarrollado. Los errores de formas escritas en desarrollo, como digamos la omisión de *h* o el trueque de *s* y *z*–los debería corregir la maestra. Con la suficiente exposición al lenguaje correcto y desarrollado, los estudiantes corregirán su propio lenguaje sin la necesidad de la constante corrección por la maestra, lo cual sólo tendrá el efecto de interrumpir las intenciones comunicativas del estudiante.

Igual al tratamiento del vocabulario dialectal deberían tratarse las construcciones gramaticales locales, tales como la regularización de la sílaba acentuada en los verbos del subjuntivo en la primera personal del plural (por ejemplo, *téngamos, vuélvamos, váyamos*) o arcaísmos como *truje* o *semos*. Estas, como construcciones legítimas dentro de la comunidad local, deben ser valoradas por la maestra, estimulando a los alumnos a usarlas, si es que ya las conocen, o si no, a aprenderlas. En forma escrita, estas formas aparecerán en textos populares y periodísticos que la maestra podrá usar en el aula.

El español normativo deberá entrar en la enseñanza solamente después que se afirme la propia variedad del alumno como válida, legítima, y digna de usarse como medio de instrucción. Las formas escritas del lenguaje estándar se introducen en textos formales primero en forma de cuentos, historias, y canciones escritos en el español general que serán muy apropiados para ciertas lecciones. Al introducirse la ciencia, la matemática, y las ciencias sociales, naturalmente la mayoría de los materiales estarán escritos en el español normativo, y en sus tareas sobre éstos, los estudiantes deben usar las construcciones formales. En presentar estas lecciones la maestra encontrará la oportunidad de discutir los usos léxicos y gramaticales sociolingüísticamente apropiados.

De todo este proceso surgirá dentro de los estudiantes la conciencia no sólo de las funciones sociolingüísticas del estándar sino también de los usos apropiados del lenguaje tanto regional como local. En fin, los estudiantes llegarán a reconocer que las palabras y construcciones usadas por su comunidad de habla son ordinarias y aceptadas mientras que las formas ajenas son extraordinarias y peculiares a ciertas regiones y a ciertos estilos del discurso formal. Nos parece a nosotros que los niños de edad escolar son perfectamente capaces de comprender estas diferencias sociolingüísticas fundamentales. De hecho, se sabe que los niños desde muy tierna edad ya empiezan a demostrar sus conocimientos sociolingüísticos, como por ejemplo cuando los niños criados en familias bilingües a los dos años empiezan a dirigirse en un idioma u otro a los hablantes apropiados.

Hay que hacer hincapié en el hecho de que la gran preponderancia de vocablos y formas gramaticales usadas en los textos dialectales siguen las normas generales internacionales. En cualquier texto dado, será mínimo el número de formas netamente dialectales. Por lo tanto, concluimos que la problemática del uso escolástico del lenguaje dialectal no es cuestión tanto de la cantidad de formas no estándar, ni tampoco de sus propiedades lingüísticas, sino del valor cultural y social que le atribuimos los educadores.

Resumen y conclusiones

El español de los chicanos forma una rama del tronco lingüístico mexicano (Cárdenas 1975), el cual es un habla regional del español general. Como todas las variedades aisladas geográfica o socialmente, el español chicano difiere de la norma culta por incluir vocablos y estructuras tanto arcaicas como innovadoras. También, por su contacto con el inglés, incluye un sinnúmero de préstamos, y los hablantes suelen mezclar los idiomas en sus interacciones cotidianas.

Además, debido principalmente a las políticas étnicas del país al que fueron anexionados los chicanos, su español ha sido desplazado por el inglés, especialmente entre las generaciones más jóvenes. El resultado ha sido la adquisición de un español parcial o incompleto en que muchos hablantes tienen una competencia en el idioma muy reducida.

Una de las consecuencias más dañinas de esta situación ha sido el desprecio por el español chicano entre los educadores. Corrigen a los estudiantes, a menudo poniéndolos en ridículo, y tratan de extirpar sus modalidades locales a favor de las normas cultas. Estas prácticas tienen repercusiones graves en la identidad cultural de los estudiantes y en sus actitudes hacia el idioma, incluso su propio modo de hablar.

El desprecio y los prejuicios hacia el lenguaje de los chicanos ciegan a los maestros a la importancia de esta variedad, no sólo para los estudiantes y su comunidad sino para el éxito de la enseñanza del idioma y de otras materias.

Por el contrario, se propone que el uso del español chicano en el aula de clase no sólo lo valoriza y le da legitimidad, sino que realza la autoestima del estudiante, dándole más motivación para aprender. De igual importancia, el aprendizaje de su variedad sirve de base para que el estudiante también logre competencia en el español normativo, con efectos benéficos tanto para el individuo como para la comunidad.

En este ensayo, no proponemos que se deje de lado el español estándar. Nuestra posición es que la enseñanza temprana y exclusiva de la variedad normativa lleva consigo ciertos riesgos muy graves para el aprendizaje del español de estudiantes chicanos, para su identidad cultural, y para el mantenimiento futuro del idioma en el suroeste de los EE.UU.

La enseñanza del español comunitario a los chicanos de una manera que fomente la competencia completa en todas las habilidades auditivas, orales, y escritas sirve varios propósitos educativos al mismo tiempo: ayuda al estudiante a mejorar su competencia en la variedad local, reforzando los vínculos con su comunidad; fortalece la autoestima del estudiante, dándole amor a su lengua y ánimo para sus estudios. Al mismo tiempo forma la base esencial para aceptar y aprender el español estándar que todo el mundo quiere que aprenda, porque después de hacerse competente en su propio lenguaje, el estudiante podrá entonces "echar sus versos del alma" como un José Martí, una Gabriela Mistral, o aun como un vato chicano de atole como José Montoya.

REFERENCIAS

Atencio, Tomás. 1988. "Resolana: A Chicano Pathway to Knowledge." Third Annual Ernesto Galarza Commemorative Lecture. Stanford, CA: Stanford Center for Chicano Research.

Bernal-Enríquez, Ysaura. 1997a. "La variedad regional primero en la enseñanza del español a chicanos: Datos de la encuesta sobre el español de Nuevo México y el sur de Colorado." En *La enseñanza del español a hispanohablantes: Praxis y teoría*, eds. M. Cecilia Colombi y Francisco X. Alarcón. Boston: Houghton Mifflin.

———. 1997b. "The Nature of Non-Pathological Native Language Loss." Examen Comprensivo para el Doctorado en Lingüística Educativa. Albuquerque: University of New Mexico.

———. 1996. "Spanish Language Loss in La Nueva México." Manuscrito de proyecto para la beca Arturo G. Ortega conferida por el Hispanic Culture Foundation. Albuquerque, NM.

——. 1995. "Establishing a Baseline of Proficiency in Native New Mexican Spanish." Manuscrito del proyecto para el Challenge Assistantship. Albuquerque, Universidad de Nuevo México.

Bills, Garland D. 1997. "New Mexican Spanish: Demise of the Earliest European Variety in the United States." *American Speech* 72:154–71.

Burt, Marina K., Heidi C. Dulay, y Eduardo Hernández-Chávez. 1976. *Bilingual Syntax Measure: Technical Handbook*. Nueva York: Harcourt Brace Jovanovich.

Campbell, Lyle, y Martha C. Muntzel. 1992. "The Structural Consequences of Language Death." En *Investigating Obsolescence: Studies in Language Contraction and Death*, ed. Nancy C. Dorian, 181–96. Cambridge: Cambridge University Press.

Cárdenas, Daniel N. 1975. "Mexican Spanish." En *El lenguaje de los chicanos: Regional and Social Characteristics of Language Used by Mexican Americans*, eds. Eduardo Hernández Chávez, Andrew D. Cohen y Anthony F. Beltramo, 1–5. Arlington, VA: Center for Applied Linguistics.

Chávez, Eliverio. 1988. "Sex Differences in Language Shift." *Southwest Journal of Linguistics* (8)2:3–14.

Cobos, Rubén. 1983. *A Dictionary of New Mexico and Southern Colorado Spanish*. Santa Fe: Museum of New Mexico Press.

Cummins, Jim. 1991. "Interdependence of First and Second Language Proficiency in Bilingual Children." En *Language and Processing in Bilingual Children*, ed. Ellen Bialystok. Cambridge: Cambridge University Press.

——. 1981. "The Role of Primary Language Development in Promoting Educational Success for Language Minority Students." En *Schooling and Language Minority Students: A Theoretical Framework*, 3–49. Departamento de Educación del Estado de California, Oficina de Educación Bilingüe Bicultural, Ed. Los Angeles: California State University, Evaluation, Dissemination, and Assessment Center.

Dorian, Nancy C., ed. 1992. *Investigating Obsolescence: Studies in Language Contraction and Death*. Cambridge: Cambridge University Press.

Dulay, Heidi C., Marina K. Burt, y Eduardo Hernández Chávez. 1978. "The Process of Becoming Bilingual." En *Diagnostic Procedures in Hearing, Language, and Speech*, eds. Sadanand Singh y Joan Lynch, 251–303. Baltimore: University Park Press.

Ferguson, Charles. 1959. "Diglossia." *Word* 15:325–40.

Fishman, Joshua A. 1967. "Bilingualism with and without Diglossia: Diglossia with and without Bilingualism." *Journal of Social Issues* 23:29–38.

Gal, Susan. 1992. "Lexical Innovation and Loss: The Use and Value of Restricted Hungarian." En *Investigating Obsolescence: Studies in Language Contraction and Death*, ed. Nancy Dorian, 313–31. Cambridge: Cambridge University Press.

Garton, Alison F. 1992. *Social Interaction and the Development of Language and Cognition*. Hillsdale, NJ: Lawrence Erlbaum Associates.

Gumperz, John J. 1964. "Linguistic and Social Interaction in Two Communities." *American Anthropologist* Parte II, 66:6, 137–53.

Gumperz, John J., y Hernández Chávez, Eduardo. 1970. "Cognitive Aspects of Bilingual Communication." En *Language Use and Social Change*, ed. W. H. Whitely, 115–25. Oxford: Oxford University Press.

Hagoort, Peter. 1990. "Tracking the Time Course of Language Understanding in Aphasia." Ph.D. diss. University of Nijmegen.

Harris, Margaret. 1992. *Language Experience and Early Language Development: From Input to Uptake*. Hillsdale, NJ: Lawrence Erlbaum Associates.

Hernández Chávez, Eduardo. 1995. "La reivindicación del español en el suroeste." Ponencia Plenaria en el First Annual Conference on Spanish for Native Speakers: New Directions for the 21st Century. New Mexico State University, Las Cruces, mayo.

———. 1994a. "Language Policy in the United States: A History of Cultural Genocide." En *Linguistic Human Rights: Overcoming Linguistic Discrimination*, eds. Tove Skutnabb-Kangas, Robert Phillipson y Mart Rannut. New York: Mouton de Gruyter.

———. 1994b. "La pérdida del español entre los chicanos: Sus raíces sociopolíticas y las consecuencias para la identidad cultural." Ponencia Plenaria en el Tercer Congreso Anual de la Sociedad Iberoamericana sobre La Lengua Española y la Identidad Social. Universidad de Nuevo México, Albuquerque, febrero.

———. 1993. "Native Language Loss and Its Implications for Revitalization of Spanish in Chicano Communities." En *Language and Culture in Learning*, eds. Barbara J. Merino, Henry T. Trueba, y Fabián A. Samaniego, 58–74. London: Falmer Press.

———. 1990. "Gracias por viniendo — Language Loss in the Spanish of New Mexico." Comunicación ante el Congreso Anual de The Linguistic Association of the Southwest, El Paso, TX, noviembre.

———. 1974. "ESL — Too Little Too Late, or Too Much Too Soon?" Congreso de CATESOL, San Francisco, CA, abril.

———. 1973. "The Home Language of Chicanos as a Medium of Instruction." En *Reading between the Lines: The Claremont Reading Conference*, ed. Malcolm P. Douglass, 26–38. Claremont, CA: The Claremont Reading Conference.

Hernández Chávez, Eduardo, Garland D. Bills, y Alan Hudson. 1996. "El desplazamiento del español en el suroeste de EE.UU. según el censo de 1990." En *Actas del X Congreso Internacional de la Asociación de Lingüística y Filología de la América Latina*, eds. Marina Arjona Iglesias, Juan López Chávez, Araceli Enríquez Ovando, Gilda C. López Lara, y Miguel Angel Novella Gómez, 664–72. México, D. F.: Universidad Nacional Autónoma de México.

Hernández Chávez, Eduardo, y Gilberto Pérez. 1991. La /-e/ paragógica en el español nuevomexicano: ¿arcaísmo o innovación? Comunicación ante el XII Congreso del Español en Estados Unidos, University of Southern California, Los Angeles, noviembre.

Hidalgo, Margarita. 1993. "The Teaching of Spanish to Bilingual Spanish-Speakers: A Problem of Inequality." En *Language and Culture in Learning*, eds. Barbara J. Merino, Henry T. Trueba, y Fabián A. Samaniego, 82–93 London: Falmer Press.

Hockett, Charles Francis. 1958. *A Course in Modern Linguistics*. New York: Macmillan Co.

Hudson, Alan, Eduardo Hernández Chávez, y Garland Bills. 1995. "The Many Faces of Language Maintenance: Spanish Language Claiming in Five Southwestern States." En *Spanish in Four Continents*, ed. Carmen Silva-Corvalán, 165–83. Washington, D.C.: Georgetown University Press.

Kloss, Heinz. 1977. *The American Bilingual Tradition*. Rowley, MA: Newbury House Publishers, Inc.

Krashen, Stephen. 1981. "Bilingual Education and Second Language Theory." En *Schooling and Language Minority Students: A Theoretical Framework*, ed. California State Department of Education. Los Angeles: California State University Evaluation, Dissemination, and Assessment Center.

Liu, Hua, Elizabeth Bates, y Ping Li. 1992. "Sentence Interpretation in Bilingual Speakers of English and Chinese." *Applied Psycholinguistics* 13:451–84.

Loftus, Goeffrey R., y Elizabeth F. Loftus. 1976. *Human Memory: The Processing of Information*. Hillsdale, NJ: Lawrence Erlbaum Associates.

Meyer, Doris L. 1977. "The Language Issue in New Mexico, 1880–1900: Mexican American Resistance against Cultural Erosion." *Bilingual Review/Revista Bilingüe* 4, 1–2:99–106.

Milk, Robert Dale. 1980. "The Issue of Language Education in Territorial New Mexico." *Bilingual Review* 7, 3:212–21.

Mycrs-Scotton, Carol. 1993. *Social Motivations for Code-Switching: Evidence from Africa*. Oxford: Claredon Press.

Ordóñez Sabido, Raúl. 1977. *Reflexiones de un lingüista inconforme*. México, DF: B. Costa-Amic.

Ortiz, Leroy I. 1975. "A Sociolinguistic Study of Language Maintenance in the Northern New Mexico Community of Arroyo Seco." Ph.D. diss., University of New Mexico.

Pfaff, Carol W. 1982. "Constraints on Language Mixing: Intrasentential Code-Switching and Borrowing in Spanish/English." En *Spanish in the United States: Sociolinguistic Aspects*, eds. Jon Amastae y Lucía Elías-Olivares, 264–97. Cambridge: Cambridge University Press.

Sánchez, Rosaura. 1993. "Language Variation in the Spanish of the Southwest." En *Language and Culture in Learning*, eds. Barbara J. Merino, Henry T. Trueba, y Fabián A. Samaniego, 75–81 London: Falmer Press.

Seliger, Herbert W., y Robert M. Vago, eds. 1991. *First Language Attrition*. Cambridge: Cambridge University Press.

Silva-Corvalán, Carmen. 1994. *Language Contact and Change: Spanish in Los Angeles*. Oxford: Claredon Press.

———. 1991. "Spanish Language Attrition in a Contact Situation with English." En *First Language Attrition*, eds. Herbert W. Seliger y Robert M. Vago, 151–71. Cambridge: Cambridge University Press.

———. 1990. "Current Issues in Studies of Language Contact." *Hispania* 73:162–76.

UNESCO. 1953. *The Use of Vernacular Languages in Education*. Paris: UNESCO.

Weltens, Bert, y Marjon Grendel. 1993. "Attrition of Vocabulary Knowledge." En *The Bilingual Lexicon*, eds. Robert Schreuder y Bert Weltens. Philadelphia: John Benjamins.

Wong-Fillmore, Lily. 1991a. "Loss of a Native Language Ability Due to Premature Exposure to English." Invited Address to the Society for Research in Child Development, Seattle, WA.

———. 1991b. "When Learning a Second Language Means Losing the First." *Early Childhood Research Quarterly* 6:323–46.

PART II

Community and Classroom-based Research Studies

Implications for Instruction K–16

6

"Spanish in My Blood"
Children's Spanish Language Development in Dual-Language Immersion Programs

Ernestina Pesina Hernández
Hinako Takahashi-Breines
Rebecca Blum-Martínez
University of New Mexico

> *"I would like to learn a lot more Spanish, 'cuz I don't like,*
> *use too much Spanish, 'cuz well, when I was little . . . .*
> *Like at the age of seven or eight, I started changing."*

—Gabriel is a ten-year-old heritage language learner in a dual-language
immersion program. He has grown up in the Southwest, in a bilingual
community where he constantly hears both English and Spanish used
in many different contexts. Learning or preserving one's heritage
language, however, is not an easy task in this country, even
in a community where both languages are present.

In this chapter, we present a view of heritage language learning in dual-language immersion elementary school settings. This is part of a larger qualitative study (Language Learning in Two Dual-language Immersion Programs) in which we are attempting to describe children's language development in both English and Spanish across three years. For the larger study, we have chosen two cohorts of children from two different dual-language immersion programs—Thoreau and Del Río Elementary Schools.* The cohorts are made up of six and five children, respectively, and reflect the population of each school. For this chapter we focus on four children, two from each cohort, in order to highlight some issues regarding the acquisition of Spanish by young students.

Dual-language immersion programs are defined as "combin[ing] the most significant features of bilingual education for minority students, and immersion education for majority students. Academic and language arts instruction is provided to native speakers of two languages using, alternatively and sequentially, both languages; one of the languages is a second language for each group of students" (Lindholm 1990, p. 95).

"The definition . . . encompasses four critical features: (a) the program essentially involves some form of dual-language instruction where the non-English language is used for a significant portion of the students' instructional day; (b) the program involves periods of instruction during which only one language is used; (c) both native English speakers and non-native speakers (preferably in balanced numbers) are participants; and (d) the students are integrated for most content instruction" (Lindholm 1990, p. 96).

It appears that in the early days of dual-language immersion programs, language majority children were thought of as also being from the ethnic majority, that is, Anglo or white students. In our experience, as the popularity of these programs has grown, we have seen increasing numbers of Chicano children with limited or no productive capabilities in Spanish comprising a large percent of the English-speaking students. What this means is that heritage language learners of Spanish are enrolled in these programs for the purpose of acquiring their heritage language, and to act as English language models for the native Spanish speakers. Although their classroom teachers may be aware of this fact, little has been done to alter the way in which these programs are implemented, or the strategies used with these children.

The field of heritage language learning has focused for the most part on high school and college students, and very little on school-aged students (Merino, Trueba, and Samaniego 1993). Questions surrounding heritage language teaching have typically centered on placement and testing, developing appropriate textbooks, the issue of different varieties of Spanish, and the appropriateness of these varieties for literate purposes (Gutiérrez 1997; Roca 1997). These concerns are more reflective of the field of foreign language, or explicit language teaching that has traditionally focused on adolescent and adult learners (Snow 1993). In the case of young heritage language learners perhaps an approach that reflects the concerns of child language development, and which sees "errors [as] a sign of progress" (p. 401) would be more helpful in developing appropriate methodologies.

The Children

Within our two cohorts we have attempted to have a wide range of language abilities represented. At Thoreau, two Spanish-dominant, two bilingual, and two English-dominant children were chosen as the members of one cohort. The designation of English or Spanish dominant represents the children's language profile when they first enrolled in the program in kindergarten. At Del Río, two Spanish-dominant, one bilingual, and two English-dominant children were chosen. Again, these are the designations given by the school at the time the children enrolled in the dual-language immersion program for the first time. Over the five years of these programs, all of the children have become bilingual, representing different points on the bilingual continuum (Valdés and Figueroa 1994).

Of the eleven children in the two cohorts, nine are heritage language students. Six of these children are first- and second-generation bilinguals who display varying degrees of fluency in English and Spanish (Rodríguez Pino 1997). Three of the children are third- or fourth-generation U.S.-born Hispanic students (considered to be receptive bilinguals) who are English dominant with limited speaking skills in Spanish. Only two of the children are learning Spanish as a brand new language.

In this essay, we focus on four of the heritage language learners. These four children began their studies in the dual-language immersion program with almost no productive abilities in Spanish. For the most part, their parents came from bilingual homes in which, over the course of their lives, English has become the language of everyday communication. For some parents, the ability to communicate in Spanish has been almost completely lost. The decision to enroll their children in a dual-language immersion program was motivated, in part, by their desire to have their children learn Spanish. Furthermore, the children we will focus on here have at least one parent who is Nuevomexicano, that is, a member of what is considered to be longtime settlers of New Mexico with few if any ties to Mexico (Gonzales-Berry and Maciel 2000). We highlight this fact because of the rapid Spanish language loss that is occurring among Nuevomexicanos, and because it is a population that is often ignored in the discussions on dual-language immersion programs.

GABRIEL

Gabriel is a bilingual student who, at present, is more comfortable using English. Nevertheless, he is able to comprehend Spanish very well, and speaks it both in school and in the community when the need arises. His father is South American. His mother is Nuevomexicana. In his infancy, Spanish was spoken in the home between his parents and grandmother. Spanish was his first language. When the family moved to the Southwest the grandmother remained on the East Coast, and English became the language of the home as a way to assist the father in learning English. Socially, Gabriel has no one close friend but participates in a soccer league and socializes with other male students who are also part of this league during recess and during group work. Among those students, some prefer to use Spanish as their social language.

ANGELIQUE

Angelique is an English-dominant speaker who will speak haltingly in Spanish when it is required. Her father is from the Caribbean and is bilingual in Spanish and English. Her mother is from New Mexico. She understands Spanish and speaks English. Angelique has contact with Spanish-speaking relatives who live in the same city. Socially Angelique has several close friends, all of whom prefer English as their language for most functions. She loves seasonal sports and joins in football and soccer games during recess time. She is liked by her classmates and volunteers to help them with their Spanish work, when she can. She is very proud of her heritage. She readily admits that her parents want her to learn Spanish since they no longer use it much at home. She is the oldest child in the family and states that her sisters do not speak any Spanish.

ANABEL

Anabel began the program as an English speaker. Her mother, a Nuevomexicana, speaks mostly English. She is raising Anabel by herself. Although Anabel has Spanish-speaking relatives, she has infrequent contact with them. Most of her exposure to Spanish is through the program. Anabel is more comfortable and talkative in English. However, over the past two years, she has begun to participate more during Spanish time. She has no trouble in social communication and she is able to comprehend most of the academic Spanish used in class. When she participates in class discussions, she speaks slowly, making sure she enunciates each syllable. Anabel is friendly with most of the students in the class. She seems most comfortable with those who prefer English. Anabel received a great deal of attention in the class and in the school when she played a leading role in the Shakespeare production, which was presented to the school, to the community, and at a national educational conference.

ROLANDO

Rolando also began the program as dominant in English. Both of his parents are Nuevomexicanos. His mother only speaks English, and his father is bilingual in both Spanish and English, as are his grandparents and other relatives.

Rolando's older sister, who is now in middle school, was also enrolled in the dual-language immersion program for several years. Rolando feels more comfortable in English. Nevertheless, he participates and is equally talkative during Spanish and English time. Over the last two years, he has shown tremendous growth in both oral and written Spanish. In third grade he was quiet during the Spanish class time. This year he stands out for his willingness to speak out and to take the lead in many activities. Rolando is also a leader in the school. During fourth grade, he was the president of his grade. He also played a leading role in the Shakespeare production, reciting all of his lines in Spanish. He is friendly with most of the male students in the class, both English and Spanish-speaking students, and will use Spanish socially when the need arises.

The Schools

The two schools in which the children in this study are enrolled are very different. Like other bilingual programs, there is a great deal of variation between the two dual-language immersion programs. Much of this is due to the distinct populations each school serves, and the neighborhoods in which the schools are located. These differences have a profound effect on the amount of Spanish that is used in each school and the opportunities the children have for using Spanish in their social and academic lives.

THOREAU ELEMENTARY SCHOOL

Thoreau is a magnet school for the visual and performing arts with a strand within the curriculum for Spanish language development utilizing a dual-language immersion program (effective 1995). The school is located in an established urban, Hispanic neighborhood that is being encroached upon by federal and local offices and businesses. The school enrollment consists of children from the surrounding neighborhood as well as many magnet students who are from varying parts of the city and who must apply for admission into the school. Many local students are from low-income families. Those who come from other parts of the city are mostly middle class. Regardless of class, the majority of students are Hispanic but English is their first language. There are also African-American, Anglo, Asian, and Native American students enrolled in the school. The dual-language immersion program model begins with immersion in Spanish and then increases the use of English instruction each year until each language is used equally (kindergarten: 90/10; first grade: 90/10; second grade: 80/20; third grade: 70/30; fourth grade: 60/40; fifth grade: 50/50). Given the population of this school, it is very difficult to achieve a balance between minority language speakers (Spanish) and majority language speakers (English). English speakers far outnumber Spanish speakers in each classroom.

DEL RÍO ELEMENTARY SCHOOL

Del Río Elementary School is located in a Hispanic community in the older part of town. The school serves mostly Hispanic, low-income families, including both recent immigrants from Mexico and other Latin American countries, and Nuevomexicano families who have been in the community for several generations.

Del Río is a bilingual school. It is bilingual in the sense that both English and Spanish are used publicly throughout the school and by the faculty, staff, and students. The school implements a dual-language immersion program and a regular English program. The dual-language immersion strand begins in kindergarten and goes through fifth grade; except for kindergarten, which begins with a 90/10 distribution of Spanish and English, all other grades employ a 50/50 model, so that Spanish and English are each used for 50 percent of the schedule.

At Del Río, they have been able to maintain almost equal numbers of minority language students (Spanish) and majority language speakers (English) in the program. As the children have progressed it is often difficult to discern which language is the language of greater facility or preference. In great part this is due to the balance that is achieved with equal numbers of Spanish and English speakers in each class.

The two schools also differ in the way that they organized the fourth grade classes (the focal classes for 2000–2001). At Thoreau, the focal children were placed in two different classes with two different teachers. These teachers worked together, sharing the teaching of reading, social studies, math, and science. One teacher taught Spanish reading and social studies (in either language). The other taught English reading, math, and science (in either language). The children would go to one teacher in the morning, and then switch at noon, in order to ensure that they received the entire curriculum.

At Del Río, all of the focal children attended Spanish in the morning with one teacher and then English time in the afternoon with another teacher. The Spanish teacher was responsible for Spanish language arts, including literacy circle, math, and social studies. The English teacher was responsible for English language arts, including literacy circle, math, science, PE, and library in English.

Another difference between the two schools was that at Del Río a school-wide literacy program that included oral language skills, reading, and writing had been adopted into the dual-language immersion program. The literature that children read was a mixture of authentic Spanish language texts and translations from other languages.

Each teacher at Thoreau implemented a language arts program in slightly different ways. Some focused more on Writers' Workshop, others on Daily Oral Language messages. Furthermore, almost all of the literature children read were translations from English, for example, all of the children in both classes read *La Telaraña de Carlota* (*Charlotte's Web*). As we will discuss later in this chapter, we believe that interaction with authentic Spanish texts (those written originally in Spanish) provide students with more examples of natural and more varied samples of different registers and varieties of Spanish.

A fourth difference between the schools was the teachers' stricter adherence at Del Río to the separation of languages. Given the greater number of fluent Spanish-speaking students at Del Río, it was easier for teachers to maintain Spanish because they had students who could easily respond to any question or request that might arise. At Thoreau, on the other hand, with so many fluent English speakers, the teachers had to frequently remind their students to speak in Spanish. Furthermore, students often requested assistance or translations, and the teachers often acquiesced, providing students with English translations during class discussions.

ORGANIZATION OF CLASSROOMS

Another significant difference that was found between classrooms was the way in which the classes were organized. These differences are more a reflection of individual teacher preference, and not necessarily a reflection of the philosophy of the school or program.

At Thoreau, both teachers tended to prefer a looser structure to their classrooms. Learning activities were generally introduced by the teacher to the whole classroom. Then students were expected to complete their work at their desks as the teachers walked around the room providing assistance as needed. Students were seated in small groups and they could move as they desired to work with peers. Cooperative groups were used extensively in the classrooms, allowing many opportunities for students to talk to each other. For the most part, this student talk was in English, regardless of the designated language, reflecting the make-up of the students in the class.

At Del Río, while cooperative groups were also used extensively, they were organized differently. Each student in a cooperative group was given a specific role with explicit responsibilities. Each student was graded according to the criteria of the role and responsibilities they were assigned. The teacher kept close track of the time, moving students to the next set of activities at designated time intervals. As a consequence, there was much less talk between students, and when it occurred it was related to the task and was generally in the designated language — in this case, Spanish.

We have outlined some of the major differences that existed between the two schools and the focal classrooms. There was, however, one important similarity between the focal classrooms: all three teachers who were responsible for the Spanish language instruction were non-native speakers of Spanish. Two of the teachers appeared quite comfortable in Spanish, having spent considerable time in Spanish-speaking countries. However, even in their case, there were times when they did not know an academic term or a particular idiomatic phrase. In the case of one teacher, there were numerous occasions when he did not seem to know how to express certain concepts, and would switch to English.

At Del Río, having a nonnative speaker of Spanish as the Spanish language instructor was not as critical an issue for Spanish language learning, given the make-up of the student and faculty populations. Children were able to hear and interact with many other fluent Spanish-speakers each day and throughout the school year. However, in a school like Thoreau, where native Spanish-speakers are scarce, the quantity and quality of the Spanish they do receive appears to be of some importance. As children are constructing their second language, they need strong and numerous language models who can guide them and give them appropriate feedback (Wong Fillmore 1982, 1991; Swain 1986). There were few opportunities for feedback at Thoreau, both orally and in the children's written texts.

Methodology

The data that is utilized for this chapter was collected as a part of a larger study designed to document children's language growth for both language-majority children and language-minority children, in Spanish and in English as they participate in a dual-language immersion program. The research project began last year when the children were in third grade. Thus the data reported here is for a two-year period in which the two cohorts were observed and audiotaped weekly.

The methodology used in gathering this data has been qualitative, attempting to understand the experience of participating students, with their teachers as they live it. This has required that we *discover* the patterns of language use by teachers and students, rather than entering with preconceived notions of how such programs should function, or developing language measures a priori (Erickson 1982; Hymes 1972; Mehan 1982). By spending as much time as possible carefully observing and recording participating students in classrooms and in areas of the school where children and faculty interact (the cafeteria, playground, library, teachers' lounge, etc.), we have been able to gather natural language samples which are more realistic indicators of children's language abilities in real communicative situations (Benjamin 1994; Dyson 1997; Valdés and Figueroa 1994). Moreover, we have gathered samples of children's written schoolwork over the course of the two years and analyzed their growth in the written mode of both languages.

DESIGN

The design of this study is guided by the objective described above. Moreover, several theoretical assumptions help to frame data collection and analysis:

1. The nature of individual bilingualism must be understood as a function of its use in everyday lives and not as an infrequently realized ideal (Fishman 1968; Mackey 1972a, 1972b; Valdés and Figueroa 1994). This means that as we study the students' language use these patterns must be analyzed within the context of each community and the linguistic experiences of participating individuals (Benjamin 1994; Fishman 1968; Mackey 1972; Valdés and Figueroa 1994).

2. Developing bilinguals' language competence is spread across two languages (Grosjean 1985). Additionally, each language may function in complementary fashion with the other. For this reason standardized tests and measures that were designed for monolinguals can never capture the real linguistic competence of bilinguals. Therefore, a large part of this study will focus on developing appropriate ways to capture the language competence of young bilinguals (Valdés and Figueroa 1994).

3. Relationships between teachers, children, administrators, and parents are reflexive and multidimensional (Erickson 1982). Consequently, while the adults in the school are very influential in establishing the organizational system of that institution, children and their parents structure and modify the school environment as well (Mehan 1982). For this reason, language as it is used by the children in both public and private exchanges will be studied.

METHOD OF ANALYSIS

The analysis found in the profiles below is based on representative audio recordings and transcriptions that were chosen for each focal child within each cohort. Many of these transcriptions have other focal children participating in the talk; therefore, there is a great deal of data on each child. We report here on the talk during Spanish instruction time.

A great deal of the talk that was transcribed is of an academic nature. The children, to a very large degree, responded to the teacher during presentations, or during seatwork. At Del Río children initiated little private talk. They were on-task much of the time and their talk reflects this. At Thoreau, while children did discuss their academic work frequently, much more of the private talk was social. Most of this talk was in English, reflecting the linguistic make-up of the class.

The analysis of children's talk was based in large part on a previous study that focused on children's talk in a fifth-grade bilingual class in another school (Benjamin 1994). In that study, children's communicative competence was examined by analyzing the functions or purposes for which they used their two languages, that is, what they were able to accomplish through their talk. The categories and speech acts that were identified for the previous study were examined for their applicability to these classrooms. Although in these classrooms there is a good deal less of personal talk, the academic functions and speech acts identified in the previous study were helpful in analyzing the talk in these two cohorts. Over the course of the two years, an additional function has been added—Talk with the Teacher—as we have observed children responding to teachers' requests, answering questions, reading aloud, and bidding for a turn. Furthermore, across several language functions we have heard children practicing new words, phrases, and grammatical constructions, either before or after a public or private exchange. Detailed descriptions of the functions and speech acts are found in the appendix (see also Benjamin 1996).

Using a functional analysis of language allows one to discern the purpose for which children use particular languages and the characteristics of their language usage. Other child language scholars, such as Halliday (1973, 1980), Tough (1977), and Dore (1977), have also utilized a functional approach as a way of describing children's competence. Language functions can be broken down further into smaller units of analysis. In this case, following the previous study (Benjamin 1994, 1996), speech acts were utilized to identify what children could actually do in both languages.

For each focal child a tally of speech acts was made so as to summarize all of the information about each child's language use. From this summary, individual profiles are included that help to explain how the child used Spanish, and for what purposes, and how their language use changed from one year to the next. We believe that this kind of analysis allows for a more detailed and realistic description of children's language behavior: what they understand, how they participate, and how well they are able to accomplish their communicative intentions, both with their teacher and with their classmates.

Two of the major language functions in which children were involved, in both classes, were Getting Their Work Done ("used for accomplishing the academically-related tasks and activities that are assigned or are part of the responsibilities in school") and Talk with the Teacher ("talk either in response to the teacher's request, or made by the student to initiate an exchange"). In both schools, children were involved in seatwork, class discussions, small-group problem solving, paired computer work, etc. Students provided their teacher and their classmates with information, explanations, assistance, clarifications, and confirmations. Additionally, they requested these same actions from those around them. Students read aloud, planned out their work strategies, and assisted themselves by talking to themselves during seatwork. Profiles of children's oral Spanish are provided below.

GABRIEL

In third grade, Gabriel spoke very little in classroom discussions. Most of his talk was to classmates as he wandered around the room, socializing and, less frequently, attempting to get some work done. Nevertheless, he was the only student within the focal group to initiate conversations in Spanish, and provide information and guidance to his classmates. Furthermore, he read aloud to the teacher upon request.

In fourth grade we found some of the same tendencies; for example, Gabriel still liked to go from table to table conversing with his classmates, mostly in English. However, he was still one of two children in this cohort to initiate conversations in Spanish. In fourth grade, Gabriel was much more engaged in class discussions — displaying his knowledge for the teacher, reading aloud, and providing information. Furthermore, he also requested assistance and clarification in Spanish, using the appropriate language during Spanish language instruction time. When sitting at his desk, Gabriel also talked himself through the assignments (Monitoring His Own Thinking) in Spanish. In his conversations with his classmates, he used the Talking to Others function, asserting himself, correcting others, and alerting them about impending trouble.

ANGELIQUE

Angelique is a Spanish heritage language learner who has very little productive usage of Spanish, either at home or at school. Like her classmates, she utilizes English as her primary language of communication, even during Spanish time. During third grade, Angelique was very quiet in both languages. Most of her talk was with her classmates, and very rarely did she volunteer to answer her teacher's questions. Despite her reserve, she did attempt to speak in Spanish when it was required. Most of this talk consisted of Requests for Explanations and Assistance, responding to the teacher's requests, and Reading Aloud.

In fourth grade, Angelique continued to confine most of her talk to academic functions Getting Their Work Done and Talk with the Teacher. She was able to Provide Information, Suggest a Plan of Action to her classmates, and Read Aloud. The only other speech act used with any frequency was Monitoring Her Own Thinking, which was done principally when she was composing a written text in collaboration with her classmates. During these same events, she Attempted to Correct her classmates. It was during this same activity that Angelique had seven instances of Spanish language practice.

ANABEL

During third grade, Anabel was very reserved in class, speaking far less than any other student in her cohort. Most of her public language use was in response to the teacher's questions and requests (Talk with the Teacher) and was confined to short one- or two-word phrases. Some of these speech acts were: Knowledge Displays, where she would spell out a word, and Read Alouds. She was able to confirm the teacher's or her classmates' questions and very few instances of Providing Information or Requesting Explanations.

In fourth grade, Anabel became more vocal, although she was still the most reserved student in her cohort. Most of her Talk with the Teacher continued to be confined to simple phrases, which she could say easily. Often, when she was called upon she would delay somewhat as she searched for the correct word or until others gave her assistance. Most of her talk in Spanish class consisted of Knowledge Displays for the teacher, and displaying politeness during her presentations to the class. There were also several instances where she Provided Information, Provided Explanations, and Requested Action. Additionally, there were several examples of Interpreting and Language Practice. Significantly, although Anabel feels more comfortable in English, there were several instances during *English instruction* when she initiated *Spanish* interactions with several of her classmates during a science project.

ROLANDO

In third grade, Rolando struggled a great deal to communicate effectively in Spanish. Most of his talk occurred in Talks with the Teacher and was confined to Knowledge Displays (answering questions to which there was already a known answer), and to Confirming the teacher's questions and requests (simple one- or two-word answers). Nevertheless, he tried repeatedly to speak in Spanish, despite a great deal of inaccuracy.

In fourth grade, Rolando made a dramatic leap both in the quality and quantity of his Spanish output. Rolando participated often, and was constantly bidding for an opportunity to speak. This occurred both with the teacher and with his classmates, and he was often eager to assist those who either did not know the answers or had difficulty expressing themselves in Spanish. He offered information, assistance, and confirmations. Significantly, he also initiated these speech acts with both his teacher and his classmates, even during seatwork, or at other times when it wasn't required. He and another of the focal students, who is a native Spanish speaker, often vied for the leadership role in the class. He was able to use full phrases that were often complex. He utilized past, imperfect, and subjunctive tenses when describing facts and events from his study of history, although these were not always used consistently. At times he had difficulty maintaining agreement between noun and verb forms (*los negros tenia*). Nevertheless, he was able to use Spanish to communicate most of what he wanted to say.

Profiles of Students' Writing

Before describing individual students' writing abilities, it is important to underscore, once again, the great difference that existed in the curriculum between the two schools. In Thoreau, students were required to keep notebooks for the different subject areas: language arts, reading, social studies, science, math, and drama. The two teachers varied in the kind of work that they assigned to students, and in the amount of writing required. In one class, children were required to discuss and then write about a Daily Oral Language message. This message was usually focused on a topic that children were currently studying, but always had several grammatical and orthographic errors that the students were expected to correct. In this class students also were required to write in their journals, and were often given a topic to write about. Language usage was also stipulated (Spanish or English). In the other class, children also wrote in their journals, but there was less control both over topic and language. In both classes a lot of writing took place during drama class. The children had a different teacher for this class who was a native Spanish speaker.

At Del Río, reading and writing were based on literature and those topics related to language arts and social studies content areas. The activities tended to be prescribed activities from a literacy program that was being implemented school-wide. Generally the period started with a teacher-centered lesson, which focused on word study, or grammatical or orthographic lessons, which then broke up into small groups where students either worked individually or with their group members. Students were given very specific roles in these groups, such as discussion leader, secretary, investigator, or illustrator.

The differences between each school's (and each teacher's) approach to writing were evident in the work that we were able to collect from each student. Generally, at Del Río, all five students had completed the same work, and there were samples from both social studies and language arts units of study. At Thoreau, there was a great deal of variation from one student to another. Some students had a great many creative stories in their journals, others had only a few. Some had more written pieces in English, others had written texts in both languages.

The profiles describing students' written work reflect those differences, although we have endeavored to describe their work in similar ways. We have utilized the National Council of Teachers of English Standards Exemplar Series (Myers and Spaulding 1997) in order to help us understand the developmental issues involved for young writers. While we have sought similar guidance from the Spanish-speaking world, we have been unable to find descriptions of young writers who have already passed the incipient literacy stage. We recognize that there may be some difficulties in our analysis of the children's writing in Spanish, using what are essentially English rubrics. We hope that this chapter and the assessments that are being done on other dual-language immersion programs (Howard and Christian 1997) would encourage others to work in this area.

GENERAL TENDENCIES

Generally, over the course of two years, children have shown a greater ability to develop their topic more consistently and coherently. There is also a growing ability to organize their writing according to the genre that they are using. In fourth grade, children are increasingly able to present well-developed ideas, maintain a focus, and provide supporting details. This is especially true in their essays and creative stories. In fourth grade, children are much more conscious of correct punctuation and paragraphing. Their spelling is generally conforming to the standard, with the exception of those developmental errors that are usually found in Spanish—confusion of b/v, s/z/c, g/j, h/o, and in quite a few cases an influence from English—confusion between i/e, c/qu, r/rr, futball/*futbol*.

Gabriel

Over the course of two years, Gabriel has grown from a very basic writer, who would write strings of sentences, to one who is able to maintain a focus on a single subject with supporting details. His texts have never been very lengthy, but they have grown. Gabriel writes complete sentences, consistently uses capitals and correct punctuation, and is the only student in his cohort who seems to have a real consciousness of accent marks. His work when it is completed is usually done neatly. There is evidence in his writing of his vocabulary increasing, especially in academic discourse (*planetario*, *fósil*, etc.) He enjoys writing about his family and their visits to family members or trips to the mountains. We include a sample from his journal in which he was asked to introduce himself to an imaginary visitor:

> Yo me llamo Gabriel Santos. Yo tengo nueve años y vengo a la escuela de Thoreau. Mi materia favorita es la ciencia.
> A mi me gustan futbol y futbol Americano. Yo estoy en un ecipo de socer el ecipo se llama Prairie Dogs.
> Mi comida favorita es pizza para comer. A mi me gusta tambien Mec danal.
> Mi amigo es Juaquin. Juaquin y yo casi cenamos la casa.
> Mi familia es lo mas importante. Fin.

Angelique

Angelique is able to write very well in English. She adheres to a clear topic and is able to use details, as well as actions, in a logical sequence of events. This ability is reflected in her Spanish writing. Her writing in Spanish is coherent and organized and she is able to write about a variety of topics. She is able to express her feelings and describe the feelings of others. She uses quotation marks to signify dialogue. Her entries show originality and she discusses her point of view, as well as that of the characters. The difficulty Angelique has is with the Spanish language itself. She is learning subject-verb agreements, and is still unsure of the possessive. Like other learners of Spanish, she confuses *ser/estar*, and often uses the third person for the first (*yo fue*). At other times, she translates directly from English into Spanish; "*voy a nombrar a el despues de su papa.*" We include a sample from her journal about her dog Ox.

Hase como 3 anos, cuando mi perra Snowball tenia perritos. Ellia tenia como 9 perritos. El papa Ox mato dos. El tenia que ir al veterinario.

Mi nana no le gusta perros. Entonces ella tenia una venta de jardin. Ella no estaba ventando ella estaba dando los a personas que venia al venta de jardin. Una persona se olvido a el perrito entonces mi papa me deije "Angelique tu puedes detener a este perro" Yo dije a mi papa "Voy a nombrar a el despues de su papa, Ox."

Un dia por la manana Ox estaba muy enfermo. El era vomitando y todo cuando mi mama me llamo, "Angelique tienes que ir a la escuela." Yo fue con Monica.

Cuando yo vine patras de la escuela mi mama me dije, "Angelique Ox se murio de parvo." Yo me senti muy triste.

Yo queria a tener tres perros haora pero mi mama y mi papa no agare su inyiecciones para parvo.

Extrano a Ox muchisimo. El no cumplo 1.

Anabel

In third grade, Anabel was able to write full sentences in Spanish, although she had a tendency to string multiple independent clauses together with "y." At times her writing in Spanish was unclear. There was a strong influence of English in her Spanish spelling and sentence structure. This improved in fourth grade, and Anabel was able to develop stories and expository texts with greater cohesion, and less English influence. While Anabel's spelling was still not on a par with her classmates, it showed improvement from third to fourth grade.

In fourth grade, Anabel continued to have difficulties maintaining the same tense in her narratives, and at times, like some of the other children, she would utilize the third person for the first. In addition, she rarely maintained gender and number agreement in Spanish.

In terms of punctuation, Anabel had difficulties maintaining good punctuation throughout a text. She was able to use complete sentences most of the time, but her grammar and punctuation "petered out" towards the end of most of her written texts, a tendency that also existed in her English writing. The sample we have included is a short story students were asked to create, based on their social studies report on a particular country. In Anabel's case, she wrote a report on Morocco.

Holla mi nombre es Anabel y estos es mi a amgos Liz y Eli. Liz le gusta mucho los animales. Eli le gusta futball. Esta es mi animal. Shania el pantre es negro.

Nosotrs vamos a Fez en Marruecos. Nosotrs fuemos en un barco. Mis amigos y yo vamos a tener fiesta cuando agmos.

Cuando nosotrs estabamos en el barco un gran pulpo agaro el barco y nos metio en la agua. Ya mero nos comta en la agua.

Cuand nosotros estabamos en la agua un pez queria ayudar pero no pondia ayudarnos. El pez llamo un caballito del mar el no podia ayudarnos tampoco. Cabllito del mar llamo un tiburon el tampoco podia ayudar. El tiburon llamo un delfen el tampoco no podia ayudar. El delfen llamo un starfish pero el no puden anden.

El starfish llamo un wahal y si audamos. Thran a fez en Marruecos. Tene un gran fista.

La festa esta bueno. Nosotros tene amigos aye. Nosotros dece ados y se fueron.

Rolando

In third grade, Rolando's Spanish writing reflected the strong influence of his knowledge of English. This was especially the case when his writing was done quickly, and on an assigned topic by the teacher. In these kinds of texts he also had difficulty maintaining Spanish, and using the appropriate punctuation. On pieces where he had more time, he successfully composed the entire piece in Spanish and with no apparent English influence. An interesting aspect of Rolando's writing in third grade was his conscious use of code-switching for added rhetorical effect.

In fourth grade, Rolando's written texts were lengthy, detailed, and imaginative. He took risks as a language learner and user, attempting various registers (formal, informal, poetry, etc.) and describing events that were sometimes beyond his linguistic ability.

Rolando used full sentences that were often complex. At times, he confused present and past. And he had difficulty maintaining agreement between noun and verb forms (*los negros tenia*). His spelling improved. Any difficulties he had were similar to those native Spanish speakers have: *s/c*, *s/z*, *g/j*, and an inconsistent use of *h*. Nevertheless, he was able to use Spanish to communicate most of what he wanted to say.

After reading a story about a woman with supernatural powers, Rolando and his classmates were asked to explain something about this character. The question posed was: *¿Qué es lo que los científicos no pueden explicar sobre la Tia Zulema?*

Los cientificos no pueden explicar que tia Zulema puede hacer cosas misticos. Tia Zulema puede pronosticar el tiempo sin ver el television o los noticias. Y tambien no pueden explicar los cientificos que tia Zulema tiene un tercer ojo pero el tercer ojo de ella se ceco. Ella tambien puede abrir una puerta sin manos solo con sus anteojos y en el libro dice que puede abrir la puerta con una carta. Y estos son los cosas misticas que tia Zulema puede hacer.

The data that has been presented on the four focal children allows us to see the ways in which children have grown in their spoken and written Spanish over a two-year period. Generally we see growth in the children's oral abilities and a greater willingness to take risks by participating in class discussions and in interactions with classmates. All four children participated more frequently and used more complex language in the second year of the study. In the same way, there is growth in the children's written Spanish. Their texts are longer; they are better able to focus on a topic and provide the supporting details that are necessary to carry their writing to a conclusion. Furthermore, they are better able to utilize more complex grammatical and idiomatic structures.

Pedagogical Implications for Teaching Spanish as a Heritage Language

From our examination of children's Spanish language usage in two dual-language immersion programs, it is clear that the programs are providing children with an opportunity to learn their heritage language. The children are being exposed to complex and challenging language at the same time that they are learning content material—social studies, math, science, etc. Over the two years that we have observed and audiotaped them, the focal children have shown an increasing ability to use Spanish for their own purposes as they participate in academic study.

We believe that several factors have contributed to the growth they have experienced thus far. Below we highlight those that we feel have been critical. Additionally, we discuss those elements that we feel still need to be addressed by both teachers and administrators, particularly in regards to the Nuevomexicano students.

SPANISH-SPEAKING CLASSMATES

At Del Río where there are a great many native Spanish-speaking children, the heritage language learners have had multiple opportunities to interact with their classmates in various settings: the classroom, the playground, the cafeteria, and the neighborhood in general. This means that Anabel and Rolando have been able to hear many different kinds of Spanish, both in terms of register and dialect, and by people of different ages. They are also able to see that Spanish is useful both within and outside of the classroom, and for many different purposes.

Language learning in a classroom seldom provides these additional opportunities, and makes the teacher's job that much harder. For heritage language learners who may be learning the language so that they can communicate and interact with their families and their culture, having many opportunities to hear and speak the language probably comes closest to living in a Spanish-speaking country.

For those students at Thoreau, these opportunities are few and far between. This means that teachers and administrators need to consider additional means for having students interact with native Spanish-speakers who can be of their same age and interest groups, either during school hours, or as after-school activities.

SPANISH LANGUAGE TEXTS THAT REFLECT REAL AND AUTHENTIC SPANISH

Much of the material used in bilingual programs consists of texts, both expository and fiction, that have been translated from English. Some of these translations attempt to utilize authentic Spanish expression, others simply mimic the English phrasing (for example: *En un bosque obscuro, obscuro*, for "In a dark, dark wood"). Spanish language texts are an important source of language input for students, particularly when they represent a specific content area such as social studies or language arts. In authentic texts, students will have better models of language usage, especially for their written compositions. This will assist them in creating Spanish compositions that reflect the structure, phrasing, and rhetoric of Spanish language cultures.

CLEAR SEPARATION OF LANGUAGES

In those classrooms where teachers kept a strict separation of languages, students tended to utilize more Spanish both with the teacher and with their classmates. This in turn provided them with greater opportunities for practice and feedback. Setting these boundaries also had an additional benefit. It allowed the children who are native Spanish-speakers to act as language models or "teaching assistants," thus elevating their status in the classroom and the school.

Maintaining this separation requires an agreement among all of the teachers in the program, and across the grades. The program administrator can play an important role here. Furthermore, it requires that teachers have a high level of Spanish language proficiency in order to maintain the separation of languages in each of the content areas they are teaching.

CHALLENGING ACADEMIC MATERIAL

Public schools have long treated language minority children as if they were intellectually incapable of dealing with complex academic study, simply because they did not have the English language abilities to deal with school texts (Brisk 1998). Most research done on successful programs and strategies agree that what language minority children need are high expectations and challenging materials and activities, provided that children are given the linguistic assistance they might need. It is clear in both of the programs we have observed that all of the children—both English-speakers and Spanish-speakers—were required to interact with cognitively challenging texts and materials. Because both languages were used, both groups of students were able to participate at times as student leaders, and other times, as learners. These different roles were also factors in language learning.

REMAINING CHALLENGES

We have discussed those elements that assisted children in their acquisition of Spanish. There are still some issues to consider, particularly in the case of these four Nuevomexicano students. Valdés has pointed out that one difficulty dual-language immersion programs have is meeting the needs of two groups of students—language minority and language majority children. We believe a "third" group of children must also be considered, namely, those who are either (re)acquiring the language or learning it as a part of their heritage which has been lost to their families.

SPANISH FOR SOCIAL PURPOSES

While the children are definitely developing their Spanish language skills within the academic functions, we do not see an accompanying development of Spanish in social situations. Like the (single) immersion students in Canada, the minority language (Spanish) has yet to become an equal language of socialization, especially at Thoreau (Tarone and Swain 1995). This issue must be viewed in terms of the differential power each language has in the society, and the children's ability to perceive these differences. Nevertheless, if Spanish is to be truly revitalized for heritage language learners, there will need to be social purposes for the use of Spanish. It may well be that schools are not the vehicle for such a purpose, as Fishman has pointed out (1972). However, if revitalization is one of the expressed or implicit goals of the program, this issue must be considered with the parents of the children and the surrounding neighborhood or community members who have similar concerns.

ATTENTION TO LOCAL SPANISH LANGUAGE VARIETIES AND CULTURE

The focal children have definitely profited from the consistent and long-term exposure to Spanish, and have acquired considerably more Spanish than if they had been placed in a more traditional "bilingual program." However, there was no particular focus or strategy in place to address the particular needs of Nuevomexicano students to (re)acquire or revitalize the particular Spanish spoken by the families of focal children. At times, certain teachers who for personal reasons had knowledge and awareness of different dialects of Spanish would address the issues of dialects. However, there was no programmatic attention to these issues, or the particulars of how to teach Spanish as a heritage language.

Similarly, while the history of New Mexico was studied as a part of the social studies units, there was no particular attention given to the Spanish-speaking Nuevomexicano population. Little, if any, serious attention was given to the contributions and funds of knowledge that exist in the families of the Nuevomexicano children (Moll et al. 1992).

ATTENTION TO LANGUAGE LEARNING IN THE CLASSROOM

Programmatically, there is great deal of discussion in the dual-language immersion programs about following a 90/10 or 50/50 model. Administrators and teachers spend considerable time making sure that they adhere to the prescribed language schedules. However, these schedules were developed with a specific student population in mind, notably 50 percent minority-language speakers and 50 percent majority-language speakers. This, however, in our experience is rarely the case, even at Del Río. What might be more beneficial would be to examine the particular student populations, the linguistic resources available (both in terms of faculty and students), and the particular ways in which classrooms are structured to see how well all of these elements combine to provide for second language learning possibilities.

As Fillmore has pointed out, it is the ratio of language learners to speakers, the quality and quantity of teacher talk, and the opportunities for interaction (as provided by the structure of the class) that may be more helpful in designing the particular program that meets the needs of all of the students (Wong Fillmore 1991).

Getting Work Done

Used for accomplishing the academically related tasks and activities that are assigned or are a part of the responsibilities of children in school.

SUBCATEGORY: GETTING HELP

These are used for requesting any kind of assistance for the purpose of completing academic or other types of work. Within this subcategory are included both direct and indirect requests. The speech acts listed in this subcategory are self-explanatory. Examples taken from the data are given after each speech act.

Speech Acts

- *Request for Assistance:* "¿Cómo se dice *take care?*" "Veronica, ¿tenemos que poner los otros países?" (How do we say take care? Veronica, do we have to write down other countries?)
- *Request for Clarification:* "¿Otro grupo u otras personas?" "¿Tenemos que saltar líneas?" (The other group or other people? Do we have to skip lines?)
- *Request for Information:* "¿Dónde viven los incas?" "¿Cuántos años duró Nelson Mandela en la cárcel?" (Where do Inca people live? How many years did Nelson Mandela stay in prison?)
- *Request for Confirmation:* "¿Número tres, estás?" (Are you in number three?)
- *Request for Interpretation:* "¿Moneda? ¿Qué es moneda?" "¿Cómo se dice *A plus?*" (Currency? What is currency? How do you say A plus?)
- *Request for Action:* "Y tú haces uno." (And you do one.)

SUBCATEGORY: WORKING TOGETHER

These are the statements, comments, and other utterances that are made while working with peers who assist the accomplishment of the task. They are often responses to the requests listed above, but may be uttered without a preceding request.

Speech Acts

- *(Provides) Assists:* Usually made after a request for assistance. An utterance that directly assists in a given activity or task, for example, "¿La moneda de Francia? La moneda de Francia se llama franco francés." (The currency of France? The currency of France is called French franc.) *"You don't have to put that actually. You could put* primero . . . las arañitas nacieron primero que todos." (You don't have to put that actually. You could put first . . . the little spiders were born before the others.)

- *(Provides) Informs:* A statement or comment that provides information that is related to the accomplishment of a given activity or task, for example, "Seis por seis es igual a treinta y seis." "La capital de Polonia se llama Varsovia." (Six times six equals thirty-six. The capital of Poland is Warsaw.) "Okay, Jack, Sara, y Elias fue a la, fue para, fue para a ver que grado estás." (Okay, Jack, Sara, and Elias went to, went for, went to see what grade you are in.)

- *(Provides) Confirms:* An utterance made in response to a request for confirmation, for example, "Teacher: Rolando, ¿tú dices que no? Rolando: No." (Teacher: Rolando, you say no? Rolando: No.)

- *(Provides) Clarifies:* An utterance that assists in clarifying the procedures or tasks that are being undertaken. They are not always given upon a request, for example, "Carlos: What do we need to draw? Anabel: "Las Américas." (Anabel: The Americas.)

- *(Provides) Interprets:* Utterances that can be both an interpretation from one language to another, or a personal or given interpretation of some part or whole of an activity. For example, "No. Es un(a) opinión porque hay muchas personas que dicen que hay muchos tornados y hay personas que dicen que no hay muchos." "Es extension en inglés." (No. It's an opinion because there are many people who would say that there are many hurricanes and there are people who would say there aren't many. It's extension in English.)

- *(Provides) Explains:* An utterance used to explain what they know to get work done in whole or small group contexts. For example, "Estaba en la cárcel porque luchó para los negros." "Arqueología es como un arqueólogo que ellos pueden estudiar como agarrar historias del pasado." (He was in the prison because he fought for the black people. Archeology is like an archeologist who can study how to find histories of the past.)

- *Suggests Plan:* These are utterances in which the child suggests a plan for proceeding on a given task. For example, "Puedes usar éste para poner las líneas." (You can use this to draw the lines.) *"You guys, let's just* say, 'Vamos a ver.' *Hey James, James, James, why don't we just put,* 'Vamos a ver?' " (Hey James, James, James, why don't we just put, 'Let's see'?)

- *Assessment of Work:* These are utterances that refer to either the quality or the quantity of work accomplished at a given point. For example, "Tú eres (estás en) el número dos también? Yo soy (estoy en) en número dos." (Are you in number two also? I'm in number two.)

Talking to Myself: Intrapersonal Language

Speech Acts

- *Provides Plan:* An utterance that assists the child to plan his or her next step in a given activity or task. For example, "Nomás necesitamos Canadá de aquí." (We only need Canada from here.)
- *Self-Assesses:* An utterance in which the child evaluates his or her own ability to do something or the quality of his or her own work. For example, "Juan: Buena suerte. Gabriel: Okay, I got it, Juan. Bueno, su . . . no, I got it Juan. Buena suerte, Buena . . ." (Juan: Good luck. Gabriel: Okay, I got it, Juan. Good, lu . . . no, I got it Juan. Good luck, Good . . .)
- *Monitors Own Thinking or Speech:* These are utterances that assist the child to monitor himself or herself as a given task progresses, or in thinking out a task or problem. They can often be heard as incomplete sentences or "snatches" or self-talk. For example, "O, yo sé." (Oh, I know.) (talking to herself as she writes a sentence to answer question) "Había una brisa cuando . . . It's HABIA una brisa . . ." (There was a breeze when . . . It's there WAS a breeze . . .) "¿En qué grado estarás. ¿En qué grado estarás? ¿En qué grado estarás? Estarás, estar, estarás en el segundo or . . ." (trails off to silent thinking) (In what grade are you? In what grade are you? You are, to be, you are in the second or . . .)
- *Reports Internal State:* These are utterances that the child says to himself or herself that refer to the internal state and feelings of the child. For example, "¿Cómo enseñaste? hm, hm, me olvidé mi pregunta." (How did you teach, hm, hm, I forgot my question.)
- *Performs:* The only instances in which the child is reading out loud to himself or herself.
- *Direct Behavior:* Utterances that children use to alter what they are doing at the moment.
- *Practices Language:* These are utterances that the child says to himself or herself to practice language.

Getting Along with Others

Used to establish and maintain social relations among class members. Three subcategories are subsumed within this function.

SUBCATEGORY: CHALLENGING OTHERS

Utterances that involve attempts to raise the status of one child vis-à-vis another or others. These are accomplished through the speech acts below:

Speech Acts

- *Asserts:* A statement of opinion or purported fact, often an essential part of a dispute (Brenneis and Lein 1977). For example (responding to teacher question during instruction), "Cinco! Cinco, cinco, cinco." (Five! Five, five, five.)
- *Displays:* These are utterances in which the children display either a material item or share an anecdote that elevated their status in some way. For example, "Yo agarré A plus." (I got A plus.)
- *Teases:* Utterances that call into question the abilities or personality traits of an individual, but in a softened joking manner. For example (when Javier was getting ready to present in front of the class), "Javier es Romeo." (Javier is [like] Romeo.)
- *Insults:* Utterances that insult an individual's abilities or personality traits or family members. At times the utterances may be similar in content to teases, but they are said in an aggressive manner. For example, "Tu eres una COCHINA!" (You are a PIG!)
- *Questions:* Utterances that question the proposition that another has endorsed (Labov and Fanshel 1977). "Sr. Smith, ¿qué es un intervalo?" (Mr. Smith, what is an interval?)
- *Accuses:* Utterances that accuse another of some undesirable action.
- *Demands for Explanation:* Utterances that request an explanation, often from an opponent (Brenneis and Lein 1977).
- *Denies:* Utterances that are used commonly in response to an accusation.
- *Protests:* Utterances in which the child protests another's actions. For example, "No, no, we should put narrador first so that we can say um . . . entonces Elias dijo . . ." (No, we should put narrador first so that we can say um . . . then Elias said . . .)
- *Refuses:* Utterances in which the child refuses to comply with a request or go along as intended by others.

- *Contradictory Assertions:* An utterance that is in direct contradiction to a preceding assertion, but that is not simply a negative statement (Brenneis and Lein 1977).

- *Supportive Assertions:* Statements presenting evidence in support of an argument (Brenneis and Lein 1977). For example:
    Justin: rusco, crusco. (Rusco, crossed)
    Gabriel: cruzó. (He crossed)

- *Placates:* Utterances that are meant to placate or appease.

- *Apologizes:* Utterances in which a child directly apologizes to another.

SUBCATEGORY: DIRECTING OTHERS

Language used to regulate and influence the behavior of others. Similar to Halliday's regulatory function (Halliday 1973).

Speech Acts

- *Corrects:* Utterances that are meant to correct the language or behavior of others. For example:
    Michael: What is guestaría?
    Logan: I don't know.
    Angelique: GUSTAría! (LIKE!)
    Logan: Lookat! Estaba decenas y decenas de arañitas! And you says, Decenas . . . (Lookat! There was tens and tens of little spiders! And you says, Tens . . .)
    Angelique: Decenas? (Tens?)
    Logan: Or whatever!
    Angelique: Docenas! (Dozens!)

- *Gossips:* Utterances that refer to actions of or experiences with a third party or parties.

- *Tattles:* Utterances that report the actions of a third party or parties to someone with greater status or power than the individual speaking.

- *Alerts:* Utterances that alert another of something they may not be aware of, e.g., being called by another, possible trouble, etc. For example, "Jorge, did you hear? No comida afuera de la cafetería." (Jorge, did you hear? No food outside of the cafeteria.) "Maestra, hay una (un) problema más. (Teacher, there is one more problem.)

- *Negotiates:* Utterances in which the child attempts to negotiate the outcome of a given situation, without confronting the other about it.

For example, "I helped you on this one and this one. You should give me some cheetos. Yes, because I'm the one who came up with this, 'Docenas de arañitas se fueron.'" (Dozens of little spiders left.)

- *Reports:* Utterances in which the child recounts a personal experience or action. The difference between reports and gossip is that in reports, the child is the focus, while in gossip it is someone else. For example, "Then Elias says, 'Vamos a la escuela para firmar la forma.'" (Then Elias says, "We are going to school to sign the form.") "Yo soy parte católica. Y también cristiano, parte cristiano." (I'm part Catholic. And I'm also Christian, part Christian.)

- *Threats:* Utterances in which the child threatens another with some future action.

SUBCATEGORY: BEING FRIENDS

Language used for establishing or maintaining positive relations with others.

Speech Act:

- *Compliments:* Utterances in which one child compliments another. For example, Sergio: "Dos sugerencias?" Anabel: "Sugerencias." (Sergio: Two suggestions? Anabel: Suggestions.)

- *Jokes:* Utterances that are funny and/or are meant to amuse others. For example: "Es la araña, la aroña, la roña." (It's the spider, the aroña, the mange.)

- *Flirts:* Utterances whether serious or funny that serve to promote or maintain romantic ties between boys and girls.

- *Requests for Attention:* These are utterances that are used to request or call attention to the speaker. For example, "Mr. Smith, Señor Smith."

- *Request for Reports of Internal State:* Utterances in which a child requests that another speak of their feelings.

Conversational Devices

"Language that is used to establish, maintain or otherwise regulate . . . conversations" (Dore 1977).

Speech Acts

- *Initiates:* Utterances that initiate or attempt to initiate conversation.

- *Responds:* Utterances that serve as a response to another's move. For example, "Diez!" "Punto diez." "Es igual." (Ten! Point ten. It's the same.)

- *Delays:* Utterances that delay the need for a particular response. For example, "A . . . ja . . . " "y, y, y." (And, and, and)

- *Bids for Turn:* Utterances that serve as a bid for speaking. These are often single words or fragments, particularly when the bid is not successful. For example, "Mi, mi, mi." (Me, me, me.)

- *Supports:* Utterances that show that the child is attending to another and supports the continuation of the exchange. These are often single words or sounds that show such support.

- *Accompanies:* Utterances that "signal closer contact by accompanying a speaker's actions" (Dore 1977).

- *Redirects:* An utterance that either redirects the topic of conversation or points the participants to another topic or action. For example, "James, James, we're gonna put, estás en el segundo grado." (James, James, we're gonna put, 'You are in the second grade.')

- *Interrupts:* Utterances that are spoken out of turn before another has finished. These often consist of one word or a fragment because the interruption may be ignored by others.

- *Politeness Markers:* Utterances that are explicit markers of politeness (Dore 1977). For example, " Gracias." (Thank you.)

Talks with Teacher

Language used by the students when they address or respond to their teacher.

Speech Acts

- *Displays Knowledge:* These utterances are used by the child to show his or her knowledge to the teacher in response to the teacher's request. For example, Teacher: "¿Otro detalle que habla sobre la ubicación dentro de la región de los Four Corners, Anabel?" Anabel: "Las reservación." Teacher: "Ok." (Teacher: The other detail that talks about the habitat of the Four Corners region, Anabel? Anabel: The reservation.) Teacher: "Mmmmmjum. Gracias. ¿Y tres por siete, Gabriel?" (Teacher: Mmmmmjum. Thank you. And three times seven, Gabriel?) Gabriel: "Veintidos. Veintiuno!" (Twenty-two. Twenty-one!) Teacher: "¿Gracias, y luego que hacemos aquí?" (Thank you, and then what do we do here?) Gabriel: "Sss..ssuu..suub..sub . . . subtración." (Sss..ssuu..suub..sub . . . subtraction.)

- *Requests Clarification:* Utterances in which the student asks the teacher for a clearer definition or direction.

- *Indirect Complaint:* Utterances where the student bemoans what the teacher or another student is asking them to do. This is usually done by talking under their breath.

- *Direct Complaint:* Utterances where the student talks directly to the teacher to tell them how they feel about what they are required to do.

- *Provide Assistance:* Utterances in which students give the teacher information to help with the lesson.

- *Attempt Correct:* Utterances where the student will correct the teacher's use of Spanish or attempts to clarify what the teacher is saying.

- *Repeat:* Utterances where the student says what the teacher does.

- *Practice Language:* These utterances are used by the child to repeat the teacher's pronunciation or choice of word or words while doing their work. For example:

  Angelique: El forma. (The form.) masculine article
  Teacher: No, la forma. (No, the form) feminine article
  Angelique: La forma. (The form) feminine article

- *Politeness Marker:* Utterances that are explicit markers of politeness (Dore 1977).

- *Read Aloud:* "La calaca flaca es una persona tradicional. Es una verdu, las cosas de los muertos. Chocolates y carne muerto son tradicional de del Día de los Muertos. Aquí no treta, trata, tratamos tantas fiestas como en México."

NOTE

*All the names used for children and the schools in this chapter are pseudonyms.

REFERENCES

Benjamin, Rebecca. 1996. "The Functions of Spanish in the School Lives of Mexicano Bilingual Children." *The Bilingual Research Journal* 20 (1):135–64.
———. 1994. The Maintenance of Spanish by Mexicano Children and Its Function in their School Lives. Ph.D. diss., College of Education, University of California at Berkeley.
Brenneis, Donald Lawrence, and Laura Lein. 1977. "'You Fruithead': A Sociolinguistic Approach to Children's Dispute Settlement." In *Child Discourse*, eds. C. Mitchell-Kernan and S. Ervin-Tripp. New York: Academic Press.
Brisk, María Estela. 1998. *Bilingual Education: From Compensatory to Quality Schooling*. Mahwah, NJ: Lawrence Erlbaum Associates.

Dore, J. 1977. "'Oh Them Sherriff': A Pragmatic Analysis of Children's Responses to Questions." In *Child Discourse*, eds. C. Mitchell-Keman and S. Ervin-Tripp. New York: Academic Press.

Dyson, Ann Haas. 1997. *Writing Superheroes: Contemporary Childhood, Popular Culture, and Classroom Literacy.* New York: Teachers College Press.

Erickson, Frederick. 1982. "Taught Cognitive Learning in Its Immediate Environment: A Neglected Topic in the Anthropology of Education." *Anthropology and Education Quarterly* 13:149–80.

Fishman, Joshua A. 1972. "The Relationship between Micro- and Macro-Socio-linguistics in the Study of Who Speaks What Language to Whom and When." In *Language in Sociocultural Change: Essays by Joshua A. Fishman*, ed. J. A. Fishman. Stanford, CA: Stanford University Press.

———. 1968. "Sociolinguistic Perspectives on the Study of Bilingualism." *Linguistics* 39:21–49.

Gonzales-Berry, Erlinda, and David R. Maciel. 2000. *The Contested Homeland: A Chicano History of New Mexico.* Albuquerque: University of New Mexico Press.

Grosjean, Francois. 1985. "The Bilingual as a Competent but Specific Speaker-Hearer." *Journal of Multilingual and Multicultural Development* 6 (6):467–77.

Gutiérrez, José R. 1997. "Teaching Spanish as a Heritage Language: A Case for Language Awareness." *ADFL Bulletin* 29:33–36.

Halliday, Michael A. K. 1980. "Three Aspects of Children's Language Development: Learning Language, Learning through Language, Learning about Language." In *Oral and Written Language Development Research: Impact on the Schools*, eds. Y. M. Goodman and D. S. Strickland. Chicago: National Council of Teachers of English.

———. 1973. *Explorations of the Functions of Language.* London: Edward Arnold.

Howard, Elizabeth R., and Donna Christian. 1997. "The Development of Bilingualism and Biliteracy in Two-Way Immersion Students." ERIC Document Reproduction Service: No. ED405741.

Hymes, Dell. 1972. "Models of Interaction of Language and Social Life." In *Directions in Sociolinguistics*, eds. J. Gumperz and D. Hymes. New York: Holt, Rinehart and Winston.

Labov, William, and D. Fanshel. 1977. *Therapeutic Discourse: Psychotherapy as Conversation.* New York: Academic Press.

Lindholm, Kathryn J. 1990. "Bilingual Immersion Education: Criteria for Program Development." In *Bilingual Education: Issues and Strategies*, eds. H. Fairchild and C. Valadez. Newbury Park, CA: Sage.

Mackey, William F. 1972a. *Bilingual Education in a Binational School.* Rowley, MA: Newbury House.

———. 1972b. "The Description of Bilingualism." In *Readings in the Sociology of Language*, ed. J. Fishman. The Hague: Mouton.

Mehan, Hugh. 1982. "The Structure of Classroom Events and Their Consequences for Student Performance." In *Children In and Out of School*, eds. P. Gilmore and A. A. Glatthorn. Washington, D.C.: Center for Applied Linguistics.

Merino, Barbara, Henry T. Trueba, and Fabián A. Samaniego. 1993. *Language and Culture in Learning: Teaching Spanish to Native Speakers of Spanish*. Washington, D.C.: Falmer Press.

Moll, Luis C., C. Amanti, D. Neff, and N. Gonzalez. 1992. "Funds of Knowledge for Teaching: Using a Qualitative Approach to Connect Homes and Classrooms." *Theory into Practice* 31 (2):132–41.

Myers, M., and E. Spaulding, eds. 1997. *Standards Exemplar Series: Assessing Student Performance Grades K–5*. Urbana, IL: National Council of Teachers of English.

Roca, Ana. 1997. "Retrospectives, Advances, and Current Needs in the Teaching of Spanish to United States Hispanic Bilingual Students." *ADFL Bulletin* 20:37–43.

Rodríguez Pino, Cecilia. 1997. *Teaching Spanish to Native Speakers: A New Perspective in the 1990s*. Eric/CLL News Bulletin 1997 (cited September 1997).

Snow, Catherine E. 1993. "Bilingualism and Second Language Acquisition." In *Psycholinguistics*, eds. J. Berko Gleason and N. Bernstein Ratner. New York: Harcourt Brace College Publishers.

Swain, Merrill. 1986. "Communicative Competence: Some Roles of Comprehensible Input and Comprehensible Output in Its Development." In *Bilingualism in Education*, eds. J. Cummins and M. Swain. New York: Longman.

Tarone, Elaine, and Merrill Swain. 1995. "A Sociolinguistic Perspective on Second Language Use in Immersion Classrooms." *Modern Language Journal* 79:166–78.

Tough, Joan. 1977. *The Development of Meaning: A Study of Children's Use of Language*. New York: Wiley.

Valdés, Guadalupe, and Richard A. Figueroa. 1994. *Bilingualism and Testing: A Special Case of Bias*. Norwood, NJ: Ablex Publishing Corporation.

Wong Fillmore, Lily. 1991. "When Learning a Second Language Means Losing the First." *Early Childhood Research Quarterly* 6:323–46.

———. 1982. "Instructional Language as Linguistic Input: Second Language Learning in the Classroom." In *Communication in the Classroom*, ed. L. C. Wilkinson. New York: Academic Press.

7

Minority Perspectives on Language
Mexican and Mexican-American Adolescents' Attitudes toward Spanish and English

Karen Beckstead
Dos Pueblos High School,
Santa Barbara, California
Almeida Jacqueline Toribio
Pennsylvania State University

Introduction

Over the past years, increasing attention has been devoted to educational programs and practices that serve linguistic and cultural minority students. Recent treatments such as those of Ladson-Billings (1994), Haberman (1995), and Olsen (1997) have yielded a consistent profile: successful teachers are those who demonstrate the following:

- a strong belief in students' ability to learn and high expectations for achievement
- skill in scaffolding between what students know and knowledge to be acquired
- skill in using students' linguistic strengths to teach a second language
- an orientation to the specific community of which the students are members.

These research findings are consonant with the views of parents and other community members about how education should be most profitably delivered to linguistic minority children. Especially noteworthy is the ethnographic study carried out by Soto (1997), in which Latino families speak out on what constitutes equitable and quality education for their Spanish-speaking children. It should be readily apparent to all concerned that the wisdom of families and insights of community leaders can be valuable to educators and researchers.

Quite significantly, however, in these aforementioned research and community efforts to identify the best teaching practices, the researchers', educators', and parents' views of how children learn best do not include the views of the students themselves. This disregard for the sentiments of those most directly affected by educational practices is at odds with popular educational missions, especially those espoused in middle and junior high schools, where adolescents are granted increased rights and privileges. For example, the mission statement at Goleta Valley Junior High School, articulated in the Annual Report to the Community (1997–98), requires students to:

- respect themselves and others
- take responsibility for their individual development as lifelong learners
- participate in the diverse community as informed and conscientious citizens.

This work seeks to afford language and cultural minority students at Goleta Valley Junior High School the requisite voice for achieving this vision.[1]

More specifically, our aim is in exploring and presenting quantitative and qualitative information about the language history, language attitudes, and other cultural attributes of the Latino adolescents enrolled in English-as-a-Second-Language (ESL) courses at Goleta Valley Junior High School. These Latino youth are at a particularly critical point in their attitude toward language and language instruction because they may be exposed to conflicting sets of norms and values in the home and educational settings. Moreover, the linguistic attitudes they hold in junior high school will impact their educational achievement in high school, and their ability to enter into and succeed in higher education and/or the world of work.

The Study

THE SCHOOL COMMUNITY

The study was carried out in the context of the ESL program at Goleta Valley Junior High School in 1998.[2] Goleta, a suburb of Santa Barbara, California, has a considerable Hispanic population, which is reflected in the school enrollment. In the 1998–99 academic year, the school enrolled an estimated

900 students, of which approximately one-third were classified as Hispanic.[3] Many of the Hispanic students had families that had resided in the area for generations, and as a result had been born and raised in California; others had arrived at a young age and had significant English language proficiency when they entered junior high; and still others were recent newcomers who had immigrated to the U.S. as adolescents, speaking little or no English.[4] The Hispanic students represented the continuum from those who had limited Spanish language proficiency, to those who were functional Spanish-English bilinguals, to a smaller number who were classified as non-English-speaking. Students were assessed upon entering the school and biannually, using several instruments to measure fluency in both English and Spanish (speaking, writing, reading, and listening proficiencies). In accordance with their scores, students were placed in appropriate classes, and could receive instruction and materials in Spanish, or attend "sheltered" classes that implemented specifically designed academic instruction in English for content areas such as math, science, and social studies.[5]

The ESL program at Goleta Valley Junior High School was unique for several reasons. First, the ESL Department employed dedicated and committed teachers who were sensitive to the demands and challenges of English language learners.[6] Once students successfully completed the primary language program, as determined by language testing and class work, they were transitioned into a class with a teacher who had been trained to work with second language learners. Second, two of the ESL Department's teachers held multiple subject credentials, in addition to single subject credentials. As a consequence, ESL students could remain with the same teacher for two, three, or four periods each day, studying English, math, science, and history. This situation helped create an environment in which students were at ease with the teacher and with each other and were not afraid to experiment with their newly acquired language skills.

THE SAMPLE

The forty-three students who participated in this study fall into two groupings. The first group consists of students who had arrived within the twelve months preceding observation. These students received three periods per day of primary language instruction from a teacher proficient in Spanish, employing Spanish-language materials; they also received three periods per day of English, delivered by two teachers, only one of which was proficient in Spanish. The second group consists of those students who had arrived as school-aged children at varying times and ages and demonstrated beginning through advanced English-language competency; this latter category is further subdivided by the students' length of residency in the U.S.

Of these forty-three students, only twenty-eight had completed the full complement of survey materials at the time of the writing of this report.[7] Of these twenty-eight, twelve had lived in Santa Barbara County for a period from four months to two years, nine had lived in the U.S. for three to seven years, and seven had lived in the U.S. for nine to fourteen years, including four born in Southern California.[8] We maintain this three-way division in order to explore what correlation, if any, obtains between length of residency and linguistic behaviors:

- Group 1: 12 participants; 0.4–2.11 years U.S. residency
- Group 2: 9 participants; 3–7 years U.S. residency
- Group 3: 7 participants; 9–14 years U.S. residency, including four born in California

THE TEST INSTRUMENTS

A four-part battery was designed and administered to each student:

- Part I: Extensive background component
- Part II: Language proficiency and usage measure
- Part III: Language attitudes surveys
- Part IV: Open-ended questions on instrumental and integrative value of language

The extensive background questionnaire explored personal history, e.g., place of birth, length of residence, and family occupational history. The component on language proficiency and language usage referenced educational background and language(s) of instruction, language use patterns in the home (who speaks what to whom and where), frequency of access to language(s) across domains (e.g., popular press and media, and leisure and play activities), and a scale of proficiency across receptive and productive modalities. The third component incorporated surveys on language attitudes, including items referencing linguistic (in)security, self-identity, and perceived language vitality in the local community. The final component presented open-ended questions on the instrumental and integrative value of Spanish and English. All materials were prepared in Spanish and English to promote students' comfort with the tasks.[9] The ensuing discussion will focus on selected items from the various questionnaires, rather than a discussion of the full battery for all twenty-eight students to avoid extreme concision.

The Results

These direct measurements have yielded valuable data concerning the relationship between language background, language usage, language attitudes, and other cultural attributes of the Latino adolescents sampled. In the discussion of the results, each respondent is assigned a number and letter; the number corresponds to the group (e.g., Groups 1–3 as described above), and the letter further specifies their length of U.S. residence.

- Participants 1a–1l (twelve participants in Group 1: 0.2–2.11 years in U.S.)
- Participants 2a–2i (nine participants in Group 2: 3–7 years in U.S.)
- Participants 3a–3g (seven participants in Group 3: 9–14 years in U.S.)

LANGUAGE USAGE

The general language profiles revealed in the surveys reflect the balancing of two main factors: the necessity for communicating with the dominant English-speaking society, and the benefits associated with Spanish language retention. As shown in (1), "Language of the home," Spanish language use is maintained in the home by all of the participants, owing to interactions with Spanish-dominant speakers, such as older adult relatives and younger siblings—all of them interact exclusively in Spanish with at least one relative at home; Spanish may be used in favor of English with one parent; and Spanish and English both may be used equally with siblings, or English may displace Spanish altogether, especially with other peers.

1. Language of the home/Lengua en casa

   1=All Spanish/Todo en español; 2=More Spanish than English/Más español que inglés; 3=Same amount of both/Ambos en igual medida; 4=More English than Spanish/Más inglés que español; 5=All English/Todo en inglés

   1: all (1a-1l; 2a-2i; 3a-3g) interact exclusively in Spanish with at least one relative
   2: 2b, 3b, with father only
   3: 1l, 2b, 2d, 2f, 2h, 2i, 3b, with siblings; 3f
   4: —
   5: 3b, 3d, 3g, with siblings

2. Language with close friends/Lengua con amigos íntimos

   1: 1a, 1f, 1g, 1h, 1j, 2a, 3d
   3: 1b, 1e, 2g
   3: 1c, 1d, 1i, 1l, 2b, 2c, 2f, 2i, 3f
   4: 1k, 3b, 3c, 3e
   5: 2d, 3g

3. Language with school peers/Lengua con compañeros de escuela
   1: 1a, 1c, 1f, 1i, 1j
   2: 1b, 1e, 1g, 1l, 2g
   3: 1d, 1h, 2b, 2c, 2f, 3c, 3d, 3f
   4: 1k, 2i, 3b, 3e
   5: 2a, 2d, 3g

4. Language of the neighborhood/Lengua del vecindario
   1: 1a, 1f, 1g, 1h, 1j, 1k, 2a, 2f, 3b, 3g
   2: 1b, 1e, 2g, 2i
   3: 1c, 1d, 1i, 2b, 2c, 3a
   4: 3c, 3e, 3f
   5: 1l, 2d, 3d

Notably, Group 3 participants (those with nine to fourteen years U.S. residency) tend toward greater English-language usage, at home with siblings, with close friends, and with school peers, although they reserve Spanish for the home. Thus, for Group 3 adolescents, as for many U.S. Latinos, Spanish and English together constitute their linguistic competence in a singular sense, and their linguistic performance may draw primarily upon English, primarily on Spanish, or on a combination of the two, as required by the speech situation and interlocutors. We must caution, however, that this reduction of domains of Spanish-language usage could be a sign of incipient language shift.[10]

Despite the decrease in Spanish-language usage with increased length of U.S. residency, the data in (5) and (6) inspire some degree of optimism: all of the adolescents regularly avail themselves of Spanish-language media. However, many had received limited formal instruction in Spanish, and demonstrate Spanish-language abilities that are largely receptive or conversational. Without sustained effort to develop and advance Spanish-language literacy, the language will be subject to attrition (as will become evident in the transcripts presented later in the section under the heading "Language Attitudes").[11] In this respect, the data in (7) are cause for concern: a good number of the adolescents are not regularly reading in Spanish, and it is likely that those who report reading Spanish language materials are doing so only in the classroom, rather than developing more extensive reading habits.[12]

5. How often do you listen to radio in Spanish?
   ¿Con cuánta frecuencia escucha la radio en español?

   1=Every day/Todos los días; 2= A few times a week/Algunas veces por semana; 3= Once a week/Una vez a la semana; 4= Once or twice a month/Una o dos veces al mes; 5=Once every three or four months/Una vez cada tres o cuatro meses; 6=*Once in six months/Una vez en seis meses;* 7=*Once a year/Una vez al año;* 8=*Once every few years/Una vez dada varios años;* 9=*Never/Nunca*

1=*Every day/Todos los días*

1: 1d, 1g, 1h, 1i, 1j, 1k, 1l, 2a, 2c, 2e, 2g, 3f

2: 1c, 1e, 2b, 2f, 2h, 2i, 3a, 3b, 3c, 3d

3: 1a, 1f

4: 3e

5: —

6: —

7: —

8: —

9: 1b, 2d, 3g

9=*Never/Nunca*

6. How often do you watch television programs in Spanish?
   ¿Con cuánta frecuencia ve programas de televisión en español?

   1=*Every day/Todos los días*

   1: 1a, 1b, c, 1d, 1e, 1f, 1g, 1h, 1j, 1k, 1l, 2a, 2b, 2c, 2e, 2f, 2g, 3b, 3c, 3d, 3e, 3f, 3g

   2: 1i, 2h, 2i, 3a

   3: —

   4: —

   5: —

   6: —

   7: —

   8: —

   9: 2d

   9=*Never/Nunca*

7. How often do you read magazines or books in Spanish?
   ¿Con cuánta frecuencia lee revistas o libros en español?

   1=*Every day/Todos los días*

   1: 1a, 1b, 1c, 1d, 1h, 1i, 1j, 3a

   2: 1e, 1f, 1g, 2a, 2c, 2f, 2g, 2h, 3b, 3d

   3: 3f

   4: 3c

   5: 3e

   6: —

   7: 2e

   8: —

   9: 1k, 1l, 2b, 2d, 2i, 3g

   9=*Never/Nunca*

LANGUAGE VITALITY

We also sought to measure the students' perception of the status of Spanish and English in their communities. The vast majority of our adolescent participants attach a high value to Spanish, as shown in (8).[13] A contributing factor, to be sure, was the positive school environment in which there is little ambivalence or negative judgment associated with Spanish.

8. How highly do you regard Spanish?
   ¿Qué consideración tiene usted del español?

   1=*Low/Baja*

   1: —

   2: 1g, 3g

   3: 2i

   4: 2d

   5: 1e

   6: 3f

   7: 1a, 1b, 1c, 1d, 1f, 1i, 1j, 1k, 2a, 2b, 2c, 2e, 2f, 2g, 2h, 3c, 3d

   7=*High/Alta*

English is also highly valued, although to a somewhat lesser degree than Spanish, as shown in (9). This finding is significant, especially in light of misinformed claims about students' reluctance toward or opposition to English.

9. How highly do you regard English?
   ¿Qué consideración tiene usted del inglés?

   1=*Low/Baja*

   1: 1d

   2: —

   3: 1a, 1e

   4: 1j, 1k, 2f

   5: 1f, 1g, 1i, 2a, 2c, 2h

   6: 1c, 2e, 3d, 3g

   7: 1b, 1l, 2b, 2d, 2g, 3c, 3f

   7=*High/Alta*

The responses of participant 2d—neutral on the status of Spanish and highly positive on English—merit attention, as this adolescent also revealed an English-language dominance across speech domains (with close friends, with peers, and in the neighborhood). Save such exceptional cases, the generally positive view of Spanish is in keeping with its extensive use in Latino homes and neighborhoods.

LANGUAGE ATTITUDES

As the models show, all of the adolescents sampled recognize the importance of English. The impressions gleaned from these quantitative measures are confirmed in the students' introspective responses. Students' candid comments relate explicit information that is useful to researchers and educators. When asked why it is important to study English, the adolescents' answers converged on instrumental factors, as shown in (10a–e); but there are also integrative factors manifest in the positive disposition toward English (10f–h).[14] Note that these responses are faithfully reproduced, without editing.[15]

10. Why is it important to learn English?
    ¿Por qué es importante aprender inglés?

    a. Te alluda a superarte no solo en los Estados Unidos también en Mexico porque puedes conseguir megor trabajo. (PN)
    It helps you to excel not only in the United States but also in Mexico because you can get better employment.

    b. Porque con el ingles puedes ir donde tu quieras. (VA)
    Because with English you can go anywhere you want.

    c. Para tener una carrera que nosotros quieramos como doctor. (DU)
    To have a career that we want like (being a) doctor.

    d. Porque ya sabiendolo puedes trabajar en muchas partes del mundo. (SC)
    Because knowing it you can work in many parts of the world.

    e. Para mi es muy importante para alguna profecion. (DG)
    For me it is important for some profession.

    f. Porque puedes agarrar un buen trabajo y tender una educacion y puedes comunicarte con norte americanos. (CC)
    Because you can get a good job and have an education and you can communicate with North Americans.

    g. Porque en EUA se habla ingles. Tambien porque mis clases no todo el tiempo las boy a tener en español. (CM)
    Because in the USA English is spoken. Also because I won't always have my classes in Spanish.

    h. Porque es necesario en los Estados Unidos. (RT)
    Because it is necessary in the United States.

The students eagerly embrace English and the opportunities it presents, unaware of the nonlinguistic obstacles to social and economic advancement that await them. However, their innocent enthusiasm is buttressed by a strong work ethic and tempered by a maturity and worldview that is unexpected in thirteen- and fourteen-year-old children.

  Our students' attitudes are well defined: they don't want their educational advancement to be compromised because of language. When asked whether and why they preferred to have instruction delivered in Spanish, they offered the responses in (11):

11. Why do you prefer classes in Spanish?
    ¿Por qué prefiere las clases en español?

    a. Por que le entiendo mas a la maestra y no repruebo mis examenes y tengo mas posibilidades de pasar megor a la High School. (PN)
       Because I understand the teacher better and I don't fail my exams and I have greater possibilities to pass to high school.

    b. Por una parte si las prefiero porque asi aprendo mas rapido de Mate, Social Studies y todas las demas materias. Pero por el otro lado prefiero tender clases en ingles para aprenderlo porque si sigo con clases en español nunca voy aprender. (RR)
       In one respect I do prefer them [in Spanish] because that way I learn math, social studies and other subjects more quickly. But in another respect I prefer to have classes in English to learn it because if I continue with classes in Spanish I will never learn.

    c. En el ingles . . . me pongo nerviosa y no entiendo. (LM)
       In English I get nervous and I don't understand.

    d. Porque me gusta entender mis clases y en el ingles pienso que no entenderia todo lo que el maestro ponga de trabajo y bajaria mis calificaciones . . . (CM)
       Because I like to understand my classes and in English I think that I would not understand all of what the teacher gives for work and it would lower my grades.

    e. Para aprender mas el ingles y el español porque unas clases nomas tienen puro ingles y yo quiero aprender los dos idiomas. (CM)
       To better understand English and Spanish because some classes have only English and I want to learn both languages.

    f. (1)Por que me ciento mas agusto (2) por que ciento que el ingles no es para mi. (DG)
       (1) because I feel more comfortable (2) because I feel that English is not for me.

    g. Porque es nuestro idioma. (CC)
       Because it [Spanish] is our language.

Thus, while students are anxious to learn to speak and understand basic English, they are equally concerned about developing the skills needed for academic participation and success, in junior high school and beyond. As clearly articulated by the students, notably RR in (11b), they feel pressure to gain sufficient English language development for acceptance in the U.S., but feel a strong desire to gain access to the full core curriculum. However, they are not discouraged by the apparent contradiction, and they recognize that they may have to sacrifice one for the other. In resolving the dilemma, most students link their native Spanish language with their potential academic success: the comments in (11a–e) indicate that when instruction is delivered in Spanish, students are less anxious, less confused, less likely to fall behind, and less likely to fail.[16] Also implied in the students' expressions, particularly (11f–g), are views that speak to more affective themes surrounding culture, identity, and self-worth, factors that are also clearly implicated in academic success. These responses beg the question: should English or Spanish take precedence?

Turning to English, we've observed that these Latino adolescents endorse the English language on instrumental grounds, and some of them support English on integrative grounds as well. Still, only a handful promote English on affective grounds, as shown in (12); a majority recognize the difficulty in developing English proficiency and literacy, and feel that the language will remain "foreign" to them:

12. How do you feel when you speak English?
    ¿Cómo se siente cuando habla inglés?

   a. Me siento que ya voy aprendiendo mas ingles, tambien orguyoso de mi mismo porque el ingles es muy importante aprender. (VA)
      I feel that I am learning more English, also proud of myself because English is very important to learn.

   b. Porque con el ingles tu puedes ir a todas partes y no te da verguensa preguntar por algo y no te sientes mal. (KW)
      Because with English you can go anywhere and you don't get embarrassed to ask for something and you don't feel bad.

   c. Me siento bien porque pienso que lo que e vivido aqui no a sido a lo tonto y siento que si e avansado bien mucho. (RR)
      I feel good because I think that what I've lived here hasn't been for nothing and I feel that I have indeed advanced quite a lot.

   d. Yo quiciera entrar alas clases de ingles cuando lla supiera hablar mas, saber un poquito mas. (CM)

I would like to enroll in English classes when I will already know more, to know a little more.

e. Me siento un poco raro porque no se si lo estoy diciendo o pronunciando correctamente. (PN)
I feel a little odd because I don't know whether I am speaking or pronouncing correctly.

 f. Yo casi no me gusta hablarlo mucho porque hay veces que creo que no lo digo bien y pienso que la gente se va a burlar. (SC)
I almost don't like to speak much because there are times when I think that I don't say it right and I think that people will make fun of me.

g. no estoy acostumbrada atodo esto . . . cuando hablo ingles me siento muy rrara. (DG)
I am not used to all of this . . . when I speak English I feel very strange.

Again, students' responses manifest the belief that if they learn English and work hard, they will be successful; they demonstrate a strong desire to overcome the English language barrier as quickly as possible in order to advance in their studies.

CULTURAL IDENTITY

The hypothesis linking students' language attitudes to achievement is one that can easily be made: students' views of their own language is assumed to be strongly linked to self-concept, which is, in turn, related to achievement (consult the vast literature that is attempting to explain the educational achievement of some ethnic groups). We have already documented that our students have a highly positive disposition towards their heritage language. The data in (13) and (14) demonstrate that they value their Latino culture as part of their self-identity:

13. Latino culture is an important reflection of who I am.
    La cultura latina es un reflejo importante de quien soy.

    1=Agree/Completamente de acuerdo
    1: 1b, 1c, 1d, 1f, 1g, 1j, 1k, 2d, 2g, 2h, 3a, 3b, 3d, 3f
    2: 1h, 1i, 2c
    3: 2a, 2i, 3g
    4: —
    5: 1e, 3e
    6: 2b
    7: 1a, 1l, 2f, 3c
    7=Strongly disagree/Totalmente en desacuerdo

14. Latino culture is an important part of my self-image.
    La cultura latina es un reflejo importante de mi propia imagen.

    1=Agree/Completamente de acuerdo
    1: 1a, 1c, 1d, 1f, 1k, 2a, 3d, 3f
    2: 1g, 1h, 1i, 2d, 3b
    3: 1e, 1j, 2b, 2c, 2g, 2i, 3a, 3e
    4: 1b, 2f, 2h, 3g
    5: —
    6: —
    7: 1l, 3c
    7=Strongly disagree/Totalmente en desacuerdo

Thus, the students' attested language loyalty is likely due to their value systems; they may wish to maintain their native Spanish because they associate it with their Latino identity. These findings should serve to allay the fears commonly voiced by Latino parents who believe that their children's shift toward English will occasion a shift in cultural values and identity.

Summary

In summary, the findings suggest that students place a high value on both the native Spanish and the socially dominant English. Students recognize the value of Spanish in the preservation of their Latino identity, while recognizing that wider educational and employment opportunities are available to them through English. Though instrumental and integrative factors favored English, our findings additionally revealed a strong preference for Spanish in the classroom; students articulated empowering agendas that could ultimately benefit them and their school and home communities. Of course, the extrapolation of generalizations from this to other settings or communities may be limited. However, the present study has already made a significant contribution in accessing, validating, and reporting the perspectives of Spanish-speaking students—those most directly affected by educational programs and philosophies—toward the role of Spanish and English in their education and in their lives.

Pedagogical Implications for Instruction of Spanish as a Heritage Language

The findings reported here may be appreciated as an exhortation to educators to carry out similar exercises. Language attitude surveys may be incorporated into middle and high school curricula as questionnaires to be completed individually or collaboratively, in the classroom or at home. Alternatively, the survey questions can provide the basis for teacher-facilitated peer discussions. The mere act of acknowledging that students' heritage language is worthy of examination will foment an affective environment that translates into greater engagement on the part of the students. The positive findings towards the Spanish language may be posted on student-generated classroom bulletin boards dedicated to works reflecting cultural heritage and pride. In future classroom activities, students may be motivated to work together towards the common goal of advancing their Spanish language skills. The advantages of bilingualism should be emphasized for all—not only for those who may wish to maintain a heritage language, but for those who will acquire a foreign language as well. A career day could showcase the benefits of bilingualism in the workforce; and an alliance with local community organizations could further foster the desire to develop the local minority language among all students. Finally, a workshop or lecture series could guide students and teachers towards a greater understanding of minority language situations; especially relevant for the Spanish-speaking community at issue would be talks delivered by scholars in Mexican-American studies, sociology, anthropology, and linguistics. More generally, the information and insights gathered from these activities can serve to educate practitioners and administrators about students' perceptions of the role of heritage language instruction and, in turn, assist educators in more adequately meeting the needs of linguistic minority children.

NOTES

1. Karen Beckstead served as ESL Department chairperson at Goleta Valley Junior High School.

2. Owing to changes in instructional design, this particular program model is no longer being implemented.

3. School records indicated that the population of the school was predominantly middle and lower middle class, with approximately 52 percent white, 35 percent Hispanic, 6 percent Asian, 2 percent Filipino, and 1 percent Native American.

4. Other languages were also represented in the school: Korean, Swedish, Portuguese, and Taiwanese.

5. Sheltered classes were those in which dependence on the English language as a medium of instruction was reduced, thereby "sheltering" limited English proficiency students; curriculum content in these classes was not diminished. The premise was that students could not learn academic content if they could not understand the language of the teacher or the language in the textbook.

6. The ESL teachers were trained in SDAIE instruction and bilingual methodology, and held CLAD and/or BCLAD credentials as required by the State of California in order to teach English language learners.

7. Participation in the study was voluntary, so not all of the students in these classes elected to participate. Moreover, the difficulty level of the questionnaire, which was designed for use with university students, proved to be a significant challenge for the adolescents, especially given the constraints of the class period. Finally, participants were encouraged to disregard those survey items that proved confusing or otherwise unsettling.

8. All but one of the Latino pupils sampled were of Mexican origin.

9. The surveys were administered during the regular school day, with the authorization of the school principal and the permission of the parents. The time required to complete the surveys was approximately two nonconsecutive hours.

10. Home language use is the only area in which a noticeable disparity emerged in cross-group comparisons. Overall, there is a high level of comparability among the three groups (although a different picture could have emerged had we incorporated supplementary data from these and remaining participants). In addition, the lack of categorical agreement across survey items serves to remind us that the adolescents' attitudes, beliefs, and behavioral patterns are in formation.

11. The vast research literature on second-language learning shows that literacy in one's home language is the best basis for developing literacy in a second language.

12. Of course, this represents normal behavior for the age group and not behavior specific to these Latino adolescents.

13. Note that some participant responses are not recorded here due to the improper completion of particular items on the questionnaire.

14. In safeguarding students' anonymity, we failed to cross-code these introspective questionnaires with the personal background, language proficiency, and language attitudes questionnaires; the reader can, however, draw comparisons across items by noting the participants' (fictitious) initials.

15. As amply attested in their writing samples, these adolescents have had little opportunity to develop advanced Spanish-language literacy, and as such, they demonstrate greater variation in form. The heritage language must not only be protected and maintained, but advanced in educational practice.

16. The attitudes expressed by participants may not coincide with those of students outside of the "sheltered" courses in the school, where classes that address language issues may be stigmatized. As noted, students in these classes receive identical curricular content as their seventh- and eighth-grade counterparts, although the teacher's approach may be modified to accommodate the needs of the English-language learners.

REFERENCES

Haberman, Martin. 1995. *Star Teachers of Children in Poverty*. West Lafayette, IN: Kappa Delta Pi.

Ladson-Billings, Gloria. 1994. *The Dreamkeepers*. New York: Jossey-Bass.

Olsen, Laurie. 1997. *Made in America: Immigrant Students in Our Public Schools*. New York: The New Press.

Santa Barbara High School District. *Goleta Valley Junior High School, An Annual Report to the Community*. 1997–98 School Year.

Soto, Lourdes Díaz. 1997. *Language, Culture, and Power: Bilingual Families and the Struggle for Quality Education*. Albany: State University of New York Press.

8

META: A Model for the Continued Acquisition of Spanish by Spanish/English Bilinguals in the United States

Roberto Luis Carrasco
Florencia Riegelhaupt
Northern Arizona University

Introduction

META is a holistic model for the acquisition of languages (Carrasco and Riegelhaupt 1992), and it is at once a research design, a curriculum, and a pedagogy. It is particularly useful for the continued acquisition of Spanish by heritage learners. While META was first developed and tested in language and culture immersion contexts in Mexico (Carrasco and Riegelhaupt 1994; Riegelhaupt and Carrasco 2000), it was also refined and tested in American university Spanish language classrooms in which heritage speakers were participants. This article describes the approach in the context of its appropriateness and usefulness to heritage language and culture acquisition.

We begin with a review of the literature on the acquisition of Spanish by heritage/native Spanish-speaking bilinguals followed by a historical overview on the development of the META model. The next section describes META. It includes an explanation of four underlying theoretical concepts, followed by a description of the curriculum design and a summary. In the conclusion, along with recommendations, we discuss pedagogical implications for instruction of heritage language in the United States, and research implications of employing the META approach for the further acquisition of Spanish by heritage learners.

A Brief Review of Literature on the Acquisition of Spanish by Heritage/Native Spanish-Speaking Bilinguals in the United States

Research on the Spanish of Chicano heritage speakers began to receive special attention in the 1970s (Hernández Chávez, Cohen, and Beltrano 1975; Elías-Olivares 1976; Riegelhaupt-Barkin 1976; Carranza 1977; Valdés-Fallis 1975; Valdés-Fallis and Teschner 1977; Elías-Olivares and Valdés-Fallis 1979; Teschner, Bills, and Craddock 1976). In the late 1970s through the 1990s, high schools and institutions of higher education implemented courses for heritage speakers and with them came more related studies on (1) the linguistic characteristics of heritage speakers (Barkin and Brandt 1980; Barkin 1978, 1979, 1980 a–d, 1981 a–b; Carrasco 1979, 1981a–b, 1984; Carrasco and Riegelhaupt, 1992; Carrasco, Vera, and Cazden 1980; Floyd 1981; Villa Crésap 1997; Valdés and Geoffrion-Vinci 1998), (2) an appropriate pedagogy for teaching Spanish to Native Speakers (Barkin 1981a; Riegelhaupt-Barkin 1985; Faltis 1990; Rodríguez Pino 1993; Rodríguez Pino and Villa 1994), (3) the placement, and the oral and written Spanish language proficiency of heritage students (Teschner 1990; Valdés 1997, 2001; Valdés and Geoffrion-Vinci 1998), (4) professor, family, community, and student attitudes toward local U.S. varieties of Spanish and the learning of Spanish in U.S. classrooms (Hidalgo 1990; Delany-Barmann 1997), and (5) discourse analysis of planned and unplanned speech and Mexican and Chicano students (Valdés and Geoffrion-Vinci 1998).

These studies have contributed knowledge and insights about psychological, cultural, social, and linguistic issues regarding heritage speakers' continued acquisition of Spanish. They also have proposed various pedagogical approaches that seek to address the needs of heritage learners studying in traditional high school, community college, and university classrooms. The literature on heritage language acquisition coupled with our documented teaching experiences in both immersion and classroom settings led us to develop the META teaching and learning activities based on four interrelated key concepts that will be discussed in a later section.

Historical Overview of the Development of META

In the 1970s very few textbooks were available for heritage language populations. These textbooks tended to use a corrective, comparative, standard/nonstandard approach and included numerous exercises directed at pointing out nonstandard characteristics and eradicating them. Correcting of oral language was also commonplace. Correcting, especially of speech during discourse, can be detrimental to the self-esteem of heritage learners, and may discourage the use and further acquisition of Spanish (Riegelhaupt and Carrasco 2000).

Knowledge about the strategic importance of affective variables in language acquisition was unavailable. Many U.S.-born bilinguals themselves became Spanish language teachers and linguists. They recognized the need to inform the profession about the issues involved in the continued maintenance and acquisition of U.S. native languages. Their own Spanish-language learning experiences did not build upon their linguistic and cultural knowledge. Rather, they experienced what Peñalosa (1980) coined to be "languagism," or prejudice toward Spanish and especially toward their dialects and informal registers.

Researchers began to point out the need for special programs for Spanish-English bilinguals (Valdés-Fallis 1981; Merino, Trueba, and Samaniego 1993). Teachers and students alike, be they native or non-native Spanish speakers, also recognized that these two populations had different needs and desires. Discussion about problems in being overly critical and correcting oral speech began to unfold. How should we treat the home language? How should we build on it rather than criticize and/or eradicate its nonstandard aspects? Why do Spanish-English bilinguals experience difficulties in typical Spanish classes?

Sociolinguistic knowledge began to inform classroom practices, especially in the case of minorities in bilingual elementary education programs. Similar issues were surfacing for adolescent and adult bilingual populations. Were they being treated equitably? Was their language recognized and given the respect it deserved? What should be the role of Spanish language educators in the teaching of Spanish to native speakers?

In 1981, Barkin (1981a) designed a course sequence directed at meeting the specific needs of this population. This sequence concentrated principally on literacy development, with emphasis on productive writing skills. Instead of a textbook, a personalized, individualized methodology that built on existing linguistic skills was developed. Reading selections included essays, poems, and stories about contemporary sociopolitical and educational issues. Writing assignments involved documenting oral speech on tape and in transcribed form, allowing students to understand the principal differences between speech and writing, writing about their own life and that of members of their bilingual communities, writing poetry that reflected their hopes, dreams, and difficulties as minorities in the U.S. A "whole language" approach (Goodman, Goodman, and Flores 1979) was adopted and all material used came from original sources. Students realized that there was a purpose and an audience for their work.

In addition to prior research and teaching experimentations, META also was informed by important findings about heritage language learners' experiences in their continued acquisition of Spanish during immersion in Guanajuato, Mexico. Spanish/English Arizona bilingual teachers were immersed in a five-week summer language and culture program (Carrasco and Riegelhaupt 1985, 2000). To maximize the benefits derived from their immersion experience, instructors Carrasco and Riegelhaupt utilized the context of the Mexican host family and daily activities in and around the Guanajuato community as the principal teaching and learning environments. Rather than typical Spanish language classes, class meetings took on the form of language seminars, where observations and recordings from family and community experiences became principal topics of discussion and analysis.

There were bilingual teachers in the summer immersion program who were heritage speakers of a variety of Chicano Spanish at various levels of proficiency. The program also had second-language learners who learned Spanish in school. META activities revealed that students were receiving differential treatment by their Guanajuato host families (Carrasco and Riegelhaupt 1994; Riegelhaupt and Carrasco 2000). While the non-Chicano bilingual teachers appeared to be receiving preferential treatment, the Chicano teachers were experiencing an identity crisis as the result of a language and culture clash with their Guanajuato host families. Through META interviews and interactive journals, Chicano bilingual teachers (all heritage learners) revealed discomfort in speaking Spanish with their host families. These heritage learners noted that correction strategies were far more harsh when directed at them than when directed at their second-language learner colleagues.

META data collection and analyses helped instructors not only to identify the type of errors committed, but also to document the manner in which the families corrected their guests. Instructors, armed with this knowledge, were able to implement effective strategies to help heritage learners learn from their interactions with Guanajuato native speakers of Spanish.

Mexican host family interviews with us revealed their contrasting attitudes toward their non-Hispanic and Hispanic American guests. Such instructor research and involvement during the first week of immersion allowed us to construct and propose a set of expectations, a paradigm that these Mexican host families were employing with their Mexican American guests (see table 8.1). Later, when using the META approach in our language classes we noted that the paradigm based on the Guanajuato data was identical to that found in university Spanish language classes. The same expectations of a more standard, formal variety, a generic Spanish, existed (see figure 8.1).

The Mexican host families' paradigm demonstrates that Mexican host families had the same expectations for educated Chicanos as they did for educated Mexicans and that these families did not expect as much from educated American non-Hispanics. Through interviews, the families cited the lack of finesse in language. "Hablan como de rancho; un español mocho, hablan pocho." After all, these Mexican families saw a brown face, a person who seemed to speak Spanish without an American accent, whose last name was Hispanic, who could communicate in Spanish, who was doing graduate work at a university and who was a professional teacher. They expected him/her to speak Spanish like educated people from their own community. They never even considered the fact that these same individuals could communicate in two languages and that they had been educated principally through English, rather than Spanish, as the language of instruction.

Housing a non-Hispanic American teacher guest, in spite of lack of language proficiency and cultural knowledge, was viewed by the Mexican families as more socially prestigious than housing a Chicano guest. "Mándenos unas güeritas la próxima vez" ("Next time send us some [blue-eyed] blonde girls"), they stated in family interviews with the researchers/instructors.

These U.S. Spanish-English bilinguals also documented their own language experiences in the surrounding Guanajuato community. A similar dialect of Spanish, where archaisms such as *vide, truje, traiba, muncho,* etc., occurred, was spoken by uneducated Guanajuato residents both in Guanajuato proper and the surrounding *pueblitos* and *ranchos.* If uneducated people in their own community spoke Spanish with similar characteristics, their Chicano heritage learner guests must also be uneducated, they thought. Yet, this was not the case at all. They simply were using their own cultural and sociolinguistic knowledge to detect social class and cultural differences.

Once this knowledge was made explicit to all parties, a potentially negative psychological, cultural, and linguistic experience was short-circuited. The host Mexican families began to work closely and effectively with their Chicano teacher guests once they recognized the various factors that had caused them to develop negative attitudes toward the variety of Spanish spoken by these heritage learners. Knowing that they were helping the teachers of Mexican immigrant children, perhaps the teachers of their own grandchildren living in the United States, also contributed to their desire to reevaluate their own negative attitudes and reactions about the Spanish of these individuals.

Like Mexican host families' expectations, many Spanish university in-

Table 8.1 *University Spanish Teacher and Mexican Host Families Expectations*

UNIVERSITY SPANISH TEACHER EXPECTATIONS: A PARADIGM FOR SPANISH NATIVE/HERITAGE SPEAKERS AND MONOLINGUAL ENGLISH STUDENTS	MEXICAN HOST FAMILIES EXPECTATIONS: A PARADIGM FOR MEXICAN AMERICAN AND OTHER AMERICAN GUESTS

A. If you are an "American" college/university student:

1. The type of Spanish or levels of proficiency are not considered important. There is a class available to you that takes into consideration your past formal (classroom) and informal experiences with Spanish.	1. The type of Spanish or levels of proficiency are not important.
2. "Mexican" social and cultural knowledge is not expected from you.	2. "Mexican" social and cultural knowledge is not expected from you.
3. You are not expected to be aware of dialect and register differences as expressed. Social class differences through language are not detected in either English or Spanish.	3. You are not expected to be aware of dialect and register differences as expressed. Social class differences through language are not detected in either English or Spanish.

B. If you were born, raised, and educated in Mexico or any other Spanish-speaking country and are a university student:

1. Your Spanish language should reflect that of an educated person (i.e., "standard" Spanish is expected).	1. Your Spanish language should reflect that of an educated person (i.e., "standard" Spanish is expected).
2. You are expected to have the social and cultural knowledge (etiquette, knowing how to behave in social and academic settings, etc.) and be able to demonstrate it both orally and in writing utilizing the dialect and register appropriate for the social/academic situation.	2. You are expected to have the social and cultural knowledge (etiquette, knowing how to behave in social and academic settings, etc.) and be able to demonstrate it both orally and in writing utilizing the dialect and register appropriate for the social/ academic situation.

C. If you were born in Mexico or any other Spanish-speaking country and immigrated to the U.S. at an early age (before exposure to extensive education in Spanish) or if you were born in the United States and were/are exposed to Spanish in family and/or community contexts (especially if your last name is typically Hispanic, and/or if your accent in Spanish appears native):

1. Your Spanish language oral and written skills are expected to reflect those of an educated native speaker even when you enter beginning Spanish classes.	1. Your Spanish language should reflect that of an educated person (i.e., standard Spanish is expected).
2. You are expected to possess social and cultural knowledge (etiquette, knowing how to behave appropriately in social and academic settings, etc.) and be able to demonstrate such knowledge through your choices of appropriate dialects and registers.	2. You are expected to possess social and cultural knowledge (etiquette, knowing how to behave appropriately in social and academic settings, etc.) and be able to demonstrate such knowledge through your choices of appropriate dialects and registers.

structors also expect heritage students who look, sound, identify with, and/or have typical Hispanic last names to understand, speak, read, and write Spanish at levels beyond non-Hispanic peers or at least at levels appropriate to their age and education (see table 8.1). Similarly, non-Hispanic student peers in the same classroom also assume that heritage learners have an edge on Spanish. They tend to use the same identifying variables as do some teachers of Spanish.

While META served as a model for the acquisition of Spanish for all participants, the above findings, among many others, suggested that it would also be particularly useful for the continued acquisition of Spanish by heritage learners in both immersion and in U.S. high schools and institutions of higher education. Riegelhaupt, who is both a Spanish instructor and linguist, implemented META for Spanish native speakers at Northern Arizona University following its use in the Guanajuato immersion experience. She also used it in special classes devoted to the further acquisition of Spanish for heritage learners, as well as in classes where both heritage and nonheritage learners were enrolled.

The META approach produced longitudinal and analytical documentation on heritage language and culture acquisition. It also produced META acquisition portfolios that informed both instructors and students about the acquisition process and provided knowledge to the student and the new instructor about what to do next.

What Is META?

META is at once a research design, a curriculum, and a pedagogy. The term META is derived from "meta-analysis" or an analysis of self. It involves continuous data collection and analysis of students' language acquisition process. Student portfolios document their linguistic needs and achievements, cognitive strategies used to maximize acquisition, as well as cultural and psychological insights that inhibit or promote language acquisition. This knowledge allows the instructor to create a more relevant and culturally responsive teaching and learning environment for heritage learners. It also allows heritage speakers to be responsible for and to take charge of their own language learning.

META is based on four underlying, highly interdependent, and interrelated key concepts that affect language acquisition: Metapsychological, Metacultural, Metalinguistic, and Metacognitive knowledge (see figure 8.1). These four "meta" knowledges play important roles in the acquisition of heritage languages. The use of any one of these meta knowledges or a combination of more than one can either hinder or promote acquisition.

Figure 8.1 *Interrelated Key META Concepts*

METAPSYCHOLOGICAL KNOWLEDGE

Metapsychological knowledge refers to psychological reactions that promote or inhibit language acquisition.

- It encourages heritage learners to look at their own emotional reactions to linguistic situations (i.e., insecurities about using their heritage language with family and native speakers; insecurities which prevent them from traveling and participating in other Spanish-speaking countries).
- It makes explicit the relationship between attitudes *and* the cultural perspectives and traditions that caused them.
- Often just knowing that one's emotive reactions are normal helps to facilitate and promote their further acquisition.

METACULTURAL KNOWLEDGE

Metacultural knowledge is knowledge about the sociolinguistic and socio-political history of heritage learners in the United States. It also makes explicit the present heritage culture community norms and expectations.

- It begins with the exploration of heritage learners' own family history.
- It explores differences in language use, registers, and dialects across time, places, and situations.
- It compares language and culture content of language courses with language and culture of home and community.
- It includes sociocultural perspectives on the importance of maintaining the family/ community language.
- It takes into consideration the need to expand heritage learners' sociolinguistic repertoire to include the standard and other registers and dialects.

METALINGUISTIC KNOWLEDGE

Metalinguistic knowledge is the awareness of an individual's own language use. Metalinguistic knowledge refers to the ability to talk about language, analyze it, and use such information to help acquire it.

- It includes recognizing other dialects and registers and where, when, and how to use them.
- It identifies the various problems in heritage learners' communicative style during authentic interactions in an effort to help eliminate them.
- It provides heritage learners with the skills necessary to help them analyze their own conversations with native speakers.
- It equips students with strategies to increase their communicative effectiveness when interacting in their heritage language with their family, community, other students, and professors.

METACOGNITIVE KNOWLEDGE

Metacognitive knowledge, or "learning how to learn," refers to an awareness of cognitive abilities, strategies, and learning styles that promote or inhibit heritage language and culture acquisition.

- It identifies those learning strategies that help to maximize language and culture acquisition.
- It identifies and helps to eliminate cognitive barriers to acquisition.
- It identifies the most effective personal learning style.

METAPSYCHOLOGICAL KNOWLEDGE

Metapsychological knowledge refers to knowledge about oneself and one's reactions when exposed to the language experience. It encourages language learners to look at themselves, their own reactions and interactions as they observe and/or participate in new or different cultural and linguistic situations. Heritage learners' insecurities about using Spanish and their fear of being criticized and corrected often prevent them from taking Spanish classes and/or traveling to Spanish-speaking countries, including to their heritage country. Such information provides students and their instructors with important knowledge that can be used to help them overcome such obstacles.

Metapsychological knowledge makes explicit the relationship between attitudes/feelings and the events that cause them since such knowledge helps promote the further acquisition of Spanish. Often just knowing that one's reactions are normal facilitates language acquisition.

METACULTURAL KNOWLEDGE

Metacultural knowledge in immersion settings refers to making explicit cultural expectations from one cultural/social situation and how they influence reactions to the new culture. Such reactions may impede language acquisition, if not understood and processed by instructors and students. When continuing to acquire a family/community language in the United States, metacultural knowledge takes on a modified definition. It includes making explicit familial, cultural, and linguistic knowledge and how it differs from knowledge necessary to successfully function in the university community, as well as the society at large. It also includes cultural attitudes about the continued acquisition of the family/community language: Do members of the community desire and support the maintenance of Spanish in their families and communities? Do they encourage their children to acquire or further acquire Spanish? How do they react to learners' Spanish?

METALINGUISTIC KNOWLEDGE

Metalinguistic knowledge is the awareness of an individual's own language use. It refers to the ability to talk about language, analyze it, and use such information to help acquire it. It also includes becoming aware of dialect differences and developing expanded register and dialect ranges. Students use META to analyze their own conversations with native speakers of Spanish. On a weekly basis, students record at least one hour of their interactions in Spanish and transcribe approximately fifteen minutes of their conversations. Instructors review transcriptions and tapes and provide students with input about how they can incorporate strategies to increase their communicative effectiveness. For example, after a word count of each participant speech, students are able to determine their own quantity of speech as compared to their conversational partners. They are then encouraged to try to equalize their contributions to the conversation. Once students are made aware of the various gaps in their communicative style, they are often able to increase their communicative effectiveness.

METACOGNITIVE KNOWLEDGE

Metacognitive knowledge refers to an awareness of the cognitive strategies and learning style that promote or inhibit language learning/acquisition and cultural awareness. Metacognitive processes include a person's thoughts in problem-solving situations. The person employs such strategies as self-planning, self-monitoring, self-regulating, self-questioning, self-reflecting, and/or self-reviewing (Hyde and Bizar 1989). The learner explores his/her cognitive capacities, ascertains the level of difficulty of the specific language problem, and employs various strategies to enhance and promote language acquisition. Conditions and environments that maximize and facilitate one's learning are made explicit. Learning styles may be different for each student. One of the principal roles of the instructors/directors is to help students identify those metacognitive strategies that most effectively lead to continued acquisition of Spanish.

CURRICULUM DESIGN: META TEACHING AND LEARNING ACTIVITIES

META activities were developed for the purpose of conducting research that directly informs the curriculum. They serve both as the curriculum and as a research design that generates information on the four META key concepts.

Figure 8.2 *META Teaching, Learning, and Research Activities*

A. Language and Culture Workshops and Seminars (Classes)

B. Interactive Journals

C. Audio- and/or videotaped interactions with native speakers/family

D. Transcriptions of audiotaped interactions done by students from taped conversations with native speakers/family

E. Weekly interactive analyses of transcriptions, done by students following model provided by program directors/instructors

F. Interviews with instructors, questionnaires, etc. (beginning, middle, end of semester)

G. Personal Language and Culture Student Portfolios

H. Book for Relatives: *Caminos, Encuentros y Recuerdos de Nuestra Cultura*

These data can be analyzed in the classroom. These activities can be implemented in immersion and nonimmersion settings. The nature and intent of the eight teaching and learning activities that provide the framework for the curriculum are described below.

A. Language and Culture Workshops and Seminars (Classes)

Language and culture workshops, seminars, and/or classes are at the core of META since they provide the contexts and opportunities for students to process their experiences and to share them with each other and with the instructor. The atmosphere is very relaxed so students feel comfortable expressing their feelings. The following summarizes the nature and purpose of these learning environments:

- Language and culture are integrated into each class session.
- Students share personal experiences and insights regarding their acquisition of Spanish and cultural realizations and knowledge.
- Dialects and registers of Spanish brought into the classroom are valued and respected.
- Opportunities for student contact with Spanish in natural settings in their homes and communities are provided.
- Students are required to read and write for at least thirty minutes daily out of class.
- Students initiate class topics directly and indirectly as they relate to their own and other students' experiences.
- Redrafting and correcting are seen as editing for the authentic purpose of publishing a final book to be given to their families.
- Students learn how to identify categories of their own errors.
- Student transcriptions of oral conversational language, stories, and legends as told by their family and friends serve to develop an understanding of standard writing conventions for what students already know and use orally.
- Differences between oral and written language become obvious as students listen, read, and analyze transcriptions and compare them to work meant to be read, such as stories, essays, and poems.
- Instructor serves more as a language analyst and counselor than as a typical language instructor. He or she guides and directs students to understand and develop their own language learning strategies.
- Class Readings: The U.S. Hispanic experience is the focus, and writing activities are designed to develop a META awareness of the psychologi-

cal and cultural issues involved in being a Spanish-English bilingual in the United States. Rather than write critiques of the material, students utilize readings as models for their own creations. The main objectives for the readings are:

a. To provide models of writing using various dialects and registers.

b. To demonstrate that concerns of U.S. Hispanic writers about linguistic, cultural, social, and political realities are similar to their own.

c. To allow students to compose pieces of immediate interest to them and their family, through publication of a final edited book of their work.

d. To appreciate and to relate to poems, essays, and short stories by U.S. Hispanic authors and other representatives of the ethnic/national/ cultural heritage of the students.

e. To read and hear each other's work on a regular basis to enhance oral comprehension, performance style, and reading skills.

B. Interactive Journals

This activity involves journal writing with the knowledge that the instructor will be reading and commenting on the journal's content, if and when appropriate or desired. Instructor comments are reactions and expansions to the information provided by the student. Corrections are made indirectly (unless students request that the instructor point out their errors) by using the correct form as part of a response to a student comment. Interactive journals also serve as a source of data for analysis of the acquisition of Spanish orthography, fluency, accuracy, and syntactic, morphological, and discourse development.

Student interactive journals:

• provide a context for daily informal writing.

• offer an opportunity to express feelings about new language and culture experiences.

• encourage students to document daily activities and realizations, and observations.

• offer an authentic, interactive opportunity to communicate in writing with instructors.

• provide a record of new vocabulary and other linguistic information.

ADVANTAGES TO THE INSTRUCTOR

Information in the journals:

• develops an awareness of student interests, goals, and needs.

- provides a broader sociolinguistic and cultural context for understanding students' present language abilities and attitudes.

- allows instructor to witness a personalized written form.

- helps to develop and maintain a closer teacher/student relationship.

C. Audio and Videotaped Interactions with Family and/or Community Members and Speakers from Other Parts of the Spanish-Speaking World

META provides real interactive data that instructors and researchers cannot otherwise be privy to. These sessions provide a link between the students and their linguistic communities, and between their past and present linguistic experiences. These audio- or videotaping activities:

- provide opportunities for frequent interactions in Spanish.

- provide opportunities for learning from relatives about linguistic and cultural experiences in the United States and in their places of origin.

- expose students to a variety of registers of their own dialect, as well as other dialects.

ADVANTAGES TO THE INSTRUCTOR

- They allow for the opportunity to hear students interacting with those closest to them.

- They provide instructor with information about the students' dialects as spoken by family members.

- They link family, community knowledge with academic knowledge.

D. Transcriptions of Audio- and Videotaped Interactions Done by Students

Transcriptions provide both instructor and student with the opportunity to see speech in written form. They challenge students to understand how what they say looks when put into writing so that they may also learn that writing conventions are important tools for standardization. This activity helps students to:

- use an authentic, well-known context as a take-off point for understanding the differences between oral and written language.

- familiarize themselves with their own dialect in writing.

- illustrate the conventions necessary to put conversational language into writing, e.g., punctuation, spelling, etc.
- learn how to identify and classify errors, and to correct and edit written work.

ADVANTAGES TO INSTRUCTOR

By allowing the instructor to witness student interpretations of speech, the instructor is privy to linguistic and cultural contexts unavailable in the classroom. The instructor is able to:

- observe the degree of knowledge about written conventions.
- further tailor the curriculum to the individual needs of the student.
- allow for a successful transition between speech and writing.

E. Interactive Analyses of Transcriptions

Similar to the approach taken with the interactive journals, instructors provide comments on interesting aspects of the content communicated during taped conversations. Corrections concerning students' linguistic production occur principally in an effort to "edit" transcriptions for final publication in the book to be given to their family members (see section H, "Book for Relatives").

Instructors make students aware of the nature of their interactions and how native speakers may inadvertently provide them with new vocabulary and grammatical forms. This enables students to develop an increased meta-linguistic awareness. As the semester progresses, students are able to spot these forms on their own, when they review their transcriptions. An example of common orthographic errors made in tape transcriptions follows. A similar list is also required in areas of verb morphology and tense, aspect, mood acquisition, etc.

An interactive analysis of transcriptions:

- provides comments on interesting aspects of the content communicated during taped conversations.
- informs students about how to better structure their communication to avoid such problems in future conversations.
- points out errors, and provides the appropriate correction where appropriate.
- trains students how to document errors.
- requires students to redo their transcriptions incorporating corrections into their second draft, resulting in a final copy written with standard

punctuation and orthography that will be included in the book to their family.

· teaches students how to identify the sociolinguistic strategies that they use (and that are used with them) during conversations.

· develops an increased metalinguistic, metacognitive, and metacultural awareness.

ADVANTAGES TO THE INSTRUCTOR

· They give the instructor an opportunity to provide comments and questions about linguistic production and topics of mutual concern.

Figure 8.3 *Examples of Transcription Errors from Week 1 Conversation*

The following examples from a heritage learner's transcription of her first tape-recorded conversations include common errors documented in the writing of many United States bilinguals and Spanish-speaking monolinguals who have not studied Spanish in a formal setting. The most common errors, misplacement or elimination of the written accent, will not be included here.

TRANSCRIBED FORM	CORRECT FORM	TRANSCRIBED FORM	CORRECT FORM
1. queaseres	quehaceres	19. conponer	componer
2. oyir	oír	20. desaugarse	desahogarse
3. ayá	allá	21. as ido	has ido
4. parese	parece	22. asta	hasta
5. enterumpir	interrumpir	23. deci	decía
6. vas aser	vas a hacer	24. resivo	recibo
7. ayí	allí	25. siervienta	sirvienta
8. circumstancias	circunstancias	26. hiba venir	iba a venir
9. hasen	hacen	27. train	traen
10. cres	crees	28. conose	conoce
11. horita	ahorita, orita	29. quiaser	quehacer
12. tubieron	tuvieron	30. empuntando	apuntando
13. hibas	ibas	31. eror	error
14. haora	ahora	32. iva sentir	iba a sentir
15. tiera	tierra	33. allado	hallado
16. abnormal	anormal	34. ayo	halló
17. vas sentirte	vas a sentirte	35. siguiste	seguiste
18. oes	oyes	36. verda	verdad

· They permit instructor to "eavesdrop" on authentic situations and treat them as objects of investigation to enlighten students and enhance their language learning experience.

· They provide longitudinal analysis of errors for individual students.

· They serve to inform pedagogy.

F. Audio- and Videotaped Interviews with Instructors, Periodic Questionnaires, and Evaluations

Teacher interviews with students represent one of the principal sources of personal, psychological, cultural, linguistic, and demographic information. Often, it is through these interviews that instructors become aware of student problems. These instructor/student interviews also provide linguistic data and allow instructors to further evaluate the level of Spanish proficiency of their heritage students. Pre- and post-META Self-Reflective Strengths and Goals Essays and final META Questionnaires provide additional data. What follows is an example of the Final META Questionnaire administered as part of the final examination.

Figure 8.4 *Final Evaluation Questionnaire*

ESPAÑOL 312
PROFESORA FLORENCIA RIEGELHAUPT
EVALUACIÓN FINAL

Please answer as completely as possible:

1. Discuss how you felt about SPEAKING Spanish at the beginning of this semester.
2. Discuss how you felt about WRITING Spanish at the beginning of this semester.
3. Discuss how you felt about READING Spanish at the beginning of this semester.
4. Discuss how you felt about COMPREHENDING oral Spanish at the beginning of this semester.
5. After taking this class, discuss any personal affective changes about SPEAKING Spanish, i.e., your attitudes toward speaking Spanish.
6. After taking this class, discuss any personal affective changes about WRITING Spanish, i.e., your attitudes.
7. After taking this class, discuss any personal affective changes about READING Spanish, i.e., your attitudes.
8. After taking this class, discuss any personal affective changes about COMPREHENDING oral Spanish, i.e., your attitudes.

Figure 8.4 *Continued*

9. What are your strengths in Spanish?

10. What are your weaknesses in Spanish?

11. What problems with VERBS did you have at the beginning of this course and what is the status of these problems now at the end of the course?

12. What problems with ADJECTIVES did you have at the beginning of this course and what is the status of these problems now at the end of the course?

13. Read over your first few writing assignments and compare them to your last few. What are the areas of improvement?

14. Given your present status in Spanish, describe a method of INSTRUCTION that would most likely meet your needs.

15. Has learning more Spanish and about Spanish issues in this class affected you psychologically? How? Explain.

16. If you were to travel to a Spanish-speaking country (other than the United States), discuss how you think you could survive given the Spanish you already know.

17. If you had to continue your Spanish studies on your own, what would you do? Outline a plan so that you could increase or maintain your present level.

18. Please discuss any aspect of Spanish, learning Spanish, or this class that would be helpful to future teachers/students of Spanish.

19. Are there some personal psychological issues and concerns you must overcome to continue to learn/acquire Spanish? What are they? Please explain.

20. What are the maximal conditions for your acquisition of Spanish? What are some strategies that you have learned to maximize learning Spanish?

21. What historical, cultural, social, and political background knowledge that you learned in class helped you in the acquisition of Spanish? Explain.

22. What strategies do you recommend to maximize communication with your Spanish-speaking relatives and friends?

These questionnaires and interactive journals also serve as a source of data for analysis of the acquisition of Spanish orthography, fluency, accuracy, and syntactic, morphological, and discourse development. The primary goal for these activities is to provide students with an opportunity to express their opinions and concerns both orally and in writing about issues affecting their language learning experiences.

- They offer instructor and student the chance to together examine and analyze linguistic proficiency.
- They allow instructor to help students, "one-on-one," with any past, present, and future issues and apprehensions affecting their continued acquisition of Spanish.
- They help establish a close relationship of trust and caring.
- They give instructor an opportunity to provide students with feedback about their experiences as recounted and processed in interviews.

G. Personal Language and Culture Student Portfolios

Portfolios serve to inform both student and teacher about the total student linguistic oral and written production over the course of the semester. If continued across all language learning experiences, they provide documentation for long-term analysis.

- They provide a longitudinal record of students' continued acquisition of Spanish.
- They document student linguistic growth, strengths, needs, and goals.
- They allow new instructors to have a context and background knowledge of student proficiency.
- They allow students to continue their acquisition in situations outside of the classroom, i.e., with family and community members, and in other natural, authentic settings.

ADVANTAGES TO THE INSTRUCTOR

- They enable instructors to revisit student work and examine progress across the semester and in subsequent semesters of study.
- They provide instructors with raw data for analysis.

H. Book for Relatives: Caminos, Encuentros y Recuerdos de Nuestra Cultura

META utilizes a "whole language" approach to literacy acquisition much in the same way that whole language is used in bilingual elementary school programs (Goodman, Goodman, and Flores 1979; Flores 1981; Edelsky 1986; Faltis and DeVillar 1993). Rather than concentrate on discrete item exercises such as those often found in language textbooks, whole language incorporates authentic materials with authentic purposes into the curriculum. When students know that there is a reason to write, with a real audience, with a particular interest in their work, "correcting" their work becomes a necessity, and is a required part of the "editing" process.

Written assignments for "authentic purposes" in a class for heritage speakers include such assignments as:

- ¿Quién soy yo? (Who am I?)

- Mi lengua y mi cultura (My language and my culture)

- Mi casa: una descripción (My house: a description)

- Una persona importante en mi vida: una descripción (An important person in my life: a description)

- "Borges y yo": una aventura en el descubrimiento personal ("Borges and I": an adventure in personal discovery). This assignment uses "Borges y yo" by Jorge Luis Borges, the famous Argentine writer, as a model.

- Cartas formales e informales (Formal and informal letters)

- Un ensayo inicial y final sobre "Mis fuerzas y mis metas" (An initial and final self-reflective essay, "My strengths and goals")

All of these assignments are for authentic communicative purposes, since students include them in an edited volume, to be read by their families, friends, teachers, and community members. The knowledge that there is a reason for editing makes even the redrafting process an authentic activity. Corrections, or final "editing," of their written work is of personal value, while also being essential for the book authored by classmates.

Writing assignments and various literary selections from U.S. Hispanic authors on similar topics are designed to enhance language acquisition by allowing students to explore various aspects of themselves and their culture. This leads to both development of linguistic and cultural pride and increased self-esteem, as well as increased accuracy and linguistic proficiency.

The book directed at family members and named and organized by students:

- provides them with a "real" reason to write, and a real audience to write for.

- allows them to understand why they have to utilize standard conventions, even for conversational speech in their own dialect.

- permits them to share their university experiences with their family.

- gives them an opportunity to demonstrate their knowledge of written Spanish to their family.

- encourages their family to begin to write and/or orally share their own family experiences and stories.

- provides their families with an important source of literacy materials to read.

- gives the student and family members a source of pride in their own stories.

ADVANTAGES TO THE INSTRUCTOR

- The book connects the university to the community.

- The book creates a forum for literacy, where writing and reading become part of everyday life experiences.

- It allows for an opportunity for continued family involvement in their children's education after high school.

Summary

META serves to develop students' awareness of their linguistic, psychological, social, cultural, and cognitive behaviors as they document their growth through an analysis of their interactions with native speakers in their families and communities, and with host families abroad. They analyze their language use, their communicative strategies, their oral and written comprehension skills, their state of mind, their attitudes, cultural differences, and their preferred learning styles to maximize their acquisition of language and culture. Through data analyses, instructors also become aware of their students' linguistic needs and cultural concerns, and they use these insights to provide a more efficient and relevant teaching and learning environment. Since students are actively engaged in self-analysis, the developing portfolios are seen not as mere class assignments but rather as "personal" language and culture profiles to accompany them as lifetime language learners.

The four interrelated concepts that underlie this approach—metacultural, metapyschological, metalinguistic, and metacognitive knowledge—are necessary considerations for both the learner and the instructor. Data and analyses culled from these four concepts serve to promote and enhance heritage language acquisition. The following heritage language comments show the importance and the effects of recognizing these meta-concepts in the heritage acquisition process. In actual examples below, we identify the four types of meta-knowledge by using brackets.

Florina Flores expresses how metacultural and metapsychological knowledge interact to promote language acquisition.

> . . . este año yo gané más fuerzas en mi lengua y en mi cultura [metacultural knowledge]. Ahora me siento con más confianza en escribir una carta en español o en escribir una nota cuando no pueda estar presente. Se siente muy bonito poder escribir el español [metapsychological] (META Database 2001a).

The importance of revitalizing the heritage culture is best expressed by Laura Lenma:

> Cuando tuve que escribir sobre mi cultura y mi lengua me di cuenta que yo no sabía nada de mi cultura. Pensé en todos los momentos que mi pobre madre intentó decirme de las costumbres de su pueblo, gente y país. Yo no quería saber. Pensaba yo: 'Estamos en los Estados Unidos. No necesito saber esas cosas.' El hecho que yo soy resultado de mi cultura no se me había ocurrido antes. Al escribir este ensayo sentí un gran deseo de oír los cuentos de mi mamá (META Database 2001b).

Lissette Valle documents how she overcame the psychological barrier to speak and write in Spanish and María Elena Contenas's comments show the importance of reconnecting with family as part of her language and culture acquisition process.

> I was very reluctant to speak Spanish around campus because I felt like no one wanted to hear it [metapsychological]. Now, I feel proud of it and I have found that there is a lot of non-Spanish-speaking people who like to hear it and learn more about it . . . I would always try to write in Spanish but I knew my grammar was horrible [metalinguistic]. I did not know how to use accents. Whenever I wrote e-mails to my family in Mexico I felt embarrassed about my grammar [metapsychological] (META Database 2001c).

> Una cosa que creo que sea interesante y triste es que mis abuelos son de México, y no hablan el íngles y por muchos años ni podía hablar con ellos. Ni les entendía ni nada, pero ahora estoy muy orgullosa porque por fin, puedo hablar con ellos — más o menos — en español [metapsychological and metacultural] (META Database 1992).

Exploring and writing about one's own cultural background, e.g., one's family, sets the frame for expanding Spanish writing skills because it is personal and authentic.

Mi trabajo largo lo escribí sobre mi abuelita, Florentina. Me acordé de muchas experiencias que tuve con ella, momentos que estaban enterrados en lo más profundo de mi memoria. Me sentía tan cercas de ella que se me olvidó incluir el hecho que ella ya no vive [metapsychological and metacultural].

. . . Aprendí a apreciar mi cultura [metacultural] y a mi misma [metapsychological]. Esta clase me forzó experimentar sentimientos muy personales y profundos. Tuve que crecer. Para mí esta no fue una clase, fue un viaje [metapsychological] (META Database 2001b).

También me gustaría darle la sorpresa a mis padres de poder escribir el español correctamente [metalinguistic, metacultural, and metapsychological] (META Database 2001a).

Finally, Teresa Onman expresses the importance of a low anxiety level and a relaxed teaching and learning environment where heritage students are not ridiculed for their lack of Spanish and or for their Spanish dialect. META works toward increasing students' self-esteem about their Spanish by promoting its oral and written use without fear of being criticized for a variety of Spanish with which they were brought up.

La clase ha sido . . . un lugar de aprendizaje en donde los estudiantes no son presionados ni riduculizados frente a los demás [metacognitive and metapsychological] (META Database 2001d).

Conclusions

Sharing the same concern about heritage language acquisition, META data-generated theories are immediately applicable and acted upon, both by the instructors and by the students, as action researchers. The following pedagogical implications for instruction, and research recommendations, that can be derived from this theoretical and applied approach to heritage language acquisition, are presented.

Pedagogical Implications for Instruction of Spanish as a Heritage Language in the United States

- Objectives and activities for heritage Spanish speakers should reflect their cultural and linguistic background and knowledge.
- Developing awareness involves utilizing authentic reading and writing activities with a "real" audience, a real reason to communicate orally as well as in writing.

- Writing about and orally describing "who you are" and "where you come from" provides an opportunity for the student to develop his/her individuality, while at the same time to develop relationships and identification with other Hispanic students with similar backgrounds and linguistic, cultural, and academic concerns.
- META allows students to hear/see their dialect and that of their family and community in writing. This factor alone provides them with an understanding that their dialect is a perfectly viable one with a history of its own.
- Awareness about their own history and cultural roots leads to pride in students' varieties of Spanish.
- Knowledge that a student's dialect is one of many dialects and registers of Spanish allows for an increased willingness to accept the fact that people speak in different ways in different regions.
- Sociolinguistic awareness that people frequently speak more than one register of a given language points out the importance of learning additional registers as student interactions expand from contact with Spanish-speaking people in local and regional towns to contacts in other parts of the Spanish-speaking world.
- Becoming aware of who you are individually and culturally builds self-esteem. Knowledge of self and your culture provides a strong foundation and motivation for continued language acquisition at home, at school, and in immersion settings abroad.
- Teachers of heritage learners need to show respect for student linguistic and cultural knowledge while providing them with access to and knowledge about a Spanish language global "standard."
- Extensive experience in Spanish in all modes, registers, and in a variety of dialects is essential; and university and high school programs need to recognize that the task of developing literacy and increasing dialect recognition and knowledge and register use requires far more than one or two courses. Indeed, according to Avila (as quoted by Hidalgo 1990) approximately 600 hours of literacy training are necessary to develop literacy skills in Spanish by monolinguals in Mexico.

IMPLICATIONS FOR RESEARCH

This applied and theoretical research model:

- proposes that there is a relationship between "meta" awareness and the continued acquisition of Spanish by heritage learners.

- serves as a basis for understanding oral and written language for authentic purposes.
- documents language use *in situ*.
- provides data for placement and curriculum development.
- documents language in whatever contexts it is used and therefore it can be used for analysis of acquisition.
- helps to ensure an individualized, culturally appropriate Spanish language curriculum for native speakers.
- yields longitudinal language data on individual learners and across learners to investigate the process of acquisition of heritage languages.
- generates various oral and written language samples that serve as data for a multitude of linguistic studies.

Efforts to regain and maintain Spanish connect students to the rich cultural and linguistic heritage of their own Hispanic families and communities, while also providing them with the necessary linguistic skills to interact with other Spanish speaking communities throughout the United States and the world. META focuses on an immediate purpose: that of communicating with people important to students, such as family, in a language medium seldom, if ever, used before. The primary goal of courses for Spanish for native/heritage speakers is the transmission of Spanish to the next generation. Students need to know that using the language, above all else, is a prerequisite to its maintenance as a viable means of communication for present and future generations. Feeling comfortable and confident in Spanish will help to ensure its continued acquisition and use in future generations.

REFERENCES

Barkin, Florence. 1981a. "Establishing Criteria for Bilingual Literacy." *Bilingual Review* 8 (1):1–13.

———. 1981b. "Problems of Language Education: Language Switching in Chicano Spanish: Norms for Awareness." In *Social and Educational Issues in Bilingualism and Biculturalism*, eds. R. St. Clair, G. Valdés, and J. Ornstein-Galicia, 102–22. New York: University Press of America.

———. 1980a. "Testing Language Proficiency of Future Bilingual Teachers." In *Teaching Spanish to the Hispanic: Issues, Aims, and Methods*, eds. G. Valdés, A. G. Lozano, and R. G. Garcia-Moya, 215–35. New York: Teachers College Press.

———. 1980b. "The Role of Loanword Assimiliation in Gender Assignment." *Bilingual Review* 7:105–13.

———. 1980c. "Research in Phonology and Lexicon of Southwest Spanish." In *Bilingualism and Language Contact: Spanish, English and Native American Languages*, eds. F. Barkin, E. Brandt, and J. Ornstein, 123–38. New York: Teachers College Press.

———. 1980d. "Testing Bilingual Spanish Language Proficiency for Future Teachers in Bilingual Programs." In *Speaking, Singing, and Teaching: A Multidisciplinary Approach to Language Variation*, ed. F. Barkin and E. Brandt, *Anthropological Research Papers* No. 20:262–63. Tempe: Arizona State University.

———. 1979. "Loanshifts: An Example of Multilevel Interference." In *Proceedings of the Seventh Southwest Area Language and Linguistics Workshop. SWALLOW VII*, ed. A. Lozano, 1–11. Boulder: University of Colorado.

———. 1978. "Language Switching in Chicano Spanish: A Multifaceted Phenomenon." In *Proceedings of the Sixth Southwest Area Language and Linguistics Workshop. SWALLOW VI*, eds. H. H. Key, G. McCullough, and J. B. Sawyer, 1–10. Long Beach: California State University.

Barkin, Florence, and Elizabeth Brandt. 1980. *Speaking, Singing and Teaching: A Multidisciplinary Approach to Language Variation. SWALLOW: Anthropological Research Papers* No. 20. Tempe: Arizona State University.

Carranza, Michael A. 1977. "Language Attitudes of Mexican American Adults: Some Sociolinguistic Implications." Ph.D. diss., University of Notre Dame.

Carrasco, Roberto L. 1984. "Collective Engagement in the Segundo Hogar: A Microethnography of Engagement in a Bilingual First Grade Classroom." Ed.D. diss., Harvard University.

———. 1981a. "Expanded Awareness of Student Performance: A Case Study in Ethnographic Monitoring in a Bilingual Classroom." In *Culture and the Bilingual Classroom: Studies in Classroom Ethnography*, eds. H. Trueba, C. Guthrie, and K. Au. Rowley, MA: Newbury House.

———. 1981b. Review of *Chicano Sociolinguistics: A Brief Introduction*, by Fernando Peñalosa. *Harvard Educational Review* 51(1):191–93.

———. 1979. "Expanded Awareness of Student Performance: A Case Study in Ethnographic Monitoring in a Bilingual Classroom." In *Working Papers in Sociolinguistics, Sociolinguistic Paper 60*, eds. R. Bauman and J. Sherzer. Austin, TX: Southwest Educational Development Laboratory.

Carrasco, Roberto L., and Florencia Riegelhaupt. 1994. "Language and Culture Clash: Chicano Teachers' Identity Crisis during Immersion in Mexico." Paper presented at the conference Spanish in the United States/El español en los Estados Unidos, University of Colorado at Boulder, October 28–29.

———. 1992. "META: un modelo holístico de la adquisición del español." In *Aspectos de la enseñanza del español como lengua extranjera*, ed. Pedro Barros, 81–90. Granada, Spain: University of Granada Press.

———. 1982–85. *The Training of Bilingual Personnel in Language Theory and Research, Testing and Curriculum Development: A Field-based Practicum*. ESEA Title VII, Office of Bilingual Education and Minority Language Affairs (OBEMLA), U.S. Department of Education.

Carrasco, Roberto L., Arthur Vera, and Courtney B. Cazden. 1980. "Aspects of Bilingual Students' Communicative Competence in the Classroom." In *Latino Language and Communicative Behavior*, ed. Richard Duran. Discourse Processes: Advances in Research and Theory, vol. 4. Norwood, NJ: Ablex Publishing.

Delany-Barmann, Gloria. 1997. "United States Native Spanish Speakers and Their Spanish Language Education: Needs, Attitudes, and Characteristics." Ed.D. diss., Northern Arizona University.

Edelsky, Carole. 1986. *Writing in a Bilingual Program: Había una vez*. Norwood, NJ: Ablex Publishing.

Elías-Olivares, Lucía. 1976. "Ways of Speaking in a Chicano Speech Community: A Sociolinguistic Approach." Ph.D. diss., University of Texas at Austin.

Elías-Olivares, Lucía, and Guadalupe Valdés-Fallis. 1979. "Language Diversity in Chicano Speech Communities: Implications for Language Teaching." *Working Papers in Sociolinguistics* 54:1–23.

Faltis, Christian. 1990. "Spanish for Native Speakers: Freirian and Vygotskian Perspectives." *Foreign Language Annals* 23 (2):117–26.

Faltis, Christian J., and Robert A. DeVillar. 1993. "Effective Computer Uses for Teaching Spanish to Bilingual Native Speakers." In *Language and Culture in Learning: Teaching Spanish to Native Speakers of Spanish*, eds. Barbara J. Merino, Henry T. Trueba, and Fabián A. Samaniego. Washington, D.C.: The Falmer Press.

Flores, Barbara. 1981. "Bilingual Reading Instructional Practices: The Three Views of the Reading Process as They Relate to the Concept of Language Interference." *Journal of Teacher Education* 8:45–52.

Floyd, Mary Beth. 1981. "Language Variation in Southwest Spanish and Its Relation to Pedagogical Issues." In *Teaching Spanish to the Hispanic Bilingual: Issues, Aims, and Methods*, eds. G. Valdés-Fallis, A. Lozano, and R. García-Moya. New York: Teachers College Press.

Goodman, Ken, Yetta Goodman, and Barbara Flores. 1979. *Reading in the Bilingual Classroom: Literacy and Biliteracy*. Rosslyn, VA: National Clearinghouse for Bilingual Education.

Hernández Chávez, Eduardo, Andrew Cohen, and Anthony Beltrano, eds. 1975. *El Lenguaje de los Chicanos*. Arlington, VA: Center for Applied Linguistics.

Hidalgo, Margarita. 1990. "On the Question of 'Standard' versus 'Dialect': Implications for Teaching Hispanic College Students." In *Spanish in the United States: Sociolinguistic Issues*, ed. J. Bergen, 110–26. Washington, D.C.: Georgetown University Press.

Merino, Barbara J., Henry T. Trueba, and Fabián A. Samaniego. 1993. *Language and Culture in Learning: Teaching Spanish to Native Speakers of Spanish*. Washington, D.C.: The Falmer Press.

META Database. 2001a. Participant Florina Flores, Self-Reflection and Final META Questionnaire. NAU Spanish 312.

META Database. 2001b. Participant Laura Lenma, Final META Questionnaire. NAU Spanish 312.

META Database. 2001c. Participant Lissette Valle, Final META Questionnaire. NAU Spanish 312.

META Database. 2001d. Participant Terese Onman, Final META Questionnaire. NAU Spanish 312.

META Database. 1992. Participant Maria Elena Contenas, Final META Questionnaire. NAU Spanish 314, Conversation and Composition.

Peñalosa, Fernando. 1980. *Chicano Sociolinguistics: A Brief Introduction*. Rowley, MA: Newbury House Publishers.

Riegelhaupt, Florencia, and Roberto Luis Carrasco. 2000. "Mexico Host Family Reactions to a Bilingual Chicana Teacher in Mexico: A Case Study of Language and Culture Clash." *Bilingual Research Journal* 24 (4):405–21.

Riegelhaupt-Barkin, Florence. 1985. "Testing Bilingual Language Proficiency: An Applied Approach." In *Spanish Language Use and Public Life in the United States*, eds. L. Elías-Olivares, E. Leone, R. Cisneros, and J. Gutiérrez, 165–80. New York: Mouton Publishers.

———. 1976. "The Influence of English on the Spanish of Bilingual Mexican American Migrant Workers in Florida." Ph.D. diss., State University of New York, Buffalo.

Rodríguez Pino, Cecilia. 1993. *Selected Bibliography of Spanish for Native Speaker Sources*. Funded by the National Endowment for the Humanities for the grant project "Teaching Spanish to Southwest Hispanic Students" Summer Conference, July 14–18.

Rodríguez Pino, Cecilia, and Daniel Villa. 1994. "A Student-Centered Spanish for Native Speakers Program: Theory, Curriculum and Outcome Assessment." In *Faces in a Crowd: Individual Learners in Multisection Programs*, ed. C. Klee. Boston: Heinle and Heinle.

Teschner, Richard. 1990. "Spanish Speakers Semi- and Residually Native: After the Placement Test Is Over." *Hispania* 73 (8):16–22.

Teschner, Richard, Garland Bills, and Jerry Craddock. 1976. *Spanish and English of the United States Hispanos: A Critical, Annotated Linguistic Biliography*. Arlington, VA: Center for Applied Linguistics.

Valdés, G. 2001. "Heritage Language Students: Profiles and Possibilities." In *Heritage Languages in America: Preserving a National Resource*, eds. J. K. Peyton, D. Ranard, and S. McGinnis. McHenry, IL, and Washington, D.C.: Delta Systems and Center for Applied Linguistics.

———. 1997. "The Teaching of Spanish to Bilingual Spanish-Speaking Students: Outstanding Issues and Unanswered Questions." In *La enseñanza del español a hispanohablantes: Praxis y teoría*, eds. M. C. Colombi and F. X. Alarcón. 8–44. Boston: Houghton Mifflin.

Valdés, Guadalupe, and Michelle Geoffrion-Vinci. 1998. "Chicano Spanish: The Problem of the 'Underdeveloped' Code in Bilingual Repertoires." *The Modern Language Journal* 2 (4):473–501.

Valdés-Fallis, Guadalupe. 1981. "Pedagogical Implications of Teaching Spanish to the Spanish-Speaking in the U.S." In *Teaching Spanish to the Hispanic Bilingual: Issues, Aims, and Methods,* eds. G. Valdés, A. Lozano, and R. García-Moya, 3–20. New York: Teachers College Press.

——. 1975. "Teaching Spanish to the Spanish Speaking: Classroom Strategies." *System* 3:54–62.

Valdés-Fallis, Guadalupe, and Richard Teschner. 1977. *Spanish for the Spanish-Speaking: A Descriptive Bibliography of Materials.* Austin, TX: National Education Laboratory Publishers.

Villa Crésap, Daniel. 1997. *El desarrollo de futuridad en el español.* México, D.F.: Grupo Editorial Eón, S.A. de C.V.

9

La enseñanza del español a los hispanohablantes bilingües y su efecto en la producción oral

Marta Fairclough
University of Houston

N. Ariana Mrak
University of Houston, Downtown

Durante las últimas décadas, numerosos estudios sociolingüísticos se han enfocado en la situación de contacto entre el español y el inglés en los Estados Unidos. En muchos casos, los resultados de las investigaciones se obtuvieron a partir del análisis de la covariación de varios factores sociales y lingüísticos. Sin embargo, teniendo en cuenta el considerable aumento en el número de cursos de español para hispanohablantes, y el hecho de que para muchos la enseñanza constituye la solución a la pérdida de la lengua española que se observa en los estudios de tipo generacional, uno de dichos factores no ha recibido la atención merecida: el nivel de enseñanza formal recibida en el dialecto estándar.

Antecedentes

Antes de enfocarnos en el estudio propiamente dicho, es necesario clarificar ciertos conceptos y encuadrar nuestra investigación dentro de un marco teórico apropiado. Al hablar de enseñanza formal del español nos referimos a todo tipo de cursos de español de nivel básico, intermedio y avanzado, pero en particular, a los cursos para hispanohablantes conocidos como *Spanish for Native Speakers* y más recientemente como *Spanish for Heritage Learners*.

Si bien, como lo indica Valdés (1997), el interés en la enseñanza del español a hispanohablantes bilingües ha existido desde los años treinta, no fue sino recién en las décadas de los setenta y ochenta que dicho interés se consolidó. Hoy día, a pesar de que los programas de español para hispanohablantes han aumentado considerablemente en todos los niveles académicos y de que los estudios demográficos calculan que la comunidad hispana en los Estados Unidos va a triplicar su número hacia mediados de siglo (Delany-Barmann 1997), el español sigue perdiendo terreno con cada nueva generación, dando lugar a una extensa diversidad entre los hispanohablantes que poseen una variada gama de conocimientos (Aparicio 1983; Hidalgo 1993; Lipski 1993; McQuillan 1996; Roca 1997; Valdés 1997; Villa 1996; Walqui 1997; entre otros).

Los cursos para hispanoparlantes bilingües han tratado de superar dichas dificultades a través de una multiplicidad de enfoques, textos y pedagogías (Aparicio 1983; Faltis 1981, 1984, 1990; Faltis y DeVillar 1993; Hidalgo 1993; Merino y Samaniego 1993; Rodríguez Pino 1997; Valdés 1981, 1988; Villa 1996; y muchos otros), aunque no siempre con resultados totalmente favorables (Merino 1989; Roca 1997).

Dentro de los propósitos de este tipo de cursos, además del mantenimiento de la lengua española, la expansión de las habilidades bilingües, y la transferencia de las destrezas en la lecto-escritura (Valdés 1997), se destaca la adquisición de la variedad de prestigio del español, en otras palabras el español estándar. Si bien parece haber consenso con respecto a qué debe respetarse el dialecto que el estudiante trae al aula (Porras 1996, 1997; Sánchez 1993; Villa 1996), también se reconoce que el dominio de la modalidad estándar presupone innumerables ventajas (Porras 1997).

La variedad estándar constituye la modalidad prestigiosa (Danesi 1986), es decir un dialecto social o regional que por razones económicas o políticas se convirtió en el instrumento de la administración, la enseñanza y la literatura; es aquella que provoca actitudes positivas de parte de los hablantes; es la norma ideal: una abstracción (Hidalgo 1997).

Para otros (Cheshire y Stein 1997) la variedad coloquial hablada y las formas estándar constituyen un continuo con las formas sintácticas de la prosa escrita en un extremo y el habla vernácula en el otro. Entre ambos polos existe una amplia gama de variantes imposibles de delimitar claramente las cuales para algunos son coloquiales mientras que para otros constituyen dialectos o formas no-estándar. Van Marle (1997) también ve la diferencia entre el dialecto y el estándar como una secuencia de niveles interrelacionados: (1) el estándar escrito; (2) el estándar en su forma hablada, (a) formal, (b) informal; (3) los dialectos. Mientras que el estándar escrito no llega a ser la lengua nativa de nadie, sí ejerce influencia sobre la variante estándar hablada, la cual a su vez se manifiesta en un estilo o registro formal (semejante a la forma escrita) y uno informal (que se aproxima a los dialectos). Finalmente es posible definir la forma vernácula dado su valor sentimental en oposición a la forma estándar que puede ser definida de acuerdo con su valor intelectual (Escure 1997).

Con respecto a un marco teórico apropiado para esta investigación, es evidente que el aprendizaje de la modalidad estándar por hispanohablantes bilingües constituye un proceso de adquisición de un segundo dialecto. Sin embargo, es muy poco lo que se sabe acerca de cómo los hablantes de una variedad no prestigiosa adquieren un dialecto estándar. Politzer (1993) por ejemplo, trata de situar la adquisición de un segundo dialecto dentro de los marcos teóricos para la adquisición de una segunda lengua y lo encuentra sumamente difícil. Si bien al compararse la adquisición de una segunda lengua con la de un dialecto, especialmente en su modalidad estándar, existen varias semejanzas, hay numerosos puntos en los que difieren (Chambers 1992; Danesi 1986; Escure 1997; Fairclough 1998; Larsen-Freeman y Long 1991; Politzer 1993; Valdés 1997). Valdés (1997), por su parte, indica que aún no se han desarrollado teorías que intenten explicar la adquisición de un dialecto estándar.

Para poder formular principios y teorías es necesario llevar a cabo numerosos estudios empíricos de la producción oral y escrita de individuos en el proceso de adquirir un dialecto estándar. A pesar del aumento en el número de cursos para hispanohablantes bilingües, mejores materiales, una pedagogía más apropiada y la dedicación esmerada del personal docente, con frecuencia los resultados de la enseñanza no han sido completamente satisfactorios, sobre todo en la producción oral de las formas estándar. Merino y Samaniego (1993), por ejemplo, cuestionan si la adquisición de dichas formas se enfoca de manera adecuada en el aula tradicional, sobre todo a causa de la importancia que representa para muchos la adquisición de la forma estándar en el discurso oral.

Por este motivo, el propósito de nuestro estudio consiste en analizar la covariación entre el nivel de enseñanza de la lengua minoritaria recibida en el aula (en este caso, el español) y el porcentaje de formas consideradas "no-estándar" en la producción oral de hablantes méxico-americanos residentes en el área de Houston.

Utilizando como técnica metodológica el análisis de errores, intentaremos calcular las principales diferencias morfosintácticas en el habla de aquellos entrevistados que han completado cursos de español y aquellos que nunca han recibido algún tipo de enseñanza formal en dicha lengua. Necesitamos aclarar que usamos el término "errores" para referirnos a usos que se apartan de la norma estándar, y que dichas formas pueden ser sistemáticas del dialecto bajo estudio. Investigaciones que comprobaran esta sistematicidad respaldarían la noción de la variedad analizada aquí como un código aparte del estándar. Sin embargo, nuestro objetivo es intentar contestar la pregunta postulada por Merino y Samaniego (1993, 117–18): *Can the acquisition of standard oral forms be addressed adequately in a traditional classroom?* y a la vez determinar qué formas o estructuras deben reforzarse en el aula para que se encuentren disponibles en la producción oral del hispanohablante bilingüe en los Estados Unidos.

Metodología

PARTICIPANTES

De un corpus de 40 entrevistas hechas a hablantes méxico-americanos bilingües pertenecientes a tres grupos generacionales con un mínimo de 10 años de residencia en Houston, seleccionamos para esta investigación a aquellos que nacieron en México y emigraron a los Estados Unidos antes de los seis años de edad, o que nacieron en este país de padres nacidos en México. Algunos son estudiantes universitarios mientras que otros se localizaron a través de estos mismos estudiantes, empleados de la universidad y contactos que se hicieron en la comunidad por parte de los entrevistadores. Descartamos a los hablantes nacidos en México que emigraron a los Estados Unidos después de los once años de edad debido a que ya habían recibido enseñanza en español en su país de origen. Reagrupamos a los restantes, un total de 21, dentro de tres categorías basadas en el nivel de enseñanza recibida en español: grupo (I) hablantes sin instrucción formal, grupo (II) con un año o menos, y grupo (III) con más de un año (en nuestra muestra, un promedio de tres años y medio). En el Cuadro 1 se presentan las características de los hablantes.

Procedimiento

Se condujeron entrevistas de tipo semi-dirigido, de una hora cada una, hechas en cintas magnetofónicas. Cada hablante fue entrevistado una sola vez y se le hizo un número mínimo de preguntas tratando de lograr una situación relajada en que el hablante hablara de su vida personal, trabajo, etc. El entrevistador dirigió la conversación sólo con la intención de producir una variedad amplia de discurso que incluyera pero no necesariamente se limitara a narrativas, discurso condicional y futuro. Se transcribieron las 21 grabaciones basadas en la selección previamente mencionada.

Cuadro 9.1 *Datos de los hablantes*

HABLANTE	GRUPO[a]	SEXO	EDAD	PROFESIÓN	EDUCACIÓN	ESPAÑOL
Blb	I	F	56	Oficinista	1 Técnic.	0
Clg	I	F	18	Estudiante	12 Secun.	0
Gum	I	F	25	Oficinista	1 Univ.	0
Lug	I	F	58	Técnico	8 Secun.	0
Yvz	I	F	42	Estudiante	1 Técnic.	0
Dar	I	M	32	Policía	4 Univ.	0
Isr	I	M	18	Estudiante	12 Secun.	0
Hec	II	F	26	Estudiante	3 Univ.	1 semestre
Maf	II	F	21	Estudiante	2 Univ.	1 semestre
Cac	II	M	19	Estudiante	1 Univ.	1 semestre
Res	II	M	20	Estudiante	3 Univ.	1 semestre
Rie	II	M	23	Estudiante	2 Univ.	1 semestre
Roh	II	M	31	Estudiante	3 Univ.	1 semestre
Vif	II	M	19	Estudiante	1 Univ.	1 año
Arj	III	F	23	Estudiante	5 Univ.	5 años
Cam	III	F	25	Estudiante	3 Univ.	3 años
Keo	III	F	21	Estudiante	3 Univ.	3 años
Mag	III	F	28	Estudiante	3 Univ.	2 años
Nec	III	F	38	Biblioteca.	4 Univ.	3 años
Car	III	M	25	Estudiante	3 Univ.	4 años
Jop	III	M	21	Estudiante	3 Univ.	4 años

[a]Los hablantes se agruparon de acuerdo al número de años de instrucción formal que han recibido en español: I=sin instrucción formal, II=con un año o menos, III=con más de un año.

Análisis

El estudio consiste en un análisis de la producción oral de los entrevistados. Partiendo de la técnica del análisis de errores (Corder 1973; Danesi 1986; Dulay, Burt, y Krashen 1982; James 1998) se procedió a detectar, localizar, describir y finalmente, clasificar y cuantificar los errores producidos por los hablantes. La motivación (o sea la causa de los errores) no será incluida en este estudio.

De acuerdo con James (1998) y Ellis (1994), el análisis de errores como método para organizar datos ha sido criticado con frecuencia principalmente debido a problemas de metodología y a limitaciones en el alcance que puede lograr resaltando: (1) el hecho de que no ofrece un cuadro completo del lenguaje del individuo, (2) que los estudios de muestras representativas no han considerado las distintas etapas de desarrollo y (3) que el hablante tiende a evitar las formas que no domina ya sea por medio del silencio o la circunlocución o paráfrasis.

Si el hablante elige evitar una forma debemos agregar que otra herramienta que puede utilizar en este tipo de situación es el cambio de código; sin embargo, ya que se ha demostrado efectivamente que las razones por las cuales los hablantes recurren a esta estrategia son variadas y dependen de razones pragmáticas a la vez que lingüísticas (Pfaff 1979; Poplack 1980) preferimos excluir de nuestros datos todos los cambios de código y reservar la oportunidad de sugerir en la sección final de este trabajo algunas consideraciones futuras basadas en este fenómeno. Para poder tener un panorama completo intentamos representar la producción de nuestros hablantes de una manera total, no solamente analizar las desviaciones que producen pero también la cantidad de formas que son paralelas a la norma estándar. Finalmente, queremos corregir la falta de distintas etapas de desarrollo en estudios previos incluyendo en nuestra muestra a los hablantes en 3 etapas diferentes de instrucción que confiamos, una vez presentados los resultados, probarán ser oportunas.

Partiendo de numerosos estudios sociolingüísticos que analizan el desgaste del español en contacto con el inglés en los EE.UU. (Lipski 1993; Sánchez 1982; Silva-Corvalán 1994; y otros) dividimos las desviaciones de la norma estándar en 9 categorías de errores: (1) concordancia dentro de la frase nominal (C.N.), (2) concordancia entre el sujeto y el verbo (C.V.), (3) tiempo o modo (T.M.), (4) adverbios (AD.), (5) clíticos (CL.), (6) ser o estar (S.E.), (7) preposiciones (PR.), (8) que (relativo) (QU.), (9) otros (OT.). Dentro de esta taxonomía de categorías lingüísticas subdividimos cada una en tipos de error: (a) omisión, (b) adición, (c) sustitución, (d) orden y (e) combinación (en nuestros datos se limita a dos o más adverbios o frases adverbiales juntos, creando una mezcla o "combinación" de formas que no se encuentran en el español estándar). Tomamos cada una de las categorías lingüísticas de los tres grupos por tipo de error y calculamos el porcentaje que representa comparado con el total de enunciados producidos. La categoría (9), "otros", es donde colocamos las formas que no se ajustaban a ninguna de las 8 primeras y, debido a que consta de un número muy bajo de formas (4 categorías, 33 sucesos), decidimos no crear categorías aparte. Dentro de este grupo colocamos construcciones con sujetos silentes, donde el artículo que precede al sujeto elidido también se ha omitido o sustituido. Estas construcciones son del tipo *lo, la, los, las + que*, como en el ejemplo (1); o *el, la, los, las,* como en el ejemplo (2). Además esta categoría incluye casos de sustitución de *estar* por *haber*, (3) y de *tener* por *ser*, (4).

1. Esto es parte del problema del presidente. El presidente tiene que decidir. ¿Qué podemos hacer nosotros, no nomás compañías grandes? Muchas veces son las compañías grandes que toman los beneficios. (Hec/F/26/II/7)[1]

2. Lo que yo pienso de esa, de eso es que pienso que sí, pues no sé nada, no conozco los otros planetas pero como en real . . . nadie de nosotros puede conocer otros planetas pero yo pienso que si tenemos vida aquí, pueden tener vida allí también. Es, parece que va a ser muy diferente que de nosotros pero pienso que sí. (Car/M/24/II/8)

3. M: ¿Puedes describir tu habitación, qué cosas tiene?[2]
   V : [. . .] Luego voltiando a la izquierda hay un *fireplace*, una chimenea, sí, y arriba están los este, los *rewards*, los *awards* que me gané en la escuela y todo, yo y mi hermana N. y luego volteando de vuelta a la derecha está el comedor. 'Ta una mesa grande y luego 'ta un gabinete con trastes lujosos y luego **está** un *hallway* y luego la cocina 'ta pequeña la cocina, pero el comedor a la derecha 'ta un un *hallway* luego dos recámaras y un baño. (Vif/M/19/II/4)[3]

4. . . . y ella, yo creo lo que le daba co . . . le gustaba a ella salir . . . y mi papá . . . **tenía** 15 años mayor que ella . . . él tendría sesenta y . . . siete años, sesenta y ocho ahorita, si, si todavía estuviera viviendo. (Keo/F/21/III/12)

Para contabilizar el número total de enunciados se sumó el número total de palabras eliminando las siguientes: (1) repeticiones que no son de naturaleza enfática, (2) los intentos fallidos, (3) las muletillas, (4) los enunciados en inglés, (5) los clíticos cuando forman parte de una expresión fija. Por el contrario sí se incluyeron: (1) palabras en inglés que son parte de la cultura, (2) nombres propios en inglés, (3) oraciones incompletas que dan significado al discurso (y por eso no las podemos considerar intentos fallidos), (4) las interjecciones cuando no son usadas como muletillas y (5) los clíticos, antepuestos o cliticizados, cuentan como una palabra.

Resultados

Los datos se dividieron en 9 categorías lingüísticas y 5 estrategias de superficie que se pueden ver en el Cuadro 2 para los 3 grupos de hablantes. La primera categoría, C.N., con un porcentaje de 0.26% en el grupo sin instrucción formal (I) aumenta a un 0.60% en el grupo con un año o menos de instrucción (II) y disminuye a un 0.44% en el grupo con más de un año de instrucción (III). Bajo esta categoría se dan los siguientes tipos de errores: (a) omisión de determinantes, (b) adición de determinantes, (c) sustitución de determinantes, (d) sustitución de género o número (que es donde colocamos la falta de concordancia), y por último, (e) reordenamiento dentro de la frase nominal que es el caso ejemplificado bajo el número (5).

5. Pero la cosa más rara también, es que cuando me volví para Houston, viví aquí en la calle xxx, en un apartamentito chiquito, por dos, **dos y medio meses**, y luego regresé para atrás . . . (Yvz/F/44/I/3)

El mismo tipo de variación se da en las dos categorías siguientes: las frecuencias en la C.V. pasan de un 0.19% en el grupo I a 0.22% en el grupo II y a un 0.18% en el grupo III. En T.M. el grupo I produce 0.28%, el grupo II 0.40% y el grupo III 0.27%. Volviendo a la C.V., tenemos casos de sustitución, es decir, falta de concordancia de persona y número como en el ejemplo (6):

6. Pues me **gusta** diversos tipos de música porque toco el saxófono. (Jop/ M/22/III/7)

La categoría T.M. incluye la omisión de un verbo y la sustitución de un tiempo por otro o de un modo por otro como también la adición de una forma nueva, que ejemplificamos con el número (7).

7. . . . yo quiero continuar con francés pero nomás aquí **tenen**, nomás de literatura entonces, bueno no me interesa. (Roh/M/31/II/5)

La frecuencia en el uso no-estándar de AD. va de 0.10% en el primer grupo a 0.08% en el segundo grupo y a 0.05% en el tercer grupo. Esta es quizás la categoría más variada ya que además de las cuatro estrategias de superficie que hemos venido discutiendo, aparecen aquí las mezclas, como en el ejemplo (8).

8. Las personas en Houston, como te dije antes, me gustan. Soy más Houstonian **de más de Californian**, pero . . . (Res/M/23/II/11)

La categoría que disminuye en el porcentaje de errores es la de CL., que pasa de 0.31% en el grupo I, a 0.21% en el II y luego sube ligeramente a 0.26% en el grupo III. Aquí también se dan casos de omisión, adición y sustitución. El ejemplo (9) muestra la omisión de un clítico.

9. Este, yo no soy experta pero creo que mi español es un poco más, no Tex-Mex, que le nombran. Trato de eliminar esas palabras de mi vocabulario pero a veces tiene uno que comunicar con la persona así es que tiene que adaptarse al (claro), me imagino que usted . . . (Nec/F/3X/ III/2)[4]

Cuadro 9.2 Frecuencias de errores por grupo

CATEGORÍAS LINGÜÍSTICAS[a]

TIPO DE ERROR	C.N.			C.V.			T.M.			AD.			CL.			S.E.			PR.			QU.			OT.			TOTALES		
	I[b]	II	III	I	II	III	I	II	III	I	II	III	I	II	III	I	II	III	I	II	III	I	II	III	I	II	III	I	II	III
Omisión	32[c]	63	40	–	–	–	2	7	8	1	5	3	34	23	29	–	–	–	51	131	98	8	8	28	2	17	4	130	233	210
Adición	14	8	12	–	–	1	5	9	5	20	13	11	24	17	30	–	–	–	50	63	35	7	4	1	–	–	–	120	114	95
Sustitución	42	126	113	65	76	70	90	123	91	10	5	5	46	30	39	11	6	30	77	73	60	–	–	–	–	5	5	345	444	413
Orden	1	8	3	–	–	–	–	–	–	1	3	–	1	3	–	–	–	–	–	4	–	–	–	1	–	–	–	3	18	4
Combinación	–	–	–	–	–	–	–	–	–	4	1	–	–	–	–	–	–	–	–	–	–	–	–	–	–	–	–	4	1	–
Totales	89	205	168	65	76	71	97	139	104	36	27	19	105	73	98	11	6	30	178	271	193	15	12	30	2	22	9	598	831	722
% Total	.26	.60	.44	.19	.22	.18	.28	.40	.27	.10	.08	.05	.31	.21	.26	.03	.02	.08	.52	.79	.50	.04	.03	.08	.01	.06	.02	1.74	2.42	1.88

[a] C.N.=concordancia nominal, C.V.=concordancia verbal, T.M.=tiempo y modo, AD.=adverbios, CL.=clíticos, S.E.=ser y estar, PR.=preposiciones, QU.=que relativo, OT.=otros.

[b] Nivel de instrucción formal de los hablantes: I=sin instrucción formal, II=con un año o menos, III=con más de un año.

[c] Número de formas lingüísticas producidas.

La frecuencia de errores en la categoría de las cópulas verbales, S.E., pasa de 0.03% en el grupo I, a 0.02% en el grupo II y a 0.08% en el grupo III y son todos casos de sustitución que incluyen tanto *ser* por *estar* como *estar* por *ser*, este último en el ejemplo (10).

10. También yo, cuando yo tenía como 10 años yo **estaba** un niño malo en la escuela. Siempre quería hablar o pelear o jugar. Nunca hacía nada. Una vez yo, mi profesor o mi maestro, me dio una mala nota del, del conducto, de cómo yo porté esa semana. (Jop/M/22/III/7)

Las PR. van de un 0.52% en los hablantes sin instrucción formal a 0.79% en los hablantes con un año o menos a 0.50% en los que tienen más de un año de instrucción formal. Reportamos casos de omisión, sustitución y adición; un ejemplo de este último aparece en el número (11).

11. La primera casa que viví . . . sí me acuerdo pero **de** seguramente tienes unas que son las más favoritas casas que vivistes y la primera no era más favorita. (Hec/F/2/II/2)

Los usos de QU. con 0.04% en I, 0.03% en II y 0.08% en III, bajan en el grupo intermedio y luego aumentan en el grupo con más instrucción. Esta categoría incluye omisión de QU., como en el ejemplo (12), pero también adición y orden.

12. So, entonces este, este verano aahh pienso yo que aahh ya cuando de, acabe el año escolar en mayo, la voy a sacar de su escuelita, y yo creo la quioro meter como en una *YMCA* o algo. (Gum/F/25/I/15).

Finalmente, el primer grupo tiene 0.01% de variación en la última categoría, OT., el grupo II tiene 0.06% y el grupo III tiene 0.02%.

Al enfocarnos en los totales debemos señalar que los hablantes del grupo sin instrucción formal (I) produjeron un total de 34.404 enunciados de los cuales 602 o un 1.74% se cuantificaron como errores. En el grupo con un año de instrucción o menos (II) vemos un ligero aumento en la frecuencia de errores, 2.42% con 832 formas de un total de 34.337 enunciados, mientras que el grupo con más de un año de instrucción baja a un 1.88% con un número de errores de 718 de un total de formas de 38.389, aproximándose al nivel del grupo I.

Discusión y conclusión

La información que nos parece de mayor interés al estudiar los resultados obtenidos es la frecuencia casi igual de errores entre el grupo sin instrucción formal del español y el grupo con más años de instrucción, el cual tiene un promedio de 3.5 años. Esto nos lleva a sugerir que la enseñanza formal en la modalidad estándar no produce resultados observables en la producción oral. Sin embargo, reconocemos que se necesitan estudios de la producción escrita para determinar si está sucediendo lo mismo o si esto es un fenómeno que sólo ocurre en el habla. Si se limita a la producción oral, sugeriría que la enseñanza formal permite que el individuo pueda adaptarse según las circunstancias y utilizar la variante que considere más apropiada (Politzer 1993; Chambers 1992).

Al mismo tiempo hace falta destacar que la frecuencia de errores es baja, un promedio de 2.01% del total de enunciados para los tres grupos. La necesidad de un grupo de control se hace más obvia aún ya que no hemos determinado el porcentaje de desviaciones que se dan en una variedad monolingüe. Reconocemos por supuesto que los cambios de código que excluimos de nuestros cálculos ayudan a diferenciar la variedad de nuestros hablantes del estándar.

Algo que justamente mencionamos al principio de este trabajo y que queremos retomar brevemente es la posibilidad de que el hablante evite formas que no conoce o que ha perdido a través de cambios de código. En este estudio no tomamos en cuenta este fenómeno pero creemos que sería de interés en el futuro encarar este tema y considerar cuáles de los cambios se deben a la falta de conocimiento y cuáles son parte de la cultura norteamericana como sugiere Otheguy (1993) ya que basándose en estos números podríamos aumentar el interés en cursos de español para situaciones específicas.

Implicaciones pedagógicas para la enseñanza del español como lengua heredada en los Estados Unidos

El bajo porcentaje de errores morfosintácticos y la presencia del cambio de código en el habla de los entrevistados parecen indicar que resultaría de mayor utilidad dedicarle más tiempo a la expansión del léxico en lugar de concentrarnos en la enseñanza de la gramática. En todos los niveles de estos programas deberíamos incorporar más materiales que contribuyan a ampliar el vocabulario que manejan los estudiantes para mejorar su habilidad de comunicarse con hablantes monolingües de español. En esto seguimos la sugerencia de Hernández Chávez de aumentar la enseñanza del léxico para disminuir la inseguridad lingüística de los hablantes bilingües (1999).

Los resultados de este estudio vuelven a resaltar la necesidad de metodologías más comunicativas y funcionales, algo que ya todos consideramos im-

prescindible en la enseñanza de segundas lenguas pero que no parece trans-
ferirse a la enseñanza de lo que aquí hemos estado denominando segundo
dialecto. Muchos nos hemos formado la impresión de que lo que necesitamos enseñar es gramática debido a que la mayoría de los hablantes bilingües no han recibido instrucción formal en español. La evidencia aquí
presentada indica que debemos cambiar el énfasis del salón de clase y ofrecer
al estudiante una gama más amplia del léxico al que pueda tener acceso
cuando su interlocutor es un hispanoparlante monolingüe.

De ninguna manera cuestionamos la legitimidad del dialecto que el estudiante ya posee; nos alineamos con Hidalgo (1993) y Villa (1996) al sugerir
que la meta principal de los cursos de español para hispanos debe ser la de
identificar la variación morfosintáctica ya que es ésta área de la producción
oral (y escrita) la que permite que se estigmatice a los hablantes asociándolos
con un grupo socioeconómico no privilegiado. Lo que nos interesa lograr es
la adquisición de la variedad estándar por parte del hablante para que tenga
la capacidad de adaptación, siguiendo la explicación de Chambers (1992), de
modificar su producción oral de acuerdo con el interlocutor y el medio
ambiente.

Es esencial seguir insistiendo en que el uso de la forma no estándar por
parte del hablante no debe interpretarse como falta de conocimiento o habilidad sino una opción que el hablante tiene disponible (Politzer 1993). Porras
(1996, p. 57) propone "diseñar e implementar un programa de educación bidialectal de la lengua española en escuelas y universidades, de tal manera
que garantice tanto la supervivencia del habla local de las comunidades hispánicas, como la adquisición de la modalidad formal general de la lengua española por parte de hablantes en edad escolar". Si logramos la adquisición de
la forma estándar como un dialecto de la L1 en el plano diastrático o sociocultural, llegaremos a una formación lingüística bidialectal comprensiva y
funcional que le permite al hablante usar, independientemente uno u otro
dialecto, según la ocasión.

NOTAS

1. Los ejemplos vienen seguidos entre paréntesis por: las iniciales del hablante, el
sexo (F=femenino, M=masculino), la edad, el nivel de enseñanza (I=sin instrucción formal, II=un año o menos, III=más de un año), el número de página en la
transcripción.

2. Pregunta del entrevistador.

3. Palabras en cursiva son enunciados en inglés.

4. Los datos entre paréntesis son comentarios del entrevistador.

REFERENCIAS

Aparicio, Frances. 1983. "Teaching Spanish to the Native Speaker at the College Level." *Hispania* 66:232–38.

Chambers, J. K. 1992. "Dialect Acquisition." *Language* 68 (4):673–705.

Cheshire, Jenny, y Dieter Stein. 1997. "The Syntax of Spoken Language." En *Taming the Vernacular*, eds. Jenny Chesire y Dieter Stein, 1–12. London: Longman.

Corder, S. Pit. 1973. *Introducing Applied Linguistics*. Harmondsworth, UK: Penguin.

Danesi, Marcel. 1986. *Teaching a Heritage Language to Dialect-speaking Students*. Toronto: OISE Press.

Delany-Barmann, Gloria. 1997. *United States Native Spanish Speakers and Their Spanish Language Education: Needs, Attitudes, and Characteristics*. Ph.D. diss., Northern Arizona University.

Dulay, Heidi C., Marina K. Burt, y Stephen D. Krashen. 1982. *Language Two*. Rowley, MA: Newbury House.

Ellis, Rod. 1994. *The Study of Second Language Acquisition*. Oxford: Oxford University Press.

Escure, Genevieve. 1997. *Creole and Dialect Continua: Standard Acquisition Processes in Belize and China (PRC)*. Amsterdam: John Benjamins.

Fairclough, Marta. 1998. "En busca de un marco teórico para la adquisición del español estándar como segundo dialecto en una situación de contacto." Unpublished manuscript.

Faltis, Christian J. 1990. "Spanish for Native Speakers: Freirian and Vygotskian Perspectives." *Foreign Language Annals* 23 (2):117–26.

———. 1984. "Reading and Writing in Spanish for Bilingual College Students: What's Taught in School and What's Used in the Community." *The Bilingual Review/ La Revista Bilingüe* 11 (1):21–32.

———. 1981. "Teaching Spanish Writing to Bilingual College Students." *NABE Journal* 6 (1):93–106.

Faltis, Christian J., y Robert A. DeVillar. 1993. "Effective Computer Uses for Teaching Spanish to Bilingual Native Speakers: A Socioacademic Perspective." En *Language and Culture in Learning: Teaching Spanish to Native Speakers of Spanish*, eds. Barbara J. Merino, Henry T. Trueba y Fabián A. Samaniego, 160–70. London: The Falmer Press.

Hernández Chávez, Eduardo. 1999. "Imperativo para la sobrevivencia cultural: La revitalización del español chicano de Nuevo México." Paper presented at the XVII National Conference of Spanish in the United States. Marzo 11–13, 1999. Miami, FL.

Hidalgo, Margarita. 1997. "Criterios normativos e ideología lingüística: Aceptación y rechazo del español de los Estados Unidos." En *La enseñanza del español a hispanohablantes: Praxis y teoría*, eds. M. Cecilia Colombi y Francisco X. Alarcón, 109–19. Boston: Houghton Mifflin.

———. 1993. "The Teaching of Spanish to Bilingual Spanish-Speakers: A 'Problem' of Inequality." En *Language and Culture in Learning: Teaching Spanish to Native Speakers of Spanish*, eds. Barbara J. Merino, Henry T. Trueba, y Fabián A. Samaniego, 82–93. London: The Falmer Press.

James, Carl. 1998. *Errors in Language Learning and Use: Exploring Error Analysis*. London: Longman.

Larsen-Freeman, Diane, y Michael H. Long, eds. 1991. *An Introduction to Second Language Acquisition Research*. New York: Longman.

Lipski, John M. 1993. "Creoloid Phenomena in the Spanish of Transitional Bilinguals." En *Spanish in the United States: Linguistic Contact and Diversity*, eds. Ana Roca y John M. Lipski, 155–82. Berlin: Mouton de Gruyter.

McQuillan, Jeff. 1996. "How Should Heritage Learners Be Taught?: The Effects of a Free Voluntary Reading Program." *Foreign Language Annals* 29 (1):56–72.

Merino, Barbara J. 1989. "Techniques for Teaching Spanish to Native Spanish Speakers." *Español para triunfar/Spanish for Success: A Summer Institute for High School Spanish Teachers of NSS Students*. Davis: UC. Seminar at the University of California, Davis.

Merino, Barbara J., y Fabián A. Samaniego. 1993. "Language Acquisition Theory and Classroom Practices in the Teaching of Spanish to the Native Spanish Speaker." En *Language and Culture in Learning: Teaching Spanish to Native Speakers of Spanish*, eds. Barbara J. Merino, Henry T. Trueba, y Fabián A. Samaniego, 115–23. London: The Falmer Press.

Otheguy, Ricardo. 1993. "A Reconsideration of the Notion of Loan Translation in the Analysis of U.S. Spanish." En *Spanish in the United States: Linguistic Contact and Diversity*, eds. Ana Roca y John Lipiski, 21–45. Berlin, New York: Mouton de Gruyter.

Pfaff, Carol W. 1979. "Constraints on Language Mixing: Intrasentential Code-Switching and Borrowing in Spanish/English." *Language* 55 (2):291–318.

Politzer, Robert L. 1993. "A Researcher's Reflections on Bridging Dialect and Second Language learning: Discussion of Problems and Solutions." En *Language and Culture in Learning: Teaching Spanish to Native Speakers of Spanish*, eds. Barbara J. Merino, Henry T. Trueba, y Fabián A. Samaniego, 45–57. London: The Falmer Press.

Poplack, Shana. 1980. " 'Sometimes I'll Start a Sentence in Spanish y Termino en Español': Toward a Typology of Code-switching." *Linguistics* 18 (7–8):581–618.

Porras, Jorge E. 1997. "Uso local y uso estándard: un enfoque bidialectal a la enseñanza del español para nativos." En *La enseñanza del español a hispanohablantes: Praxis y teoría*, eds. M. Cecilia Colombi y Francisco X. Alarcón, 190–97. Boston: Houghton Mifflin.

———. 1996. "Proyecto de enseñanza bidialectal del español para estudiantes nativos." En *First Annual Conference on Spanish for Native Speakers: NMSU May 17–19, 1995*. Working Papers, 56–62. Las Cruces, NM: New Mexico State University.

Roca, Ana. 1997. "La realidad en el aula: logros y expectativas en la enseñanza del español para estudiantes bilingües." En *La enseñanza del español a hispano-hablantes: Praxis y teoría*, eds. M. Cecilia Colombi y Francisco X. Alarcón, 55–64. Boston: Houghton Mifflin.

Rodríguez Pino, Cecilia. 1997. "La reconceptualización del programa de español para hispanohablantes: estrategias que reflejan la realidad sociolingüística de la clase." En *La enseñanza del español a hispanohablantes: Praxis y teoría*, eds. M. Cecilia Colombi y Francisco X. Alarcón, 65–82. Boston: Houghton Mifflin.

Sánchez, Rosaura. 1993. "Language Variation in the Spanish of the Southwest." En *Language and Culture in Learning: Teaching Spanish to Native Speakers of Spanish*, eds. Barbara J. Merino, Henry T. Trueba, y Fabián A. Samaniego, 75–81. London: The Falmer Press.

———. 1982. "Our Linguistic and Social Context." En *Spanish in the United States: Sociolinguistic Aspects*, eds. Jon Amastae y Lucía Elías-Olivares, 9–46. Cambridge: Cambridge University Press.

Silva-Corvalán, Carmen. 1994. *Language Contact and Change: Spanish in Los Angeles*. Oxford: Clarendon Press.

Valdés, Guadalupe. 1997. "The Teaching of Spanish to Bilingual Spanish-Speaking Students: Outstanding Issues and Unanswered Questions." En *La enseñanza del español a hispanohablantes: Praxis y teoría*, eds. M. Cecilia Colombi y Francisco X. Alarcón, 8–44. Boston: Houghton Mifflin.

———. 1988. "The Language Situation of Mexican Americans." En *Language Diversity: Problem or Resource*, eds. Sandra Lee McKay y Sau-Ling Cynthia Wong, 113–39. New York: Newbury House.

———. 1981. "Pedagogical Implications of Teaching Spanish to the Spanish Speaking in the United States." En *Teaching Spanish to the Hispanic Bilingual: Issues, Aims, and Methods*, eds. Guadalupe Valdés, Anthony G. Lozano, y Rodolfo García-Moya, 3–20. New York: Teachers College Press.

Van Marle, Jaap. 1997. "Dialect versus Standard Language: Nature versus Culture." En *Taming the Vernacular*, eds. Jenny Chesire y Dieter Stein, 13–34. London: Longman.

Villa, Daniel J. 1996. "Choosing a 'Standard' Variety of Spanish for the Instruction of Native Spanish Speakers in the U.S." *Foreign Language Annals* 29 (2):191–200.

Walqui, Aída. 1997. "Algunas consideraciones acerca de la enseñanza del español a hispanohablantes a nivel secundario." En *La enseñanza del español a hispanohablantes: Praxis y teoría*, eds. M. Cecilia Colombi y Francisco X. Alarcón, 45–54. Boston: Houghton Mifflin.

10

Academic Registers in Spanish in the U.S.
A Study of Oral Texts Produced by Bilingual Speakers in a University Graduate Program

Mariana Achugar

School for International Training

The relationship between the social contexts where language is used and the language produced in these contexts can help us understand how discursive communities are constructed. Gee (1996) and Street (1999) argue that in order to become a member of the academic discourse community, individuals need to learn something more than the language appropriate for academic situations. They have to become practicing members of the community, in order to adopt the rest of the social practices that together with the language make that community's identity. On the other hand, other researchers such as Martin (1993) and Schleppegrell (2001) propose that learning the language of the academic community allows individuals to have access to this community's meaning-making practices. Having the tools to understand how language works in academic settings allows learners to use language for their own purposes. In this study, the focus is on how linguistic features contribute to signaling membership in a discourse community; acknowledging, however, that other social practices also help construct a member's identity.

Several studies have focused on how students are socialized into academic discourse in English-speaking contexts (Atkinson and Ramanathan 1995; Halliday and Martin 1993; Morita 2000). However, little research has been carried out on the characteristics of Spanish academic discourse in bilingual contexts in the U.S. (but see Schleppegrell and Colombi 1997; Colombi 1997; Valdés and Geoffrion-Vinci 1998). This study focuses on the linguistic and discursive features of Spanish academic discourse in the U.S. university context in order to better understand how bilingual speakers can develop their academic language skills in a broader setting (Spanish as a minority language in the U.S.) where there are few opportunities to be socialized into this discourse.

Building on Valdés and Geoffrion-Vinci (1998), the present study analyzes the characteristics of the language produced by bilingual speakers of Spanish and English during oral presentations for two graduate seminars in a U.S. university in the western region. This task is considered an example of an academic genre that is used to socialize students into the discourse community of their discipline. Becoming proficient in this academic activity entails not only developing the appropriate language for the situation but also presenting themselves as experts on the topic. The objective of this paper is to point out how linguistic features contribute to the presentation of the self as an "expert" within a discourse community.

Academic Registers

The concept of academic registers refers to a language variety associated with situations that occur in educational institutions. The notion of register in systemic functional linguistics implies a "systematic correlation between the organization of language itself and specific contextual features" (Eggins 1994, p. 52). From this perspective, three aspects of a situation have a linguistic consequence: the topic that is being addressed (field), the role relationship between the participants in the situation (tenor), and the role that language plays in the situation (mode) (Eggins 1994; Halliday 1994). In academic registers some of the distinguishing features associated with these aspects of the situation are: a technical vocabulary (field), a distance between the participants that produces a level of formality (tenor), and a tendency towards the written aspects on the oral/written continuum (mode). These general characteristics of academic registers are realized through specific and systematic lexico-grammatical structures. The purpose of this study is to identify some of the linguistic and discursive features that realize academic registers in Spanish.

Learning the language of academic contexts such as the school and the university constitutes a second socialization. This language is permeated by writing in all of its modes. Thus educational knowledge is heteroglossic, constituted out of the dialectic between the spoken and the written (Halliday 1996). The process of becoming a member of an academic community then entails learning how to use language in a different way from its ordinary uses.

Although learning to use the language of the academy does not guarantee success in it, it has been shown to be a relevant aspect when predicting access and achievement in this discourse community.

Several researchers have pointed out the relationship between learning these academic registers and being able to succeed in school (Bernstein 1972; Cummins 1984; Melgar, Carlino, and Finocchio 1999; Colombi 2000; Schleppegrell 2001). These authors have distinguished between context-embedded language and context-independent language (Cummins 1984), restricted and elaborated codes (Bernstein 1972), and "oral based" and "text based" codes (Ong 1982). These distinctions point to the priority the written end of the orality-literacy continuum has in educational contexts. Through ethnographic research in communities and schools some studies have found continuity between the language and other social practices of white middle class families in the home and in schools. The discursive practices used by middle class groups tend to coincide with the language favored in schools (Bernstein 1972, 1990; Brice-Heath 1982). In consequence, in order to succeed in school students need to master not only the content matter of the different disciplines they study but also the ways this knowledge is displayed and constructed through language. Learners need to develop their skills to use language as "experts" in the field. With this in view, learners need to become aware of the ways in which the discourse community of a discipline uses language to signal its identity. A deconstruction of academic registers in order to identify some of its distinguishing features can make this discourse more understandable to the new members of the community.

Studies of the difference between oral and written language have informed research on academic registers in English since this type of language has been associated with the characteristics of the written end of this continuum (Chafe 1985; Tannen 1985; Chafe and Tannen 1987; Halliday 1990; Biber 1995). Some of the general characteristics associated with academic language include: detachment, technical lexis, grammatical simplicity (structurally embedded discourse), lexical density, and the use of technical action processes and attributive processes. At the lexico-grammatical and discursive level some of the structures associated with these registers in English (Biber 1995; Gibbons 1997) are the packaging of information in noun phrases or nominal groups (nominalization) and the increased explicitness in logical structure (more integration and less coordination). By packaging information in nominal groups, language users are able to abstract more and construct scientific concepts (Halliday and Martin 1993). Nominalization allows language users to organize texts in terms of ideas, reasons, causes, etc. (Eggins 1994). And through use of more integration academic discourse makes the system of interdependence between clauses and the system of logico-semantic relations more evident and explicit. This characteristic is what allows speakers to construct a text that is more independent from the context in which it is produced.

The linguistic and discursive features associated with certain communicative goals and functions reflect the way linguistic resources are allocated to carry out certain functions in each culture (Biber 1995; Halliday 1996). Nevertheless, even if similar communicative goals and functions exist across cultures their differing linguistic resources will result in variations across languages within parallel registers. This is why it is relevant to investigate the linguistic and discursive features associated with the realization of academic registers in Spanish, and specifically in a bilingual context.

Academic Discourse in a Bilingual Context

There have not yet been many studies of the linguistic and discursive features that realize Spanish academic registers in monolingual or in bilingual contexts. Gibbons's study (1997) is one of the few studies attempting to find the lexico-grammatical features that realize Spanish academic registers in order to help in the development of Spanish in bilingual learners in the Australian context. In this study Gibbons compared school textbooks used in monolingual academic contexts (Argentina and Uruguay) to teach natural and social sciences in primary and secondary school. The hypothesis was that early primary texts would be closer to the learners' everyday language than the language of secondary school textbooks. Texts that covered similar topics from both levels were selected. Gibbons found that the characteristics of Spanish academic registers resemble those of English, but that the formal resources to realize this register are not exactly the same due to differences between the languages. Some of the particular forms of realization of these registers in Spanish are:

1. Spanish uses fewer passives and creates detachment through "se" constructions. For example, "Se hicieron cambios importantes" (important changes were made).

2. Spanish uses specialist adjectives to package information instead of compounding two nouns as English does. For example, "energía eólica" versus "wind power."

This study has shown that there are differences between the way academic registers are realized in Spanish and English. As a result, further investigation of these registers in Spanish is necessary.

Research on academic registers in Spanish in the U.S. have focused on identifying lexical choices in spoken language (Valdés and Geoffrion-Vinci 1998) and on clause-combining strategies and nominalizations in written language (Schleppegrell and Colombi 1997; Colombi 1997, 2000). All of these studies were carried out with participants in undergraduate university language courses. These projects advocate for the explicit instruction of academic registers in order to develop the Spanish bilingual's linguistic repertoire.

The investigation on oral academic language (Valdés and Geoffrion-Vinci 1998) contrasted the oral presentations of monolingual working class first-generation university students in Mexico with those of second- and third-generation bilingual working class first-generation university students in the U.S. Their findings suggest that both groups were aware of the existence of academic registers that both groups tried to approximate. The main difference between the performances of these groups appeared in the use of less proficient technical vocabulary and transitional phrases by the bilingual group. In addition, according to Valdés and Geoffrion-Vinci, the group of bilingual students avoided code-switching in their presentations since this was perceived as inappropriate academic Spanish. In their conclusions the authors mention that the bilingual students "appear to be young, unsophisticated, and sometimes even inarticulate" (Valdés and Geoffrion-Vinci 1998, p. 494). Some of the elements that contribute to the impression of inarticulateness are: limited lexical range, few strategies for managing academic interactions, restricted resources for characterizations of one's or others' contributions to the discussion, and difficulty presenting oneself as a competent and knowledgeable academic.

The goal of the present study is to better describe the linguistic and discursive characteristics that enable speakers to portray themselves as members of the academic community of their discipline. This goal was explored through analysis of the academic registers produced by graduate students of a particular discipline when they performed oral presentations as part of their course work.

Participants, Setting, and Data Collection

The texts selected were analyzed using the systemic functional model (Halliday 1994). This type of analysis entails a very detailed level of discourse analysis; therefore, few texts were selected for in-depth analysis. As a consequence, the findings of this study can only be suggestive; however, they can contribute to the description and understanding of the lexico-grammatical and discursive features that realize Spanish academic registers.

To explore academic discourse, data were collected through video and tape recordings of oral presentations in two graduate seminars. The classes from which the texts were taken were two linguistics seminars conducted in Spanish with some instances of code-switching. One of the professors was from South America and the other was from the U.S. Both professors expected Spanish to be used as the language of presentations. The presentations were a requirement in both seminars and they entailed reading a specialist's article and reporting on it. Most of the readings in both classes were in English, so the presenters had to translate and adapt the technical terms to Spanish in order to carry out the oral presentation.

This analysis paid attention to the cultural context and the insiders' perspectives on academic registers. Acknowledging that academic registers vary from discipline to discipline and from one institution to another, the participants in this discourse community were asked to complete a questionnaire in order to establish what the expectations for this specific academic genre are in this particular setting. The results of the interview were used to characterize the genre of academic oral presentation and to select the presentations.

According to the participants in this academic community an oral presentation is a way of displaying knowledge and practicing a skill that will be necessary in a future professional career. In the questionnaire participants were asked about the characteristics of an effective oral presentation and about what they expected to find in an oral presentation. Their answers included the following:

- organization around the main topic of the article
- communication of the main ideas of the article
- use of examples and explanations
- clarity of delivery
- use of formal and technical language
- presentation completely in Spanish
- fluency
- confidence
- use of visual aids (OHP, handouts, blackboard)
- eloquence
- good command of the audience

These characteristics are the result of the analysis of thirteen completed questionnaires out of sixteen participants in the classes, including the professors. Based on this description two "effective" presentations were selected to be analyzed in depth. The selection was also based on the characteristics of the participants' language socialization. According to Valdés and Geoffrion-Vinci (1998) students who have experiences with Spanish predominantly in bilingual contexts are not able to develop the type of language expected by the academic discourse communities. Their project specifically addressed the status of Chicano students in graduate programs of Spanish in the U.S. According to their study Chicano students were not perceived as competent speakers of these registers, which affected their standing as students in the university. For these reasons the language socialization of participants in this study was considered in order to select the texts because the students have had different experiences with Spanish academic language.

The presentations selected for in-depth analysis are by a student in the program who has been socialized in Spanish monolingual (SSM) contexts up to the graduate level and by one socialized in English during high school and in bilingual (SEB) contexts during his university studies. Both students were in their first year of a Ph.D. program in Spanish linguistics and they did the oral presentations as part of their course requirements. However, their experience in the academic community differed. The student who had been schooled in Spanish monolingual contexts up to the graduate level also had been a teacher educator in her country. The student schooled in English-dominant environments majored in American literature in college and began to study Spanish linguistics only in his graduate studies. These students not only differ in their language socialization histories but also in their experience with the content matter of their disciplines. The participants' language socialization history and their familiarity with the field of study they were presenting on were key variables that affected their performance.[1] Language has an important function in the construction of knowledge and in the enactment of social roles. As a consequence, the linguistic performances of these participants can be taken as an indication of their knowledge of the topic as well as of their identity as members of the academic community.

Information about the community's expectations regarding an oral presentation was used in interpreting the texts chosen to be analyzed more in depth. Through interviews with two people who read the transcripts of the two presentations and from the comments professors made of these presentations it was found that there were differences in the way the participants' texts were perceived. The text produced by the person socialized in a mostly monolingual academic context was perceived as a sample of a more competent user of academic registers than that of the presenter whose language socialization was in a bilingual academic setting. The perceived difference between the texts is interpreted as a sign of the presenters' academic competence in general and, as a result, an index of their membership in the community is affected. Their competence in using academic registers affects their status in the discursive community.

Analysis

A comparable stretch of text without significant interruptions was taken from both presentations. These texts are the beginning of the oral presentation where the presenters hold the floor for an extended period of time almost without interruptions. The analysis of these texts revealed that there is a difference in the construction of logico-semantic relationships in the texts, in the ways authority is brought in, and in the use of code-switching to position the speaker and establish contact with the audience. These features are relevant in the realization of discourse in academic contexts, since one of the main characteristics of academic registers is to present the speaker/writer as an expert. The linguistic resources mentioned before show how authority is established through the grammar of the language produced.

The texts were divided into clause complexes using the grammar to identify the interdependence of clauses shown by explicit signals like conjunctions (Thompson 1996). Then, two dimensions were considered in analyzing how clauses relate to each other: interdependency and logico-semantic relations. The logico-semantic relations can be analyzed as being two types of relationships which function in different ways: expansion or projection. Expansion is a type of logico-semantic relation through which one clause expands the meaning of another in different ways: elaborating, extending, or enhancing it. Projection is "a representation of a (linguistic) representation" (Halliday 1994, p. 250). Projection corresponds to the prototypical reported speech (direct speech, indirect speech, free indirect speech). In these texts projection serves as one of the linguistic resources the speaker uses to mark his or her authority and portray himself or herself as an expert.

Text #1 (SEB), produced by a person socialized mainly in an English academic context, shows a greater number of projection than the other text, as shown in table 10.1. By directly quoting the article he is presenting, the speaker tries to position himself as a source of knowledge. He also presents indirect representations of the original text; through this device he is able to comment on the content he is presenting without really indicating his opinion about the propositions he presents. For example:

1. "Entonces eh . . . dice que el hablante nativo usa oraciones como: '¿dónde es la casa?' y '¿dónde es el correo?' y 'mi casa está aquí'" [then, uhm . . . she says that the native speaker uses sentences such as 'where is the house?' or 'where is the post office?' and 'my house is here']

2. "Afirma ella que existe una diferencia que el hablante nativo la reconoce pero que es muy difícil de explicar porque . . ." [she states that there is a difference that the native speaker recognizes but which it is very difficult to explain because . . .]

The first example shows how the presenter cites the article by directly presenting the information in a neutral way. In this case of direct citation the presenter is merely a vehicle to transmit the information to the audience. In contrast, the second example represents a more evaluative remark because he expresses agreement with the author's proposition. The verb the presenter chose for this projection, "afirma" (states), is more evaluative than the verb "dice" (says), which is the one predominantly used in this presentation. However, there is not a clear critical stance towards the text that is being presented in either example.

Most of the information from the article is presented without further elaboration or commentary by the presenter of text #1. The speaker (SEB) mainly relies on the text as a source of validation for his presentation. The verbs that the presenter selects tend to be very "objective" (verbal processes), for example: "dice" [says], "afirma" [states], "habla" [talks]. There are not clearly stated points of view or stances taken by the presenter (see table 10.2). He merely comments on the controversial aspects of the content being presented by stating his agreement with the author of the article. By agreeing with the expert who wrote the article he himself becomes a part of that interpretative community and uses its language without having to make the propositions directly his own. This allows him to maintain some distance from the information presented without really being critical. For instance, when he comments on a controversial example presented in the article he agrees with rather than challenges the information:

3. "allá usamos muchas de las cosas que ella estuvo usando entonces no me pareció tan . . . no me pareció tan radical como les haya parecido quizás a ustedes" [there we use many of the things she was using and that is why it didn't seem so radical to me as it might have seemed maybe to you all]

Table 10.1 *Use of Projection in the Presentations*

Presenter 1	20 in 58 clauses (20 clause complexes)
Presenter 2	14 in 92 clauses (28 clause complexes)

Table 10.2 *Verbs Used for Projection*

	VERBAL PROCESSES	MENTAL PROCESSES
Presenter 1 (SEB)	15	5
Presenter 2 (SSM)	8	6

It is important to note that in this example he addressed the audience with reference to a commentary that someone had made before the presentation. He is referring to a discussion that happened before the article was presented in class. This is another example of the dubious ground on which the presenter stands since he does not feel comfortable presenting the information and commenting on his interpretation without addressing the audience's reaction. This direct reference to the audience is something that the oral medium permits and demands, in a way, since having the audience present requires trying to engage them and considering their reactions to the presentation.

In contrast, the other presenter (SSM), the person who was socialized mainly in a Spanish monolingual academic context, resorts to projection to a much lesser degree (see table 10.1) and utilizes other discursive devices to present herself as an expert. She uses projection to cite the article and other references that apply to the subject she is presenting on. For example:

> 4. "Y ella habla que lo que ve en la gente de Puerto Rico es una estabilidad bilingüe y un patrón de migración circular" [and she says that what she sees in the people from Puerto Rico is a bilingual stability and a pattern of circular migration]

But she also uses expansion. This type of logico-semantic relation is very different from projection in that the expanded clause would not change meaning radically if the expansion is taken away, but, on the other hand, in a projection the information projected is an essential part of the meaning of the clause (Thompson 1996). In text #2 the relationship of expansion is used to elaborate, extend, and enhance the information presented in the article she is reporting on. For example:

> 5. "Ella quiere ofrecer un modelo sociolingüístico, para explicar . . . eh este fenómeno de la alternancia." [She wants to offer a sociolinguistic model to explain this . . . uhm this phenomenon of code-switching.]

This difference in the construction of logico-semantic relations in the text realizes a higher level of academic register. This is because the speaker not only relies on someone else's words to present herself as an author, but because she also demonstrates an understanding and a critical stance towards the information presented. For example:

> 6. "Entonces quiere combinar las dos cosas . . . las funciones sociales y pragmáticas . . . y en eso yo creo que todas las lecturas que estamos haciendo están de acuerdo . . . ." [then she wants to combine the two things . . . the social and pragmatic functions . . . and in that I believe that all the readings we are doing agree . . . .]

In example #6 we can see how this speaker not only presents the content of the article, which is about the combination of social and pragmatic functions of code-switching, but also adds a remark that connects this information to other readings on the topic. Through the use of projection, using the mental verb "creo" (I believe), this presenter makes a logico-semantic connection between the content of the article and her previous knowledge. In this use of a linguistic resource the presenter is evidencing her critical thinking skills, the ability to connect new information to already known information.

Another important linguistic resource this speaker deploys is the use of a form of projection that packages a lot of information into a clause. For example:

> 7. "Pero entonces ella se plantea [lo mismo que Timm se plantea] entonces podemos encontrar en este modelo . . . podemos aportar con factores lingüísticos que aclaren algo más esto de la alternancia . . . ." [but then she presents the same as Timm presents . . . then we can find in this model . . . we can contribute with linguistic factors that clarify something more about this code-switching issue . . . .]

The linguistic resource she is using, transforming a clause into a nominal group through the addition of the neuter pronoun "lo" allows her to not only present the information in the article but also establish a relationship between the content she is presenting and her previous knowledge on the subject. By presenting information as facts, propositions construed as having previous existence, the speaker partly packages the material she is presenting without making it into a nominalization. This resource allows her to challenge the information presented since it is not represented as an entity but as a proposition. This possibility allows the presenter to have a critical stance towards the text, which subsequently portrays her as an expert on the information she is presenting. This ability to make connections between ideas and sources is a reflection of an academic discourse practice.

Another interesting difference in the way the texts are structured appears in the use of conjunction[2] to establish logical relations between the ideas. The text of the second presenter (SSM), the person mainly socialized in Spanish academic contexts, uses a variety of connectors to establish relationships of addition, contrast, and cause predominantly. Among the most prevalent conjunctions are: "pero" (but), "porque" (because), "también" (also), "entonces" (then/so), "así que" (so), "por otro lado" (on the other hand). For example:

> 8. "Hay otra persona que ha estudiado mucho esto que es Pedraza, que lo cita en el artículo con otra perspectiva . . . pero también es interesante porque ella va a tomar los datos de Pedraza que es una persona de la comunidad como pasó con Zentella . . . ." [There is another person that has studied this a lot that is Pedraza, who she cites in her article with another perspective . . . but it is also interesting because she is going to take the data from Pedraza who is a person from the community as it happened with Zentella . . . .]

In this example the presenter establishes connections of contrast and cause, displaying an integration of ideas.

However, the first text (SEB) does not establish this type of relationship between the ideas as often; there is a tendency to organize ideas as independent clauses. And when there are connections between the clauses the presenter relies mostly on connectors that establish chains of information as is characteristic in oral language. In this text the connector that predominates is "y" (and) which reflects a trait that makes this text more oral and thus less academic. For example:

> 9. "///Dice //en 'mi casa es aquí' se expresa identidad ah . . . miembro de un conjunto. ///Básicamente eso es . . . [lo que dice durante todo la el artículo . . . el artículo . . . identidad y miembro de un conjunto] //y por supuesto evento que lo dice más tarde." [She says in 'my house is here' identity is expressed ah . . . member of a group. Basically that is what she is saying in the whole article . . . the article . . . identity and member of a group. And of course event that she says later.]

Text #9 shows the tendency of this speaker to explain information without integrating it into a clause complex, that is, using no subordination and creating coordination through the use of "y" (and) as the most frequent conjunction. The construction of causal relationships is more prevalent in the second presenter's (SSM) text (19 percent) than in the first presenter's (SEB) text (12 percent). This difference together with the previously mentioned usage of projection provides grammatical evidence for the perceived difference in competence of these speakers.

Text #1 (SEB) does use some forms that can function as causal conjunctions, but in most cases they are not used to produce the integration of clauses. For instance, one of the lexical items that appears very frequently in this text is "entonces" (then/so) which is used as a discourse marker (so/well) to signal the continuation of the speaker's turn more than to establish a logical relationship between ideas. For example:

10. "Entonces eh . . . dice que el hablante nativo usa oraciones como '¿dónde es la casa?' y '¿dónde es el correo?' y 'mi casa es aquí' o . . ." [so . . . she says that the native speaker uses sentences such as 'where is the house?' and 'where is the post office?' and 'my house is here' or . . .]

In this case "entonces" signals a continuation of the previous utterance, not a logical relationship between the propositions.

Another difference between these texts appears at the interpersonal level in the way the speakers use modalization to hedge the information that is being presented. In the first presenter's (SEB) text his modalization portrays the speaker as an insecure presenter or a novice in the field. For example:

11. "Entonces el semántico en verdad lo . . . lo desarrolla de una manera bastante sencilla que se entiende . . . bueno, yo al menos pensé que sí se entendía. . . ." [So, the semantic really she develops it in a way that is pretty simple . . . that is understandable . . . well, at least I thought that it was understandable . . . .]

Modalization appears in text #2 (SSM) in a more indirect form, many times as an interpersonal grammatical metaphor[3] as illustrated by this example:

12. "Pareciera que eso es lo más claro." [It would seem that that is the clearest.]

The speaker's opinion regarding the probability of the proposition appears as a projecting clause in a hypotactic clause complex (Halliday 1994, p. 354). The presenter construes the probability as objective, presenting the information as a projection. By presenting information as objective the presenter does not put into question the reliability of the information she is presenting and as a result she may be perceived as a reliable source.

The use of code-switching by these presenters is another notable aspect. Studies in Spanish-English code-switching reveal it as a sign of proficiency in both of the languages mixed. And when distinguishing the different types of code-switching the mixing at the level of the word is referred to as "emblematic code-switching." This type of code-switching is related to establishing intergroup solidarity and membership. In the texts studied here, both speakers resort to English for similar functions, clarifying information or not having the resources in one of their available codes, Spanish. According to previous studies in code-switching, the less competent speaker in Spanish academic registers would be expected to resort to English more frequently since he or she would not have the linguistic resources to carry out a presentation in only one of his or her two available codes. Surprisingly in these texts the opposite occurs. The speaker who has been socialized mostly in Spanish academic (SSM) contexts shows more tokens of English than the one mostly socialized in English (SEB). However, the text of the less-experienced Spanish speaker (SEB) is perceived as more "tainted" by English than the one which in fact has more tokens (SSM). The reason is that the text produced by the person with more experience in English academic contexts (SEB) uses discourse markers and examples in English to clarify and expand the information presented in Spanish. For example:

13. "ok . . . so . . . entonces el siguiente ejemplo que usa es el mismo . . . similar: 'This garden is a paradise' . . . entonces el garden es una categoría del paraíso . . . los dos son . . . ." [ok . . . so . . . then the following example that she uses is the same . . . similar: 'This garden is a paradise' . . . then the garden is a category of paradise . . . they both are . . . .]

This finding seems relevant in demonstrating that differentiating code-switching by the "amount" of language that is mixed, single word alternation or the mixing of longer stretches of language, is not a useful distinction in all cases. In this case analyzing the status of Spanish as a minority language in the larger community would explain some of the code-switching choices of presenter #1 (SEB). In the larger community switching to English has ideological connotations associated with power and authority (Sánchez 1994). However, in this situation where Spanish is the dominant language of the academic discourse community this mechanism has the opposite effect—instead of signaling authority and power, switching to English signals inappropriate evaluation of the situation.

Since most studies of code-switching have been carried out analyzing casual conversation, the use of this practice in more formal settings has not been explored. This analysis reveals that in this formal situation the type of language used (e.g., interjections, fillers, etc.) and the discursive functions of code-switching are more important in affecting the social meaning of the text produced. It seems necessary to do more research on code-switching and its social meanings and perceptions in different registers.

In previous studies of academic registers, texts with a low level of grammatical intricacy (i.e., less coordination and more embedding) and high lexical density (i.e., more content words per total number of words in the text) are shown to have a high level of academic language (Gibbons 1997; Colombi 2000). However, in this study there is no significant difference in grammatical intricacy or lexical density between the two texts. One possible cause for this result is the type of activity in which these texts were produced. The oral presentation as a genre provides the speakers with a chance to plan the text they will be delivering, which would account for the high level of lexical density. On the other hand, the fact that it is an oral presentation in front of an audience makes it likely that the presenters will want to engage the audience. As a result, the texts produced in this situation end up being a mixture of written and oral registers. More differences between the way they organized the text at the logical and lexical levels might have surfaced if the presenters had been producing a written text.

Other aspects that surface from the analysis of the texts at the macro level include the presenters' adoption of different roles during the presentation and the types of sources used for citations or references to support their ideas. The presenter of the second text (SSM) adopts several roles during the presentation but most of the time she acts as an expert. This presenter elaborates on the information in the article and makes connections to other texts and even becomes a teacher who explains technical terms to the audience. For example:

> 14. "y como acá hay mucha gente que no está en lingüística . . . muy muy rapidito . . . de del morfema nada más, por ejemplo una palabra, un verbo ¿sí? Como comer en español . . . ." [and since here there are a lot of people that are not from linguistics . . . very very quickly . . . about the morpheme only, for example a word, a verb yes? Such as 'comer' in Spanish . . . .]

There is, however, an exchange with the audience in which the "expert" becomes a "peer," when she requests assistance with the translation of some terms that she is using in English. This role changing reveals the presenter's ability to move from one register to another without hesitation.

Another resource by which authority is brought into the presenter's discourse is through the naming of other authorities and bibliographical sources besides the article that is being reported. These features portray the presenter as a knowledgeable and experienced speaker who the audience can trust.

On the other hand, the first presenter (SEB) barely cites any authority in the field besides the one writing the article he is reporting on. The roles of this participant range from presenter of information to peer of the audience, but his authority as an expert on the subject is never played out. For example:

> 15. "[. . .] entre estas dos oraciones: "mi casa es aquí" y "mi casa está aquí" afirma ella que existe una diferencia que el hablante nativo la reconoce pero que es muy difícil de explicar porque: Ah . . . ya que las cualidades semánticas, la referencia a

un lugar específicio y la pragmática . . . . . Ah . . . son las mismas entonces no hay . . . este es difícil ¿no?" . [. . . between these two sentences "my house is here" and "my house is here" she states that there exists a difference that the native speaker recognizes but which is very difficult to explain because: Ah . . . since the semantic qualities, the reference to a specific place and the pragmatic ah . . . are the same then there isn't . . . this is a difficult one, isn't it?]

When he presents information there is always hesitation or engagement of the audience to receive approval or support.

Discussion

Power relations are expressed in language through difference. In the case of oral presentations the differences are in formal knowledge (Kress 1990). Because knowledge is constructed and displayed through language, however, in cases where the participants have different discursive histories, knowledge is not the only difference that affects a presenter's status or membership in the discourse community. In the cases analyzed here the presenters' performance is both a way of practicing their future participation in the academic community of their discipline and a way of being assessed in their present condition as students. As a result, their proficiency in academic registers has an impact in their present situation as apprentices as well as in their future situation as members of the academic community. Developing the language appropriate to participate in the social practices of the academic community is an important aspect when constructing a person's identity as an "expert" in her or his field. This analysis has shown that there are particular linguistic and discursive features that mark a person's identity as a member of the academic community. In the case of Spanish academic registers in bilingual contexts, features such as the use of projection and expansion, conjunctions and embedding to integrate ideas, and the use of code-switching appear to be relevant signals when constructing the identity of an "expert."

As it stands now, many learners who have been socialized in bilingual settings do not have the discursive experience that would position them on an equal ground with those who have had more experience in Spanish academic settings. The relation of language users to their language is constructed through their experiences of texts in social situations (Kress 1990). These experiences with language result in linguistic resources that the users have at their disposal. That means there is not an equal distribution of linguistic resources among the apprentices into the academic community. In order to contribute to the development of academic registers of Spanish speakers in the U.S., programs should develop awareness of the importance and impact of discursive features that are part of the social practices in the academic community. And they should also provide opportunities to have direct experience with the discourse and practices of the academic community. However, learning the language of the communities does not eliminate the power issues involved in the construction of academic identities.

Developing the type of knowledge about language necessary to participate in a discourse community is not a neutral activity; it implies adopting or contesting ways of doing that serve the interests of some social group (Fairclough 1995). Even when students have chosen to become members of an academic community they might not be willing to adopt their practices without having a critical stance. On the other hand, becoming a member of a discourse community is not in the hands of the "apprentice" only. Discursive communities have ways of limiting access by evaluating and judging their potential members' performance. Awareness of what constitutes academic discourse for specific disciplines can allow members to transform existing practices and also open up opportunities to incorporate new members into the community.

Pedagogical Implications for the
Instruction of Spanish for Native Speakers

The pedagogical implications of this study comprise making explicit the community's discursive practices and assessing how these practices contribute to the socialization of future members of that community. By providing learners the chance to experience the language and social practices of their discipline, programs can maximize the students' access to the academic community of their field.

The development of Spanish academic registers in a bilingual context where there are not many situations in which students can be naturally socialized into it requires an explicit concert of efforts on the part of teachers and curriculum designers. Approaches to language that focus on content and consider the different genres students need to use in order to be active participants in academic communities should inform curricular and class design (see, for example, Mohan 1986; Martin 1993).

When considering in particular the development of oral academic discourse, pedagogies that engage learners as partners in the analytical discourse are necessary. This means that students have to become aware of the ways in which meaning is made and the different values these particular forms of making meaning have in different social groups. Academic language constitutes specialized forms of discourse that have more value in this society than quotidian uses. Linguistically different registers represent only variations in choices of how to instantiate the relationship between context and language. However, different registers are perceived as inherently more or less valuable in different communities. "The more specialized the action, the higher the 'capital' in Bourdieu's (1991) term and the greater the profit to the actants; by contrast, the more quotidian the action, the further removed it is from locations of social power; and by the same token, the less privileged or privileging (Bernstein 1990) any participation in it will be" (Hasan 1999, p. 298). Learners need to become aware of the ways language and power relate in our society.

The content-based and genre approach have been successfully implemented from the beginning levels of instruction. However, if we proceed from more experiential learning and practical content to more expository learning and theoretical content then we would recommend this type of focus on academic oral academic registers at the more advanced levels.

For the more advanced students this would include activities in which there is expository peer teaching, such as presenting reports to the class. In addition, students could engage in ethnographic activities such as observing and videotaping formal presentations and later deconstructing them to identify the functional stages and the discursive characteristics of the activity. As a follow-up, students could do their own oral presentations, be evaluated by their peers and themselves based on their previous findings of what the community expects and values in those types of activities.

According to Halliday (1999, p. 1), language figures in education in three different guises: as substance (learning language: mother tongue or foreign language); as instrument (learning through language: content); and language as object (learning about language: grammar, styles/registers, history of words). This implies that decisions and choices need to be made to provide a long-term immersion in relevant social practices together with explicit language instruction that provides students with "critical language awareness" (Fairclough 1995) and gives students the tools to become "discourse analysts" and social agents in their communities.

Questionnaire

EL REGISTRO ACADÉMICO EN EL ESPAÑOL DE LOS EE.UU.
[ACADEMIC REGISTERS IN SPANISH IN THE U.S.]

Por favor, toma unos minutos para responder a las siguientes preguntas.
[Please, take a couple of minutes to answer the following questions.]

I. Historia de tu repertorio lingüístico
   [History of your linguistic repertoire]

   a. ¿Qué lengua aprendiste a hablar primero?
      [What language did you learn to speak first?]

   b. ¿En cuáles contextos usas español?
      [In which contexts do you use Spanish?]

   c. ¿Con quién hablas español?
      [With whom do you speak Spanish?]

   d. ¿En qué lengua ha sido principalmente tu educación?
      [In what language has your instruction predominantly been?]

Lengua de instrucción: [Language of instruction	español Spanish	inglés English	bilingüe bilingual	otra other]
Primaria [Elementary school]				
Secundaria [Secondary school]				
Universidad (4 años) [University (4 years)]				
Estudios graduados [Graduate studies]				

   e. ¿Te consideras un/a bilingüe balanceado/a? Si no, ¿cuál consideras
      tu lengua dominante?
      [Do you consider yourself a balanced bilingual? If not, which is
      your dominant language?]

   f. ¿Cómo evaluarías tu proficiencia en español?
      [How do you evaluate your Spanish proficiency?]

II. Presentaciones orales. [Oral presentations]

    a. ¿Cómo describes una presentación oral en el contexto universitario? ¿Qué se espera encontrar en una presentación oral? [How do you describe an oral presentation in the university context? What do you expect to find in an oral presentation?]

    b. ¿Cuáles son las características de una "buena" o "efectiva" presentación oral en una clase universitaria? (Considera vocabulario, actitud hacia la audiencia, modo de interacción con la audiencia, tipo de organización.) [Which are the characteristics of a "good" or "effective" oral presentation in a university class? (Consider the vocabulary, attitude towards the audience, mode of interaction with the audience, and type of organization.)]

NOTES

1. Selinker and Douglas (1985) propose the discourse domain hypothesis that says that interlanguage performance can vary with context. Linguistic performance does not occur globally across interlanguage (or any language) but rather differentially within discourse domains. There is then a relationship between topic knowledge and linguistic production on those topics. Whyte's (1995) findings give further evidence of the relationship between expertise on topics and interlanguage production. She found that this relationship is associated with the effects of domain (topic, interest and opportunity to practice) on language behavior.

2. By conjunction I refer to the structural cohesive bond used to establish relationships between clauses. See Halliday 1994, p. 324.

3. A grammatical metaphor according to Halliday (1994) is an incongruent mode of expression. "The expression of a meaning through a lexico-grammatical form which originally evolved to express a different kind of meaning" (Thompson 1996, p. 165). Interpersonal metaphors are a mode of expression in which the grammar accommodates metaphors of mood and modality. It is a way to objectify opinion by nominalizing it (Thompson 1996).

ACKNOWLEDGMENTS

I would like to thank Mary Schleppegrell, Cecilia Colombi, Teresa Oteíza, and Brian Carpenter for their comments and suggestions. And a special recognition goes to the professors and students who opened their classrooms to contribute to the understanding of academic registers in Spanish.

REFERENCES

Atkinson, Dwight, and Vai Ramanathan. 1995. "Cultures of Writing: An Ethnographic Comparison of L1 and L2 University Writing/Language Programs." *TESOL Quarterly* 29 (3):539–68.

Bernstein, Basil. 1990. *Class, Codes, and Control 4: The Stucturing of Pedagogic Discourse*. London: Routledge.

———. 1972. "Social Class, Language and Socialization." In *Language and Social Context*, ed. P. Giglioli. Middlesex: Penguin Books.

Biber, Douglas. 1995. *Dimensions of Register Variation. A Cross-Linguistic Comparison*. New York: Cambridge University Press.

Brice-Heath, Shirley. 1982. "What No Bedtime Story Means: Narrative Skills at Home and School." *Language in Society* 2:49–76.

Chafe, Wallace. 1985. "Linguistic Differences Produced by Differences between Speaking and Writing." In *Literacy, Language and Learning*, eds. D. Olson, N. Torrance, and A. Hildyard, 105–23. Cambridge: Cambridge University Press.

Chafe, Wallace, and Deborah Tannen. 1987. "The Relation Between Written and Spoken Language." *Annual Review of Anthropology* 16:383–407.

Colombi, M. Cecilia. 2000. "En vías del desarrollo del lenguaje académico en español en hablantes nativos de español en los Estados Unidos." In *Research on Spanish in the United States: Linguistic Issues and Challenges*, ed. Ana Roca. Somerville, MA: Cascadilla Press.

———. 1997. "Perfil del discurso escrito en textos de hispanohablantes: teoría y práctica." In *La enseñanza del español a hispanohablantes: Praxis y teoría*, eds. M. C. Colombi and F. X. Alarcón, 175–89. Boston: Houghton Mifflin Co.

Cummins, Jim. 1984. "The Role of Primary Language Development in Promoting Educational Success for Language Minority Students." In *Schooling and Language Minority Students: A Theoretical Framework*. Sacramento: California State Department of Education, Division of Instructional Support and Bilingual Education. Office of Bilingual Bicultural Education.

Eggins, Suzanne. 1994. *An Introduction to Systemic Functional Linguistics*. London: Pinter.

Fairclough, Norman. 1995. *Critical Discourse Analysis*. London: Longman.

Gee, James P. 1996. *Social Linguistics and Literacies: Ideology in Discourses*. London: Taylor & Francis.

Gibbons, John. 1997. "Registers Aspects of Biliteracy in a Minority Language." Unpublished manuscript.

Halliday, Michael A. K. 1999. "The Notion of 'Context' in Language Education." In *Text and Context in Functional Linguistics*, ed. Mohsen Ghadessy, 1–24. Amsterdam: John Benjamins Publishing Company.

———. 1996. "Literacy and Linguistics: A Functional Perspective." In *Literacy in Society*, eds. R. Hasan and G. Williams, 339–76. New York: Addison Wesley Longman.

———. 1994. *An Introduction to Functional Grammar.* 2d ed. London: Edward Arnold.

———. 1990. *Spoken and Written Language.* Rev. ed. Oxford: Oxford University Press.

Halliday, Michael A. K., and James R. Martin. 1993. *Writing Science: Literacy and Discursive Power.* Pittsburgh: University of Pittsburgh Press.

Hasan, Ruqaiya. 1999. "Speaking with Reference to Context." In *Text and Context in Functional Linguistics,* ed. Mohsen Ghadessy, 219–328. Amsterdam: John Benjamins Publishing Co.

Kress, Gunther. 1990. *Linguistic Processes in Sociocultural Practice.* Second Impression. Oxford: Oxford University Press.

Martin, James R. 1993. "Genre and Literacy: Modeling Context in Educational Linguistics." *Annual Review of Applied Linguistics* 13:141–72.

Melgar, S., P. Carlino, and S. Finocchio. 1999. Con el profesor de lengua no basta. *Zona educativa en el aula.* Ministerio de Cultura y Educación de la Nación. Argentina. Available at www.zona.mcye.gov.ar/ZonaAula/ZonaAula03/1.html. Accessed on June 10, 2001.

Mohan, Bernard A. 1986. *Language and Content.* Boston: Addison-Wesley.

Morita, Naoko. 2000. "Discourse Socialization through Oral Classroom Activities in a TESOL Graduate Program." *TESOL Quarterly* 34 (2):279–310.

Ong, Walter. 1982. *Orality and Literacy: The Technologizing of the Word.* London: Routledge.

Sánchez, Rosaura. 1994. *Chicano Discourse: Socio-Historic Perspectives.* Rev. ed. Houston: Arte Público Press. University of Houston.

Schleppegrell, Mary J. 2001. "Linguistic Features of the Language of Schooling." *Linguistics and Education.*

Schleppegrell, Mary J., and M. Cecilia Colombi. 1997. "Text Organization by Bilingual Writers." *Written Communication* 14 (4):481–503.

Selinker, Larry, and Dan Douglas. 1985. "Wrestling with 'Context' in Interlanguage Theory." *Applied Linguistics* 6 (2):190–204.

Street, Brian. 1999. "Academic Literacies." In *Students Writing in the University. Cultural and Epistemological Issue,* eds. C. Jones, J. Turner, and B. Street, 193–227. Amsterdam: John Bejamins Publishing Company.

Tannen, Deborah. 1985. "Relative Focus on Involvement in Oral and Written Discourse." In *Literacy, Language and Learning,* eds. D. Olson, N. Torrance, and A. Hildyard, 124–47. Cambridge: Cambridge University Press.

Thompson, Geoff. 1996. *Introducing Functional Grammar.* London: Arnold.

Valdés, Guadalupe, and Michelle Geoffrion-Vinci. 1998. "Chicano Spanish: The Problem of the 'Underdeveloped' Code in Bilingual Repertoires." *The Modern Language Journal* 82 (iv):473–501.

Whyte, Shona. 1995. "Specialist Knowledge and Interlanguage Development." *SSLA* 17:153–83.

11

¡No me suena!
Heritage Spanish Speakers' Writing Strategies

Ana María Schwartz
University of Maryland, Baltimore County

"¡**A**y! Pero es que no me suena." Chances are that every teacher who has worked with heritage Spanish students has heard this refrain as students attempt to transfer to paper the thoughts they hold in their head only to find that it just doesn't sound "right." We know that although heritage language learners present a wide range of knowledge of and competencies in their heritage language they generally exhibit a higher degree of oral proficiency than competency in literacy skills (Valdés 1995; Campbell and Rosenthal 2000). Thus it is the process of "composing," of finding the right words and arranging them in sentences and paragraphs in such a way that they accurately reflect the thoughts of the writer in a manner consistent with the norms of the language, that is usually the most troublesome for many of our heritage language students.

At the same time, writing is a key component of most heritage language courses, and in the classroom the teaching of grammar, register, vocabulary expansion, and other language issues is approached through reading and through writing skills instruction. It is therefore crucial that we understand how heritage language learners write in the heritage language so we may design instructional approaches that are appropriate to these students' needs.

As we examine the literature on how to teach writing,[1] we see that the shift from a focus on the final product to a focus on the process of writing—prewriting, writing multiple drafts, revising, editing—that prevails in first (L1) and second (L2) language writing instruction (Silva 1990) has also been embraced by the heritage language field. According to Zamel (1983) this approach offers writers the opportunity to "discover and reformulate their ideas as they attempt to approximate meaning" (p. 165). Yet, even a process writing approach only affords us a view of what the students write *after* they have written it. We can only guess how the students arrived at what they wrote, leaving us to extrapolate the strategies they used from the drafts we read. The exploratory case studies presented in this paper, conducted with three of my heritage Spanish university students, attempt to open a window into these students' writing processes by identifying the strategies they use when they compose in Spanish. It is my hope that through this research we may gain a more intimate understanding of the struggles heritage learners face and of the strategies[2] to which they turn in order to handle the challenges of writing in Spanish.

The following section will present a brief overview of the research on what language learners do while writing or composing discourse-level texts. As will be seen, the studies cited only involve English as a second language (ESL) and foreign language (FL) learners. While these studies are relevant to us as a point of departure, our heritage students are not second language learners, they are bilinguals with varying degrees of abilities in each of their languages. We must therefore build upon the existing research and, as Valdés (1995) argues, "be more precisely focused" (p. 317) on our heritage students' needs. The overview of research will be followed by an explanation of the think-aloud protocols, the research methodology used to gather the students' composing data, and profiles of the students' writing processes. Lastly, implications of the study for the classroom will be presented.

Background

Research on writing processes emerged from the recognition that in order to teach writing it is necessary to understand how people write (Zamel 1982). The process model of writing combines three general categories of strategies: planning, composing, and revising or editing. Each category comprises a particular set of strategies that the writer may use. This overview focuses on several issues that may be of particular importance to us as heritage language teachers and which we will see reflected in the composing profiles that follow. What strategies do good (skilled) and weak (unskilled) L1 and L2 writers use? How do second and foreign language writers revise their work? Do writing strategies transfer from L1 to L2? What is the effect of planning in the L1 when writing a composition in the L2?

Vivian Zamel's (1982, 1983) observations of skilled and unskilled ESL writers were among the first studies of L2 writers' processing strategies. She noted that all writers, L1 and ESL writers and skilled and unskilled writers, followed similar processes: prewriting and revising strategies were used throughout; the writers reread their texts as a means of evaluating what they had written as well as to construct meaning; they often commented on what they were doing; and they didn't use the strategies in a sequential fashion, but in a repeating or recursive manner. Yet, Zamel also found that the skilled ESL writers made more global or meaning changes to their texts: they marked words to later check for spelling or meaning; they wrote in words or phrases in their first language, or left blank spaces so as not to interrupt the flow of the writing. On the other hand, as the less-skilled writers composed, they paused often, reviewing more at the sentence rather than the text level and making local changes (e.g., spelling, grammar) more often; they edited their texts as they wrote, and paused to use the dictionary more often.

Ann Raimes (1985, 1987) followed Zamel's observational studies with think-aloud protocols similar to those used in this study. Although she agreed with Zamel that there were parallels between L1 and ESL writers, she found a great deal of variability within the ESL group and, according to Krapels (1990), cautioned against thinking that "the L2 writer was . . . [a] definable type" (p. 44). Raimes found that her subjects did not spend much time pre-writing or planning; they rescanned (rereading what they had just written) a great deal but made no major revisions at the global level; they made few local changes that did not alter the meaning of the text; and they edited and revised their texts while writing rather than at the end, as a separate stage. Raimes (1987) notes that the ESL students' rescanning activities "were directed more to rehearsal [trying out ideas] than to editing" (p. 462), speculating that, as second language learners, the ESL students did not feel as inhibited about making errors and thus focused more on generating ideas than on correcting their texts.

Elizabeth New's (1999) research on revision strategies with FL subjects yielded findings opposite to Raimes's. New found that all of her subjects, skilled and unskilled, made many more local, surface changes than global meaning changes. The revisions were mostly at the word level and consisted of "changes for form rather than for content" (p. 92) but surprisingly for so many local edits, few grammatical changes were made in the compositions. New concludes that foreign language students may benefit from instruction on the process of revising for meaning, as either the students may not have mastered this skill in the L1 or perhaps revision skills may not transfer from the L1. She also speculates that some of the surface level revisions may be due to the fact that the students were composing on the computer.

John Hedgcock and Natalie Lefkowitz's (1996) research on FL and ESL writers' "attitudes, expectations and values" toward revision and feedback support Raimes's and New's findings and yield further insights into how different populations approach revision. Hedgcock and Lefkowitz found that while ESL students tended more toward a process approach to writing, FL students viewed composing and revision as grammar practice; they believed that "form should precede and have priority over expression of meaning, concepts, or original ideas" (p. 298). Furthermore, for the FL writers (as well as for some of the ESL writers) revision was synonymous with eliminating ungrammatical constructions and with word choice.

Several FL studies suggest that writers transfer their knowledge about writing from their L1 to their L2 and vice versa. For example, Alister Cumming's (1989) research suggests that writing expertise is a cognitive ability that is separate and not dependent on language proficiency; thus writers are able to apply their writing expertise regardless of the language in which they are composing. Similarly, research with Turkish EFL students (Akyel and Kamişli 1997) and a study of university students of French (Kern and Schultz 1992) indicate that writing skills instruction in the L2 has a positive effect on L1 as well as on L2 writing, suggesting that the transfer of writing skills may be bidirectional. Kern and Schultz conclude that "writing skill in a foreign language may in fact be more closely tied to one's ability to write in the native language than to one's general level of linguistic competence in the foreign language" (p. 6).

Other research suggests that the use of the L1 in the planning stages of the composing process may facilitate rather than constrain writing in the L2. In separate studies, Alexander Friedlander (1990) and Carolyn Gascoigne Lally (2000) looked at the effects of planning in the L1 on L2 compositions. Friedlander's study involved L1 Chinese students who were writing on a topic related to Chinese culture and planning in the L1 or English. He found that when the writers planned in Chinese they were able to produce longer and more detailed plans and longer texts, and that their essays received higher ratings than when they planned in English. Building on Friedlander's research, Gascoigne Lally hypothesized that the effects of prewriting in the L1 would not be as pronounced if the topic was language and culture neutral, but her results were similar to Friedlander's. She found that while there was no difference in vocabulary or expression between the L1 or L2 prewriting condition, there was a greater difference in organization and overall impression for L1 prewriting. She suggests that students will benefit from organizing and planning their compositions "free from the linguistic limitations of the L2" (p. 431).

As we build a research base on heritage language writing instruction, it is fitting that we begin with research on writing processes. The research described above gives this study some direction, but it doesn't answer our over-riding question: how does language interact with the writing process of in-dividuals who don't fit strict definitions of L1 or L2 speakers? The study de-scribed next begins to answer this fundamental question.

The Study

The purpose of these exploratory case studies was to investigate the writing strategies used by three English-dominant heritage Spanish speakers while writing an essay in Spanish. Multiple sources of data—questionnaires, think-aloud protocols, and interviews—were collected to enhance the validity of the study and provide a more complete picture of the students' strategy use (Færch and Kasper 1987).

The participants in the study, Johana, Micaela, and Rosaura[3] (not their real names), were nineteen-year-old women born in the United States and second-year university students enrolled in Spanish 304, my Spanish for Na-tive Speakers (SNS) course. As "second-generation bilinguals" they fit a pro-file commonly found in SNS classes: "no [or basic] academic skills in Span-ish, good academic skills in English, fluent but limited speakers of contact variety of [urban] Spanish" (Valdés 1997, p. 14).[4]

INSTRUMENTS USED TO COLLECT THE DATA

Prior to writing their essays, the students filled out two questionnaires: the *Self-Efficacy Questionnaire*, which assesses the students' level of self-confi-dence with the four language skills (National Foreign Language Resource Center 1996); and a writing strategies questionnaire, where the students re-ported the type and frequency of their strategy use (table 11.1).

The students' composing data were gathered with think-aloud protocols, a verbal report research technique.[5] A think-aloud is a person's verbal descrip-tion of the thoughts entering her or his attention while performing a task (Cohen 1998). The think-aloud procedure was chosen because it allows the teacher or researcher to go beyond the student's performance by allowing a glimpse of the hidden processes underlying that performance,[6] giving a more complete picture of the student's strategic strengths and weaknesses. Therefore, the students were asked to verbalize their thoughts as they wrote the essay—not explain what they were doing or why they were doing it, but just to give voice to their thoughts. The students' running monologue was tape-recorded to be later transcribed and analyzed for strategy use. Interviews were conducted immediately after the students finished their essays and were also tape-recorded.

Table 11.1 *Writing Strategies Questionnaire*[a]

How often do you do each of the following when you are writing in Spanish?

W1. I make notes on what I want to say before I start writing.
  □ *Never* □ *Rarely* □ *Occasionally* □ *Often*

W2. I make an outline before I start writing.
  □ *Never* □ *Rarely* □ *Occasionally* □ *Often*

W3. It takes me a while to come up with what I want to say before I start writing, but I keep those thoughts in my mind instead of writing notes or outlining.[b]
  □ *Never* □ *Rarely* □ *Occasionally* □ *Often*

W4. I start writing right away and let the ideas come to me as I write.[b]
  □ *Never* □ *Rarely* □ *Occasionally* □ *Often*

W5. I say my ideas out loud to try them out before I write them.
  □ *Never* □ *Rarely* □ *Occasionally* □ *Often*

W6. I reread what I have just written before I continue writing.
  □ *Never* □ *Rarely* □ *Occasionally* □ *Often*

W7. I reread the entire paper after I have written it.
  □ *Never* □ *Rarely* □ *Occasionally* □ *Often*

W8. I cross out or erase words and phrases and substitute other words and phrases as I write.
  □ *Never* □ *Rarely* □ *Occasionally* □ *Often*

W9. I add words and phrases to what I have already written.
  □ *Never* □ *Rarely* □ *Occasionally* □ *Often*

W10. I change around the order of paragraphs or sentences as I write.
  □ *Never* □ *Rarely* □ *Occasionally* □ *Often*

W11. I change around the order of paragraphs or sentences after I have finished the text.
  □ *Never* □ *Rarely* □ *Occasionally* □ *Often*

W12. I combine two or more sentences into one.
  □ *Never* □ *Rarely* □ *Occasionally* □ *Often*

W13. I write the entire text in English and then translate it into Spanish.[b]
  □ *Never* □ *Rarely* □ *Occasionally* □ *Often*

W14. I write whole paragraphs in English and then translate them into Spanish.[b]
  □ *Never* □ *Rarely* □ *Occasionally* □ *Often*

W15. I write sentences in English and then translate them into Spanish.[b]
  □ *Never* □ *Rarely* □ *Occasionally* □ *Often*

W16. I think of whole chunks of the text in English and then write it in Spanish.
  □ *Never* □ *Rarely* □ *Occasionally* □ *Often*

W17. I think of words and phrases in English and then write them in Spanish.
  □ *Never* □ *Rarely* □ *Occasionally* □ *Often*

W18. I use an English-Spanish dictionary . . . while I'm writing.
  □ *Never* □ *Rarely* □ *Occasionally* □ *Often*

Table 11.1 *Continued*

W19. I use a Spanish-Spanish dictionary . . . while I'm writing.
  □ *Never* □ *Rarely* □ *Occasionally* □ *Often*

W20. I edit for spelling while I'm writing.[b]
  □ *Never* □ *Rarely* □ *Occasionally* □ *Often*

W21. I edit for spelling after I'm finished writing.
  □ *Never* □ *Rarely* □ *Occasionally* □ *Often*

W22. I try to put the accents on while I'm writing.[b]
  □ *Never* □ *Rarely* □ *Occasionally* □ *Often*

W23. I go back and put the accents on after I'm finished writing.
  □ *Never* □ *Rarely* □ *Occasionally* □ *Often*

W24. I check for article/noun/adjective and verb/subject agreement as I write.[b]
  □ *Never* □ *Rarely* □ *Occasionally* □ *Often*

W25. I check for article/noun/adjective and verb/subject agreement after I'm finished writing.
  □ *Never* □ *Rarely* □ *Occasionally* □ *Often*

W26. I'm pleased with my writing strategies.
  □ *Never* □ *Rarely* □ *Occasionally* □ *Often*

W27. I'm pleased with the compositions I write.
  □ *Never* □ *Rarely* □ *Occasionally* □ *Often*

W28. I think I'm a good writer.
  □ *Never* □ *Rarely* □ *Occasionally* □ *Often*

Other approaches you use to write in Spanish:

[a]W1–5, Planning; W6, 7, Composing/Monitoring; W13–17, Composing/Translation; W20–25, Revising, surface; W10–12, Revising, deep; W8, 9, 18, 19, Revising, surface and deep; W26–28, Self-evaluation.
[b]These *may* be unproductive strategies, depending on how they are used.

The think-aloud essay consisted of a descriptive task. The prompt was: "Tu prima está pensando venir a UMBC el año que viene. Descríbele la universidad." It was felt that a description of the university would be a topic well within the students' experience and would therefore generate longer samples and be representative of the processes learners employ when writing in this discourse mode.[7]

PROCEDURES FOR WRITING THE THINK-ALOUD ESSAYS

After completing the strategy and self-confidence questionnaires in class, the participants made individual appointments to do the think-alouds in my office. They were asked to reserve a block of time of at least three hours to make sure they would have ample time to complete the essay. Once settled at a desk with a tape recorder, pencils, pens, and paper, I explained the purpose of the research and described the think-aloud procedure more fully. I modeled the protocol for a few minutes and asked the students to do a short practice think-aloud. They were told they should verbalize their thoughts in whichever language they were thinking. The students then received the topic of the essay and were given an opportunity to ask questions, and then the tape recorder was turned on. I remained in the office, but outside of their line of vision, to make sure the students maintained the monologue and spoke loudly enough to be picked up by the tape recorder.

ANALYSIS OF THE DATA

The think-aloud protocols were transcribed and analyzed with a coding scheme adapted from Pennington and Brock (1992), Perl (1979), and Raimes (1987) (see table 11.2). This coding scheme reflects the process approach to writing, or "composing" mentioned earlier. Three general categories of strategies were used: prewriting, composing, and surface and deep revision, which, according to the process model, writers apply recursively as they form and re-form ideas to express their meanings. The strategies in the coding scheme served as the basis for the questions in the *Writing Strategies Questionnaire* (WSQ) (see table 11.1). The essays were also evaluated for fluency, "the rapid production of language"; grammatical complexity; and accuracy—"error-free production" (Wolfe-Quintero, Inagaki, and Kim 1998, p. 117). Additionally, two Spanish native speakers holistically rated the essays for content and organization.

OVERVIEW OF THE WRITERS AND THEIR ESSAYS

Johana and Rosaura spoke only Spanish until they started school; Micaela spoke English as her L1. However, by the time of the study the most any of them spoke Spanish at home was 50 percent of the time. This course was Johana's first formal instruction in Spanish, but Micaela and Rosaura had taken Spanish in high school. Based on class performance, I judged Johana to be the most orally proficient, followed by Rosaura and then Micaela. All three stated that they felt most confident about their listening and least confident about their ability to write, mentioning that this was the skill they practiced the least. Interestingly, both Rosaura and Johana felt very unsure of their speaking ability, rating it lower than reading and lower than Micaela did.

Although Micaela's essay was the longest she wasn't particularly fluent. Johana was by far the most fluent of the three writers; she wrote for the shortest

Table 11.2 *Coding Categories*

STRATEGY/DEFINITION	EXAMPLE
Prewriting Strategies	
General Planning: organizing one's thoughts for writing	*Uhm, I'm taking notes on what UMBC, some things that I know about UMBC, and about . . . well . . . my . . . well . . . my cousin*
Interpreting: rephrasing the topic to get a handle on it	*Mary-lou, Mary-lou . . . uhm . . . está pensando venir a UMBC el año que viene . . .*
Questioning: asking a question of the topic	[no examples occurred in the data]
Talking leading to writing: voicing ideas on the topic; brainstorming	*Uhm, ay, UMBC . . . es . . . es small, so yo sé que eso le gustaría porque no es tan grande y uno puede como . . . y puede tener . . . las . . . las clases son grandes, pero no hay tanto 'confusion' como a big school. So . . . uhm . . . okay . . . <u>UMBC aunque es pequeña</u> . . .* [a]
Composing Strategies	
Planning: working out what to do in the piece of writing	
Global Planning: discussing changes in drafts	*Voy a escribir ésto otra vez . . . en la, en la otra página . . .*
Local Planning: talking out what idea will come next	*. . . son mayor de edad . . . they're, they're not very, very old, they just . . .*
Commenting: sighs, any comments	*. . . that's it . . . uhm . . . ah, pues quédese . . .*
Assessing: positive and negative judgments about one's writing	*. . . gym, activities, the library, and surrounding area. I can't, it's too much . . . if I just put . . . uhm . . .*
Questioning: asking a question of oneself	*. . . ¿dirictir? . . . . . . how do you say 'overall'? . . .*
Repeating: repeating a word, phrase, part of a sentence, a number of times: write and say it again	*<u>no es</u> . . . <u>tan complicada</u> . . . complicada . . . <u>como yo pienso</u> . . . uhm . . . <u>ella dice</u> . . . <u>que</u> . . . <u>la gente aquí</u> . . . en . . . gente aquí . . .*
Rescanning: going back in the text and rereading a few words, sentences, paragraphs	*y se puede . . . allí, se puede usar la tarjeta . . . que te dan . . . . si compras <u>el plan de comida</u>*

Table continues on following page.

Table 11.2 *Continued*

STRATEGY/DEFINITION	EXAMPLE
Composing Strategies	
Rehearsing: development of content, trying out ideas and words in English or Spanish	*UMBC . . . es una . . . es una buena decisión . . . quiero dar mi opinión . . . pero no le quiero decir, uh, ya, I think . . .UMBC es una buena decisión* . . . (with Local Planning) . . . *café, agua, leche, y tam-* . . . *y* . . . *uhm* . . . hot chocolate . . . *uhm* . . . cocoa? *chocolate* . . . *y* . . . *leche y chocolate* . . . *cho-co-la-te*
Comments specifically directed to the topic, going back to the topic	(sigh) . . . let me see, the library . . . internet . . . uhm . . . let me go back to the main question, *tu prima está pensando venir* . . . *a UMBC el año que viene* . . .
Reading the draft: reading the draft after the 4th sentence	
Writing silently	
Editing (Revision) Strategies	
Surface (local) Level Revision—do not alter the meaning or gist of the whole text	
Addition	. . . *tiene [una]*[b] *buena reputación* . . .
Deletion	. . . *los días que* . . . *los días cuando* . . .
Grammar	. . . *no es en* . . . *en la el centro* . . .
Punctuation	. . . *hay una variedad de bebidas como,* coma
Sentence structure	*Donde está localizado UMBC* . . . *UMBC está localizado*
Verb: form or tense	
Spelling (includes accents)	*aquí, aquí* . . . *acento*
Look up in dictionary (for spelling/accents)	
Deep (global) Level Revision—alter the meaning or summary of the entire text	
Addition	*han habido muchas personas* . . . *han habido OTRAS personas*
Deletion	*que tiene* . . . *reputación* . . . *de fiestas* . . . *hay pocas* . . . *[hay pocas]* . . . *actividades* . . . *todavía ofrece actividades* . . .
Substitution	*no ¡ay! no ayudado, me ha, me ha influenciado*

Table continues on facing page.

Table 11.2 *Continued*

STRATEGY/DEFINITION	EXAMPLE
Editing (Revision) Strategies Deep (global) Level Revision—alter the meaning or summary of the entire text	
Look up in dictionary (from English)	
Reorganization: major reorganization within a paragraph or across paragraphs which alters meaning	
Combination: putting two sentences or two paragraphs together	

ªUnderlines indicate that the student was writing as she was talking.
ᵇBrackets indicate additions or deletions, according to context.

amount of time. On the other hand, Rosaura wrote the longest amount of time and produced the shortest essay. It appears that her fluency rate was brought down by the many interruptions to consult the dictionary. The range of grammatical complexity (the total number of clauses in the essay divided by the total number of T-units or idea units—that is, main clauses plus subordinate clauses) for the three essays was very close—1.8 (J), 1.7 (R), and 1.6 (M). Micaela's accuracy ratio (E/T=total number of errors by total number of T-units) was almost double that of the other two students. Her errors were distributed over all of the categories: agreement, verb tense, spelling, and word/phrase choice. Johana and Rosaura had almost the same E/T ratio but while Rosaura's errors were also evenly distributed, almost all of Johana's errors were spelling errors. Rosaura received the highest scores in the holistic composition ratings. The raters noted that her essay was easier to read than the other two, but that she needed to pay more attention to agreement, word choice, and spelling. Johana's and Micaela's averaged ratings were very similar, but the raters could not agree on Johana's essay, each rater giving her very different scores for content and for organization. For Micaela's essay they noted that the main ideas were not adequately developed and that she lacked transitions, resulting in abrupt changes in her presentation.

Use of Strategies

As can be seen in table 11.3, Johana used the least number of strategies and Micaela the most. Of the four types of strategies, the students used composing strategies the most, and of those they most frequently used: (1) rehears-

Table 11.3 *Total Frequency of Type of Strategy Use by Student and Category*

CATEGORY	JOHANA	MICAELA	ROSAURA	TOTALS
Prewriting	3	6	3	12
Composing	65	202	113	380
Editing—Surface Level	22	39	31	92
Editing—Deep Level	12	18	29	59
Totals	102	265	176	543

ing—before writing, to try out ideas; (2) repeating—after having written a word or phrase; and (3) rescanning—rereading a larger chunk of text to see how what they had written fit in. Contrary to the other two, Micaela used all of the composing strategies, also using the commenting and questioning strategies frequently.

There was a great deal of variability in the students' use of planning. Planning can be a prewriting as well as a composing strategy depending on when it is used. Micaela was the only student who really did any prewriting before starting her essay: for four-and-a-half minutes she brainstormed and made a list of possible topics (in English), which she periodically consulted, checking off items as she wrote. Johana and Rosaura did some planning, but not as prewriting. Johana started writing immediately, but then stopped to brainstorm for two minutes after writing the first sentence; she didn't write anything down. It wasn't until she had written three paragraphs that Rosaura stopped to write a list of five topics on the margin. She consulted the list later in her essay and crossed out the topics she had addressed.

As a proportion of the total number of strategies each used, Johana and Rosaura used more revision strategies than Micaela, but all three students did more surface level edits than deep level (meaning) revisions. Johana did most revisions as she wrote the essay, editing at the surface level with deletions, additions, and grammar edits. She used only two of six deep level strategies: deletion and addition. Rosaura was very interactive with the text. As she wrote, she went back to the beginning and read her draft three times, making many surface and deep level changes each time. Her surface level revisions were, in descending order: spelling (including accents), deletions, dictionary look-ups for spelling and accents, and additions. For deep level she looked up words in the dictionary for meaning, and added, deleted, and substituted words, phrases, and sentences. Most of Micaela's surface level revisions were for punctuation, spelling (including accents), and dictionary look-ups for spelling and accents. Contrary to the other students, she underlined words as she wrote and made the surface edits on those words at the end, when she reread the draft. Micaela used a greater variety of deep level strategies than surface strategies but surprisingly, while she saved the local edits until the end, she revised for meaning only as she wrote rather than when she reread the completed draft.

Discussion

The profiles of these three students provide an insight into the very distinct worlds of our heritage Spanish writers. Therefore, as we examine the results of this study we should remember Raimes's admonition that we not "type" any one group of writers, for as many commonalities as we find in these profiles we find differences. It is clear that each student has developed idiosyncratic and well-established writing procedures, not all of which are productive.

Perhaps the most interesting finding of the think-aloud study is how each student dealt with searching for the "right" way to express her ideas in Spanish so that the language she used satisfied her inner L1/HL model, that "ear" which too frequently led the students to abandon words, phrases, and in some cases whole chunks of already written text because it didn't sound right to them. This process of "sounding out" primarily involved a recursive cycle of rehearsing, repeating, and rescanning. The students used rehearsing not only to develop content or try out ideas, but also to access the "right" words and phrases to express their ideas: [Micaela] *hay una variedad de . . . uhm . . . de . . . uhm . . . de c . . . cosas de tomar . . . de bebidas . . . .;*[8] and to monitor or check translations to and from Spanish: [Micaela] *desserts . . . uhm . . . desserts, desserts, desserts . . . también tienen . . . uhm . . . ¿dulce . . . no, that's candy . . . uhm . . . .* Once the students wrote the word or phrase they would often repeat it several times, presumably to see how it sounded: [Rosaura] *entonces . . . ellos siempre . . . te pueden . . . ¿te puedan . . . ¿te pueden? ¿te puedan? te puedan . . . ellos siempre te puedan ayudar.* Rescanning would be used lastly, to hear how what they had written sounded in the context of one or more sentences. This rehearse-repeat-rescan process was repeated by all three writers throughout the think-alouds. It should be noted that the verbalizations were in Spanish, English, and Spanish-English.

Although all of the students followed the same composing process, they weren't all as successful. As mentioned above, the writers abandoned text when they weren't able to satisfy themselves that they had written what they wanted to say. Johana abandoned the largest amount of text—38 percent of the total number of words she wrote. This included two separate times that she started writing paragraphs only to discard them because, as she said in one instance, *ay no, ay no me sale bien . . . lo que quiero decir.* Micaela and Rosaura also abandoned text, although more at the word and phrase level. While the greatest constraint for these two students was lack of vocabulary, their approaches were very different. Micaela, the most linear of the three, suffered the least when she couldn't find the right word. She forged ahead laboriously, not allowing herself to get frustrated and encouraging herself as she went, *I know! I know!; yeah!; I'll get back to it.* On the other hand, Rosaura's lack of confidence in her Spanish skills led her to overly depend on the dictionary as she translated from English. These searches for the right word in Spanish became extremely frustrating for her. In some instances she couldn't recognize the correct word, but at the same time she could tell that the one she had chosen was not correct—*provide . . . (. . .) siempre está creciendo para provenir . . . para . . . provenir . . . I don't like it . . . provide . . . let's look it up . . . (. . .) proveer . . . (. . .) supply, furnish . . . provide . . . but I never heard it like that . . .*

While all of the students made more surface than meaning changes as they revised, the total number of surface strategies used was lower than expected (17 percent of all strategies), especially considering the stress placed in class on spelling and accents. It was also interesting to see that more than once each student verbalized a correct form and then wrote it incorrectly (e.g., verbalization: *que no sea*; written text: *que no se*), a common problem attributed to interference of the oral language on the written form, that is, the students are writing what they hear. As with New's subjects, there were very few grammar-related changes and no verb form or tense edits, and both Micaela and Rosaura had a number of uncorrected verb errors in their essays. The percentage of deep level revisions was even lower (11 percent of all strategies), and the deep level strategies the students most frequently used—deletions and dictionary look-ups for meaning—seem to reflect the students' continuing search for the "right way" to phrase their ideas rather than how to best structure the essay.

Another unexpected finding was how extensively the students thought in English while composing in Spanish. This was especially true of Johana and Rosaura. While on the surface it seemed that they were rehearsing in Spanish, both students mentioned in the interviews that they were "reprocessing" (Cohen 1998) their verbalizations from English to Spanish *as they verbalized them.* It seems that the students felt pressured to verbalize in Spanish even though they had been told that they should use any language or combination of languages in which their thoughts occurred. During the interview Johana indicated that she had discarded large chunks of text because *[if] it doesn't sound right in Spanish . . . I don't, like, put it in. If I can't say [it] . . . I don't put it in.* She explained that she was, in fact, thinking in English all along and wasn't able to convey her ideas in Spanish in the paragraphs she abandoned, *to write* **write** [her emphasis], *unless it's those little phrases that come to me in Spanish, I have to think about it in English.* In different ways both Johana and Rosaura said that this thinking in English and *trying to say it* (Rosaura) or verbalize it in Spanish may have produced a sort of cognitive overload which led to frustration and affected their writing. The implication was also that if they hadn't been doing the think-aloud, except for very familiar language, they would have thought through and rehearsed their ideas in English first.

This brings us to a related issue: writing text through translation. Micaela and Rosaura had different views on this issue and followed opposite approaches. Although most of Micaela's planning was in English—*ok, I've talked about . . . places to eat . . . uhum, let me think about sports*—her rehearsal was mostly in Spanish and in the interview she indicated that she hardly used translation strategies except for words or short phrases. She explained that, *a mí me tom[a] más tiempo en escribirlo en inglés, y después cómo traducirlo, no suena bien. Y después me falta mucho tiempo a pensar, como puede ser esto asi si no suena bien, y estoy . . . and I'm stuck on it, that same idea, no lo puedo poner en español. Por eso me gusta a pensarlo en español y después es más fácil a cambiarlo, a poner otras palabras.*

The other approach to translation comes from Rosaura, who initially wrote parts of her essay in English. She "warned" me before she started the think-aloud that she wrote in a very "weird" way: all of her work was first written in English and then translated to Spanish. Although she wrote the first paragraph in Spanish (perhaps as a concession to me), she quickly switched to English for the next two paragraphs. These three paragraphs became her "first" draft. She then wrote the Spanish essay by recombining the Spanish paragraph with translated and new text, and adding a last paragraph and a concluding sentence directly in Spanish.

Micaela's approach—planning and organizing through her dominant language but writing in the not-dominant language—is supported by Friedlander's and Gascoigne Lally's research discussed earlier, and although Rosaura's technique may be controversial to many, it is also supported by research. Cohen (1998) reports on two studies where intermediate-level essays written through translation were rated higher than essays written directly in the FL. In his conclusions he speculates that "the attempt to think directly through the L_T [the target language, in our case the not-dominant language] may in fact detract from the production of good writing" (p. 176). Whether attributable to her translating technique or not, the transcript analysis showed that Rosaura used the most deep level strategies (she made the most meaning changes), and she received by far the highest ratings for organization and content. The think-aloud transcript also shows that her translation was not word for word. It would seem that translating for meaning led her to process the material much more deeply, to further elaborate the ideas, and to make substantive changes as she rewrote the paragraphs.

As we reflect on these findings we must take into consideration that the think-aloud protocol intervened in the composing processes of all three students. For example, Micaela explained in the interview that normally she writes her compositions longhand (an amazing fact, as she is an information systems major!) and then types them into the computer, putting in paragraphs and reorganizing the text when necessary. For the think-aloud we agreed that instead of recopying she would just indicate paragraph breaks and any other changes on the draft she had written, and in fact she added a sentence to the first paragraph. Yet, not following her usual composing routine may have kept her from the more substantive changes that we saw in Rosaura's transcript. It is impossible to attribute the relative quality of the essays to how the authors used English as they composed the essays. Yet, these findings are tantalizing and deserve to be looked into further.

As we saw earlier, research also supports the position that writing ability may be more dependent on writing expertise than on language proficiency. If we believe in the importance of writing as process, it is unlikely that we will advocate writing in translation. Nevertheless, we will need to offer students like the ones profiled in this study other means to achieve the same level of writing competence in Spanish as they may have developed in English, while at the same time helping them draw on the content and sociolinguistic knowledge, the language competence, and the strategies they already bring to the task.

Implications of the Study for the Classroom

This exploratory study has attempted to uncover the strategies that three Spanish heritage learners use when writing a composition in Spanish. It would be improper to generalize from these students to all of the population of Spanish heritage learners, yet it is hoped that readers have seen snatches of their own students reflected in these pages. The following recommendations for classroom activities suggest themselves from what we've learned from these students.

· It is important that we include instruction *and* practice on writing strategies in our SNS curricula. One can begin by creating an awareness of the process of writing in Spanish. Teachers can share the processes they use when they write, as well as ask students to describe their own strategies. This can be followed up with a discussion on the distinction between writing for practicing grammar or other formal aspects of the language and, as Johana said, writing *to write* **write** or composing. Lastly there should be a discussion of what difficulties the students encounter when writing in Spanish, what strategies they use to get around their problems, and which strategies don't seem to work for them—it is important that the students understand that not all strategies are productive and that they need to match strategy to task. This last step can be done with the class as a whole or in small groups or pairs, but it is necessary that the results be shared with the class and that a written record be kept of the strategies mentioned.

    Awareness activities should be followed by an examination of the writing process from the standpoint of the three major categories of strategies. Although somewhat time consuming, think-alouds may be used to illustrate the composing and revising processes. A more realistic way of including think-alouds in the classroom is to have the teacher or a student pre-record a think-aloud of a short writing task and use it later for discussion (individual think-alouds can also be used for diagnosis of writing difficulties or to monitor strategy use). The planning-composing-revising process should be presented as a recursive process of constructing meaning and working out ideas rather than as an opportunity for spelling practice. At this point, the strategies the students generated during the awareness-raising discussions can be fit into the planning-composing-revising process model. Lastly, activities should be devised that model and practice strategies individually (e.g., brainstorming activities for prewriting or word/ phrase substitution exercises for deep level strategies) and in combination (e.g., revising a paragraph using several surface strategies), teaching students to evaluate the effectiveness of their strategies and how to use them flexibly, depending on factors such as task, audience, and purpose.

· We've seen that students tend to concentrate on surface editing and ignore meaning revisions. It is important to discuss the need for both types of editing and to practice both surface and deep editing strategies separately and in combination. For example, save uncorrected first drafts from previous classes and use them to practice revision strategies. Also discuss strategies that help the students compensate for spelling or vocabulary problems so that they can keep the flow of ideas and the writing going. Suggestions may include underlining a word to check later for spelling or accent, or inserting an English word in parentheses to look up in the dictionary when they have finished the draft.

· Lack of vocabulary is a major stumbling block for many heritage students. Research by Keiko Koda (1993) indicates that there is a "strong relationship between vocabulary knowledge and quality ratings" (p. 343). Koda suggests that vocabulary knowledge provides linguistic scaffolding for the task and allows the writer to manipulate and express concepts. Vocabulary development should be one of the cornerstones of SNS courses and should be integrated with writing instruction, especially as part of prewriting activities. Reading on the topic of the composition and developing a list of key vocabulary that they may use later and doing semantic webs both to develop vocabulary and to organize the structure of the essay are excellent techniques to follow.

· Practice should also be provided on how to use a dictionary effectively, including recognizing parts of speech and making decisions on which meaning best fits the intent of the writer. Simple monolingual paperback dictionaries like those published for school-aged children (i.e., *diccionario escolar*) are usually accessible to even first level heritage language students. Diccionarios de sinónimos y antónimos are also excellent tools for vocabulary expansion. An effective activity is to give students an excerpt from an article or story with certain words underlined. The students must then find an appropriate synonym to substitute for the underlined word and rewrite the sentence making the necessary changes in the word so that it fits the context. After the students gain practice, more complex substitution activities in which they have to reword the sentence in order to use the synonym can be included.

· Another important type of classroom activity is practice on paraphrasing from written or oral texts, and paired paraphrasing activities in which students have to orally rephrase a partner's ideas. These activities should be short and frequent. They will give students multiple opportunities for online "reprocessing" and, together with vocabulary expansion activities, will enhance the students' abilities to phrase their own thoughts in Spanish and rely less on direct translation strategies.

- The students' responses to the Writing Strategies Questionnaire closely cross-checked with the processes the students revealed in the think-alouds and with their answers in the post—think-aloud interviews. Assuming that students will answer the questions truthfully, the WSQ may give a reasonably complete picture of the students' strategy use without taking the time to do think-alouds. If the strategy training program suggested above is followed, the WSQ could be administered before doing the awareness-raising activities.

- Lastly, by providing students with the tools to develop their writing skills we are helping them develop confidence in their abilities as language learners. Far too many students have poor self-images as Spanish writers and, as in Rosaura's case, this lack of confidence constrains them from using the language and taking risks. All teachers must be cognizant of their students' needs, but as teachers of heritage language learners we "must go beyond only teaching to also being [the] students' mentors and advocates" (Schwartz 2001, p. 239).

Conclusion

Research on heritage language speakers' writing processes and instruction is in its infancy. As stated by the Heritage Language Research Priorities Conference (2000) *Executive Report*, "pressing research gaps" exist in all areas related to heritage language speakers, including "how best to encourage and provide effective and efficient language learning." Many more studies are needed by teachers as well as researchers. Of special importance are action research studies by the teachers in the classroom who are trying out new methods and techniques and seeing firsthand what works and what doesn't. We must work together to share our knowledge and insights into this key area of heritage language education.

NOTES

1. For very complete reviews of L2 writing research see Susan M. Gass and Sally Sieloff Magnan (1993) and Alexandra R. Krapels (1990).

2. In this study the terms writing processes and writing strategies will be used interchangeably to mean what writers do as they compose.

3. My deepest appreciation goes to the three students who so generously gave of their time to share their thoughts with me. ¡Muchísimas gracias a todas!

4. According to Valdés (1997), second- and third-generation bilinguals' instructional needs include "maintenance, retrieval, and/or acquisition of language com-

petencies (e.g., oral productive abilities); expansion of bilingual range; transfer to Spanish of literacy skills developed in English; acquisition of prestige variety of the language" (p. 15). The students selected for the study displayed all of these characteristics.

5. The think-aloud (also called self-revelation) is one of three types of verbal report techniques. Cohen (1998) lists two other verbal report measures: self-reports, which yield generalized statements of how the respondents believe they learn languages—self-reports include questionnaires such as the ones used in this study—and self-observation techniques through which learners reflect on or analyze their language behavior either immediately after the event (introspection) or some time after (retrospection). The interviews conducted after the think-alouds were retrospective interviews.

6. Kasper (1998) reminds us that "cognitive processes are not directly manifest in protocols, but have to be inferred" (p. 358). It is suggested that use of reliable methods of data collection such as providing instructions and training in the procedure, monitoring the verbalizations and reminding the participants to speak (Ericsson and Simon 1987), as well as presenting a theoretically grounded analysis of the data (Kasper 1998) and thorough reporting of procedures (Cohen 1998), will increase understanding of the processes under study and allow for greater generalizability.

7. L1 writing research suggests that a writer's competence varies according to mode of discourse, with narrative and descriptive tasks being easier. Furthermore, when the topic is familiar writers seem to generate more ideas (Scott 1996).

8. The text in italics is taken directly from the student think-aloud transcripts. Underlining signals when the word/phrase was written; ellipses signal pauses; ellipses in parentheses (. . .) signal that part of the think-aloud has been left out.

REFERENCES

Akyel, Ayşe, and S. Kamişli. 1997. "Composing in First and Second Languages: Possible Effects of EFL Writing Instruction." *Odense Working Papers in Language and Communication* 14:69–105.

Campbell, Russell N., and J. W. Rosenthal. 2000. "Heritage Languages." In *Handbook of Undergraduate Second Language Education*, ed. J. W. Rosenthal, 165–84. Mahwah, NJ: Lawrence Erlbaum Associates.

Cohen, Andrew D. 1998. *Strategies in Learning and Using a Second Language*. New York: Addison Wesley Longman.

Cumming, Alister. 1989. "Writing Expertise and Second-Language Proficiency." *Language Learning* 39:81–141.

Ericsson, K. Anders, and H. A. Simon. 1987. "Verbal Reports on Thinking." In *Introspection in Second Language Research*, eds. C. Færch and G. Kasper, 24–53. Clevedon, UK: Multilingual Matters.

Færch, Claus, and G. Kasper. 1987. "From Product to Process—Introspective Methods in Second Language Research." In *Introspection in Second Language Research*, eds. C. Færch and G. Kasper, 5–23. Clevedon, UK: Multilingual Matters.

Friedlander, Alexander. 1990. "Composing in English: Effects of a First Language on Writing in English as a Second Language." In *Second Language Writing: Research Insights for the Classroom*, ed. B. Kroll, 109–25. Cambridge: Cambridge University Press.

Gascoigne Lally, Carolyn. 2000. "First Language Influences in Second Language Composition: The Effect of Pre-Writing." *Foreign Language Annals* 35 (July/August):428–32.

Gass, Susan, and S. Sieloff Magnan. 1993. "Second-Language Production: SLA Research in Speaking and Writing." In *Research in Language Learning: Principles, Processes, and Prospects*, ed. A. Omaggio Hadley, 156–97. Lincolnwood, IL: National Textbook Co.

Hedgcock, John, and N. Lefkowitz. 1996. "Some Input on Input: Two Analyses of Student Response to Expert Feedback on L2 Writing." *The Modern Language Journal* 80 (autumn):287–308.

Heritage Language Research Priorities Conference. 2000. *Executive Report*. Available at www.cal.org/heritage/priorities.html. Accessed on April 2, 2001.

Kasper, Gabriele. 1998. "Analysing Verbal Protocols." *TESOL Quarterly* 32 (summer):358–62.

Kern, Richard G., and J. M. Schultz. 1992. "The Effects of Composition Instruction on Intermediate Level French Students' Writing Performance: Some Preliminary Findings." *The Modern Language Journal* 76 (spring):1–13.

Koda, Keiko. 1993. "Task-Induced Variability in FL Composition: Language-Specific Perspectives." *Foreign Language Annals* 26 (fall):332–46.

Krapels, Alexandra R. 1990. "An Overview of Second Language Writing Process." In *Second Language Writing: Research Insights for the Classroom*, ed. B. Kroll, 37–56. Cambridge: Cambridge University Press.

National Capital Language Resource Center. 1996. *The Language Self-Efficacy Questionnaire (Secondary and Higher Education)*. Washington, D.C.: Author.

New, Elizabeth. 1999. "Computer-Aided Writing in French as a Foreign Language: A Qualitative and Quantitative Look at the Process of Revision." *The Modern Language Journal* 83 (spring):80–97.

Pennington, M. C., and M. N. Brock. 1992. "Process and Product Approaches to Computer-Assisted Composition." In *Computers in Applied Linguistics: An International Perspective*, eds. M. C. Pennington and V. Stevens, 70–109. Clevedon, UK: Multilingual Matters.

Perl, Sondra. 1979. "The Composing Processes of Unskilled College Writers." *Research in the Teaching of English* 13 (December):317–36.

Raimes, Ann. 1987. "Language Proficiency, Writing Ability, and Composing Strategies: A Study of ESL College Student Writers." *Language Learning* 37:436–68.

———. 1985. "What Unskilled ESL Students Do as They Write: A Classroom Study of Composing." *TESOL Quarterly* 19 (June):229–58.

Schwartz, Ana María. 2001. "Preparing Teachers to Work with Heritage Language Learners." In *Heritage Languages in America: Preserving a National Resource*, eds. J. K. Peyton, D. A. Ranard, and S. McGinnis, 229–52. McHenry, IL and Washington, D.C.: Delta Systems and Center for Applied Linguistics.

Scott, Virginia M. 1996. *Rethinking Foreign Language Writing*. Boston: Heinle & Heinle.

Silva, Tony. 1990. "Second Language Composition Instruction: Developments, Issues, and Directions in ESL." In *Second Language Writing: Research Insights for the Classroom*, ed. B. Kroll, 11–23. Cambridge: Cambridge University Press.

Wolfe-Quintero, Kate, S. Inagaki, and H. Kim. 1998. *Second Language Development in Writing: Measures of Fluency, Accuracy and Complexity*. Honolulu, HI: University of Hawai'i Press.

Valdés, Guadalupe. 1997. "The Teaching of Spanish to Bilingual Spanish-speaking Students: Outstanding Issues and Unanswered Questions." In *La enseñanza del español a hispanohablantes: Praxis y teoría*, eds. M. C. Colombi, and F. X. Alarcón, 8–44. Boston: Houghton Mifflin.

———. 1995. "The Teaching of Minority Languages as Academic Subjects: Pedagogical and Theoretical Challenges." *The Modern Language Journal* 76 (autumn):301–28.

Zamel, Vivian. 1983. "The Composing Processes of Advanced ESL Students: Six Case Studies." *TESOL Quarterly* 17 (June):165–87.

———. 1982. "Writing: The Process of Discovering Meaning." *TESOL Quarterly* 16 (June):195–209.

12

Navegando a través del registro formal
Curso para hispanohablantes bilingües

Rebeca Acevedo

Loyola Marymount University, Los Angeles

En este ensayo quiero compartir con el lector los resultados obtenidos en un curso piloto de español para hispanohablantes bilingües. Este curso fue diseñado para estudiantes subgraduados a un nivel intermedio avanzado, cuarto semestre de español y último prerrequisito de lengua para ser aceptado en la especialidad. Los estudiantes fueron ubicados por medio del examen estandarizado de la Universidad de Wisconsin (800 + puntos), a falta de un examen especialmente diseñado para bilingües, más una entrevista personal. Estos estudiantes crecieron en un hogar hispanoparlante y pertenecen a la 1a. y 2a. generaciones de hispanohablantes bilingües en los Estados Unidos. Todos fueron capaces de mantener una conversación informal, completamente en español, antes de inscribirse en el curso. Durante el mismo semestre se ofrecieron dos cursos de nivel intermedio-avanzado, uno de español como lengua extranjera y nuestro curso piloto; los estudiantes participaron en este curso piloto de manera voluntaria y para la mayoría se trataba de un curso optativo. Los estudiantes reportaron un interés personal por perfeccionar su español, principalmente en lo que se refiere a contextos formales y el registro escrito.

La meta principal que persigue este curso es la de conservar y fortalecer el idioma español. El medio seleccionado para lograrlo es la transferencia al español de los niveles de alfabetización adquiridos en el inglés. Partimos del supuesto de que al incidir en los niveles de alfabetización del español, se amplía de manera evidente la escala bilingüe del estudiante y, con ello, se alcanza la meta del curso.

El enfoque del curso es la escritura, pero eso no implica que dejemos de lado las otras habilidades; ya que a través del proceso de la composición, los estudiantes leen varios textos modelos y hablan entre sí para describir los objetivos de sus textos o sugerir y hacer ediciones a las composiciones del compañero. También se llevan a cabo múltiples actividades orales en grupo. Existe una fuerte relación entre el desarrollo de las destrezas de la escritura y el desarrollo de otras áreas de la habilidad lingüística. Es decir, que al enfocarnos en fomentar la escritura, se afectan directamente otras habilidades indispensables para el dominio de la lengua en su conjunto.

Como señalamos anteriormente, se seleccionó este enfoque por el interés expreso de los estudiantes, pero también por la importancia que en nuestra cultura se le da al texto escrito. Nadie puede negar que la escritura en la sociedad occidental se ha convertido en un fetiche. Se considera ésta como una condición necesaria para el desarrollo del pensamiento abstracto, científico e histórico porque permite la comunicación a través del tiempo y el espacio (Goody 1982). Se dice que el registro escrito representa lo objetivo, lo analítico y lo cronológico. La escritura, así definida, se contrasta con la oralidad. Ésta última ha sido equiparada con lo acumulativo, redundante, tradicionalista, cercano a la realidad (es decir, no abstracto), subjetivo, imaginativo, mítico y orientado hacia el presente o lo ahistórico (Ong 1982). Un buen análisis puede desmantelar de inmediato esta concepción de valor radicalmente opuesta entre el lenguaje oral y el escrito: se trata únicamente de dos registros diferentes. No obstante, la palabra escrita sigue gozando de enorme prestigio al mantener autoridad y peso en nuestra sociedad y transmitir a la vez fuerza al que se adjudica su dominio.

El prestigio adquirido por la escritura a través de la historia occidental está relacionado con la equiparación común entre ésta y los contextos formales en que aparece. La relación entre formalidad y escritura es producto de las circunstancias en que se da la modalidad escrita; se trata de un acto solitario y sin restricciones temporales que permite una mayor abstracción, manipulación y estructuración de las ideas. Sabemos que el estudiante bilingüe ha tenido mayor exposición en el idioma español a las interacciones familiares y coloquiales a través del discurso oral. Por otra parte, su familiaridad con textos escritos en español es generalmente limitada. En este curso se busca que el estudiante desarrolle los niveles de alfabetización en español que ya ha adquirido en el inglés. Se propone trabajar con textos escritos formales para ofrecer, a la vez, una mayor exposición a ese tipo de registro. Consideramos que por medio de estos documentos escritos se le permite al estudiante, no sólo balancear su escala bilingüe inglés español con el desarrollo de la lectoescritura en español, sino también que a la vez, se familiarice con el registro formal al que ha tenido limitado acceso.

El discurso escrito en un curso universitario de español para estudiantes bilingües representa el área del idioma que mayor desarrollo requiere para cumplir con las exigencias de la especialidad. Por medio de los documentos escritos el estudiante recibe la exposición necesaria a los ámbitos formales. Además, esta exposición se lleva a cabo bajo condiciones muy controladas, a diferencia del discurso oral, por ejemplo. Cuando se manipulan documentos impresos se trabaja con material que se mantiene fijo, sin variación; material que podemos analizar detalladamente y en su totalidad. Por otro lado, la manipulación y producción del discurso escrito permite al estudiante desarrollar al máximo su capacidad expresiva y su repertorio lingüístico. Como se dijo, nuestro objetivo es que el estudiante bilingüe fortalezca las habilidades de la lectoescritura en español. Esperamos que, con resultados positivos, el estudiante logre también una autoevaluación más positiva por su manejo del español en general.

Transferencia de habilidades

Presuponiendo una aceptación de la premisa propuesta en la introducción de que al incidir en los niveles de alfabetización en español, se amplía la escala bilingüe del estudiante, nos enfrentamos aún ante un problema común: en la enseñanza de la composición de los cursos de español para estudiantes bilingües no se han reportado resultados muy halagadores. Los textos escritos que el estudiante bilingüe produce en las aulas, como lo describe Colombi (1997), se ubican más cerca de las narrativas orales que de los registros escritos (p. 175). En mi opinión, esta falta de resultados positivos se debe al uso de metodologías de enseñanza que dan por sentado conocimientos en español no adquiridos aún por el estudiante modelo. No podemos olvidar que nuestros estudiantes presentan proficiencia en el discurso oral en español y que, además, poseen las destrezas para manipular la escritura formal, pero enfocadas primordialmente al inglés. La transferencia de este tipo de habilidades de una lengua a otra no ha sido confirmada. De darse, la experiencia en las aulas nos confirma que tal transferencia no se presenta de manera automática.

Para lograr la transferencia de estas habilidades, necesitamos desarrollar un programa en el que se exponga ampliamente al estudiante a diversos textos escritos en la lengua modelo, para que, a través de esta intensa exposición, logre identificar las características particulares del registro escrito en español. Recomiendo que durante este programa se empleen principalmente textos que representen la norma formal del español en los EE.UU. Es necesario insistir, sin embargo, que la simple exposición intensiva a este registro no será suficiente. Se requiere crear en el estudiante una actitud crítica que le permita decodificar los textos y analizar el sistema de escritura, reconocer sus principios e identificar las técnicas y herramientas empleadas. Solo por medio de un análisis crítico, el estudiante será capaz de manipular y reproducir dicho registro. Este conocimiento no se debe dar por sentado, no importa si el estudiante modelo se considera o no poseedor de un sistema de alfabetización avanzado en el inglés. Paso a describir, a continuación, las características que debe incluir el método propuesto.

Metodología

DISTINGUIR ENTRE EL REGISTRO ORAL Y EL ESCRITO

El primer elemento indispensable para que el alumno logre manipular el sistema de lectoescritura del español es la clara distinción entre el registro oral y el escrito. Durante las primeras clases y sin escatimar el tiempo dedicado a ello, se tendrá que discutir ampliamente y de manera obvia las diferencias entre la modalidad oral y la modalidad escrita de la lengua. Esto se logra no sólo con base en una mayor exposición al registro escrito, sino, como ya lo enunciamos, a través de un análisis deductivo. Tenemos que llamar la atención del estudiante para que identifique el enorme conocimiento que emplea en su manejo del inglés y que puede aplicar también al español. Para cumplir con este objetivo, se sugiere analizar ejemplos en que el mismo mensaje se transmita por medio de las dos modalidades, oral y escrita, para de esa manera contrastar la estructura correspondiente a cada una de estas modalidades.

Necesitamos atacar un error frecuente en los libros de texto que clasifican las tareas escritas como "temas para redactar y conversar". Los autores de los libros justifican esta estrategia porque ofrece "the students the opportunity to express themselves either in oral or in written form" (Marqués 1986, p. 191). Con ello, se hace una equiparación errónea entre ambos registros. Estos enfoques están reflejando una metodología tradicional de la enseñanza de lenguas extranjeras la cual sugiere iniciar la enseñanza de la escritura con actividades simples, como son el transcribir o imitar cosas que sean capaces de decir, como reflejo sólo del habla. El problema estriba en que la redacción se percibe sólo como un apoyo para las habilidades orales, no como un objetivo en sí mismo. Esa misma metodología, sin embargo, propone un enfoque diferente cuando los estudiantes ya han adquirido fluidez en la lengua oral. Se dice que a ese nivel se les podrá dar mayor apoyo en la producción escrita, por medio de instrucción sobre las convenciones retóricas y los procesos mentales que se echan a andar al escribir. No me detendré aquí a discutir las deficiencias de los métodos tradicionales de la enseñanza de la composición. Quiero solamente enfatizar la necesidad de que, en un curso para estudiantes bilingües con destreza oral en el español, se ofrezcan precisamente estas últimas técnicas citadas (las identificadas por Rivers [1975] como "skill-using activities") que incluyen el análisis de las convenciones retóricas de la lengua. Es fundamental que se entienda la producción escrita como tal y que no se vea como una simple imitación del discurso oral.

Como venimos insistiendo, será necesario destacar en clase las diferencias entre el registro oral y el escrito. Recibimos estudiantes capaces de crear con el lenguaje una amplia variedad de contextos, con una gama extensa también de tiempos verbales y estructuras gramaticales. Sin embargo, con estudiantes que no han sido expuestos a los registros escritos del español, no debemos presuponer la transferencia de su conocimiento de los géneros retóricos del inglés en la producción en español.

Sugiero que en las primeras semanas de clase se ofrezcan análisis contrastivos entre modelos que representen ambos registros. Por ejemplo, se puede trabajar con la descripción de un suceso local. Por un lado, se graba la descripción oral hecha por un estudiante a sus compañeros; por otro lado, se analiza ese mismo suceso del artículo escrito en el periódico local. Debe quedar claro para el estudiante que el tipo de expresiones y muletillas que se usan en el discurso oral para confirmar la comprensión del oyente no son las mismas que se incluyen en el texto escrito, ya que el lector no se encuentra presente. Que en el texto escrito se debe prescindir de las repeticiones, expresiones corporales y apoyo que ofrece el contorno físico compartido por hablante y oyente. Que el acto de la comunicación escrita es un acto solitario en el que la negociación establecida con el lector es indirecta y por ello requiere de mayor contextualización. Que los textos escritos exigen mayor precisión y claridad. Lo anterior se logra por medio de una mayor densidad léxica, con nominalización y uso de modificadores[1].

Recomiendo también que se analice el triángulo de la comunicación y sus elementos básicos: emisor, receptor y mensaje. Al hacer este análisis se debe enfatizar el papel que juega el medio o instrumento empleado al enviar el mensaje: el sonido cuando se trata del discurso oral, o la letra en el discurso escrito. Se sugiere también analizar los medios de comunicación que se encuentran en una posición intermedia entre los registros, como son el teléfono o el correo electrónico, que permiten, en ausencia, la respuesta simultánea del oyente lector. U otros medios más complejos como la radio y la televisión, que a pesar de emplear la voz para transmitir el mensaje, tienen una base escrita.

CONCEPTUALIZAR LA COMPOSICIÓN COMO UN PROCESO

En este curso partimos del principio de que la producción del registro escrito no se adquiere por medio de un proceso mecánico, sino a través de un proceso cognitivo en el cual el aprendiz debe tomar un papel activo. Recomiendo que se familiarice al estudiante con el concepto de la composición como un proceso y que se le motive a que trate de identificar su propio ritmo en este proceso. Afortunadamente se han escrito ya varios textos sobre la enseñanza de la composición en español que adoptan este enfoque. En este curso en particular, adopté el libro A *manera de ensayo* (1998) de Schaffer y Acevedo. El programa se organiza con base en las diferentes etapas necesarias a través de la creación de un texto escrito. Atrás debe quedar la idea de que la composición se asigna para el día siguiente y en una sentada el producto queda listo para recibir una nota. Al contrario, este curso se estructura para llevar de la mano al estudiante por las diferentes etapas que requiere la elaboración de una composición. Por fines pedagógicos, se ha determinado dividir el proceso en tres etapas. Cada una de las etapas coincide con la producción de un borrador de la misma tarea. El estudiante debe entender, sin embargo, que hay quienes requieren dedicar más tiempo a una u otra etapa; que se trata de un proceso que requiere tiempo y energía. El instructor o/y los editores de la clase revisan los borradores y hacen comentarios y sugerencias para clarificar el mensaje. El estudiante debe presentarse dispuesto a la revisión y ser flexible a los cambios y modificaciones que exija su proyecto.

La primera etapa es la de planeación que consiste en dos pasos principales: la recopilación de ideas y el descubrimiento de un enfoque apropiado. Estos procesos deben depender totalmente del estudiante. El papel del instructor en esta primera etapa será solamente fungir como facilitador para agilizar y motivar la producción de un mensaje claro y completo. Es muy importante que cuando el instructor escriba su respuesta al primer borrador, se limite a hacer comentarios exclusivamente sobre la selección y la lógica de las ideas, es decir, a la macroestructura. No se debe distraer al escritor con detalles superficiales como formas verbales irregulares o convenciones escritas, hasta no tener las ideas necesarias y el enfoque preciso para lograr la comunicación del mensaje. Se ha reportado, en investigaciones hechas con estudiantes bilingües, que las deficiencias en esta etapa de planeación afecta de manera concreta los resultados en el proceso de la redacción en español (Schwartz 1999).

La segunda etapa comprende el desarrollo y la organización de las ideas. Sugiero que no se escatime el tiempo en este paso. Una buena organización de las ideas garantiza gran parte del éxito en la escritura. Vuelvo a insistir que durante todo el proceso, sin importar la etapa en la que se esté trabajando como grupo, cada individuo debe permitirse flexibilidad y regresar cuantas veces sea necesario a etapas previas para hacer las modificaciones pertinentes. Por ejemplo, es frecuente que si esa segunda etapa no progresa de la manera esperada, se deba al hecho de que no se hizo una planeación suficiente. Eso exigirá volver a la primera etapa; se trata de un proceso recursivo.

La tercera etapa se centra en la claridad de las ideas y en la selección de un estilo apropiado para la transmisión del mensaje. Se requiere de un plan que nos permita controlar la forma en el acto mismo de la composición. Es en esta etapa en donde se lleva a cabo el proceso de la revisión, la lógica de las ideas. Finalmente, y sólo después de que se haya logrado el objetivo central de la transmisión del mensaje, se prestará atención a los aspectos mecánicos; es decir, gramática, ortografía, selección de vocabulario y deletreo. Esta última etapa se concentra en la corrección formal, la atención a lo mecánico. Debe evitarse tomar actitudes puristas en esta etapa o imponer normas ajenas. Hay que tener muy presente que las características que identifican la norma hispana estadounidense, no siempre corresponden a la de otras normas hispanas extranjeras. Será muy enriquecedor, en casos de dudas por parte del instructor, que se discuta en grupo la adecuación o no de la palabra o estructura en cuestión. El fungir como informantes de su propia lengua, permite al estudiante fortalecer la confianza en sus destrezas lingüísticas. Lo importante, como dije con anterioridad, es no anticipar este paso, ya que debe ser el mensaje y no la forma el objetivo central de una composición. La corrección formal quedará para el final del proceso.

ESTABLECER EL MENSAJE COMO PUNTO FOCAL

La composición escrita, como cualquier tipo de discurso, debe mantener como objetivo central el transmitir un mensaje.[2] Si no prestamos atención a las necesidades comunicativas del estudiante, no se podrá lograr la motivación necesaria para que desarrolle sus habilidades lingüísticas. Expresar por escrito sus propias ideas será el objetivo principal. Se debe dejar atrás, insisto, la visión mecánica de la composición como simple pretexto de apoyo para practicar el vocabulario o repasar nuevas estructuras gramaticales. Nuestro enfoque considera la redacción como un acto de comunicación, un medio para transmitir información.

Por otro lado, no debe interpretarse lo anterior como licencia a una total anarquía lingüística. Ya se dijo que este curso está limitado al registro formal académico para de esa manera partir de una norma claramente delimitada.

Sin embargo, el proceso de la escritura exige que antes de observar las convenciones formales, se atienda al mensaje y la lógica de las ideas. Es indispensable que el estudiante comprenda que la información empleada en las composiciones no debe restringirse a las experiencias personales o la inspiración de la noche anterior. Se requiere investigación previa, recopilación de información y elaboración de un esquema. Se debe aceptar que para lograr un texto claro es indispensable tener un pensamiento claro. Por ello, para facilitar el proceso de la composición, el instructor debe promover diversas actividades de pre-escritura, tales como: lluvia de ideas, presentaciones grupales sobre el tema, discusiones de grupo, debates, técnicas de investigación y acceso a recursos bibliográficos.

Para poder lograr un mensaje claro por parte de los estudiantes, se deben también dejar claras las reglas del juego. No deben dejarse espacios para que el alumno divague. Al asignar cada tarea de composición, se le tiene que ofrecer al estudiante todas las especificaciones requeridas, delimitar con precisión los parámetros con los que se trabaja y describir claramente las características del texto escrito asignado. Se debe incluir al asignar las tareas al menos la siguiente información básica: el género retórico requerido (relato, exposición, argumentación); el objetivo (expresivo, persuasivo, descriptivo, literario); la función (negociación, información, exhortación); el tema global al que debe referirse el texto y, por último, la relación establecida entre escritor lector, en otras palabras, su lector modelo. De este modo, el proceso y las etapas de edición parten de fundamentos muy claros. Incluyo a continuación un modelo de una tarea de composición asignada.

Ejemplo

La Voz es un periódico en español publicado por el Departamento de Lenguas Modernas de esta Universidad. Usted, como experto en el tema, ha sido invitado por el consejo editorial para escribir un artículo sobre "Las causas y consecuencias de la deserción escolar en la población hispana".

Características del texto
Género: expositivo
Objetivo: descriptivo
Función: informativa
Técnica: causa y efecto
Lector modelo: estudiante de español de su universidad

ORGANIZAR EL CURSO POR GÉNEROS O ESTILOS RETÓRICOS

La clasificación por géneros o estilos retóricos resulta una manera lógica y efectiva de organizar un curso de composición. El primer paso será exponer al estudiante a diversos modelos de lectura que empleen un mismo género. El estudiante, con ayuda del instructor, podrá aprender a decodificar este tipo de textos, identificar las estrategias empleadas y los objetivos que persigue. Al descubrir la macro estructura del género, el estudiante cuenta con una herramienta excelente para producir sus propios textos. Ya que se tiene una estructura modelo que sigue convenciones relativamente fijas y bien reglamentadas, sólo restará elaborar las ideas para vaciarlas en el molde.

Es muy importante, al discutir cada género, identificar el objetivo que el género persigue. Por ejemplo, si la tarea de redacción es la de elaborar un artículo editorial, se discutirá el género de la argumentación. Se deben analizar modelos de los diferentes enfoques que maneja el género argumentativo: argumentación directa o indirecta, según presente la idea central o argumento, al frente o hasta el final. Es importante contrastar también, por ejemplo, modelos editoriales que persigan objetivos diferentes y enfatizar la manera en que esas diferencias se reflejan en su estructura. Se podrán identificar diferencias entre: el editorial que busca sólo informar al público sobre cierto asunto novedoso del que toma partido ante un asunto controvertido. También es importante analizar en los textos el lector modelo al que se dirige cada editorial. Para ello, se recomienda que se emplee material de referencias claramente identificadas y de fácil acceso, para así poder confirmar las inferencias a que llegue el grupo.

El análisis de los géneros puede ser tan profundo como el tiempo lo permita. Sería recomendable, para que el estudiante tenga una idea más clara de todos los elementos que intervienen, comentar sobre las posiciones de los periódicos más populares de la región y ver de qué manera se representa esta posición en sus editoriales. El acceso a muchas publicaciones en español a nivel nacional en EE.UU. se facilita mediante la red o 'internet'. Comentar sobre el tipo de lector al que se dirige, el lenguaje que emplea para hacer predicciones, para exhortar o emitir juicios; los juicios de valor que emplea para atraer a su lector modelo y la temática que le ofrece. No se puede olvidar que el curso gira en torno al concepto de cómo transmitir mejor los mensajes por escrito. Confirmamos pues que en este proceso de aprendizaje sobre la escritura, no son ajenas las actividades de lectura, de discusión oral, y por qué no, de crítica social.

ENFATIZAR LA IMPORTANCIA DEL RECEPTOR LECTOR DEL TEXTO

Por último, se debe entender la comunicación escrita como una actividad social, comunitaria. El estudiante escritor debe tener claro que para poder lograr transmitir el mensaje, no solamente tiene que atender al tema y la forma del texto escrito, sino también atraer la atención de su lector. Para lograrlo, su texto debe cubrir información completa y pertinente; además, debe ofre-cerla de una manera clara y organizada para que las ideas fluyan hacia el lec-tor. Por ello, desde la etapa de planeación el estudiante debe saber para quién está escribiendo. Además, a través del proceso de la redacción, el escritor debe tomar el papel del lector para hacer las correcciones pertinentes.

Una actividad que ayuda a los estudiantes a orientar sus textos conside-rando al lector es el trabajo de edición de sus propios escritos por parte de los compañeros o compañeras de clase. Esta actividad obtuvo excelentes re-sultados durante mi clase. El compartir las composiciones con los compa-ñeros y recibir sus comentarios les permite enfocar mejor los textos. El hecho de diversificar el lector "real" de sus composiciones y no limitarlo a la imagen del instructor ayuda al estudiante a cumplir con las especificaciones de la composición, que comprende un lector no personalizado. Con un poco de entrenamiento, se pueden obtener excelentes editores en la clase, siempre y cuando mantengan claros los principios que rigen el proceso y se concentren en la transmisión de las ideas.

Implicaciones pedagógicas

Los resultados que obtuve al seguir este programa fueron muy productivos. Por primera vez logré en mis clases que los estudiantes identificaran y mani-pularan con consistencia las diferencias entre el registro formal académico del coloquial familiar. Lo anterior se logró, en mi opinión, porque se man-tuvo muy bien delimitado el espacio de trabajo. Puedo concluir que al crear un alejamiento de la realidad personal del estudiante, es decir, de su subjeti-vidad, se agiliza la adquisición del registro formal. Mientras permanezcamos asignando tareas limitadas a contextos personales será difícil evitar la combi-nación de registros. Es importante insistir, sin embargo, que se requiere un nivel de destreza lingüística básico para poder aplicar estos principios: por eso este programa se podrá implementar eficazmente sólo con estudiantes con cierta madurez lingüística oral en español. Cuando el estudiante haya logrado manipular el registro formal y reconocer las diferencias con el regis-tro informal o familiar, en ese momento se podrá romper la rigidez.

Por lo anterior, insisto en que a este nivel de enseñanza se ofrezca un curso de redacción limitado al registro formal escrito. Este curso puede preceder a otro curso para hispanohablantes bilingües, diseñado especialmente para desarrollar el discurso oral formal. Se sugiere iniciar con el curso descrito en el presente ensayo debido a que los cánones del lenguaje escrito están más claramente establecidos. Además, hay que reconocer que, en contraste con el habla, se facilita el proceso de la corrección y comentarios con los textos escritos, ya que es un proceso más fácilmente manipulable y en el cual las convenciones retóricas se encuentran claramente establecidas.

Otro elemento que favorece el trabajar con la redacción formal antes que con los contextos formales orales es el que se refiere al filtro afectivo. Con la palabra escrita se permite reducir el filtro afectivo que limita la confianza del estudiante ya que no le pone restricciones temporales. La composición se caracteriza también por ejercer menos presión social ya que le permite la autocorrección y la revisión a su propio ritmo y en privado.

Al terminar el curso, los estudiantes se mostraron satisfechos al entender y manipular las convenciones del registro escrito en el español. No cabe duda de que la idea occidental sobre la primacía de la modalidad escrita pervive en ellos. Tenemos confianza en que si el estudiante tiene actitudes positivas hacia el objeto de estudio, la recuperación y empleo del español serán más factibles. Los estudiantes reportaron en sus evaluaciones de fin de curso que, al aprender a manipular los textos formales, aumentó también su apreciación por la lengua heredada.

Una de las implicaciones más importantes de nuestro enfoque para el salón de clases es la necesidad de mantener el mensaje, y no la forma, como el punto focal del curso. Es primordial que el estudiante se preocupe primero por transmitir de manera clara y precisa sus ideas, antes de enfocarse en las convenciones de la norma escrita. Este programa requiere un nivel de destreza oral intermedio para poder tener efectividad. Termino con una última recomendación para los instructores que quisieran aplicar este tipo de programas. Se debe mantener siempre en mente que el perfil de nuestro estudiante es bicultural y bilingüe. Hay que evitar imponer normas lingüísticas ajenas. El instructor debe sentirse satisfecho de haber logrado el objetivo del curso tan pronto como el estudiante reconozca las herramientas del registro escrito en español y las utilice a su favor para transmitir mensajes con claridad y adecuación a su propia realidad.

NOTAS

1. Colombi ofrece una descripción detallada de las características sintácticas que demanda el registro académico en una de sus más recientes publicaciones (2000).

2. No obstante, con frecuencia los cursos de español para hispanohablantes se enfocan casi exclusivamente en la corrección formal. En mi opinión, ese enfoque puede resultar contraproducente.

OBRAS CITADAS

Colombi, M. Cecilia. 2000. "En vías del desarrollo del lenguaje académico en español en hablantes nativos de español en los Estados Unidos." En *Research on Spanish in the United States: Linguistics Issues and Challenges*, ed. Ana Roca, 296–309. Somerville, MA: Cascadilla Press.

——. 1997. "Perfil del discurso escrito en textos de hispanohablantes: teoría y práctica." En *La enseñanza del español para hispanohablantes: Praxis y teoría*, eds. Cecilia Colombi y Francisco X. Alarcón, 175–89. Boston: Houghton Mifflin.

Goody, Jack. 1987. *The Interface Between the Written and the Oral*. Cambridge: Cambridge University Press.

Marqués, Sarah. 1986. *La lengua que heredamos. Curso de español para bilingües*. New York: John Wiley & Sons.

Ong, Walter. 1982. *Orality and Literacy: The Technologizing of the Word*. New York: Methuen.

Rivers, Wilga M. 1975. *A Practical Guide to the Teaching of French*. New York: Oxford University Press.

Schaffer, Susan, y Rebeca Acevedo. 1998. *A manera de ensayo*. Boston: Houghton Mifflin.

Schwartz, Ana María. 1999. "¡No me suena! Heritage Spanish Speakers' Writing Processes." Ponencia presentada en Fifth Annual Conference on Teaching Spanish to Native Speakers. Las Cruces, Nuevo Mexico, 13–15 de agosto.

13

Spanish Print Environments
Implications for Heritage Language Development

Sandra Liliana Pucci

University of Wisconsin, Milwaukee

Introduction

This essay examines the Spanish print environments in predominantly Latino neighborhoods in two different cities: one located in Southern California and one in the Midwest. The purpose of the study is to "print map" the general print environments in the respective communities, investigating the range of reading materials available in Spanish. More specifically, it examines the availability of reading materials for adolescents and young adults in heritage language Spanish for Native Speakers classes and high school developmental bilingual settings. Although some attention has been given to access and availability of print in neighborhoods of differing socioeconomic status (Neuman and Celano 2001), to date no studies investigating Spanish print environments appear in the literature.

Language "Minority" Students and the Politics of Language

Historically speaking, schools have responded to "language minority" students in a variety of ways (Crawford 2000, 1999; Cummins 2000; Kloss 1998; Skutnabb-Kangas 2000). Present-day instructional programs, whether using the primary language or not, are situated within an overtly "compensatory" framework. Hernández Chávez (1993) is correct in his assessment of such programs as inadequate for the purposes of language revitalization. He states that "the principal (and irremediable) difficulty with these programs is that they follow an openly assimilationist philosophy that is codified into law by all the relevant federal and state statutes" (p. 68). The case of transitional bilingual education is a prime example of both an assimilationist and a compensatory agenda. The stated goals of these programs are subject-area learning and the acquisition of English. Students are "transitioned" to English-based instruction when their "reading levels" in Spanish are adequate and when they have demonstrated a determined level of oral proficiency in English. At this point, instruction in Spanish is generally discontinued. Even so-called developmental programs, those which aim to continue supporting the student's first language, usually fall short of developing a "fuller" variety of bilingualism/biliteracy. In reality, in both programs, the student's home language and culture are used as a bridge to those of the mainstream, and not seen as something having their own intrinsic value. Perhaps unwittingly, even the discourse of academics and sociolinguists has at times centered around justifying the use of the first language as an instructional vehicle for second language acquisition. Many discuss cognitive advantages of bilingualism, and the necessity of a firm language/literacy foundation in the first language in order to foster academic achievement in the second language, English (Cummins 2000; Fishman 1989; Ramírez 1992). While these are very important points, they do not contribute to the advancement or status of the Spanish language in the U.S. as a political and cultural right, independent of its relationship with the acquisition of English.

Many students in Spanish for Native Speakers (SNS) classes at the secondary and college levels are graduates of these transitional bilingual education programs, or have never had the opportunity to study in Spanish during their U.S. school experiences. Roca (1992) notes that the underdevelopment of Spanish literacy skills in U.S. Latino bilinguals is due to lack of exposure and training. An informal survey of students in SNS classes at a community college in Los Angeles (Pucci 1993) revealed that while in general the students do not feel inadequate in oral communication skills, they lack the foundations of Spanish literacy, and do not feel confident in using Spanish as a tool for written communication. This may simply indicate the lack of exposure to an academic register or style. Valdés and Geoffrion-Vinci (1998) have discussed the exposure to the various domains of English and Spanish that Chicano bilingual students, and possibly other U.S. Latinos, come into contact with throughout their lives. They maintain that the average Chicano student, descending from what the authors characterize as "ordinary Mexicans," and having grown up in an English-dominant society, has probably not acquired the registers and stylistic variations of Mexican Spanish monolinguals from similar socioeconomic class backgrounds (p. 477). Chicano students in this study produced oral texts comparable to their Mexican-born counterparts, although these were judged by researchers to have less lexical richness. Therefore, it could be feasibly argued that their situation may not be a question of overall "language competence" as such, and we should reject, as many others have, narrow notions of "restricted" and "elaborated" codes (Labov 1972). Instead, given the educational history of most students in heritage language classes, particularly those in urban working-class settings, and their probable limited exposure to *Spanish print,* as well as the potential benefit of Spanish language literacy, we should advocate for the development of Spanish literacy as a central focus of an SNS program.

However, many SNS programs have focused on the grammar and structure of the language, with the intention of moving students toward so-called standard varieties of Spanish (Hidalgo 1993). Such attempts at direct instruction or even remediation of nonstandard varieties have proved tedious. Even proponents of such instruction comment on its hardship to both teacher and pupil. Avila (cited in Hidalgo 1993) suggests that it would take 600 hours of study, outside school, to master standard Spanish spelling. In addition, this type of instruction could not promote the acquisition of a variety of Spanish "discourses" for a multiplicity of purposes, through exposure to various sources of "comprehensible input" (Krashen 1988). Other approaches have emphasized slow, methodical readings of literary texts, most of which are beyond the linguistic scope of the learner. Still other heritage language teaching approaches have borrowed from English as a Second Language (ESL) methodologies, communicative foreign language teaching models, and others (see the edited volume by Merino, Trueba, and Samaniego 1993, for a more detailed discussion). While these approaches are useful in many ways, there are also issues and needs specific to the SNS context. As previously stated, given the educational background of most adolescents and young adults in SNS classes, we should put forth a case for Spanish language literacy development as an important component of the SNS curriculum. The incorporation of extensive, free reading in Spanish, using comprehensible, high-interest texts, could take students much further than more traditional methods in promoting Spanish language and literacy.

Extensive Reading Studies — A Brief Summary

Research in different contexts has demonstrated that wide or extensive reading promotes both first and second language acquisition. Extensive reading, rather than direct reading instruction, may be the real key to improving reading ability (Krashen 1993, 1996; McQuillan 1998b). That is, as Frank Smith (1988a, 1988b) has repeatedly asserted, we "learn to read by reading." Several studies have shown that free reading may be the primary source of vocabulary acquisition, writing ability, spelling, and grammar (Hafiz and Tudor 1989; Hedgcock 1990; Krashen 1989; Nagy, Anderson, and Herman 1987; Nagy and Herman 1985, 1987). Krashen (1993) reviewed forty-one such studies and found that research into the gains made through free reading are "remarkably consistent." Furthermore, it seems that students who read extensively without direct skill instruction suffer no losses on standardized tests. He reported results of thirty-eight studies showing that "students using free voluntary reading did as well or better in reading comprehension tests than students given traditional skill-based reading instruction" (p. 2). Among such research is a report that showed that eighth graders in California who read more for pleasure scored higher on the California Assessment Program (CAP) test of English and language arts (Alexander, cited in Krashen 1996).

There is also evidence for the power of reading with other language groups. Studies undertaken by Schon and colleagues (Schon, Hopkins, and Davis 1982; Schon, Hopkins, and Vojir 1984, 1985) specifically look at Spanish speakers in the U.S. Briefly, sustained silent reading (SSR) programs were compared with traditional reading instruction and fared quite well. McQuillan's (1998a) reanalysis of data from these three studies yielded moderate to large effects. Although the 1985 study had weaknesses in treatment fidelity, the potential of sustained silent reading as a means of promoting Spanish literacy is clear.

Studies looking at the effect of self-selected reading in SNS courses are beginning to emerge (McQuillan 1996; Rodrigo 1995, reported in McQuillan and Rodrigo 1998). Rodrigo measured incidental vocabulary growth after a semester of administering an SNS curriculum combining popular literature with sustained silent reading. After fifteen weeks, the students demonstrated a 6 percent gain, which was impressive considering there was no direct instruction of vocabulary. The students also completed an "affective" survey, reporting that their confidence and facility in Spanish reading had improved over the course of the semester. McQuillan conducted two similar studies, also based on reading approaches (1996). The first looked at vocabulary growth of SNS students in a six-hour weekly, ten-week university course based exclusively on reading and discussion. He reports significant gains in vocabulary growth, averaging 8 percent. The second study was conducted in the same context and was of the same duration. This instruction differed slightly, in that an "individualized inquiry" outside reading project was also required, and there was a minimal amount of grammar instruction, less than 10 percent of class time. None of the students had reported reading for pleasure in Spanish before the course began. Seven months after the completion of the course a survey was sent to see if these students had continued to read in Spanish. For the purposes of establishing a control group, the same survey was sent to students who had received more traditional instruction. Results proved statistically significant; more students in the experimental group reported reading in Spanish. Although the number of students in this study was relatively small, the implications are promising: SNS courses should also tap the benefits of the power of reading.

Statement of the Problem

Given the potential impact extensive reading could have in the Spanish for Native Speaker context, a study was undertaken to investigate the availability and access to print in Spanish in central Los Angeles and the near south side of Milwaukee. The specific neighborhoods targeted in the study were chosen for their high concentration of speakers of Spanish, primarily of Central American and Mexican origin in Los Angeles, and Mexican and Puerto Rican origin in Milwaukee. They were also chosen on the basis of availability of SNS courses at public institutions in the general geographical area.

Settings

Our first neighborhood is in central Los Angeles. California has always been a land of cultural diversity, largely due to immigration and the increasing popularity of Los Angeles as a "first port of entry" to the United States. Los Angeles shows the biggest Latino population by county in the nation, 4.1 million, up 24 percent between 1990 and 2000 (U.S. Census Bureau 2000). Although the total U.S. Latino population hovers at around 35 million (U.S. Census Bureau 2000), the exact number is difficult to pin down due to continual migration.

Milwaukee, Wisconsin, has also had a long history of immigration, primarily from Europe. In the mid-nineteenth century thousands of people from central and southern Germany settled in the city, followed by many Eastern and Southern Europeans from the turn of the century through the First World War. Large-scale immigration from Mexico did not start until the late 1920s, and Puerto Ricans began settling in large numbers in the 1940s. Other Latino groups include Central Americans, Cubans, and small communities of Ecuadorians, Colombians, Venezuelans, and Argentines. Currently, the Latino population in the city is estimated at around 80,000 (U.S. Census Bureau 2000), approximately 15 percent of the population. It is predominantly concentrated on the near south side of the city, although Puerto Ricans and other Latinos have also clustered in other areas.

The central Los Angeles area targeted for this investigation is densely populated. An indication of this can be gleaned from the number of elementary schools in the area; there are six within a two-mile radius. Two of these schools have been built within a mile of each other over the past ten years. All are on a "year-round" school calendar, indicating that only two-thirds to three-quarters of the population is present at any one time. The school district implemented this calendar several years ago to accommodate a population too large for the sites. The overwhelming majority of children at these schools have Spanish as their first language (Pucci 1994). Spanish for Native Speakers programs, although limited, are available at both the community college and high school levels. Area residents are primarily from Central America or Mexico.

The near south side of Milwaukee is also fairly densely populated. Although the school system has yet to go "year round," the elementary schools on this side of town are the largest in the district, with between 750 and 1,200 students. Similarly, the middle and high schools are also large, with student populations of approximately 1,500, 65 percent of whom are Latinos. Bilingual education programs in the Milwaukee Public Schools are developmental or additive, rather than transitional, which allows for the continued development of academic language and literacy in Spanish. The current political climate is different from that of California: There is currently no Proposition 227 looming on the horizon to dismantle bilingual education, although the dominance and pressure of English is present in a number of different forms.

Results

A community Spanish print study was conducted to see what materials are available in Spanish in the general and adjacent areas of the neighborhood. First, a walking tour (Pucci 2000) of the neighborhoods was conducted to investigate immediate availability, that which would be readily accessible to area residents. Then, in the Milwaukee context, other areas of the city were also looked at. Since Milwaukee is considerably smaller, both as a Latino community and as an urban area, researchers investigated availability of Spanish print in the general metropolitan area. (Appendix A shows types and availability of print materials in Spanish.)

Places to access print materials in Spanish can be divided into four general categories. The first are *kiosks* (newsstands), which sell a variety of newspapers, popular interest magazines, and comic books. There are three main kiosks in the immediate Los Angeles neighborhood. Most are open every day with long hours on the weekends, especially Sunday when many people are out walking or attending religious services. Kiosks tend to carry a variety of women's magazines, such as *Vanidades* and *Cosmopolitan*, newspapers, automobile magazines, and a few other light materials. There is a small selection of comic books as well. Most magazines cost roughly the same price as their English language counterparts. Women's interest, popular, and automobile magazines generally cost between $3 and $4, comic books about $2, and "love story" comic books slightly higher. Los Angeles's Spanish language daily, *La Opinión*, is also widely sold. Occasionally newspapers from Central American countries find their way to the kiosks, but vendors sometimes find them hard to sell due to their relatively high cost, losing money when they become outdated. In Milwaukee there are no newsstands, perhaps due to the harsh climate.

Supermarkets and minimarkets are the second type of place to access print materials in Spanish. Almost all minimarkets, small "Mom and Pop" grocers, offer a small selection of reading materials in Spanish. There is some overlap with those materials accessible at the kiosks. Interestingly, although two of the minimarkets in the Los Angeles neighborhood were owned and run by Koreans, they also had a selection of reading materials in Spanish. All but one in the area sell the local Spanish language newspaper, and several have a few shelves of popular light reading materials, similar to the items carried by the kiosks. Two of these minimarkets carry a selection of *bolsilibros*, a type of small, softcover pocketbook, some written in comic book style, others as short novellas. In addition, several smaller community and commercially-oriented newspapers exist. These are generally directed at specific immigrant communities, such as the Nicaraguan or Salvadoran communities, as in the case of *Monimbo . . .* , "*Nueva Nicaragua*," or *El Salvador*, and have an unusually high number of advertisements. These publications are generally distributed free of charge and are commonly found in markets and restaurants.

Milwaukee's south side has many minimarkets that stock similar types of popular reading materials. Although there is no Spanish language daily as found in many other metropolitan areas, there are three weeklies: *The Spanish News, The Spanish Times,* and *El Conquistador*. These publications have articles in both English and Spanish, without translation. The Chicago daily *La Raza* is also widely distributed. The nationally distributed Spanish language versions of women's magazines, such as *Glamour, Vogue, Elle,* and *Cosmopolitan* are ubiquitous. Content in these publications ranges from simple translations of Anglo-oriented material to a more Latina-focused content. Due to the presence of the Puerto Rican community in Milwaukee, we find an array of popular magazines from the island, such as *Gente Artista, Vea*, and *Estrellas.*

A difference in the Milwaukee community is the presence of what could be called the Major Mexican Supermarket. There is one similar business in the Central American community in Los Angeles, the Salvadoran *Tapachulteca* supermarket, but few businesses of this type in the Greater Los Angeles area, somewhat surprising when one considers the proportional presence of Mexicanos and other Latinos. Instead, in Los Angeles the large supermarkets, usually part of corporate chains, tend to carry an array of food items catering to the tastes of the community, but extremely few reading materials in Spanish apart from some of the national women's magazines. In Milwaukee, on the other hand, there are three large Mexican-owned supermarkets within a few miles of each other that carry a variety of popular reading materials in Spanish. Surprisingly, considering how relatively small the Latino community is compared with that of Los Angeles, the range of reading materials appears to be greater. For example, Mexican magazines such as *Geomundo, México desconocido, Proceso,* and *Contenido* were found on the shelves of the largest Mexican supermarket in town. There was also a selection of Mexican newspapers, such as *Excelsior, Uno Más Uno, La Prensa,* and *La Jornada.* However, these were not always current — on a few visits we saw papers with dates from four weeks before. Only rarely were national newspapers from Central America or Mexico found at the kiosks or minimarkets in the Los Angeles neighborhood, and the range of magazines, whether published in the U.S. or abroad, was more restricted. Sellers in Los Angeles lamented that these publications quickly went out of date, and that they could not sell them for a profit. In addition, a small selection of nonfiction books and instructional materials having to do with learning the guitar or embroidery were also available at several of the small and large markets in Milwaukee. Few of such materials were located in Los Angeles.

The third category is the *public library.* There are two public libraries located within a mile and a half of the Los Angeles neighborhood, in addition to the large downtown branch. In Milwaukee there is one branch library located in the heart of the Mexican community. Although books in Spanish do not constitute a large part of the collections at any of these three neighborhood libraries, librarians report that they account for much of the circulation, reporting an extremely high demand for Spanish language materials, especially children's books. One Los Angeles library in particular, which was temporarily housed in a minimall, was often full of neighborhood residents, particularly on the weekends. The Spanish collection, especially the children's section, was often decimated by Saturday afternoon. This is not the library geographically closest to the neighborhood discussed in this study, but it is regarded as the central city "Latino" library. Indeed, on the several occasions this library was visited the only non-Latinos were the Anglo librarians. Children and other patrons reported walking a mile or more to this library. Interestingly, the minimall location may have inadvertently served to soften the intimidating nature of the library as a public institution. It was located a few doors down from the popular Pescado Mojado restaurant where several Latino-run businesses are housed. The other branch, newly reopened in a modern building just north of this neighborhood, is now regarded as the "Korean library." Although the population of the immediate surrounding area is heavily Latino, the majority of patrons at any given time are Korean, and there are Korean librarians working there. There is a small collection of Spanish language materials, but several visits to this library revealed a predominately Korean rather than Latino clientele.

The Milwaukee library is located next door to one of the largest elementary schools in the district. This neighborhood has a long history of immigration, and was once home to thousands of Polish and Eastern European immigrants. This is reflected in the modest collection of books in Polish, Ukrainian, and Russian. Although today's clientele is primarily Spanish speaking, the collection of books in Spanish is surprisingly limited, and the collection at the larger, central library offers even fewer books. The library personnel confirmed that there is a high demand, but reported that they had no way of knowing how many titles are in the total collection; nor could they determine the number checked out. An approximate count of books was taken on the four occasions the Milwaukee library was visited. There were approximately 1,400 books on the shelves in the adult collection, 42 in the "young adult section," and 500 in the children's section. In addition, many of the titles in the adult section are older, many with publication dates from thirty to fifty years ago. However, unlike the Los Angeles libraries, there are several freestanding wire racks of *literatura barata* in the *bolsilibro* format. This type of publication, as previously noted, is a type of small, softcover pocketbook, some written in comic book style, others as short novellas. The collection contained several different genres. There was quite a range, from the vaquero *Marcial LaFuente Estefanía* to the erotic *Páginas Intimas* and *Amores Amantes*. In addition, Biblioteca Rápida, a publishing house that offers a "gran colección de temas reservadas para el hombre de hoy," had a notable presence with its highly diversified collection of such series as *Delincuencia, Dracula, La tortura, El año 2001, Satanás*, and other titles of a similar nature. There was also a collection of *fotonovelas*, young love stories published in Mexico. These small books were well worn, and apparently are very popular.

Bookstores are the fourth channel of access to Spanish books. In the Los Angeles neighborhood, there is one large, well-known bookstore that deals exclusively in Spanish language materials. This shop is located approximately a mile away from the immediate neighborhood highlighted in this study, in a slightly more upscale business district on the way to "downtown." It is a large bookstore with a selection of literature from Spain and Latin America, as well as some children's and general interest books. It is the leading Spanish language bookstore in the city. The previous owners had been trying to retire for years, but the community simply had not allowed them to do so (Compte 1997; Marrero 1996). Finally, they agreed not to close until they found a buyer to take over and keep the bookstore open, which finally happened in 1998. There are also two bookstores dealing in political literature in the neighborhood. The one located on the main street in the neighborhood of this study has several shelves of books in Spanish. Not only do the booksellers have books which are congruent with their political orientation, they also stock some of the prominent Latin American writers, as well as Salvadoran books dealing with the civil war, previously banned in El Salvador. These books are in high demand, and they sell out almost before they get on the shelves. There are sometimes back orders which take months to fill (Jungers 2000). A new Catholic bookstore opened across the street from the local parish in 1998 and carries a selection of religious books in Spanish. Two other smaller bookstores went out of business during the time this study was taking place. One was on the main street and housed an eclectic variety of books with price tags in Salvadoran *colones*. Apparently a relative of the owner had operated a bookstore in San Salvador that had gone out of business. The other was a small shop attached to a "store-front" church which sold evangelical literature. The church either disbanded or relocated.

The first Spanish language bookstore in Milwaukee's history opened in September 1998. It is a small, friendly coffeehouse/bookstore located on the main avenue of the neighborhood. There is currently a small variety of titles, ranging from children's books to general interest to literature. Housed in a community center, it has been able to take advantage of existing citywide partnerships and offer educational, musical, and literary events, which have brought more community members to the bookstore. Despite its intention to be a place for Spanish books, the business has not promoted itself well as a bookstore, largely due to constant low inventory of books in Spanish. There is a bookstore located approximately three miles away on the lower east side of the city, which specializes in books in European languages. As such, it has an uneven collection of books in French, German, Spanish, Italian, and Portuguese. The books in Spanish are primarily full-length novels of renowned Spanish and Latin American authors. There are a few general interest books, translations of popular North American authors, as well as a limited collection of children's books. As far as magazines in Spanish are concerned, there is a small selection from Spain.

Several points need to be made regarding book availability in these stores. First, and most obviously, when compared to availability of English language titles in these two cities, the availability of titles in Spanish is rather marginal. The large variety of titles typically found in an English language bookstore is simply not available. Spanish titles primarily consist of literary works written by Latin American and Spanish authors, a few nonfiction general interest titles, a small selection of children's books, and a few translations of popular North American authors, such as Danielle Steele. It should also be noted that these books are not inexpensive. Books imported from Spain or Latin American countries, even an ordinary paperback, can run around $20 or more. Books published here in the U.S.—usually translations of previously published books in English—run appreciably higher than their English language counterparts. These paperback books were found to cost about 50 percent more in their Spanish translations.

Discussion

Results indicate that there are some sources of Spanish language materials available, although notable effort must be expended to locate these materials. Apart from magazines and *bolsilibros*, which are relatively inexpensive, prices for most books are appreciably higher and there are fewer titles available than those in English. Thus, the cost of accessing a large number of these materials to viably sustain an extensive reading program in SNS courses would be considerable. However, given the utility of extensive reading, which is well demonstrated in the literature, it is important that the effort be undertaken.

To begin, a good quantity of "light reading" materials should be made available to students. These are valuable both for their easy accessibility and high interest. Popular interest materials are important, as they may serve to focus students' attention and lower the "affective filter" (Krashen 1996). In the case of many SNS and heritage language students, whose literacy experiences in Spanish may not be extensive, and who probably do not regularly read in Spanish, these materials are necessary to "hook them into" Spanish reading. An excellent resource for the Los Angeles-based SNS class would be the Spanish language daily *La Opinión*. As with other newspapers, not only does it deal with world, national, and local events, but there are also supplementary sections that deal with arts and leisure. There are often attractive feature articles on popular musicians, actors, etc. There is now a Spanish language monthly edition of *People,* an easy-reading high-interest publication. This magazine is somewhat unique in that it focuses on the interests of Latinos living in the U.S., with a variety of articles about both Latino and non-Latino celebrities. Magazines such as *Eres, Gente Artista,* and *Deporte—tiro de esquina* could also prove to be of high interest to high school students and young adults. Lastly, especially in the Milwaukee context, there appears to be a viable selection of *literatura barata* and *fotonovelas,* some with less objectionable content, which also could be of great utility in developing skill and interest in reading in Spanish. These are the kinds of high-interest materials that could be incorporated into the SNS/heritage language curriculum to provide students with extensive exposure to Spanish print necessary to develop biliteracy.

What can such light reading materials contribute to the development of Spanish? In examining the variety of light reading materials available, their utility lies in their predictability, the contextual support from pictures and photographs, and the high interest and motivation students may have to read them. Predictable texts have long been recognized as an effective way to scaffold language and literacy for learners (Peregoy and Boyle 2001). In the field of reading, predictability is usually discussed in terms of books with patterned sentences that facilitate comprehension for emergent readers. However, the element of predictability can also be found in longer texts written for adolescents and adults. For example, series books such as *Marcial LaFuente Estefania* have the same "story grammar"—outlaws in the Wild West wreaking havoc only to be brought to justice—and the reader becomes aware of the highly patterned plot structure and anticipates what is to happen. The same can be said of *fotonovelas,* which contain love stories all written along similar lines. These texts, as well as romance novels, are what Radway (1984) describes as "technically novels because each purports to tell a 'new' story of unfamiliar characters and events, yet actually retell a single tale whose final outcome the readers already know" (p. 198).

Fotonovelas and other comic books also provide contextual support in the form of drawings or photos. This provides a powerful literacy scaffold, because readers can use the visual supports as an aid in understanding the text. This is an important tool, especially when trying to meet the needs of learners with little exposure to Spanish literacy.

Light reading is also important because it may serve as a springboard to more demanding reading in the future. Research on children's reading indicates that as children read more, they choose a greater diversity of texts, and that children who read widely develop tastes for what experts consider "good books" (LaBrant 1958 and Schoonover 1938, both cited in Krashen 1987). Participants in Ross's (1995) study, all North American graduate students, report having read dozens of series books yet eventually "moved on" to more demanding texts. This research also confirms the importance of giving readers personally satisfying experiences with texts so that they associate reading — in our context, reading in Spanish — with their enjoyment. It would be reasonable to assume that the pleasure reading phenomenon could also occur with reading in the heritage language. McQuillan's (1996) studies already provide valuable empirical support for such initiatives. Therefore, the tastes and interests young adults have for light reading and popular culture need to be exploited, not ignored; SNS teachers and curriculum developers would do well to discover student interest and provide appropriate readings and activities.

However, as the print environment data show, there are barriers to accessing extensive and appropriate titles in Spanish. If we accomplish the important task of "hooking them into" reading in Spanish through the use of easy-access high-interest materials, where do we go when students wish "to move on"? How do we provide students with reading materials to enable their development of "academic literacies" in Spanish?

One of our closest neighbors, Mexico, has often been cited as a possible source for additional reading resources in Spanish. In 1977 Isabel Schon discussed some of the problems facing the publication of books in this country, most of which are still true today. She comments that "there has been a long history of neglect of education in Mexico. Even in the 1970s it is highly unusual for any other than those from wealthy families to receive a privileged education" (p. 1). Although this statement may seem like a sweeping generalization, it is true that availability of books to the general populace in Mexico is an issue, one which continues to this day. One need only examine the cost of an average book compared with the daily minimum wage to understand the heavy role economics plays in education and publishing. The average cost of a general interest book that is written, published, and for sale in Mexico is several times the daily minimum wage, a wage that a large sector of society lives on. The cost of books has not escaped the economic upheaval of the country; it is not uncommon for a Spanish language novel to run anywhere from the equivalent of eight to twenty U.S. dollars or more. The minimum daily wage in the country has varied between $4 (the current 2001 daily minimum wage of forty pesos) and $10 in the last ten years. Therefore, it is doubtful whether this large sector of the population has the resources to purchase books, and this clearly does not help the publishing industry in general. However, among publishers and booksellers there is not usually a focus on the economic inequalities existent in the country, but on what they see as the average Mexican's "lack of a reading habit" (Pérez de León 1990, p. 33).

Reflective of the situation are the actual number of bookstores and the problematics of book trade in Mexico. Pérez de León (1990) comments: "there are about 400 bookstores and 147 book distributors in the country, which results in one bookseller for every 145,000 inhabitants. Countries like Spain or Argentina have a bookseller for every 10,000 or 12,000 people. These figures reflect the problematic situation confronting those who chose to work in book trade" (p. 33). Flores Rizo (1989), interviewing the Tijuana bookseller López, found that in the three businesses López owns, trade with the United States was minimal. This is not surprising, when one considers the innumerable barriers imposed in the form of internal and import taxes, shipping rates, and other forces (Bradbury et al. 1990). More recent work indicates that Mexican publishers wish to sell to U.S. markets, and look at U.S. Latinos as potentially promising customers (Kiser 2000), but recognize that there are great barriers to distribution.

One point of departure may be to examine Schon's extensive work reviewing and cataloguing books in Spanish for children and young adults (1978, 1983a, 1983b, 1984, 1985a, 1985b, 1985c, 1987, 1988a, 1988b, 1989). She has done a fine job identifying these publications, most of which come from Spain and Latin America. However, these books may not be of high interest for U.S. Latinos. In the context of children's literature a case has been made for promoting "home grown" authors who write in Spanish (Pucci 1993, 1994). It has been noted that books published in Spain for Spanish children, or in Latin America for Latin American children, as well as books which are translations of U.S. children's books, may not reflect the reality of Latinos growing up bilingual/bicultural in the United States. The SNS situation is in many ways analogous. There is relatively little published in Spanish in the U.S. for a "U.S. Latino" market. SNS students would benefit from texts that are more reflective of their lives and personal experiences. These texts would have more pedagogical utility in that the reader would be able to bring to bear more background knowledge, and thus receive more "comprehensible input" (Krashen 1993).

So is there hope for a future of Spanish language publishing in the United States? It is safe to say that the bookselling industry, like all markets in capitalist societies, operates "blindly"; that is, it gives consumers what they demand regardless of the social value of the product. Thus, theoretically speaking, if there were a U.S. market demand for a large quantity of high-interest reading materials in Spanish, as well as other types of more demanding reading materials in the language, it is possible that they would eventually become available.

It is obvious from the circulation and demand at local libraries that such a general potential market for Spanish books exists, apart from what could be the added demands from instructional programs. Both children and adults want to read in Spanish (Pucci 1994, 2000). This has been confirmed by public librarians, who have repeatedly reported that their Spanish collections, though relatively small, had a very high circulation. It is also substantiated by children and adults themselves, who report that they read in Spanish or would continue to read in Spanish if given a good selection of enjoyable materials, and that school and public libraries are a major source of their reading materials (Pucci 1994, 2000).

Pedagogical Implications for Instruction of Spanish as a Heritage Language in the United States

The most important pedagogical implication of this research is that of providing extensive reading resources in Spanish. While this concept is important to all levels of instruction, the following suggestions are particularly applicable to high school, community college, and university courses, all of which serve students who may not have very much experience with Spanish print literacy.

Several suggestions for light reading have been made throughout this essay. Instructors of Spanish for Native Speakers can enrich the Spanish literacy experiences of their students by ensuring that they have access to highly readable texts that interest them. Obtaining multiple subscriptions of popular magazines, purchasing class sets of high interest easy-reading books in Spanish, starting a classroom library with a variety of titles, are all good points of departure. In terms of classroom practice, conducting author or genre studies of popular literature are interesting ways to use these texts. This involves engaging in what Krashen (1997) calls "narrow reading . . . sticking to the same kind of text, reading the work of a single author, or reading books in a series." In our context, for example, reading several titles of the previously mentioned *Vaquero* series, or reading and discussing the *fotonovela* are ways of enhancing and supporting students' interactions with Spanish print. This narrow reading is useful, in that it gives the reader a familiar context which helps ensure comprehension. Practical techniques of conducting "read arounds," "shared reading," and "literature circles" are discussed in the bilingual and elementary education literature (Peregoy and Boyle 2001; Thompkins 1998) and are easily adapted to our context. Finally, systematically allocating class time to read self-selected texts in Spanish, a "sustained silent reading" (SSR) program, is another way to support Spanish literacy. Increased familiarity with Spanish print will build a foundation upon which to expand, as students eventually "move on to" more challenging texts. Extensive reading may also lead to more acquisition of vocabulary and grammar.

Instructional programs and school/university libraries can assume a greater responsibility in the Spanish literacy development of the SNS and bilingual education student, by making a firmer commitment to providing tangible reading resources. In turn, this commitment must evidence itself in terms of thoughtful policies informed by research in reading, language acquisition, and bilingual/heritage language education. The importance of free reading is abundantly supported in the literature. It is up to schools and universities to translate this into a practice that guarantees students access to a variety of reading materials not only in English but in their primary and heritage languages as well.

Spanish Reading Materials Accessible in Neighborhoods in Two Cities: Los Angeles and Milwaukee

TEXT TYPE	POINTS OF AVAILABILITY	APPROXIMATE COST (AS OF MAY 2001)	NOTES ON AVAILABILITY
Newspapers	Kiosks, minimarkets, major Mexican and Salvadoran supermarket	U.S. printed, 40¢; outside U.S., $3–5	LA: *La Opinión*, daily, commercial community papers; papers from Central America and Mexico unevenly/rarely. Milwaukee: Weekly *The Spanish News/Times*, *El conquistador*, Chicago's weekly *La Raza*; variety of Mexican newspapers regularly available.
Women's magazines *Eres, Cosmopolitan, Latina, Vogue, Somos, Glamour, Elle, Vanidades, Belleza*	Kiosks, minimarkets, major Mexican or Salvadoran supermarket, library, bookstores	$3–4	Approximately the same availability, more at Milwaukee library.
Popular culture magazines *People, Telenovelas, Estrellas Gente Artista, Furia, Auto, ¡Alarma!, Luz*	Kiosks, minimarkets, major Mexican supermarket	$2–4	Nat'l distribution approximately the same in the two cities; publications from Puerto Rico and Florida not found in LA.
Special interest magazines *Casa y Estilo, Conocer, Muy Interesante, Buenhogar, Geomundo, Américas*	Kiosks, minimarkets, major Mexican supermarket, bookstores	$3–5	Larger, more varied selection in Milwaukee.
Political magazines *Proceso, Contenido*	Major Mexican supermarket, bookstore, kiosk	$2–5	More variety from Mexico available in Milwaukee, lower price. Central American counterparts rarely seen in LA.

Continued on next page

Spanish Reading Materials Accessible in Neighborhoods in Two Cities: Los Angeles and Milwaukee (continued)

TEXT TYPE	POINTS OF AVAILABILITY	APPROXIMATE COST (AS OF MAY 2001)	NOTES ON AVAILABILITY
"Literatura barata" Small comic books for adults, some with "adult" themes	Major Mexican supermarket, minimarket, Milwaukee library, some minimarkets and kiosks	$2–3	Much larger variety in Milwaukee, mainly in public library.
"Bolsilibros" Many genres—most prominent is the vaquero	Major Mexican supermarket, minimarts, public library in Milwaukee	$1–3	Much larger variety available in Milwaukee, and in library.
Fotonovelas	Milwaukee library, minimarkets, Mexican supermarket	$2–3	Not as common in LA.
Children's books	Libraries, major Mexican supermarket, bookstores	$3–20	Only occasionally at places other than bookstores, libraries. Library collections poor, especially in Milwaukee.
Literature, novels, poetry, etc.	Bookstores, libraries, some supermarkets in Milwaukee	$8–25	Best selection at LA bookstore.
General interest books	Bookstores, a few at libraries	$5–25	Best selection at LA bookstore. Library collections limited.
Nonfiction, technical, academic	Bookstores, few at libraries	$8–25	Extremely limited in both cities.

REFERENCES

Bradbury, David, Marc Chauveinc, John Davies, Manuela Dournes, Willem Koops, Alexis Koutchomow, Klaus Lehman, Arie Manten, Paul Asser, Manfred Seidel, and Guust Wesemael. 1990. "Barriers to the Flow of Books." *Libri* 40:259–63.

Compte, Efrem. 1997. Personal interview. Los Angeles, CA.

Crawford, James. 2000. *At War with Diversity, US Language Policy in an Age of Anxiety*. Clevedon, UK: Multilingual Matters.

———. 1999. *Bilingual Education: History, Politics, Theory, and Practice*. 4th ed. Los Angeles: Bilingual Education Services.

———. 1992. *Hold Your Tongue, Bilingualism and the Politics of 'English Only.'* Los Angeles, CA: Bilingual Education Services.

Cummins, Jim. 2000. *Language, Power, and Pedagogy. Bilingual Children in the Crossfire*. Clevedon, UK: Multilingual Matters.

Fishman, Joshua. 1989. *Language and Ethnicity in Minority Sociolinguistic Perspective*. Clevedon, UK: Multilingual Matters.

Flores Rizo, Gabriel. 1989. "Un librero: una rara avis." *Libros de México* December: 9–11.

Hafiz, F. M., and I. Tudor. 1989. "Extensive Reading and the Development of Language Skills." *English Language Teaching Journal* 43:4–11.

Hedgcock, John. 1990. "Assessing the Role of Reading Genre in the Development of Writing Proficiency." Unpublished paper. University of Southern California.

Hernández Chávez, Eduardo. 1993. "Native Language Loss and Its Implications for Revitalization of Spanish in Chicano Communities." In *Language and Culture Learning: Teaching Spanish to Native Speakers*, eds. B. Merino, H. Trueba, and F. A. Samaniego. Washington, D.C.: The Falmer Press.

Hidalgo, Margarita. 1993. "The Teaching of Spanish to Bilingual Spanish-Speakers: A 'Problem' of Inequality." In *Language and Culture Learning: Teaching Spanish to Native Speakers*, eds. B. Merino, H. Trueba, and F. A. Samaniego. Washington, D.C.: The Falmer Press.

Jungers, William. 2000. Personal communication. Los Angeles.

Kiser, Karin. 2000. "Cómo vender al mercado en español en Estados Unidos. " *Libros de México* 57:31–39.

Kloss, Heinz. 1998. *The American Bilingual Tradition*. 2d ed. McHenry, IL: Delta Systems Co., Inc.

Krashen, Stephen. 1997. *Foreign Language Education, the Easy Way*. Culver City, CA: Language Education Associates.

———. 1996. *Every Person a Reader: An Alternative to the California Task Force on Reading*. Culver City, CA: Language Education Associates.

———. 1993. *The Power of Reading*. Englewood, CO: Libraries Unlimited.

———. 1989. "We Acquire Vocabulary and Spelling by Reading: Additional Evidence for the Input Hypothesis." *Modern Language Journal* 73:440–64.

———. 1988. "Do We Learn to Read by Reading? The Relationship between Free

Reading and Reading Ability." In *Linguistics in Context: Connecting Observation and Understanding*, ed. D. Tannen. Norwood, NJ: Ablex.

——. 1987. "Encouraging Free Reading." In *Claremont Reading Conference Fifty-first Yearbook*, ed. M. Douglass. Claremont, CA: Claremont Graduate School.

Labov, William. 1972. *Language in the Inner City: Studies in the Black English Vernacular*. Oxford: Blackwell.

LaBrant, L. 1958. "An Evaluation of Free Reading." In *Research in the Three R's*, eds. C. Hunnicutt and W. Iverson. New York: Harper and Brothers.

Marrero, María del Pilar. 1996. "Librería hispana seguirá operando en Wilshire." *La Opinión*, November 26.

McQuillan, Jeffrey. 1998a. "The Use of Self-Selected and Free Voluntary Reading in Heritage Language Programs: A Review of Research." In *Heritage Language Development*, ed. Stephen Krashen, Lucy Tse, and Jeffrey McQuillan. Culver City, CA: Language Education Associates.

——. 1998b. *The Literacy Crisis: False Claims, Real Solutions*. Portsmouth, NH: Heinemann.

——. 1996. "How Should Heritage Languages Be Taught? The Effects of a Free Voluntary Reading Program." *Foreign Language Annals* 29:56–72.

McQuillan, Jeffrey, and Victoria Rodrigo. 1998. "Literature-based Programs for First Language Development: Giving Native Bilinguals Access to Books." In *Literacy, Access, and Libraries among the Language Minority Population*, ed. Rebecca Constantino. Lanham, MD: Scarecrow Press.

Merino, Barbara, Henry Trueba, and Fabián Samaniego, eds. 1993. *Language and Culture Learning: Teaching Spanish to Native Speakers*. Washington, D.C.: The Falmer Press.

Nagy, William, and Patricia Herman. 1987. "Breadth and Depth of Vocabulary Knowledge: Implications for Acquisition and Instruction." In *The Nature of Vocabulary Acquisition*, eds. M. G. McKeown and M. E. Curtis. Hillsdale, NJ: Lawrence Erlbaum Associates.

——. 1985. "Incidental vs. Instructional Approaches to Increasing Reading Vocabulary." *Educational Perspectives* 23:16–21.

Nagy, William, Richard Anderson, and Patricia Herman. 1987. "Learning Word Meanings from Context during Normal Reading." *American Educational Research Journal* 24:237–70.

Neuman, Susan, and Donna Celano. 2001. "Access to Print in Low-Income and Middle-Income Communities: An Ecological Study of Four Neighborhoods." *Reading Research Quarterly* 36:8–26.

Peregoy, Suzanne, and Owen Boyle. 2001. *Reading, Writing, and Learning in ESL*. New York: Longman.

Pérez de León, Victor. 1990. "Problemas de la comercialización del libro en México." *Libros de México* March: 33–35.

Pucci, Sandra. 2000. "Maintenance of Literacy in Spanish by Salvadorans in Los Angeles." *Southwest Journal of Linguistics* 19:73–90.

———. 1994. "Supporting Spanish Language Literacy: Latino Children and Free Reading Resources in Schools." *Bilingual Research Journal* 18:67–82.

———. 1993. "Free Reading Resources in Bilingual Schools." Ph.D. diss., University of Southern California.

Radway, Janice. 1984. *Reading the Romance: Women, Patriarchy, and Popular Literature.* Chapel Hill: University of North Carolina Press.

Ramírez, David. 1992. Executive Summary. *Bilingual Research Journal* 162:1–250.

Roca, Ana. 1992. "Spanish for US Hispanic Bilinguals in Higher Education." Clearinghouse on Languages and Linguistics. EDO-FL-92–06. Washington, D.C.: Center for Applied Linguistics.

Ross, Catherine. 1995. "'If They Read Nancy Drew, So What?': Series Book Readers Talk Back." *Library and Information Science Research* 17:201–36.

Schon, Isabel. 1989. "Recent Children's Books about Hispanics and Recent Notable Books in Spanish for the Very Young." *Journal of Youth Services in Libraries* 2:157–64.

———. 1988a. "Hispanic Books, libros hispánicos." *Young Children* May.

———. 1988b. "Recent Children's Books in Spanish: The Best of the Best." *Hispania* 71:418–22.

———. 1987. "Referencias en Español." *Instructor* October: 88–89.

———. 1985a. "Remarkable Books in Spanish for Young Readers." *The Reading Teacher* 38:668–70.

———. 1985b. "Poetry for Spanish-Speaking Adolescents." *Journal of Reading* 29:243–45.

———. 1985c. "Notable Books in Spanish for Children and Young Adults from Spanish-Speaking Countries." *Hispania* 68:418–20.

———. 1984. "Trends in Literature in Spanish for Children and Adolescents: An Annotated Bibliography." *Hispania* 64:422–26.

———. 1983a. "Books in Spanish and Bilingual Books for Young Readers: Some Good, Some Bad." *School Library Journal* March.

———. 1983b. "Noteworthy Books in Spanish for Children and Young Adults from Spanish-Speaking Countries." *The Reading Teacher* 37:138–42.

———. 1978. *Books in Spanish for Children and Young Adults: An Annotated Guide.* Metuchen, NJ: Scarecrow Press, Inc.

———. 1977. *México and Its Literature for Children and Adolescents.* Tempe, AZ: Center for Latin American Studies.

Schon, Isabel, Kenneth Hopkins, and Alan Davis. 1982. "The Effects of Books in Spanish and Free Reading Time on Hispanic Students' Reading Abilities and Attitudes." *NABE Journal* 7:13–20.

Schon, Isabel, Kenneth Hopkins, and Carol Vojir. 1985. "The Effects of Special Reading Time in Spanish on the Reading Abilities and Attitudes of Hispanic Junior High School Students." *Journal of Psycholinguistic Research* 14:57–65.

———. 1984. "The Effects of Spanish Reading Emphasis on the English and Spanish Reading Abilities of Hispanic High School Students." *Bilingual Review* 11:33–39.

Schoonover, Ruth. 1938. "The Case for Voluminous Reading." *English Journal* 27:114–18.

Skutnabb-Kangas, Tove. 2000. *Linguistic Genocide in Education — Or Worldwide Diversity and Human Rights?* Mahwah, NJ: Lawrence Erlbaum Associates.

Smith, Frank. 1988a. *Joining the Literacy Club.* Portsmouth, NH: Heinemann.

———. 1988b. *Understanding Reading: A Psycholinguistic Analysis of Reading and Learning to Read.* Hillsdale, NJ: Lawrence Erlbaum Associates.

Thompkins, Gail. 1998. *Fifty Literacy Strategies, Step by Step.* Upper Saddle River, NJ: Prentice Hall.

U.S. Census Bureau. 2000. "The Hispanic population in the United States." *Current population report.* Available at www.census.gov/population/socdemo/hispanic.

Valdés, Guadalupe, and Michelle Geoffrion-Vinci. 1998. "Chicano Spanish: The Problem of the 'Underdeveloped' Code in Bilingual Repertoires." *The Modern Language Journal* 82:473–501.

Contributors

Rebeca Acevedo (Ph.D. in Spanish linguistics, University of Michigan, Ann Arbor, 1997) is assistant professor of Spanish linguistics at Loyola Marymount University in Los Angeles. Acevedo's area of specialization is historical Spanish and applied linguistics. Her recent publications include "Perspectiva histórica del paradigma verbal en el español de California" in *Research on Spanish in the United States* (2000), *El español mexicano durante la Colonia: El paradigma verbal en el altiplano central* (2000), and as a coauthor for *A manera de ensayo* (1998).

Mariana Achugar (Ph.D. in Hispanic linguistics, University of California, Davis, 2002) is currently teaching in the Department of Language Teacher Education at the School for International Training in Vermont. Her research interests include academic language development and critical discourse analysis focusing on Spanish.

Karen Beckstead graduated with honors from the University of California at Santa Barbara and was awarded Distinction in the Major. She earned her M.Ed. and California teaching credentials and currently serves as English language development department chair and International Baccalaureate Program coordinator at Dos Pueblos High School in Santa Barbara, California.

Ysaura Bernal-Enríquez (Ph.D. in educational linguistics, University of New Mexico, 2002). Her dissertation "Tesoro Perdido" looks at sociohistorical factors in the loss of the Spanish language of la Nueva México. Her general research interests are the linguistic, sociolinguistic, and psycholinguistic aspects in the maintenance, loss, and revitalization of Chicano Spanish.

Rebecca Blum-Martínez (Ph.D. University of California, Berkeley, 1993) is an associate professor in bilingual and ESL education in the Language, Literacy, and Sociocultural Studies Department in the College of Education at the University of New Mexico. She is currently working in the area of language revitalization.

Roberto Luis Carrasco (Ed.D. Harvard, 1985) is an associate professor of bilingual and multicultural education at Northern Arizona University. He received the outstanding dissertation competition award from the National Association for Bilingual Education in 1986. His research publications are in cultural anthropology, the ethnography of communication, second language acquisition, sociolinguistics, and bilingualism. Presently, he is the principal investigator of the White Mountain Apache/NAU Graduate Fellowship and Research program.

María M. Carreira (Ph.D. University of Illinois at Urbana-Champaign, 1990) is associate professor of Spanish at California State University, Long Beach. Her research focuses on Spanish in the U.S., teaching Spanish to Hispanic bilinguals, and phonology. She was co-organizer of the first National Conference on Heritage Languages in America, held in Long Beach, California, in October 1999. In 2000, Carreira received second place as Outstanding Latina Educator for the state of California.

M. Cecilia Colombi (Ph.D. in Spanish linguistics, University of California, Santa Barbara, 1988) is professor and associate language director at the University of California, Davis. Her research interests include second language development, educational linguistics, and sociolinguistics with an emphasis on Spanish in the United States. Recent publications for which she is a coauthor include *Developing Advanced Literacy in First and Second Language* (2002); *Palabra abierta* (2001); and *La enseñanza del español a hispanohablantes: Praxis y teoría* (1997).

Marta Fairclough (Ph.D. University of Houston, 2001) is assistant professor of Spanish linguistics at the University of Houston. Her research interests include heritage language education, language acquisition, and sociolinguistics with a focus on U.S. Spanish.

Eduardo Hernández Chávez (Ph.D. University of California, Berkeley, 1977) is associate professor of linguistics at the University of New Mexico, Albuquerque, where he also directs the Chicano Studies program. His publications include *El Lenguaje de los Chicanos* (1975), a seminal work in the field of Chicano sociolinguistics, along with numerous articles on the Spanish of the Southwest. His current work focuses on the maintenance and loss of Spanish and the language policies that motivate language loss, with a view toward establishing educational programs for the revitalization of the heritage language.

Ernestina P. Hernández is currently a doctoral candidate at the University of New Mexico in the department of Language, Literacy, and Sociocultural

Studies. Her research interests include bilingual education, heritage language learners, and dual language immersion education.

Andrew Lynch (Ph.D. in Hispanic linguistics, University of Minnesota, 2001) is assistant professor of Spanish and linguistics at the University of Florida. His research focuses on sociolinguistic aspects of Spanish in the U.S. and on the acquisition of Spanish as a heritage and second language.

N. Ariana Mrak (Ph.D. University of Houston, 2000) is assistant professor of Spanish at the University of Houston, Downtown. She specializes in sociolinguistics and second language acquisition. Her research interests focus on language contact phenomena in U.S. Spanish.

Sandra Liliana Pucci (Ph.D. in Language, Literacy, and Learning, University of Southern California, 1994) is associate professor of bilingual education at the University of Wisconsin, Milwaukee. Her research interests lie in primary language literacy development in linguistic minority communities, language policy and planning, and secondary bilingual/heritage language education.

Florencia Riegelhaupt (Ph.D. State University of New York, Buffalo, 1976) is an associate professor of Spanish and educational foundations at Northern Arizona University. She has published numerous sociolinguistic research papers on bilingualism, codeswitching, Spanish of the Southwest, Spanish for native speakers, and L1/L2 acquisition. Her current work centers on Spanish heritage language and culture acquisition and reacquisition theory.

Ana Roca (Doctor of Arts, University of Miami, 1986) is professor of Spanish and linguistics at Florida International University, Miami. Roca's main areas of teaching and research interest are Spanish, Spanish in the United States, bilingualism and heritage language education issues in Spanish, language teaching, language education policy issues, and undergraduate teaching of Hispanic culture and film. Selected publications include *Research on Spanish in the United States* (2000), *Nuevos mundos* (1999), *Spanish in Contact: Issues in Bilingualism* (1996), and *Spanish in the United States: Linguistic Contact and Diversity* (1993). She is the new chair of the Spanish for Native Speakers Committee of the AATSP.

Ana María Schwartz (Ph.D. in second language acquisition, University of Maryland, College Park, 1992), a native of Cuba, is associate professor of Spanish and second language pedagogy at the University of Maryland, Baltimore County, where she teaches Spanish for Native Speakers, intermediate Spanish courses, and graduate courses in language, methodology, and second language acquisition and learning. Her research interests include heritage Spanish speakers, writing and listening strategies, and teaching language with video. Recent publications include "Preparing Teachers to Work with Heritage Language Learners" in *Heritage Languages in America: Preserving a National Resource* (2001) and as a coauthor for *Noticias: An Advanced Intermediate Content-Based Course* (2002).

Hinako Takahashi-Breines is currently a doctoral candidate in the Department of Language, Literacy, and Sociocultural Studies at the University of New Mexico. In different stages of her life she has been immersed in three different languages and cultures: Japanese, Spanish, and English. Her research interests are bilingual education, second language acquisition, and heritage language learning.

Almeida Jacqueline Toribio (Ph.D. in linguistics, Cornell University, 1993) is associate professor of linguistics in the Department of Spanish, Italian, and Portuguese at the Pennsylvania State University. Her research interests include language contact, bilingualism, microvariation, and the sociology of language.

Guadalupe Valdés (Ph.D. in Spanish, Florida State University, 1972) has a joint appointment in the Department of Spanish and Portuguese and in the School of Education where she is the Bonnie Katz Tenenbaum Professor of Education. Much of Valdés's work has focused on the English-Spanish bilingualism of Latinos in the United States and on discovering and describing how two languages are developed, used, and maintained by individuals who become bilingual in immigrant communities.

Index

A

AATSP, 5, 15
ABC, 58
academic discourse community
  achievement in, 215
  membership in, 213, 228–29
  studies on, 213–14
academic discourse study
  code-switching, 225–26
  data collection, 218
  oral presentation expectations, 218
  participants, 219
  pedagogical implications of, 229
  practice, 223
  text analysis, 217–18, 219–28
academic language, 226, 229–30
academic registers
  academic language, 226–227
  academic oral, 230
  characteristic of, 215, 220
  features of, 214
  lexico-grammatical level, 215-16
  logico-semantic relations, 220, 222
  oral academic language, 217
  proficiency in, 228
  Spanish, 216
  of Spanish speakers in U.S., 228–29
academic skills, basic, 75n. 2
Acevedo, Rebeca, 12–13, 257–68, 291
Achugar, Mariana, 12, 213–14, 291
actividades de pre-escritura
  debates, 264
  discusiones de grupo, 264
  lluvia de ideas, 264
  presentaciones grupales, 264
  recursos bibliográficos, 264
  técnicas de investigación, 264

adquisición parcial
  aprendizaje dilatado, 103
  aprendizaje interrumpido, 103
  condiciones que conducen a la, 97
  inatención a la, 105–06
  olvido, 103–04
  préstamos en la, 104–05
  procesos psicololingüísticos en la, 104
advanced literacy, 9, 159
alfabetización, 110, 260
A manera de ensayo, 262
American Association of Teachers of Spanish and Portuguese (AATSP), 5, 15
American Council on the Teaching of Foreign Languages (ACTFL), 16–17
análisis deductivo, entre el registro oral y escrito, 260
análisis funcional, de los recursos gramaticales, 89
anglicismos, 43, 100
aparato, 84
aprendizaje dilatado, 103
aprendizaje interrumpido, 103
arcaísmos, ejemplos, 99
Arizona, 7, 9
Arizona, Proposition 203, 61
aspectos mecánicos
  deletreo, 263
  gramática, 263 (*ver también* gramática)
  ortografía, 263
  selección de vocabulario, 263 (*ver también* vocabulario)
aural skills, 41–42

B

Beckstead, Karen, 11, 154–69, 291
Bernal-Enríquez, Ysaura, 10, 96–120, 291

BICS, 112–13
bilingualism, 9, 28
  and education, vii, 61
  fallacy of theoretical approaches, 34
  individual, 131
  language attrition, 32
  Proposition 187, 6–7
  Proposition 227, 6
  in schools, 128
  societal, 8, 32, 40–41
  Spanish academic registers, 228
  and structuralism, 34
  terminology, 30
bilinguals, 7
  linguistic competence of, 131
  needs of, 172, 253–54n. 4
  professional opportunities for, 63
  transition to English, 270
  in the U.S., viii
bilingüismo
  culto, 102
  natural, 102
biliteracy, 9, 280
Bills, Garland D., 56, 64
Blum-Martínez, Rebecca, 10–11, 123–53, 291
bolsilibros, 275

C
calcos del inglés, 105
California, 9
  Proposition 187, 6–7
  Proposition 227, 6, 60–61
cambio de códigos, 203, 208 (*ver también*
    code-switching)
  y la enseñanza de la escritura, 111
  y la enseñanza del español, 110
  intraoracional, 102–03
  situaciones donde ocurre el, 102
campo, 79, 82, 84, 88, 90
Carrasco, Roberto Luis, 11, 170–97, 292
Carreira, María M., 8–9, 51–97, 292
CBS, 58
Center for Applied Linguistics (CAL), 15–
    16
Chicanos
  desprecio por el español chicano,
    106–07

heritage speakers, 171
  metas lingüísticas, 108
  Spanish, 60
Chomskyan paradigm, 33
Cien años de soledad, 108
civil liberties, English-only movement, 6
classrooms
  encouraging reading, 283–84
  focus in, 26
  helpful environment, 156
  and heritage language pride, 166–67
  instruction in (*see* teaching practices)
  language learning in, 140, 143
  multicultural, 3
  Spanish for Native Speakers (SNS) (*see*
    Spanish for Native Speakers)
  Terrell's methodology, 26
  writing skills instruction, 235, 250–53
CNN, 58
code-switching, 225–226 (*see also* cambio
    de códigos)
Cohen, Andrew D., 249
cohesión
  estructural, 86, 87
  gramatical, 87 (*ver también* gramática)
  léxica, 87
  textual, 87
college education, 75n. 1
  bilingualism, 6
  first language acquisition, 6
  pedagogical issues, 6
  Spanish teachers, 6
Colombi, M. Cecilia, 1–22, 78–95, 292
Colorado, 9
comic books, 280
composición
  actividades de pre-escritura, 264 (*ver tam-
    bién* actividades de pre-escritura)
  aspectos mécanicos, 263
  claridad de ideas, 263
  desarrollo de ideas, 262–63
  enfoque apropiado, 262
  especificaciones requeridas para la, 264
  importancia del receptor, 265–66
  objetivo central, 263
  organización de un curso de, 264–65
  organización de ideas, 262–63

recopilación de ideas, 262
selección de estilo, 263
comunidad hispana en los Estados
Unidos, 199
conclusión, 81, 88
uso de procesos relacionales en la, 89
Constitución de 1911, 96
contenido semántico, 86
contextos
de la cultura, 80
educacionales, 81
de la situación, 80
continuos de la relación interpersonal
tenor
contacto, 87, 88
envolvimiento efectivo, 87, 88
poder, 87, 88
corrupción lingüística, 97
Cubans, 66, 67
cuerpo, 81
cursos para hispanohablantes bilingües,
257–68
aplicación del manejo del inglés, 260
clasificación por géneros, 264–65
composición, 262–65 (*ver también*
composición)
y el discurso escrito, 258–59
enfoque, 257–58
meta principal de los, 199, 209, 257, 259
primeras semanas de clase, 261
registro escrito, 260, 261
registro oral, 260, 261
requisitos para, 257
resultados, 266
skill-using activities, 261

D

Del Río Elementary School, 128–29
demographics
changes in, 28
employment, 55
Hispanic birthrates, 54
trends, 57
densidad léxica, 86
desarrollo, 81
desarrollo de la escritura, en hablantes
nativos del español, 78–79

desplazamiento lingüístico, causas, 97
desprecio por el español chicano, efectos,
106–07
destrezas de la escritura
importancia, 258
prestigio adquirido por, 258
dialecto estándar
producción escrita del, 200
producción oral del, 200
dialects
sociolinguistic awareness of, 192
vs. standard Spanish, 11–12
and television programs, 59
dictionaries, 252
diglosia, 109
discontinuities, 35, 45n. 8
discurso escrito, 258–59
Dominicans, 67
dual language immersion programs, 10,
123–24, 142, 143
dual-language immersion programs study
classroom organization, 129–30
features, 124
participants, 124–27, 133–35
pedagogical implications, 140–43
research methodology, 130–33
schools involved, 127–29
separation of languages, 141
social purposes, 142
speech acts, 144–51
texts used in, 141
writing, 135–40

E

educación
bidialectal, 209
cursos para hispanohablantes bilingües
(*ver* cursos para hispanohablantes
bilingües)
y el español chicano, 105–07
education
attitude toward second language, 44n. 4
bilingual, 10, 61
college (*see* college education)
dual-language immersion (*see* dual-
language immersion programs study)
Hispanics and, 55, 62–63

language in, 230
in Mexico, 281
transitional bilingual, 270
elecciones léxicogramaticales del registro
campo, 79, 82
modo, 79, 82
tenor, 79, 82
elecciones lingüísticas
discursivas-semánticas, 81
léxicogramaticales, 81
emblematic code-switching (*see* code-switching)
Encuesta sobre el Español de Nuevo México y el Sur de Colorado, 107
English language
importance of, 162, 164
legislation promoting, 26
linguistic skills in, 62
as official language, 7, 44n. 3
as a second language (*see* Goleta Valley Junior High School study)
U.S., 26
ensayo expositivo, 78–93
conclusión, 81
cuerpo, 81
desarrollo, 81
ejemplo, 92–93
introducción, 81
y las metafunciones del lenguaje, 84
relación entre introducción y conclusión, 88
uso de las nominalizaciones, 85
enseñanza de la escritura, 111
enseñanza de lenguas extranjeras, 260–61
enseñanza del español, 110–14
curso de redacción, 266
escritura, 111
para estudiantes bilingües, 259
y la expansión del léxico, 208
formal, 198
guía de preguntas, 91
a hispanohablantes bilingües, 198
y las mezclas interlingüísticas, 110
necesidad de metodologías para la, 208–09
a nivel primario, 110, 114
ortografía, 111

práctica recomendada, 112
pronunciaciones locales, 111–12
variantes fonéticas, 111
variedades externas, 112–13
ESL study. *See* Goleta Valley Junior High School study
español
adquisición parcial del, 103–05
chicano, 98
comunitario, 110, 115
desgaste del, 203
enseñanza del (*ver* enseñanza del español)
estándar, 115
general, 98
malhablado, 43
mexicano, 98, 100–101
normativo, 113, 115
nuevomexicano, 98
español chicano, 100
arcaísmos, 99
características del, 98
desprecio por el, 105–07, 114
importancia cultural, 108
innovaciones, 99
de Nuevo México, 98
préstamos, 99
valor afectivo, 108–09
valor pedagógico, 109–10
valor sociolingüístico, 109
variación regional, 98–102
variación sociolingüística, 98–102
español comunitario, 110
y la enseñanza del español, 111
propósitos educativos del, 115
español estándar, 115, 199–200
español general, 98
arabismos, 99
indigenismos, 99
español mexicano
culto, 100
fronterizo, 101
general, 100
jergal, 100
nuevomexicano, 101
rural, 100
español nacional, 100

español normativo, 113, 115
español nuevomexicano, 100, 105
  estigmatización del, 97–98
  indigenismos, 99
  innovaciones, 99
  préstamos, 99
estilos retóricos. *Ver* géneros
estructura esquemática, 81 (*ver también*
  ensayo expositivo)
estudio en la producción oral de hablantes
  méxico-americanos
  análisis, 202–04
  conclusión, 207–08
  participantes, 201
  procedimiento, 201
  resultados, 204–07
  técnica de análisis de errores, 202–04
  técnica metodológica, 200
expansion, 220, 222

F

Fairclough, Marta, 11–12, 198 212, 292
Figueroa, Richard A., 34
filtro afectivo, 267
first language
  acquisition, 6
  maintaining, 9
Firth, Alan, 33
Florida, 7, 38
Flor Silvestre, 82
foreign languages, enrollment figures in,
  27
formas en desarrollo, 113
fotonovelas, 280
Fountain, Anne, 39, 46
Friedlander, Alexander, 238

G

García, Ofelia, 55, 67
Gascoigne Lally, Carolyn, 238
géneros, 79–82, 90, 264
  argumentativo, 265
  y el contexto de la cultura, 80–81
  estructura esquemática, 81
  modelos editoriales, 265
  relación con el lenguaje, 80
German language, 27

Gibbons, John, 216
globalization, 44n. 5
Goleta Valley Junior High School study
  community background, 155–56
  cultural identity, 165–66
  ESL program, 156
  findings, 166–67
  language attitudes, 162–65
  language usage, 158–60
  language vitality, 161
  mission statement, 155
  participants, 156–57
  Spanish vs. English, 164–65
  test instruments, 157
gramática
  análisis funcional, 89
  cohesión, 86, 87
  construcciones locales, 113
  elecciones léxicogramaticales del
    registro (*ver* elecciones léxicogramati-
    cales del registro)
  metáfora, 85, 86
  simplificación, 104
grammar
  vs. conversation, 45n. 9
  and language learning, 42–43
  and teaching, 42
grammatical metaphor, 232n. 3

H

Halliday, Michael A. K., 82, 85
Hasta no verte Jesús mío, 82
Hedgcock, John, 237–38
heritage language acquisition (HLA)
  instruction principles, 8
  principles, 35–40
Heritage Language Initiative, 16
heritage language (HL) learners
  characteristics of, 30–31
  correcting speech of, 171–72
  discouraging, 171–72
  expectations of, 176
  insecurities, 178
  oral vs. written skills, 235
  reading materials for, 279–80
  and Spanish speaking classmates,
    140–41

HL learners (*continued*)
  texts, 141
  vocabulary, 252
heritage languages
  attitudes toward, 166–67
  erosion of, 6
  importance of learning, viii
  loss, 18
  national initiatives, 14–17
  pedagogical implications, 41–43
heritage language speakers
  academic writing, 9–10
  education, 11–12
  grammar vs. conversation, 45n. 9
  language acquisition, 36–40
  language proficiency, 3–4
  teacher preparation, 6
Hernández Chávez, Eduardo, 10, 56, 96–
    120, 292
Hernández, Ernestina Pesina, 10–11, 123–
    53, 292–93
Hispanics, 2
  attitude toward Spanish, 67–68
  and education, 55, 62–63
  identity, 71
  income patterns, 57, 64
  Mexicans, 2
  population growth in U.S., 54–55
  population in U.S., 2
  population variations, 65–68
  prestige, 64–65
  professional opportunities, 63, 70–71
  in the U.S. workforce, 54
hispanohablantes bilingües, aprendizaje
    de la modalidad estándar, 200
Hudson, Alan, 56

I
immigrants
  acquisition of English, 6
  attitudes toward, vii
immigration
  vs. Hispanic birthrates, 54–55
  language attrition, 55–56
  and language use, 1
  in the 1980s, 26
innovaciones, 99

interlanguage performance, 232n. 1
interpersonal metaphors, 232n. 3
intragenerational variation, 35
introducción, 81, 88
  uso de procesos relacionales en la, 89

K
Kasper, G., 254n. 6
Krashen, Stephen D., 45n. 9

L
Labovian speech community, 44–45n. 8
LangNet Project, 15
language
  attrition, 55, 159
  in education, 230
  four basic skills, 17
  minority perspectives on, 154–68 (*see
    also* Goleta Valley Junior High School
    study)
  and national security, vii
  power relations, 228, 230
  usage study, 158–60
Language Policy Task Force, 41
languagism, 172
Latinos, vii, 273
  culture, 165
  Spanish use of, 161
Lazarillo de Tormes, 108
lector modelo, 264
Lefkowitz, Natalie, 237–38
lenguas extranjeras
  enseñanza de, 260–61
lingüística
  corrupción, 97
  despalazamiento, 97
  elecciones, 81
  sistémica funcional (LSF) (*ver* lingüís-
    tica sistémica funcional [LSF])
lingüística sistémica funcional (LSF), 79
  metafunciones del lenguaje, 83
  registro, 82–83
linguistic performance, 232n. 1
literacy
  acquisition of basic skills, 41
  advanced (*see* advanced literacy)
  developing, 13–14, 38, 281

informal learning scenarios, 61–62
in minority language, 14
promoting, 272
skills, 270
and SNS instruction, 69
logico-semantic relations
expansion, 220, 222
projection, 220, 223
Los Angeles, 273
LSF. *Ver* lingüística sistémica funcional (LSF)
Lynch, Andrew, 8, 25–50, 55, 66, 293

M
macroestructura, 262
Marcial LaFuente Estefania, 280
media, 36, 54, 159
bolsilibros, 275
children's books, 282
and dialects, 59
linguistic preservation, 58–59
newspapers, 58
print, 269, 280 (*see also* print study)
radio, 58
skill development and, 41–42
in SNS classes, 70
television, 58
META, 11
activities, 179
authentic materials, 187–88
background, 170–71
book for relatives, 188–89
and continued acquisition, 176
curriculum, 179
defined, 176
evaluation questionnaires, 185–87
function of, 189
implications of, 191–93
interactive journals, 181–82
key concepts, 176–79
language and culture workshops, 180–81
student portfolios, 187
student self-esteem, 191
taped sessions, 182, 185
transcriptions, 182–85
metacognitive knowledge, 177, 179

metacultural knowledge, 177, 178
metáfora gramatical, 85, 86 (*see also* grammatical metaphor)
metafunciones
ideacional, 83, 84, 88, 90
interpersonal, 83, 84, 88–89, 90
textual, 83, 84–87, 90
metafunción ideacional, 84, 88, 90, 91
experimental, 84
lógica, 84
metafunción interpersonal, 84, 87, 88–89, 90, 91
metafunción textual, 84–87, 90, 91
metalinguistic awareness, 183
metalinguistic knowledge, 177, 178–79
metaphors
grammatical, 232n. 3 (*see also* metáfora grammatical)
interpersonal, 232n. 3
metapsychological knowledge, 177, 178
Mexicans, 66
Mexico
availability of books in, 281–82
bilingual teachers study in, 173–74
book trade, 282
education in, 281
mezclas interlingüísticas, 110
Miami, 66, 67
Milwaukee, 273–74
modo, 79, 82, 84, 90
Morín, José Luis, 55, 67
Mrak, N. Ariana, 11–12, 198–212, 293
Myers-Scotton, Carol, 102, 118

N
National Conference on Heritage Languages in America, 16
National Foreign Language Center (NFLC), 15
national foreign language standards, 17–18
native speakers, 32–34
NBC, 58
New, Elizabeth, 237
New Mexico, 10
newspapers, 70
New York, 67

Nichols, Geraldine Cleary, 27
nominalización, 85–86
  densidad léxica, 86
nominalization, 215
Nuevomexicano, 125
Nuevo México
  enseñanza del español en, 96–119
  español chicano de, 98
  patrón típico de aprendizaje en, 103

O
olvido, 103–4
  comprensión, 104
  producción, 104
Opinión, La, 280
oralidad vs. escritura, 258
ortografía, 111

P
People, 280
poliglosia, 109
print, 271, 280
print study, 269
  accessible reading material, 285–86
  availability of materials, 274
  bookstores, 278–79
  kiosks, 274–75
  Los Angeles, 273
  Mexico, 281–82
  Milwaukee, 273–74
  newspapers, 276
  pedagogical implications, 283–84
  prices, 279, 281
  public libraries, 276–78
  results, 279
  supermarkets and minimarkets, 275–76
procesos materiales, 89
proficiency, 52, 64
  in academic registers, 228
  code-switching, 225–26 (*see also* code-switching)
  evaluating, 185
  of heritage language learners, 235
  of SNS students, 69
  and writing, 250
projection, 220, 223

pronunciaciones locales, 111–12
préstamos, 103
  en la adquisición parcial, 104–05
  calcos del inglés, 105
  ejemplos, 99
  y la enseñanza de la escritura, 111
Pucci, Sandra L., 14, 269–90, 293
Puerto Ricans, 66, 67

Q
Quixote, 108

R
radio stations, 42, 58, 59–60
Raimes, Ann, 237
REACH Project, 15
reading
  accessible, 69
  adolescents and, 159
  developing taste in, 281
  extensive, 271
  fotonovelas, 280
  free, 272
  light, 279, 280–81
  literacy development, 13–14
  narrow, 283
  power of, 272–73
  predictability, 280
  promoting literacy, 271
  sustained silent, 272, 284
  visual supports, 280
recontact, 39
registers
  academic (*see* academic registers)
  aspects of, 214
  linguistically different, 230
  parallel, 216
registro, 82–83, 90
  escrito, 260, 261
  formal, 257
  oral, 260
research
  classroom-based (*see* dual-language immersion programs study)
  data, 254n. 6
  discontinuities, 35

focus, 35, 193
L1 writing, 254n. 7
META implications, 192–93
on reading, 272
think-aloud technique, 239, 254n. 7
Riegelhaupt, Florence, 11, 170–97, 293
Riegelhaupt-Barkin, Florence. *See* Riegelhaupt, Florence
Rivera, Klaudia, 55, 67
Rizo, Flores, 282
Roca, Ana, 1–22, 293

S

Schwartz, Ana María, 13, 235–56, 268, 293–94
second language, facilitating development of, 9
second language acquisition (SLA), 25
    and language attrition, 32
    META (*see* META)
    and native speakers, 33
self-observation, 254n. 5
self-reports, 254n. 5
self-revelation. *See* think-aloud
September 11, 2001, vii
Silva, Tony, 256
Silva-Corvalán, Carmen, 32
simplificación gramátical
    uso del imperfecto, 104
    uso del pretérito, 104
simplificación fonológica, neutralización [r], 104
sistema de lectoescritura, 260
sistema educacional, y las clases multiculturales, 78
slang, 106
skill-using activities, 261
SNS. *See* Spanish for Native Speakers
social diglossia, 35
sociohistorical factors, 4–5
Spanglish, 43, 97, 103, 106
Spanish for bilinguals. *See* Spanish for Native Speakers
Spanish as a heritage language (SHL). *See* Spanish for Native Speakers
Spanish for heritage learners, 198

Spanish for Native Speakers (SNS), 30, 198
    abilities and needs of, 52, 68–69
    future generations, 63
    reading materials for, 279–80
    teaching, 5
Spanish for Native Speakers (SNS) classes, 4, 13
    culture and tradition, 71
    focus of, 271
    goal for, 72
    literacy skills, 270–71
    media in, 70
    national foreign language standards, 17
    pedagogical implications, 68–72
    and profesional opportunities, 71
    regional anchoring, 68
    and Spanish-language media, 59–60
    student composition of, 52–55
    using dictionaries, 252
    vocabulary development, 252
    writing strategies, 251 (*see also* writing strategies of heritage speakers)
Spanish language
    in academic context, 213–32 (*see also* academic registers)
    attitudes towards, 4–5
    Chicano, 60
    dialects (*see* dialects)
    economic value of, 64
    enrollment in, 27
    maintenance of, 193
    prejudice toward, 163, 172
    public perspective, vii
    social prestige, 64–65
    texts, 141
    in the U.S., 25, 35 (*see also* research)
    use of, 2, 158–60
    in U.S. history, 18
speech
    discontinuities in, 35, 45n. 8
    taping, 182
    transcribing, 182–85
Summer Institute for Teachers of Spanish for Native Speakers, 16

sustained silent reading (SSR), 272, 284
Systematic Functional Linguistics
    (SFL), 9

T

Takahashi-Breines, Hinako, 10–11, 123–53,
    294
teachers, 27, 43
    evaluating proficiency, 185
    evaluation questionnaires, 187
    expectations, 175
    flexibility, 72
    nonnative speakers of Spanish, 130
    proficiency, 10–11, 185
    and reading interests, 281
    respect, 192
    student journals, 181–82
    student portfolios, 187
    successful, 154
    summer immersion program study,
        173–74
    and taped sessions, 182
    and transcriptions, 183, 184–85
teaching practices, 5, 271
    bilingual-oriented, 172
    communicative language teaching, 26
    creating a book for relatives, 187–89
    encouraging reading, 283-84
    grammar-oriented, 42
    identifying best, 155
    journal writing, 181–82
    literacy strategies, 69–70
    META, 176
    skill-using activities, 261
    students portfolios, 187
    taped sessions, 182
    transcriptions, 182–85
    whole language approach, 172,
        187–88
    writing process, 235–36
técnica del análisis de errores
    categorías de errores, 203–04, 205–07
    limitaciones, 202
    problemas de metodología, 202–03
Telemundo, 58
telenovelas (soap operas), 59

television, 41, 58, 61
    as a family activity, 60
    in the SNS classroom, 70
tenor, 79, 82, 84, 87, 90 (*see also* registro)
teorías de aprendizaje de Vygotsky y Halli-
        day, 90
teoría semiótica, 79
think-aloud procedure, 239, 254n. 5
Thoreau Elementary School, 127–28
Toribio, Almeida Jacqueline, 11, 154–69,
    294
Torres, Lourdes, 35
triángulo de la comunicación, 261
Tudor, I., 272, 287

U

United States, 43
    English, 26
    Hispanics in, 54–55
    national identity, vii–viii
    national security, vii
    Spanish language publishing in, 282–83
Univisión, 58–59

V

Valdés, Guadalupe, vii–ix, 6–7, 29, 33–34,
    44n. 6, 52, 53t 3.1, 59–62, 198–200, 214,
    217, 270–71, 294
Valdés, M. Isabel, 58
Valdés-Fallis, Guadalupe. *See* Valdés,
    Guadalupe
variantes fonéticas, 111
vocabulario
    anglicismos, 43, 100
    arcaísmos, 99
    innovaciones, 99
    préstamos, 99
vocabulary, 41–42, 106, 252, 272, 284

W

Wagner, Johannes, 33
web resources, 15, 16, 42
Wilson, David, 44n. 5
workshops, language and culture,
    180–81

writing
  academic, 9–10
  for beginners, 69
  classroom activities, 250
  dual-language immersion study, 135–40
  editing, 180, 183, 188, 251–52
  expertise, 250
  heritage language learners (*see also*
    writing strategies of heritage
    speakers)
  in journals, 181–82
  process of, 235–36
  purpose of, 188–89
  teaching, 13
  transcribing speech, 182–83
  transfer of skills, 238
writing strategies of heritage speakers
  case studies (*see* writing strategies study)
  categories of, 236
  developing confidence, 253
  dictionary use, 252
  editing, 251–52

ESL writers, 237
foreign language writers, 237
instruction and practice, 251
paraphrasing, 252
prewriting in L1, 238
reprocessing, 248
revision, 237–38
use of, 237
vocabulary, 252
writing strategies study
  data, 239, 242, 245, 247–50
  implications of, 250–53
  participants, 239, 242, 245–47
  purpose of, 239
  questionnaire, 239–41
  strategy, 242, 245
  think-aloud essay, 241–42, 247–50
  translating, 249

Z

Zamel, Vivian, 236–37
Zentella, Ana Celia, 45n. 12